CROSSWINDS
An Airman's Memoir

CROSSWINDS
AN AIRMAN'S MEMOIR

NAJEEB E. HALABY

DOUBLEDAY & COMPANY, INC.
GARDEN CITY, NEW YORK
1978

Library of Congress Cataloging in Publication Data

Halaby, Najeeb E 1915–
    Crosswinds.

    Includes index.
    1. Halaby, Najeeb E., 1915–   2. Aeronautics—United
States—Biography—   I. Title.
TL540.H253A35   629.13′092′4 [B]

ISBN: 0-385-04963-3
Library of Congress Catalog Card Number 78-8210
First Edition

*To all those who have given more to aviation
than they have taken from it.*

ACKNOWLEDGMENTS

To Robert J. Serling, who has helped me edit random thoughts on a tape recorder into a first draft of a readable book, I offer my thanks for his work early in the project and for his candid comment as it became my own.

I want particularly to acknowledge the faith and patient, tolerant, but highly professional work of Walter Bradbury in keeping me on course, and my thanks to Doubleday for their endurance.

To my family for their forbearance in the hours stolen from them to give to the book—and with apologies to them and, in particular, to my mother, Laura W. Halaby, for not more fully sharing with her whatever glory I have enjoyed—I am extremely thankful.

To my longtime, long-suffering colleague and executive secretary, Miss Joan Nixon, and her associate, Mrs. Gloria Andresakis, for their enduring kindness in helping to convert a voice to the printed page while carrying out the relentless duties accumulating around them, I am particularly thankful.

I share with all of them credit for whatever you like about the book and take full responsibility for the rest of it.

If it pains some, I can only say that that's the way it is in my mind and memory, and if I have made any mistakes, I hope to be the first to acknowledge and correct them.

PREFACE

This book is essentially autobiographical, but I hope it will contain here and there a few principles and policies as well as memoirs.

Among airmen there has always been a laughing debate about whether God intended man to fly, but for me the answer has always been affirmative. God has given each of us a spirit that can soar, a mind that can accept the challenges of technology and a body that can cope with most of the physical elements. Anyone with some vision, some discipline of mind and body, can fly. Not everyone has the fullness of opportunity that I have enjoyed in aviation—not only to experience flight as a pilot, but also to face the opportunities and obligations of public service, and to translate the superb, constantly advancing techniques of civil aviation into service to passenger, shipper, general public, and the shareholder. It is on the latter sphere that much of this story will concentrate.

The publishers originally asked for a book about my experience as Federal Aviation Administrator, a job that ended July 1, 1965. They were intrigued with the Kennedy administration and its New Frontier as it applied to civil aviation and my participation in it. They wanted me to talk about the way in which an airman carried out a public responsibility to other airmen and the public in general during that colorful and tumultuous period. In fact, we called it originally *Washington Cockpit,* which had a nicely ambivalent quality.

I started working on the book in the summer of 1965, while I was being persuaded by one of the most persuasive men in aviation, Juan Terry Trippe, to join him on the flight deck of Pan American World Airways. After a summer of debate and ordeal within myself and with my family, I finally succumbed to Trippe's blandishments, attaching one condition—namely, that I could write this book and say what I wanted regardless of its impact on Pan Am. Trippe wasn't too pleased with that condition but accepted it. Soon, however, I found that the condition of Pan Am even as early as 1965 occupied my entire attention and so, except for occasional scribbling and taping, I set the book aside.

On March 22, 1972, I resigned as chairman and chief executive officer of Pan American World Airways, and this book was born again.

In the corporate cockpit, not to mention the jungles of bureaucracy, the word "resigned" is often a convenient euphemism for being fired. I claim no exception: I was, in effect, fired. For the first time in my life I tasted the humiliating dregs of defeat, doubly bitter because failure was not my own appraisal but that of my peers—a majority of the Pan Am directors in the spring of 1972.

In Rod Serling's memorable television play *Patterns,* an aging executive on his way out of a giant corporation tells his younger replacement:

> On our level, you don't get fired. You resign. They don't know how to say "get out" after years of service, most of them productive. So they create an atmosphere you can't work in and finally can't live in—tension, abuse, mostly subtle and sometimes violent. Chip away at your pride, your security, until you begin to doubt, then fear . . .

Those words don't reflect my years at Pan Am. But they come uncomfortably close in some respects. True, I wasn't an "aging executive" about to be replaced by a younger, more vigorous man. At fifty-six I was only three years older than the man who would succeed me. But I was at the top of a giant, globe-girdling airline, and the fall from those heights is a parachute jump in which one wonders if there's a ripcord to pull.

Part of this story is about that fall and the years and events that preceded it. In telling it, as I have said, I enlisted the editorial aid of a respected writer, Robert J. Serling, former aviation editor of United Press International, whom I got to know when I was head of the Federal Aviation Agency and he was covering it for UPI. The final approach—the opinions, views, and personal judgments disclosed in this book, however, are entirely mine.

CHAPTER ONE

In the summer of 1975, I visited the Owl's Head Museum in Rockland, Maine, and was given a chance to fly a restored Curtiss P-2 Pusher, circa 1905, rebuilt with a Franklin engine. The little Curtiss Pusher was a time machine, a catalyst for nostalgia. It all came rushing back even faster than a lone, curious, and playful seagull, who kept diving at me in my strange bird of fabric and wire. I recalled the words of Aristophanes:

> Listen, do I hear the birds?
> Nothing can be more delightful
> than the having of wings to wear!
> Introduce, then, wings in use—
> believe me, matters will be mended.

The legends of Daedalus and Icarus also sprang to my mind . . . and Besnier, the little locksmith, who in 1867 attached wings to his hands and feet and glided from French rooftops . . . the Montgolfier brothers, their balloons and the parachute that was a stunting device for descent therefrom. All those gallant airmen— Santos Dumont, Walter Wellman, Thad Loew, Otto Lilienthal, Sam Langley, Percey Pilcher, and the immortal Wright brothers.

1

I thought of machines as well as of men: the OX-5 Travel Air in which I soloed; the Waco in which I got my first commercial license; the Stearman in which I introduced dozens of Air Corps cadets to the exhilaration of stalls, spins, and rolls.

Many of us recall events in our lives by the cars we drove, as one measures the age of a tree by its rings. At about the same time I flew that ancient Curtiss, I visited an antique auto show in Mount Mansfield, Vermont. There was a Pierce Arrow roadster like the one I inherited from my elegant father in 1928, the 1929 American Austin my doting mother gave me for a Christmas present, the old Maxwell with the fallback front seat from my student days at Stanford—and the 1930 Harley-Davidson motorcycle on which I roared like Tom Swift during those college years. There was the 1932 Chevrolet convertible, like that Uncle Harry and I took to the air show at Mines Field in Los Angeles, where I was fatally bitten by the flying bug; and the marvelous 1936 Ford V-8 station wagon in which Yale Law School classmate Dick Galland and I roamed from New Haven to Smith and Vassar and the ski slopes.

When one starts out to write the story of his life, he should face up to the pitfalls of rationalization, subjectivity, and a kind of subconscious censorship. In most autobiographies, I suspect, authors avoid outright falsehoods merely through the simple process of omission—leaving out the unfavorable or the unexplainable.

I fully admit to the temptation; one *does,* in looking back, tend to alibi his failures and rationalize his mistakes. To keep an autobiography from becoming mere ego satisfaction requires mental and emotional discipline, and the task is neither easy nor enjoyable.

But one redeeming aspect of such retrospection is the opportunity to indulge in bittersweet memories. You remember those who have played major roles in your life: You search back for incidents and individuals who helped to mold your ethics, your philosophy, your character. You recall with fondness, amusement, wryness, and, occasionally, sadness.

I know that this was how I felt that last day at Pan Am awaiting the polling of the directors as they sat in judgment in the case of Halaby vs. Pan Am.

I was thinking of Charles Lindbergh, one of the directors, who would have a thumbs-up or thumbs-down vote on me. I was eleven years old the first time I saw the Lone Eagle—shortly after his flight across the Atlantic. He was touring the United States and he came to Dallas, where I lived with my family. The city gave him the usual ticker-tape parade, and my father took me downtown. I remember jumping up and down and screaming in the back seat of the family flivver as Lindbergh rode by. His dignified, youthful appearance—almost saintly-looking—was uplifting.

He was, of course, a hero to all Americans, but especially to the young. It wasn't so much the technical feat he had accomplished—by then, everyone knew airplanes could fly. It was the fact that he had done it alone, in a tiny, frail machine. Even in later years, when I saw the *Spirit of St. Louis* displayed in the Smithsonian Institution, it was hard to believe that Lindbergh could have entrusted himself alone to an aircraft whose entire fuel load would have been consumed by a jetliner taxiing out for takeoff. In 1927 Lindbergh's scrawny little airplane contrasted in size not to other aircraft but to the transportation giants of the day—the locomotive and the ocean liner. The idea that one young man, all alone in a winged pygmy of a crate, could do in thirty-three hours what took the seagoing leviathans eight or nine days—that was the chief ingredient of this hero saga.

It was typical of my father that he took the time and the trouble to escort me downtown for the Lindbergh welcome. I was an only child and was named for my father. He was Najeeb Elias Halaby and he was born in what was then Greater Syria and is now Lebanon, in a town called Zachly, which is halfway between Beirut and Damascus. His parents were Salim and Almas Halaby, and they came from Aleppo, which in Arabic is pronounced Halab. Anyone who was from Halab could be a Halaby—the latter being the anglicized spelling.

My grandmother was a very strong woman who bore a daughter and four sons—Rose, Habeeb, Salim, Camille, and Najeeb. Like all young Arabs, they were poor. But my grandfather apparently had some leadership qualities—he became the local magistrate and acquired a few family possessions of some value. In about 1900, Habeeb and Najeeb were given permission to take most of the family's worldly goods to Beirut and then to the United States for sale. The two boys traveled steerage and ended up in Brooklyn, where they sold the goods for enough money to send for the rest of the family. They must have been enterprising. At the time, my father was not more than twelve, and his brother Habeeb wasn't much older. I never knew exactly what the family treasures consisted of, but I believe they sold a small amount of gold jewelry, some copperware, a few rugs, and some damask material, which was in great demand in such cities as Boston, New York, and Washington.

I vividly remember my father telling me about the time he met the wife of the President of the United States, Mrs. Grover Cleveland. She was summering at Bar Harbor, Maine, and my father decided to go up there with a few wares because he understood it was a mecca for the wealthy. At that time he was more of a peddler than an importer, but I think he could have sold Stars of David in the middle of Baghdad. Apparently Mrs. Cleveland was intrigued by his Middle Eastern charm, because she gave him letters of introduction to other potential customers. Coming from the First Lady, such letters were the equivalent of a free full-page color advertisement in *The Saturday Evening Post*. His reputation grew by word of mouth, and he began to import more and more fine fabrics, rugs, and works of art. Eventually he decided to move to Dallas, Texas; there he figured (and quite correctly), were the cotton and oil millionaires who could both appreciate and afford what he had to sell.

He arrived in Dallas between 1910 and 1912—I was never able to ascertain the precise year—and shortly after setting up business met my mother. She was the daughter of Jim and Mamie Wilkins; her father had run away from home to enlist in the Confederate Army of Tennessee when he was sixteen. Like so many followers of the Confederate cause, he came out of the Civil War embittered but unbowed, and unwilling to go back home. He rode West to seek his fortune and homesteaded a small ranch near Graham, Texas, where he married a Scotch-English lass and raised their daughter and three sons.

Laura Wilkins, my mother, had a vision of the universe and a love of art in her blood from the time she was a small child. She designed and made clothes, saved to send herself to the Southern Methodist University Art School, where she studied interior decoration and design. She met my father at a party in Dallas; I still have a marvelous picture of them in full costume, dancing at a masquerade ball.

Their mutual cultural interests blended into a business partnership as well as a matrimonial one. They established the Halaby Galleries, which became one of the most fashionable, sought-after interior-decorator firms in the Dallas, Fort Worth, and Houston areas. It was successful enough to rent the top two floors of what was then the magnificent Neiman Marcus Building in Dallas—at the personal invitation of Stanley Marcus and his relatives, who had built the store. An Arab and Jews working together in a temple of luxury trade a half century ago!

From about 1920 to 1928, the Halaby family was financially secure enough to enjoy their share of luxuries. My parents traveled often, sometimes together, and occasionally my father by himself to France, Italy, and the Middle East on buying trips.

Dad was quite a guy. He was no great devotee of sports, with one exception: golf. He loved the game, and I'll never forget his taking me on as his Sunday caddie from the time I was only eight. One Christmas he had a handmade set of his old wooden-shafted clubs cut down to my size, and from then on I was as avid a golfer as he. My father was a handsome man, just under six feet, and very attractive to the ladies. Toward me, his only child, he vacillated between penitentiary discipline and marshmallow permissiveness. He could be very sweet, generous, compassionate, and sentimental. He also occasionally beat the hell out of me. He was loving and very emotional, with a short-fused temper and tremendous pride in his Arab heritage. Unlike many Syrians, Lebanese, and others from the Middle East, he refused to change his name or pretend to be anything he wasn't. To my later regret, we never spoke Arabic at mealtime, as did many Arab Americans, but I did pick up a few epithets in the old man's native tongue.

In those days, there were housing and private-club restrictions in Dallas against Assyrians, Armenians, and Arabs, just as there were against blacks, Jews, and, occasionally, the Irish. But Dad still managed to get into the classy Dallas Athletic Club, became a

5

thirty-second-degree Mason, and had no trouble purchasing property: He bought three homes in Dallas during the time we lived there.

My mother, an unreconstructed rebel with basically conservative southern views and beliefs, faced considerable maternal opposition when she announced she was going to marry Najeeb E. Halaby. For Mamie Wilkins, her daughter's marrying an Arab was nothing but a *Guess Who's Coming to Dinner?* situation. She regarded my father as an adventuresome stranger in a somewhat mysterious and not very solid business, with a suspicious nationality. Conversely, frontiersman Jim Wilkins always got along fine with Father, a fellow seeker of freedom and advantage.

At this writing, my mother is a very strong ninety, fiercely opinionated, and with an uncompromising nature. Without accepting all her views, I have loved and respected her as a person. She is totally fearless, honest, and imaginative. Throughout my life she has been a constant source of support, unflinching criticism, and a stimulation—what we call "needling" in the family. She is a woman of the soil, a magnificent and incredibly skilled gardener. She even has a garden in her small Manhattan apartment, and her friends marvel at the way she can make things grow indoors that most people can't grow outdoors. She is imaginative, as artistic as she ever was, and still decorates for friends. She did an office for me once when I was in Washington. Most of all, she has lived a life in the spirit of God, a devout seeker of Truth and a believer in the Divine Science of Life.

She gave birth to me on November 19, 1915, a few years after my father moved to Texas. After my father returned from the army we lived in a succession of three houses, the last one being the finest because it was decorated by Halaby Galleries. In fact, it was used as a customer showroom; my parents had great artistic ability, and even today, a half century later, there are some fine homes in Dallas that still proudly display the fruits of their talent.

But the house I remember best was an ordinary, two-story frame dwelling with a big yard in the back. We had some untroubled, carefree days in that old house. We never lacked for good food, and my father could afford to play golf at the Dallas Country Club every Sunday before church. Ours was a religious family; my parents were both Christian Scientists, my mother having converted Najeeb, who was born Greek Orthodox. I went to Christian Science Sunday school. I still remember the Sunday morning ritual (usually we got to sleep a little late—a luxury that ended for me when I started caddying for my father). We'd get up and have a light breakfast prepared by Ella, our black maid. Then it was my job to get out the ice-cream freezer, crack away at a fifty-pound chuck of ice and pack the freezer while Mother performed the culinary alchemy involved in creating homemade ice cream. Next I'd add a layer of ice, a layer of rock salt, and after she put in the ice-cream mixture, I'd have to crank away for twenty minutes. When it was packed, we'd go off to church. Ella would have fried chicken ready when we returned, with that rich, creamy ice cream as the final delight. Sometimes I can still taste that ice cream. It almost has become a symbol of those full, rich, creamy pre-Depression days of the twenties.

Ella was warm and wonderful; she weighed about three hundred pounds, most of which must have been heart. She was maid, cook, and sitter for the family in my early years and a rather formidable figure whom I'll never forget. She "lived in" but she had a husband with a fondness for the bottle and, occasionally, would go to their shack in Dallas's black ghetto to see him. Sometimes she took me along and I'd even get to spend the night there. One morning, her husband staggered home around dawn, weaving unsteadily through the milk bottles lined up in a row on the ramshackle wooden porch. Ella took one look at him, picked up a quart milk bottle, and crashed it down on his head. I still can remember how he looked—a very black, very drunk man bathed in white milk.

From knowing and loving Ella grew my affection for and sympathy toward black people. Even at that age, I resented the obviously underprivileged status of the American black, and I've always had a strong desire to improve that status—to improve it at a much faster rate than my mother or other Southerners would accept.

It's funny how certain incidents from boyhood never fade from memory even after many years. I remember another time when I had been working about two months on a scale flying model of a high-wing Stinson monoplane. I had painstakingly fashioned it out

7

of balsa wood and a silk screen fabric covering the wings and fuse-lage. The wooden propeller was handmade, and the power was provided by a strong twisted rubber band hitched to the prop. I had just completed it, the final touch being the application of dope to the wings and tail surfaces to stiffen the fabric covering. Proudly I set the plane in our driveway to dry before its first flight.

There never was a first flight. My father chose a few moments later to back the car out of the garage, not realizing that the airplane was in his path, and ran right over it. The tears shed by his nine-year-old son that day would have refloated the *Titanic*.

That ill-fated model was the first real indication that I, like so many boys in those years, was becoming fascinated by aviation. The aviation world was beginning to blossom in the midtwenties, and there were still some fresh memories of World War I—including those of the aces like Von Richtofen, Ball, Rickenbacker, and Luke. The whir of wings echoed in the ears of youngsters almost anywhere throughout the Southwest. You could go out to Love Field, for example, and see the barnstorming pilots flying their ancient Jennys. Kelly and Randolph fields of the U. S. Army Air Corps were in the San Antonio area, and some fledgling flying services had started up around Dallas and Fort Worth.

I can't say that I always wanted to be an aviator. I went through the traditional fireman-policeman-baseball/football player-locomotive engineer stages. I think my earliest ambition was to be a fireman, being greatly influenced by my first visit to a firehouse, where I was allowed to climb all over the big red engines. Next came an overwhelming desire to be a locomotive engineer; a train going through town in those days was a very exciting event. My train kick lasted only about a year, and model planes took over along with World War I pulp books such as *Battle Aces* and *War Birds* as well as the Tom Swift books. I even talked my father into taking me out to Love Field to watch the barnstormers stunting and wing-walking.

I was a happy and lucky youngster, but my parents parted company in 1927 and Dad worried about my "only child" status. He thought I was becoming a "Mama's boy," and he talked my mother into sending me away to school. An old friend of his had started a private school in Bedford Village, New York, called the Rippowam School. It was mostly a day school, but the headmistress took in three or four boarders and at my father's request she added me to her small list of live-in students. I was twelve, understandably lonely at being that far from home for the first time in my life, but it was a whole new world and I came to enjoy it. My initial reaction to "exile" had been hurt mingled with anger, but my father was right: I needed to be more self-reliant and independent, and it was a case of being tossed into the cold water of the East and swimming out of sheer self-preservation.

I stayed at Rippowam for only eight months, during which time I saw my father once when he came to New York on a buying trip and visited me. The next time I saw him was on his deathbed.

He had contracted what was supposed to be acute tonsillitis, and his Christian Science mental healing had no effect. Eventually he agreed to be hospitalized and underwent a tonsillectomy. Just as he seemed to be recovering, he developed an infection diagnosed as acute jaundice (I suspect it was really hepatitis, virtually unknown in those days), serious enough to warrant my mother's phoning me at Rippowam and telling me to come home as soon as possible.

It was a trip that took 2½ days by train, for there was no such thing as reliable air transportation in 1928. I arrived home in time; he died holding the hand of a bewildered boy.

Close friends have asked me if my father's death left me resentful of Christian Science. On the contrary, the religion had always had an important role in my life, and when Dad died, it became stronger. I regarded his having to go to a hospital as a sign of weakness and thought that if he hadn't been hospitalized, he never would have caught the infection that killed him. Even today, I still think he was more a victim of maltreatment and the then existing lack of medical knowledge than of a religion founded on the power of faith healing.

As traumatic as it was when Dad passed away, I didn't feel fear in the presence of death. I never have been afraid to die, because I regard death as nothing but transition from mortality to a kind of immortality. I'll admit I no longer practice Christian Science. But after my father's death I continued in Sunday school and attended a Christian Science school during the last two years of high school,

9

and I continue to have a deep faith in the idea that man is fundamentally spiritual, that he has a mortal life and then a spiritual life, and that death simply eliminates the body so one can achieve at death an even more interesting spiritual experience.

My religious background helped me get over the shock and pain of the divorce and the loss of my father, but there was more drastic change in store for me. Mother decided to move to California. She had become interested in an attractive gentleman who like her wanted to go West. She sold the Halaby Galleries, created a small estate for me, and headed West with a twelve-year-old who was more excited than sad. My mother remarried shortly after we moved to Santa Barbara. Her new husband was French, from New Orleans, and very suave. I never became close to my stepfather, my fondest memory of him being the fact that he took us abroad almost every summer. I do recall being the object of some resentment on his part because he felt that Mother paid more attention to me than to him. They were divorced six or seven years later. I wouldn't be surprised if my expectations and demands on her were not part of the cause.

The Depression had hit by this time, but with the money Mother got from selling the Halaby Galleries and the affluence of her new husband, we were reasonably well fixed to start life anew in Southern California.

Part of my inheritance was an automobile Dad purchased shortly before his fatal illness. It was a Pierce Arrow roadster with a black finish set off by gleaming brass and red leather upholstery. My mother had Ella's new husband, Clarence, drive it to California in the wake of the moving van, and I took formal possession of it when I became fourteen—yes, in the California of 1930, a fourteen-year-old could drive a car legally.

Maybe it was the prestige of that Pierce Arrow, but for the first time in my life I acquired a nickname free of jibes at my Arab ancestry. I had been called "Blackie," the "Persian Prince," and "Rug Merchant." In California friends began referring to me as "Jeeb," a sobriquet that has stayed with me.

Our first California home was in an area called Hope Ranch, and I went to Dean School, a private school nearby. We lived there for a couple of years before moving from Santa Barbara to the Bel Air section of Los Angeles. One of the few things I remember about that period was that I played golf with a celebrity—none other than Howard Hughes. He played at the Hope Ranch Golf Club, usually with a retinue that included movie stars, but one day he showed up alone and asked me to play a few holes with him. By that time I was fairly good at the game, shooting in the high seventies, and was able to keep up with Hughes, who was a pretty fair golfer himself. To my youthful eyes, he was a very dashing, attractive, carefree guy who dated a flock of pretty movie actresses—Katharine Hepburn at that moment—and flew his own airplane. I didn't consciously ape his playboy aura, but I was something of an underage playboy myself. I played a lot of golf and tennis, had discovered girls, and was getting downright spoiled. Mother stepped in at this point and dispatched me forthwith on a second "trip to Siberia"—Siberia being a very rigorous, work-your-own-way, do-everything-for-yourself boys' school in northern Michigan, called Leelanau, in Glen Arbor.

I spent two years at this school, which had tremendous impact on molding my character. It was run by a maverick from the Christian Science movement named William Beals, known to all the students as "Skipper." He had the inner compassion of a Jesuit priest and the outward demeanor of Vince Lombardi, and to the fifteen-year-old who came to him from the sunshine, fruits, and flowers of Southern California, he was a commanding, frightening figure, and his school a Spartan "Outward Bound."

Skipper Beals specialized in remodeling spoiled brats. He was more missionary than minister, more reformer than teacher. I hated him and his school at first. Fresh from a doting mother, the luxury of my own car, and an excess of leisure hours, I now found myself chopping wood, digging drainage canals, and building barns and dorms. The only fun I had that first year was sneaking out to hunt rabbits and deer in the nearby woods, although the Michigan winter weather was a difficult adjustment for my sun-thinned California blood.

Eventually Skipper got through to me, as he did to virtually every boy who attended Leelanau. The New Deal was under way during my last year there, and some of the exciting, stimulating mood of FDR's quiet revolution permeated all the way to the little

11

school in northern Michigan. The national spirit of reform and renewal was closely related to Beals' theme that public service was more important than private profit—that hard mental and physical work would be man's satisfaction and salvation. He did more than merely introduce me to hard work and pure living: Skipper Beals also planted a desire to perfect society and to do something about the underprivileged. He supplied me with my first real sense of ethical values and the capability to recognize in myself some capacity to persuade and lead others; to assume responsibility for someone other than Najeeb Halaby.

The tail end of the Depression had hit my mother hard. She had her fine home in the Bel Air section of Los Angeles, but her dwindling resources and matrimonial problems forced her to rent the house to movie star William Powell. He was then in the midst of his romance with Jean Harlow, and it was rather heady stuff, if vicarious, for me; I never did get to meet Miss Harlow.

Much of the money Dad had left was gone, and Mother had to start earning her own living. She moved into a smaller house in Bel Air and began a new career. She would buy up houses, renovate and redecorate them, and resell them for a $10,000–$20,000 profit. In Bel Air we lived near W. C. Fields, and although I didn't get to know him well, I met him often enough to remember him as a likable—if at times difficult—character. Fields never bought a house in his life, although he drove real-estate agents crazy by always looking and pretending he was hotly interested in purchasing expensive property. A neighbor once told us that his leased Bel Air house had thick iron bars on both the insides and outsides of all upstairs doors—why, we never found out, although it was rumored that he was inordinately suspicious and had once fired a butler because he was convinced the man was an international poisoner.

After my second year at Leelanau, I became seriously interested in flying, beyond building model airplanes or watching helmeted heroes perform crazy, hair-raising stunts. One of my mother's brothers, Harry Wilkins, helped me realize my early aeronautical ambition.

Harry always was "Unc" to me, and in some small ways he managed to take the place of the father I missed so much. I had just returned from Michigan feeling strong, pure, and confident. At sixteen one seldom realizes how much there is yet to learn. Unc ran a little store in Santa Monica, and his wife was chief operator at the telephone office there. They lived near the Douglas Aircraft Company plant, and Unc got the flying bug to the extent of taking a few lessons himself and getting to know some of the ex-World War I airmen and unemployed stunt pilots who did a little flight instruction to keep from starving.

It was the summer of 1932 and the National Air Races were being held in Southern California. The main event was a race between Los Angeles and Cleveland, and the competitors included such famous names as Jimmy Doolittle, James Wedell, Roscoe Turner, and Al Williams. The takeoff was from Mines Field on the outskirts of Los Angeles. (Mines Field today is the site of Los Angeles International Airport. Years later, when I headed the FAA and studied the multimillion-dollar noise-nuisance suits filed against the airport, I remembered when the airfield was just a cow pasture.)

Mines didn't even have a reviewing stand; the spectators stood in front of a little adobe terminal and tower building on the south side of the field (the main terminals at Los Angeles International today are all on the north side), where they could watch the takeoffs and the stunt flying staged in conjunction with the races. The runways at the time were graded mud covered with some gravel.

Unc took me to the races, but I was far more impressed by the accompanying air show and all its blood-chilling stunts. The star was a German former ace, Ernst Udet. One of his favorite tricks was to roar in low, go into a side slip, and pick up a handkerchief with a wingtip. The Army and Navy displayed some crack formation flying teams, and there were inverted flights at low altitudes, acrobatics, and the inevitable wing-walking.

No youngster of today, waiting outside a pro football team's dressing room for a glimpse of his heroic giants and, maybe, a hastily scribbled autograph, could be any more excited than I was standing in such close proximity to these romantic airmen. The uniform of the day invariably included leather helmet, goggles, white scarf, jodhpurs, and flying boots—very Hollywoodish by today's standards, but in the eyes of a sixteen-year-old boy, sufficient to conjure up images of Greek gods. Even the way those fliers walked was something special, a kind of casual, insouciant swagger. And, if I may paraphrase a line from Edna Ferber's novel *Cimarron,* a pilot in those days was the kind of man who could strut while sitting down.

On the way home I relived the day's activities with such enthusiasm that Unc announced that it was time for me to learn how to fly.

"I don't know if Mom will let me," I said doubtfully. "It must cost a lot."

"Twenty bucks an hour, usually," Unc conceded. "But I think I might be able to get a cut rate. If your mother says okay, I'll look around."

I didn't enter our house when we got home—I squirted in, like a popped watermelon seed. I confronted Mother with my avowed determination to become a pilot, and she took it rather calmly.

"How much will it cost?" she asked Uncle Harry.

"I figure I can get him about ten hours' instruction for around a hundred dollars."

"All right," she told me, "I'll give you sixty dollars of that if you'll earn the other forty dollars."

Unc went looking while I went working at various odd jobs. He located his man in a few days—an ex-crop duster who owned a second-hand OX-5 Travel Air two-place biplane. The Travel Air Manufacturing Company of Wichita, Kansas, was building mostly cabin monoplanes, and the OX-5 even then was something of an aeronautical anachronism.

The owner of this particular airplane and my first instructor, Freddy Foster, had acquired the plane on the proverbial shoestring and was most amenable to my uncle's offer of a hundred dollars for ten hours of dual instruction plus a solo flight—if I were fortunate enough to earn the latter. I showed up for my first lesson after obtaining a student pilot certificate at the Long Beach office of the Commerce Department's Aeronautic Branch, predecessor agency of what would become the Bureau of Air Commerce and later the Civil Aeronautics Authority. I was nervous when I made out the application, but I shouldn't have been—all they required of me was two dollars and the ability to stand up and sign my name.

If I had known airplanes then as I know them now, I wouldn't have stepped foot in Fred's OX-5. It was pretty beat-up; I think it had been built in 1924 and had been flown by a succession of owners, and it didn't even have a tailwheel, just a tailskid. The brakes might charitably have been called marginal, and the rear cockpit seat, where Fred parked me, had only three instruments: oil-pressure gauge, altimeter, and air-speed indicator. But as far as I was concerned, the old Travel Air could have been Lindbergh's *Spirit of St. Louis* and I the Lone Eagle himself.

The first lesson wasn't my first flight. I had flown once before from Santa Barbara to Los Angeles, but this time it was totally different. After taking off, Fred let me handle the stick and rudder, teaching me straight and level flight and a few banks and turns. Under my inexperienced hands, the OX-5 had the stability of a pogo stick, and what with my frequent slipping and skidding all over the sky, it's a wonder the instructor didn't throw up or throw me out.

In subsequent lessons, we concentrated mostly on takeoffs and landings. I suspect that Fred wanted me to solo very early so he wouldn't have to give the whole ten hours of instruction for that hundred bucks. One Sunday morning, with six hours of dual flight under my belt, I went out to the airport prepared to do some work on stalls and my first spins. It was a bright, clear day with virtually no wind, and Fred had me make a landing. I expected to take off right away again, but he suddenly climbed out, took his seat pillow with him, tapped me on the helmet, and spoke those magic words: "Take her up."

I was almost in a state of shock, but I managed to get the Travel Air off the ground, circled, and had started back into the landing pattern when I suddenly spotted a Waco cabin plane abreast of me, at the same altitude and in the same landing pattern. Luckily its occupants saw me, too, or we might have collided —I was so scared that I could have sailed into them. The Waco cut in front of me and landed. I lost the pattern completely and had to go around for another shot. This time I landed, albeit with a few bumps, and taxied over to receive Freddy's congratulations. He also told me who was in the plane I almost creamed: Will Rogers and his personal pilot.

My first call was to Uncle Harry, who sounded both pleased and proud.

"I'm not finished yet," I assured him. "Tomorrow I'll come back and really learn how to fly."

"Good boy," Unc said.

Fred gave me an appointment for the following morning. But when I arrived, there was no Freddy, and the OX-5 was showing a large, ugly red tag on its nose. He had failed to make the payments, and the plane had been repossessed. He still owed me 3½ hours of the promised 10, but that was the last I ever saw of him. Yet I think I owe him far more than he owes me. A rookie pilot's first instructor can plant seeds that sprout into future flight behavior—good and bad—and for all his peripatetic personality, Freddy was an excellent teacher who truly loved flying.

I wouldn't say that on my first solo I experienced the mystical love of the sky many pilots profess—the kind of "reached out and touched the face of God" feeling expressed by pilot/poet John Magee in *High Flight*. I was too busy worrying about the noise and the wind and the rattling of that venerable OX-5 and hoping that the battered engine was going to keep running. But on subsequent flights, as I acquired more skill and faith in my machines, I really did come to realize that Magee's poem aptly expressed the emotions of so many pilots; most of us can't put those emotions into such magnificent words, but the feeling is there nevertheless. Flight *can* be a poetical, mystical, almost religious experience; for me, flight has always evoked the biblical Genesis, in which "God gave man dominion over the earth and over every creeping thing upon the face of the earth."

I suppose I could call myself a "natural born" pilot; at least I had the natural co-ordination essential for above-average cockpit performance. Good pilots are something like natural athletes, with agile hands and legs and discipline over emotions; at least this used to be about all it took to be a pilot. Nowadays a competent pilot must exercise high mental competence as well as physical co-ordination. This had to come about as aircraft became so much more complex. But when I first learned to fly and later when I became an instructor myself, it was the athlete and not the scholar who showed the greatest proficiency.

I didn't have enough money to fly very often, not with college coming up. I enrolled as a freshman at Stanford and very quickly began to lose all the noble Spartan qualities Skipper Beals had tried to instill in me. I started out wanting to be an architect, no doubt through my mother's influence and my own artistic background, but the ambition was rather vague. For one thing, after those two years in the North Woods of Michigan, I rediscovered girls. I wasn't a very good student, did more dating than studying, and nearly flunked out of Stanford in my second semester.

In my sophomore year I met a political science professor named Thomas Barclay, who influenced me to major in political science. My admiration for Barclay also reignited the desire instilled in me at Leelanau for a life dedicated to public service. I dabbled a bit in pacifism—one of my numerous term papers, I recall, was an opus on the "Merchants of Death"—the German, French, and British armaments manufacturers in World War I. I even flirted a little with communism, mainly because I became mildly intrigued by Marxism when I was studying comparative governments. I secretly subscribed to the West Coast edition of the *Daily Worker,* known as the "Western Worker," figuring that was the only way to find out whether the Soviets really practiced Marxism. I'd go to general delivery at the Stanford post office and pick up the *Worker,* which was addressed to me under a phony name. Reading that hopelessly biased newspaper brought early conviction that while Marxism might have some theoretical value, the Kremlin's prescription would not cure the ills of America.

My grades improved enough to allow my considering a new ambition, that of going on to law school. I had no deep yearning for the office practice of law, but the trial lawyer profession seemed to be a logical stepping-stone to public service. Clarence Darrow and Earl Rogers, the great dramatic defenders, were courtroom heroes of the day. The only alternative I seriously considered was architecture. (I applied and was accepted at the University of Pennsylvania.) To this day I wonder if the latter wouldn't have been more satisfying simply because it is more creative and tangible. But in 1937 it was the drama of the law.

17

Deciding on law school was infinitely easier than getting into the one I wanted most: Yale. This was an institution with considerable political orientation, probably the outstanding one in the country in that respect. On the faculty at the time were such men as Wesley Sturgis, William O. Douglas, Thurman Arnold, and a number of prominent lawyer-political scientists such as Eugene Rostow and Myres McDougall, who were committed to the development of a policy science—in other words, the scientific development of national policies.

There were openings for 125 new graduate students when I applied for admission to the Yale Law School—along with some 600 other applicants, including 75 Phi Beta Kappas and 10 Rhodes scholars! Against such formidable competition I didn't stand a chance, and I settled for acceptance at the University of Michigan Law School; at least Ann Arbor winters weren't as Siberian as the ones at Leelanau. For the first time in my life I really studied hard, finishing up my first year in the upper 10 per cent of my class. This modest achievement won me a transfer to Yale, from where I eventually graduated in 1940.

I wouldn't have rated myself as any budding Perry Mason in those post-Yale years, but I did pass the California bar examination and was offered a job with O'Melveny & Myers, one of the two top law firms in Los Angeles. It was a kind of bullpen existence, typical of what most rookie lawyers experience—at $125 per month to start. I worked on municipal bond issues, cases involving small corporations, and occasionally went to court with one of our trial lawyers. It was good training but boring at times, and it didn't fit my concept of using the legal profession as a path to public service. So I re-enlisted—having been active in New Haven—in the Legal Aid Society, an organization devoted to helping mostly indigent blacks, poor whites, and Mexicans with marital and legal problems. I even got to conduct a couple of trials—a status that would have taken me at least five years to achieve for O'Melveny & Myers.

By this time Europe was at war, and American isolationists, mainly through the American First Committee, were trying to keep the United States out of it. But although I respected the views of men like Lindbergh, who had seen the German war machine building up, who were shocked at the weakness of France and England and who thought the French might be too decadent to be worth saving, I truly believed in the One World concept. I felt that America had made a wretched mistake in failing to back the League of Nations and that the United States was very much a part of this world.

Furthermore, I felt very close to both the British and French and was shocked at what was happening to minorities under the Fascists. I had been in Italy and Germany during the summer of 1939 and hated what I saw of the strutting Mussolini and the psychopathic Hitler. So I threw myself passionately into the Committee to Defend America by Aiding the Allies, headed by journalist William Allen White. Mostly I took on speaking assignments, which were frequent enough to start giving me a guilty conscience —the definite feeling that I should be doing something about the things I was talking about. The draft became law, and it was obvious that bachelor Halaby stood an excellent chance of becoming a lowly dogface; it was then that I decided aviation had better become more of a career than an occasional hobby.

I had found a few chances to fly when I was at Stanford, usually in airplanes owned by friends. There was also a fairly active Yale Flying Club to which I occasionally resorted, but in my eight years of college and law school I logged only a meager 140 hours of flight time. I loved flying but it was too expensive while I was going to school. When U.S. involvement in the war became a distinct possibility, however, the government started the Civilian Pilot Training Program—a plan to train instructors who, in turn, could start turning out the fledgling manpower for the bombers and fighters still unlaunched from our assembly lines.

I enlisted in the program, taking primary flight instruction in a light, single-engined Porterfield at Metropolitan Airport in Van Nuys. I picked up about fifty hours and a new private pilot's license, followed by secondary training in a Waco, which earned me a commercial ticket and instructor's license. All this time I continued practicing law, which made for eighteen-hour days. I got up at dawn to take flying lessons, worked at O'Melveny & Myers from nine to five, and went back to the airport so I could get in more flying before darkness.

With the war clouds drawing closer, I went to see the head of the Air Corps Flight School at Oxnard, California, having heard they were desperate for pilots. They must have been, for although I had only about 250 hours logged, I was given a job as an apprentice instructor and mechanic. For almost four months I held down this job along with my law practice—spending five hours a day at the Army Air Corps school helping with aircraft maintenance and occasionally ferrying Stearman trainers from one base to another. It was a killing pace, but I finally qualified as a full-fledged instructor and built up another 1,000 hours, most of them on my back or bouncing around uncomfortably while I played aerial nursemaid to some very, very green youngsters with dreams of flying B-17s or P-40s. I specialized in teaching fundamental acrobatics, and one of my students was a kid named Alvin White who, I recall, did a very good snap roll but a sloppy slow roll. Years later, test pilot Al White was to become the first man to fly the XB-70—the first triplesonic bomber—and later served on a special supersonic transport committee I set up while I headed the FAA. Teaching rookies like Al White didn't provide enough pay to finance a weekend, but my status as civilian flight instructor won me a draft deferment and kept me out of the dreaded infantry.

Pearl Harbor, of course, changed things, and my work with those eager youngsters took on new dimensions of importance and reality. We were now playing for keeps, and my hours at the flight school became longer and longer, to the extent of destroying my effectiveness as a lawyer. At about this time I got a decided break. At Stanford I had met a dashing young man named John W. Myers, whose father had served as chief justice of California and who had been a cofounder of O'Melveny & Myers. John owned an airplane and we had flown together occasionally in the Aviation Country Club of Southern California. He had gone to work for Lockheed as a ferry pilot, flying Hudson bombers to England. One night we had a drink together and he confided that Lockheed needed pilots who could read and write and that as the only lawyer pilot, he was lonely.

"Hell, I'm the only college graduate among all those test pilots, and it's like being a missionary in a den of pirates," he com-

20

plained. "How would you like to join me? They need test pilots, but bad."

His timing couldn't have been better. I wasn't of much use to O'Melveny & Myers. The prospect of test-flying for Lockheed, a prime war contractor, seemed far more important to the war effect than what I was doing for those Air Corps kids. I accepted the idea on the spot, and John arranged an interview with the chief pilot, Elmer MacLeod. Shortly thereafter, I left the law firm and the fledgling flight academy, my feelings of gratitude and regret tempered with relief that I was now able to give my utmost to the war effort. This band of brother test pilots was a motley crew, most of them too old to go into military service and too young to retire from flying. Many had been running guns, booze, and women up and down Central America. They were colorful characters who could fly a bathtub if you could put wings on one. But John Myers wasn't exaggerating when he told me they were prejudiced against college men. They ridiculed me about my inexperience and the fact that I was an intellectual (they placed all college graduates in the "intellectual" category). They were fond of calling me "instant pilot" or "paper pilot," and invariably I was assigned to the worst pilots when I started flying Hudson and Ventura bombers as a rookie copilot.

With only John Myers as a personal friend among the crew, I didn't spend most of my nights carousing with the other airmen. I enrolled in an evening course in aeronautical engineering at the University of California. It wasn't long before I knew a hell of a lot more about airplanes than these old-timers, who really didn't give a damn about power plants, structures, and systems—all they cared about was whether the wings would stay on and the engines keep running. "Aero Godamics" was what they called the theory of flight, and the how and why of it were beyond them.

My career at Lockheed expanded in direct proportion to my bookwork. I helped rewrite operating manuals. I started developing more scientific aircraft-testing techniques. Gradually the company's chief pilot began relying on me more and more and, eventually, instead of being low man on the totem pole of test-flight assignments, I was handed increasingly important duties. I was tried out in the P-38, a hot, twin-engine fighter with a double tail boom that eventually became one of our finest combat aircraft. Once I learned to fly this "forked-tailed devil," as the Germans called it, I was allowed to do some of the odd jobs around the engineering test-pilot group—then headed by a capable, totally devoted aeronautical pilot-engineer named Milo Burcham.

One of my most significant jobs involved high-altitude tests on the P-38 turbosupercharger—specifically dealing with the problem of regulating the high-speed turbine pump that permitted the P-38's Allison engine to operate effectively above thirty thousand feet and thereby capable of flying and fighting higher than any Japanese Zero or German Focke Wulf 190.

Eventually I became more an engineering test pilot than a production test pilot. The latter merely takes up regular assembly-line production models to make sure the airplane meets all promised performance specifications before delivery to the customer—the U. S. Army Air Corps, in this case. His engineering counterpart tests various gadgets and gimmicks before they are approved for the production aircraft. An engineering test pilot must have some technical background as well as flying ability, and it was a most satisfying day for me when I became a part of the more elite corps.

Lockheed started out producing the twin-engine Hudson bomber, with most of the output going to the British under Lend-Lease agreements. The Hudson was nothing but a militarized version of the Lockheed Lodestar, a commercial transport, and while it was a fine, sturdy, dependable airplane, it wasn't much of a combat aircraft. The British used it primarily in reconnaissance and antisubmarine patrols, while those flown by the U. S. Air Corps were employed mainly in the Pacific Theater. Lockheed also produced at this time the Ventura, which was an enlarged Hudson with much more powerful engines.

I flew both planes frequently, initially on production test flights and later to test out the various modifications and improvements inevitable in the development of all military aircraft. Because it is impossible exactly to simulate combat conditions in any laboratory, wind tunnel, or blueprint room, virtually no plane we ever built for duty in World War II was immune from weaknesses and drawbacks uncovered in war zone missions. The final B-17 produced for the Air Corps, for example, was a vastly different plane from the original B-17; it was better protected and better armed, faster, longer ranged, and higher flying.

One of my jobs was to compare other U.S. fighters with Lockheed's own P-38. The Navy loaned us a Corsair for such purposes, and we also did a comparative analysis of the P-51; this product of North American Aviation was about the only one I could rate ahead of the P-38 in overall performance. The P-51 was a superb fighting machine, and in the opinion of many pilots it was the best produced during the war, including any German fighter and even Britain's famed Spitfire.

My test-flight duties were actually preparing me for a career that came years later—the job of regulating civil aviation as FAA chief. As a test pilot, I was in a crossfire among the aircraft designer, the manufacturer, and the customer. The customer wanted an airplane right away, even with known deficiencies, because we were in the middle of a global war. The manufacturer was under heavy pressure to get his planes delivered. The designer invariably wanted to wait until his dreamboat was absolutely perfect. As test pilots, Myers, Ed Dillon (another distinguished gentleman-lawyer we recruited), and I were regulators by evaluation, and in the course of our Lockheed careers, we succeeded, as was our duty, in holding back several aircraft from active service until "squawks" were cleared or improvements were made.

I spent eighteen months at Lockheed specializing in high-altitude flying, which included testing the latest oxygen-pressure breathing equipment, along with the supercharger devices. One day they handed me a new assignment, which was instrumental in my later joining the Navy, although I didn't know it at the time. The latest model P-38 (which, incidentally, was being manufactured in a building that had once been a distillery) was armed with four .50-caliber machine guns and a 37-millimeter cannon mounted in the nose; it packed enormous destructive punch, capable of knocking anything out of the sky, or even sinking small ships. However, its brand-new air cannon presented a problem that required immediate attention: Every time it was fired, the ejected shell casings would strike the wings and tail surfaces.

Milo Burcham had me fly a cannon-equipped P-38 from Burbank to Muroc Air Base in California's Mojave Desert. Muroc is one of the world's finest gunnery and bombing ranges, but it was built on a clay-covered dry lake with a surface so smooth and long that pilots had to be briefed on its peculiar qualities before landing there for the first time. Rolling on it at a hundred miles an hour gave the dangerous illusion that the plane was doing less than fifty, and unwary pilots would start turning off the landing strip at speeds so high that they would ground-loop a sensitive beast like a Curtiss P-40.

After I landed—cautiously, I might add—they loaded up the nose cannon and I took off again for some firing tests. The gun was hooked to a wing camera that filmed the ejecting shell as I pressed the firing button. From these films the project engineer hoped to come up with a solution. I don't remember exactly what the "fix" involved, but I do remember that one of the items fixed was test pilot Halaby.

Before I had taken off for the firing tests, I had telephoned the Muroc Air Corps control tower to report that my radio could not receive their frequency, and I wanted to make sure they would give me a flight-plan clearance back to Burbank when I finished.

"I'll come back over the tower, rock my wings, and you'll know I'm ready to be cleared," I told the controller.

"Roger," he agreed cheerfully.

I finished the cannon firing and was feeling pretty good—it was a beautiful, cloudless day, and to an airman, feeling good is akin to feeling cocky. Instead of approaching the Muroc control tower in a normal shallow dive, I flew the P-38 almost directly over the field and then dove to pick up speed. I roared by the tower at about 350 miles an hour, only 50 feet off the ground and less than 100 feet from the tower itself. As I had promised, I rocked my wings as I flashed by, pulled the bird up to 3,000 feet in a half loop, rolled out, and in 15 minutes was landing at Burbank, highly pleased with myself.

Waiting for me was a colonel in charge of the Air Corps resident representative's office at Lockheed. In considerably less than 15 minutes, he suspended me for 90 days for "careless and reckless flying." It seems I had pulled my show-off stunt at the very moment an Air Corps general of the Safety Command was in the Muroc control tower inspecting the base's safety of operations.

The suspension meant I could no longer fly any aircraft designed for the Air Corps, but it didn't apply to Navy planes. The chief pilot, more charitable than sympathetic, had me deliver a Lockheed Lodestar scheduled to be used as a Navy personnel transport. Delivery was to be made at the Navy Flight Test Section at Anacostia, in the nation's capital, where I was supposed to check out some top Navy pilots in what was to them a brand-new airplane.

The assignment resulted in my meeting the Commander of the test facility, Paul H. Ramsey (later the admiral in charge of the Bureau of Aeronautics), his deputy, and other Navy fliers. After I had finished demonstrating the Lodestar and checking out the pilots who would fly it, I had a chance one night to relax with my new friends, and we found ourselves casually discussing the possibility of my joining up.

"I'd like to get into uniform," I admitted. "What the hell, we're in a war."

"You'd really like to get into the Navy?" the base commander asked.

"Very much," I assured him.

Three days later, I was Lieutenant Junior Grade Najeeb Halaby, United States Naval Reserve, Serial Number 106728—having been processed through headquarters in Washington at what must have been a record rate. It was a decision that cost me considerable pay and personal freedom but one I never regretted. Obviously the Navy wanted me because of my test-pilot background and experience, but I still had to learn to fly the Navy way. They sent me down to Corpus Christi, Texas, where I spent a delightful ten weeks flying the Naval N-1 biplane, the famous little Stearman-designed trainer dubbed the "Yellow Peril," which gave thousands of future warbirds their first flying experience. For a guy used to fast P-38's and relatively complicated Lodestars and Hudsons, it was like asking Rubinstein to play "Chopsticks," but I thoroughly enjoyed flying the N-1. There's nothing like an open-cockpit airplane for really *feeling* the thrill of flight. And the airplane itself had an interesting history; Boeing actually owned the manufacturing rights, having bought out Stearman sometime back, but some of the biplanes were made at the Naval Aircraft Factory

25

in Philadelphia and thus were the only government-built planes to be used in World War II.

With my first Navy orders to the Carrier Fighter Test Section, Flight Test, Naval Air Test Center, Patuxent River, Maryland, I became sort of a barnyard aeronautical engineer, a specialist on strange and exotic fighter aircraft. I spent about a fourth of my time at the National Advisory Commission for Aeronautics (NACA) at Langley Field, Virginia, the home of America's most advanced air research and development base. There I worked with such experts as Robert Gilruth, John Stack, Mel Gough, and a lot of younger men who were right on the leading edge of some exciting aeronautical developments. Overall I must have flown about fifty different types of airplanes from the time I joined the Navy to the end of the war. My skippers and mentors, Gouin, Trapnell, Ramsey, Boothe, Carl, Gayler, Owen, were the best of the naval test pilots—great fighter pilots who rotated between combat at sea and solving flight problems at the new test center.

Since there was nothing to do at this isolated, strictly secret base except eat, sleep, and work, and because it was only a few minutes from Langley Field, I immersed myself in aeronautical activities. My sense of guilt at not seeing combat action during the first twenty-two months of the war made my dedication that much more Jesuitical; moreover, I loved the duty. It represented a new challenge daily, pushing the frontiers of flight and balancing my scientific analysis with the instincts of the fleet pilots. It was, in brief, a great way to help win the war.

One experience at Langley was to prepare me for the rigors of testing a completely new type of airplane: the jet. I was first shown in 1943 a photograph of a sonic shock wave that had been generated in a Langley wind tunnel at Mach 1.1, or slightly higher than the speed of sound. After seeing the picture, I was allowed to observe the phenomenon repeated in the wind tunnel. I could actually feel the almost frightening vibration.

The word "Mach," in essence a synonym for speed of sound, is derived from the name of an Austrian physicist, Dr. Ernst Mach, whose experiments disclosed the existence of a shock wave generated by high speed. Mach discovered that when the flow of a liquid through a pipe reached the speed of sound at roughly

750 miles an hour at 60 degrees Fahrenheit at sea level, the pipe began to vibrate, and the liquid flow itself changed from smoothness to turbulence. In a similar manner, the air flowing around an airplane approaching Mach 1 no longer acts like a smoothly flowing liquid but instead begins to compress into solid chunks of air that break sharply away from the wings and fuselage. The result is severe vibration, a sharp shift in balance, loss of control, or even structural failure, with the shock wave literally bombarding the tail section. While flying for Lockheed, I had been thoroughly briefed on some of the P-38's early troubles when pilots diving in high-altitude dogfights penetrated Dr. Mach's sound waves and tore several of the sturdy fighters apart. The so-called sound barrier was a killer not just of the P-38's but of other combat planes as well; a number of P-51's and even P-47's lost their tails in dives to such an extent that the latter acquired the unhappy nickname of "Widowmaker."

The NACA and both the Navy and Air Corps, therefore, were interested in the sound-barrier menace long before jet aircraft came along. No piston engine plane could approach Mach 1 in level flight, but at the higher altitudes many propeller-driven planes were capable of diving into the speed of sound. It could be reached at 30,000 feet at about 650 miles an hour. A 400-mph fighter at 35,000 feet could easily nudge 650 mph in a dive at 30,000 feet, where temperatures were much lower than 60 degrees Fahrenheit at sea level. Compressibility was a murderer until Lockheed and an NACA team under Stack came up with a system of dive flaps that licked the compressibility problems as they affected aircraft in high-speed-dive configurations.

To understand better both the phenomenon and the solution, one only has to visualize what happens when a plane like the P-38 approaches the speed of sound in a dive. The supersonic shock waves disintegrate the pressure differential along the upper and lower wing surfaces. It is this differential that gives an airplane its lift. Once the lift is destroyed, the normal airflow pattern over the tail surfaces also deteriorates, changing from a downwash to an upward force that tends to drive the tail higher. Now we are in a deadly cycle. As the tail lifts, the nose keeps going down, and the dive increases in speed. This leads to the fearful "tuck under"—actually the start of an unwanted outside loop. There is no elevator control, and once tuck under begins, the result is frequently structural failure. Recovering from tuck under often was pure luck, not from anything a pilot could do—the fortunate ones lived only if the wings and tail stayed on, and they could regain elevator control.

The NACA dive flaps, activated electrically, increased drag and changed the airflow under the wing and thus increased the lift even in a dive. They achieved this without affecting the tail lift, and by this means provided the pilot with enough controllability to pull out of a dive. Later, of course, development of the swept-back wing and variable controls enabled jet aircraft to fly through the sound barrier with no danger whatsoever.

I became passionately involved with the war against compressibility when because of my high-altitude experience at Lockheed I was ordered to run dive tests for the Pacific Fleet. A number of Navy pilots had reported encountering such severe buffeting in high-speed dives on Japanese Zeros that they were unable to aim their gunsights. The difficulties always occurred when they were carrying certain externally mounted "stores": bombs, rockets, and drop tanks, for example. For more days than I like to remember, I took a Corsair up to 37,000 feet and went into a series of dives, reaching speeds of Mach .67, where the onset of the "shakes" occurred. Special cameras and other equipment recorded the airflow measurements and movements around various "stores." The result of these tests was an immediate cure: extension of the pylons carrying these stores and increasing their distance from the lower surface of the wing in such a way as to permit smoother flow. Out of all this came my only previous literary production, a Navy fleet-training film, *Ensign Buzzsaw Gets the Shakes!*

When I wasn't working at Langley, my main base of assignment was the new Naval Air Test Center on the Patuxent River near Washington, D.C. While I was at Patuxent, I was named project pilot of the new Bell Aerocomet, which was the first American-built jet. Originally it had been assigned to the Air Corps and it took some fierce interdepartmental brawling before a couple of these experimental planes were handed over to the Navy.

The sound barrier was no problem to the Aerocomet, or as it was officially designed, the YP-59A, simply because it was incapable of supersonic flight. It may have been the slowest jet ever built, and in truth it was more of a power-plant research airplane than anything else. For one thing, we hadn't learned much about the advantages of swept-back, thin wings in reducing drag and preventing compressibility. The Germans, in fact, were way ahead of us in that respect; not until intelligence reports gleaned from captured documents revealed German experiments on sharply swept-winged jets did our own NACA efforts get some priority for shaping the wing like an arrowhead.

The YP-59's speed deficiencies notwithstanding, it still was an exciting plane to fly. Because I knew damned little about turbines, the Navy sent me to the General Electric Turbine Division in Lynn, Massachusetts, for a cram course in "Look, Ma, no prop" technology. Participation in the crossing of the jet threshold had to be the greatest challenge of a young aviator's life, but a greater thrill was yet in store.

Sometime in 1943, after I had learned to fly the YP-59A, my commanding officer summoned me.

"Jeeb," he announced, "we've got a certain VIP coming here to be checked out in the Bell. You're about the best jet jockey we've got around here, so he's your pigeon."

"An admiral?" I ventured.

"Nope, he's not even in the military."

"How the hell does he rate flying a classified airplane?" I demanded.

"Because his name is Charles Lindbergh," my commander replied wryly.

I was in awe of the man when he showed up for ground instruction. The only reason Lindbergh wasn't in uniform was because of his isolationist record, which had earned the undying enmity of President Franklin D. Roosevelt. Walter S. Ross, in his fine biography of Lindbergh (*The Last Hero,* Harper & Row, 1968), summed up FDR's hatred most succinctly:

One cannot avoid the conclusion that Roosevelt built Colonel Lindbergh up as a pro-Nazi so he could break him. Lindbergh was a strong and dangerous political antagonist, never a potential traitor. But Roosevelt had to get rid of him at any cost. . . .

The President never did succeed in getting rid of Lindbergh. While many people—including me—disagreed with Lindbergh's isolationism, he was still regarded as a superb aeronautical technician; and he had enough behind-the-scenes support to win some highly secret assignments during World War II, mostly in the field of combat-zone flight tests. He actually flew thirty-six of what amounted to combat missions, and on one was unofficially credited with shooting down a Japanese fighter.

Anyway, for me this certainly was no case of internationalist meeting isolationist. It was a young pilot being introduced to one of the world's greatest pilots, possibly *the* greatest, and I confess to considerable nervousness at the prospect of teaching something to Charles Lindbergh. As it turned out, my qualms were soon dissipated: Lindbergh was open, modest, friendly, and intensely interested. In his questions and responses, he seemed to be looking beyond the relative simplicity of a machine into the mysteries of intuition.

I first took him through the shops where the Navy was inspecting and maintaining the GE I-16 gas-turbine engines that powered the YP-59. Then we looked over the airplane itself very carefully. It had virtually no range, I warned him, and its fuel capacity allowed only about a forty-five-minute flight. Fully loaded with fuel, guns, and ammunition, the YP-59 would have needed half of the Sahara Desert for a takeoff roll: It was no wonder the aircraft never saw combat. I also confided to Lindbergh that on the previous day, I had almost "bought the farm" in this same airplane through a combination of carelessness and zeal.

We had been experimenting with pressure breathing equipment, and the Navy wanted a new system tested in the YP-59. Also, we were anxious to see how the plane's controls and various systems would behave at about forty thousand feet—an altitude that no Navy pilot had ever reached simply because there was no Navy aircraft capable of climbing that high.

I got into a fleece-lined flying suit with boots, goggles, and heated mittens, donned the new high-pressure experimental oxygen mask, and took off, eventually staggering up to 46,900 feet—almost 500 feet higher than any previously recorded heavier-than-air flight. It took the YP-59 so long to reach 46,900 feet that my fuel ran out just shortly after I broke the altitude record. I was just too excited to notice the fuel gauges, and while I was cruising around congratulating myself, both engines quickly flamed out; with no power, the batteries ran down. This left me with no juice to extend the flaps and landing gear, and at 12,000 feet and gliding heavily, I also lost my radio. At this point I was faced with three alternatives: jumping, landing the plane on its belly, or trying to crank the gear and flaps down manually in the few moments' race with gravity. For some unknown reason—perhaps test-plane preservation—I took the third option. It took exactly 127 turns of the hand crank to lower the gear, and by then I was only 100 feet above the runway, having made a crosswind approach. The control tower was rather surprised to see me and was equally surprised when they learned later that the landing was dead-stick. It took more luck than skill, and I must have lost seven pounds just sweating it out.

I told that story to Lindbergh mostly to impress him with the YP-59's limited fuel capacity, remembering what I had heard about the Lone Eagle's sheer love of flying and boyish enthusiasm at the prospect of piloting a new type of aircraft. But while I did what I could to familiarize him with the jet's controls, systems, power plants, and assorted idiosyncrasies, I had the distinct impression that even without my instructions he could have flown that bird cold.

The checkout flight itself had to be solo because the plane was single-place, yet he had no difficulty whatsoever in handling the Bell as if he had five hundred hours logged in one. Furthermore, he impressed me in a personal as well as a professional sense.

I had half expected my earlier hero worship to collide with my distaste for Lindbergh's past isolationism, but if there was a subconscious element of the latter, it evaporated quickly under the spell of his simplicity and humility. We were to meet many times after that YP-59 briefing and we were to become good friends. But even in the relatively brief span of that first contact, I sensed what others had felt or eventually would feel about this unique man: the depth of his intellect, the incredible span of his interests, the spiritual, almost metaphysical approach he brought to every endeavor. In many ways, he was an echo of Da Vinci—scientist, philosopher, engineer, scholar, and writer, excelling not in just one field but in all.

Granted, Lindbergh's assumptions that the Germans couldn't be beaten and that the British couldn't fight turned out to be wrong. His chief weakness in those pre-World War II days was his airman's propensity for viewing Nazi Germany solely as a military threat while never really grasping its even greater moral threat. I believe that the far more mature Lindbergh of the fifties, sixties, and seventies would not have fallen into that ideological trap. As a matter of fact, there was considerable justification for both his admiration and fear of German technological prowess; the Germans were ahead of us in many engineering areas, as I found out myself, when the Navy assigned me to test and evaluate enemy aircraft.

The Japanese Zero, for instance, gave me the feeling I was flying an orange crate. Although it was light, fast-climbing and impressively nimble, structurally it left a lot to be desired. There was an awful lot of engine to fuselage, with torque so excessive that on takeoff the Zero would pull violently to the left.

Going from the flimsy Zero to the top German fighters, the ME-109 and Focke Wulf 190, was like transferring from a flivver to a Mercedes-Benz. I also flew some of the early German jet fighters and was puzzled by the amazing variation in the quality of their manufacturing. One captured test model would be superbly constructed while a second, ostensibly an identical airplane, had apparently been assembled with safety pins and glue. Not for some time did we learn the reason: The poorly built jets had been made in "salt mines" by prisoner labor.

One of the Nazi warplanes I tested almost cost me my life. American troops had captured a German air base and picked up, intact, four ME-262's. The ME-262 was a twin-engine jet fighter-bomber and one of the first planes capable of achieving 500 miles per hour in level flight. They were put on a British carrier and shipped to Newark, New Jersey, from where the Navy was supposed to ferry one of them back to the Patuxent Naval Air Base in Maryland. I was the pigeon selected for the ferry flight, apparently because I had acquired a reputation for being both scientific and crafty, two obvious requisites for flying a strange airplane that had no operating manuals and whose instruments and controls were placarded in German. Also I was one of the few American pilots who had ever flown jets.

I spent a day and a half in Newark going over the Messerschmitt with a knowledgeable Navy mechanic. Unfortunately neither one of us could read German. We did the best we could to check out the unfamiliar cockpit, and I finally decided it was reasonably safe to take off. I had a mild premonition of disaster as soon as I began taxiing, as the brakes were terrible and the steering about as agile as that of a Panzer tank. But I was committed, so I lined up on the assigned runway, which happened to be east–west, pointing me straight toward the city of Newark (runway alignments at Newark were later changed after three bad crashes in the early post-war years).

There wasn't a full fuel load; I was afraid to top the tanks, since we didn't have any idea what the maximum allowable takeoff weight was, nor did we know the best flaps and trim tab settings. We *had* determined which was the button for activating the electrically controlled trim tabs, however, and I figured the 262 was really nothing but another airplane.

I charged down the runway and got off the ground successfully, but that's when everything hit the fan. The plane just started to climb, the nose going up all the time until I was close to stalling out right over downtown Newark. I kept pressing the elevator tab switch forward to get the nose down, while simultaneously pushing the stick forward with my right knee and all my 170 pounds. No response, except that the climb got steeper. The 262 began to shake in the ominous warning of a stall—she practically was standing on her tail. Suddenly it hit me: On a German airplane, that tab switch had to be reversed. Instead of pushing forward to get the nose down, maybe it should be pulled back—the exact opposite from the American tab controls. I pressed the tab switch back instead of forward, and the nose obediently came down, a split second before I would have stalled out. I flew down to Patuxent—and only my laundry knew how scared I was.

It is my belief, based on my own test-flight experience, that the best-designed fighters we developed during World War II were the P-51 and the Grumman F8F, otherwise known as the Hellcat. I know I'd get plenty of arguments from the men who flew other types, particularly the immensely strong P-47 Thunderbolt and Lockheed's own P-38. The P-38, to which I'll always feel a sentimental attachment, may have been the best *all-around* combat aircraft we produced. It could fly any kind of mission, from photoreconnaissance to bomber escort; from high-altitude fighting to low-altitude strafing. It made no difference to this superb airplane that was born in Lockheed designer Kelly Johnson's famed "skunk works," the affectionate nickname for this colorful genius's design headquarters. But despite its incredible versatility, the P-38 still was too complicated to be a fighter. The twin engines and the turbosuperchargers were constant problems.

After a year and a half in the Carrier Fighter Test Branch, I became restless and itching to get some combat duty before the war ended. I so informed my immediate superior, tough, competent Noel Gayler, whom the pilots irreverently christened "Torque Nose." His full name was Noel A. M. Gayler, his mother's inspiration for a baby born on Christmas morning. (At this writing, he is Admiral Gayler, commander in chief of the Pacific Fleet, and still harder than chrome steel.)

To buttress my repeated requests for combat duty, I went through carrier qualification, but Torque Nose kept turning down my applications as fast as I submitted them. The more I tested, the more experienced I became in this highly specialized role and—in Gayler's eyes, anyway—the less dispensable. I even tried to transfer secretly to the Marine Corps, but got nowhere when the commandant found out what I was doing. I was doomed to spend the whole war testing rather than fighting airplanes.

One of my last Navy missions got me momentary distinction. After several weeks of plotting, I took off on May 1, 1945, from Muroc in a YP-80, the Lockheed Shooting Star and the nation's first operational jet fighter. I ended up at Patuxent, having completed the first transcontinental *jet* flight in American aviation history. The flying time was five hours and forty minutes, but three refueling stops—at El Paso, Fort Worth, and Nashville—gave me an elapsed time of eighteen hours, which was about the same as for a

DC-3. But it still proved that man could leap as well as walk and that a simpler engine combined with a clean wing could compress this nation into one quarter of its old time dimension. Since it was a classified mission, this distance-defying feat remained in the files of the U. S. Navy until it was dug out by an FAA information officer sixteen years later.

The flight was a fitting climax to my Navy life. The war in Europe was over, and Japan already was doomed. I had no desire for a military career, but I really didn't know what I wanted to do; like so many young Americans geared to the tempo of wartime, I found myself unprepared for what they called peace.

When the war ended, I entered a period of brooding that bordered on depression. It wasn't my failure to see any combat—I honestly felt my test flying constituted important and worthwhile duty—but rather the onset of doubts about whether we really had won the war . . . whether it was just like 1918, a victory without real peace. We certainly hadn't achieved a lasting partnership with the Soviet Union; even before the war was over, the Soviet-American-British alliance was coming apart at the seams.

I was a full lieutenant at war's end, but my dreams and ambitions progressed much farther than those two stripes indicated. I began studying the Russian language at Navy night school and pored over all the intelligence reports on Soviet aviation I could find. When I considered myself sufficiently versed in that difficult arena, I submitted an unusual proposal to the chief of naval operations.

Briefly, I asked that I be sent to Moscow as assistant naval air attaché but that I also be authorized to take with me two of the latest-model U.S. aircraft—the Grumman F8F and the Ryan Fireball—as a token of friendship with and trust in the Soviets, and in exchange for the Soviets' two latest models. I further proposed that I develop with Soviet aeronautical experts a joint program of peaceful engineering and flight development.

In retrospect, I was naïve and, yes, idealistic. Inevitably, my scheme had virtually no chance of success; I had no way of knowing that Stalin was about to stretch a string of broken pledges from the Balkans to Poland, that Soviet spies already had begun demolishing our atomic monopoly, and that the Soviet dictator re-

35

garded the Americans, who had helped save his skin, as targets no less than Germans or French or Italians.

Maybe, though, I could have been about thirty years ahead of my time. In one of my last acts as FAA administrator, I went to the Soviet Union on an official mission and was encouraged— almost begged—by the Soviets to bring back their Yak 40 jetliner for U.S. demonstrations. The Soviets were anxious to put together a joint venture involving American marketing of this small transport, aiming it at the local-service airlines like North Central and Allegheny, which had little or no jet equipment yet. The dreams I had three decades ago of international co-operation seem a lot closer to reality today, particularly as they affect aviation and space —witness the United States-Soviet joint space mission and the Chinese buying Boeing 707s.

At any rate, the Navy quickly spattered the mud of rejection all over my rose-colored glasses. I was told that some people in the Navy Department were intrigued by my plan, but officially it never got off the ground.

Instead, an old buddy at Yale Law School offered me a job in the State Department's new Office of Research and Intelligence, the companion of what would become the Central Intelligence Agency. The only other intriguing possibility was an invitation from McDonnell Aircraft to take the chief test pilot's job, but I didn't think it had as much future nor nearly the challenge of the State Department post. Truthfully, I would have preferred to go back to California, but the government assignment looked interesting, and I figured it wouldn't hurt to try it out for six to eight months.

Besides, by then I had fallen in love, and courtship was a higher priority than California weather.

Her name was Doris Carlquist, and she was blond, beautiful, and emphatically not dumb. I was still a lieutenant and assistant chief of the Fighter Test Section at Patuxent when we met at a Thanksgiving party in 1945 a few months after the war ended. I had been invited by a law school classmate, Ed Clapp, who had a home in Washington and whose bright and attractive wife, Jean, had decided to invite her friend Doris as the extra lady.

36

Doris came unescorted, and it was just as well I showed up in the same category, because I don't think I would have paid much attention to anyone else. Very early at the party we got into a political discussion, and I realized that for the first time I had found a quick and witty girl who enjoyed this give-and-take debating as much as I did.

She was tall, slim, and athletic (I found out later she played a California brand of tennis). Her background, like mine, was western; Doris had come East from San Francisco, where she had been working for the regional Office of Price Administration. When I met her, she was an administrative assistant in the State Department's German-Austrian Occupied Affairs branch and, also like me, had stars in her eyes about peace and international understanding. Because of the size of the Clapps' Washington apartment, I started out sitting in the only vacant spot—at her feet, which were at the ends of lovely legs.

Our courtship began immediately, and we were married only three months later. My life in bachelor officers' quarters was lonely, a new career was starting, and I reasoned that if I went back to Mother's home, I would never be on my own.

We went to New York a couple of times for dinner and shows. Once we decided to get married—at Christmas Eve services at the Washington Cathedral—we talked about going to California to meet my mother and, possibly, to Alaska, where her father was living. But we were both of age and quite independent and determined to remain so. We felt it wasn't necessary to get parental blessings. Aside from our independence, I also had the only-too-accurate conviction that no girl was going to be completely satisfactory to my mother.

CHAPTER TWO

I was discharged from the Navy just before our marriage and started my new job in the State Department. The Office of Research and Intelligence actually was a combination of the wartime Office of Strategic Services (the famed OSS) and the Army's Research and Analysis Group. To Research and Analysis had fallen not only the job of determining the values of targets to hit in Germany and Japan but also the analysis of the various guerrilla groups and incipient political forces in Southeast Asia. But in my mind the Army's G-2 Special Branch, under Colonel Alfred McCormack, was really the brains behind the nation's communications intelligence efforts: In the last three years of World War II their achievements included using the Japanese codes and revealing force movements at crucial junctures.

A good friend and Yale Law contemporary, Amory Bradford (who was also a top deputy of McCormack's), was a midwife of the State Department's new intelligence branch. An important ally was Secretary of State James Byrnes, who liked the idea of infusing the department with some young, fresh blood. Inevitable opposition came from the old-line Foreign Service officers: They were loath to accept intelligence as a separate function in the State Department, completely divorced from their traditional policymaking and foreign operations. They were openly afraid of the newcomers, just as we were somewhat disdainful of and impatient with them. We saw it as a chance to reform the subjective, conservative, tradition-bound State Department—as well as a chance for securing with wits the peace that had escaped our arms.

I reported to the Research and Intelligence Branch as a GS-7 on March 1, 1946, the intervening month being spent on a honeymoon. Our marriage had gotten off to a snowy start; we were married in Washington, and right after the ceremony a blizzard hit the capital. All planes were grounded, and we had to stay in the Wardman Park Hotel for two days while the city's inadequate snowplow force finally managed to clear some paths through five inches of white stuff.

We flew to Los Angeles on the third day for the first—and nearly the last—visit with my mother. It was an emotional disaster, Mother's open antagonism toward her new daughter-in-law conveying her distinct conviction that I had married a designing woman. To recover, we wound up in a small resort hotel, Furnace Creek Inn, in Death Valley. Most resort hotels were still being used as military hospitals, and we were lucky to find even this obscure, though rather romantic, little place. When we returned to Washington, Doris quit her job, and I went to work at the State Department, where my first duties involved the review and co-ordination of various studies of foreign technical developments, including aviation. This led to an overseas assignment late in 1947, after George C. Marshall had replaced Byrnes as Secretary of State.

Livingston Merchant, who later became an ambassador to NATO, was then heading the department's Aviation Division. He received a request from the government of Saudi Arabia to supply a civil aviation adviser to King Ibn Saud Abdul Aziz, the longtime ruler. Saudi Arabia already had contracted with TWA to serve as the technical operating support group for Saudi Arabian Airlines. The country had joined the International Civil Aviation Organization (ICAO) and was becoming an aviation-oriented nation. Saudi Arabia figuratively had great faith in Allah, the camel, and the airplane—and oil. There were abysmal or nonexistent roads, not much of a rail system, and little coastal shipping.

Saudi Arabia, indeed, had leaped over the desert into the airspace, using the airplane as the prime means of transportation. The King wanted someone with both technical and legal experience, and Merchant, after canvassing the department, nominated me. He also confessed that in addition to helping Saudi Arabia, I was to find out what the British might be up to in Saudi Arabia. They were playing a strong role in the Saudi Arabian military services, and the State Department was curious as to how deeply and for what purpose the British were getting involved in this primitive but oil-rich country.

I reported to J. Rives Child, U.S. ambassador to Saudi Arabia, in Jidda. I spent many weeks in Jidda, Dhahran, and Riyadh, the nation's three principal cities, in the winter of 1947–48, using Jidda as my base of operations.

Because I was a guest of King Ibn Saud and the Saudi Arabian Government, I was put up in the official guest house. It was ancient, but freshly whitewashed. I had a crib for a bed and a stand-up commode, but there was no plumbing nor running water, and no refrigeration. I was assigned two tall, black Sudanese servants for my personal use; they looked like a couple of spear carriers from a Cecil B. DeMille biblical epic—both were around six-six and would have scared the hell out of a pro football linebacker.

My first contacts were with the King's fourth son, Prince Ali Mansour Abdul Aziz (he has since died), who was in charge of defense and aviation activities. He hospitably escorted me on a round of visits, and our talks mostly concerned exactly what a civil air adviser might do for his country.

At this point I began to learn the difference between doing business in the West and in the East, and the lesson is still useful today. The Kingdom of Saudi Arabia is an absolute monarchy, and all final policy decisions are made by the King. He operates through the royal family, so that his sons and relatives have the major positions of power, and they, in turn, appoint from the civilian population domestic and foreign advisers, staff officers, and the like. Since theirs is a completely controlled economy and a tight, blood-knit Administration, the King can only delegate to a prince or to a few highly educated and motivated young public servants; thus the only way the King can decentralize his authority is to

40

share some power with those closest to him. Perhaps more importantly, the best way for his monarchy to develop an economy is to distribute and redistribute the wealth through trusted hands. So he adopts the simplest, most direct means available—and in this specific case, he delegated to his loyal and capable son, Prince Mansour, responsibility and decentralized authority over a function of government: namely, the state airline. He was not only permitted but also expected to "earn" a reasonable return from this investment and to distribute it among his wives, children, relatives, and retinue. In this fashion, the money trickles down to the lowest servant as well as to those who make a substantial contribution to the operational earnings of the airline. This was not considered unethical—simply pragmatic. It works for their society and economy, and they cannot and never will be able to understand why this could be called corrupt by the West. It is not a question of ethics, but rather a question of whether, at this stage in their development, this is a good way to operate.

The three TWA technical aides had a fascinating airline going. The equipment consisted of surplus World War II airplanes, mostly DC-3s, with a single DC-4. TWA pilots flew the planes, although they were trying to train some Saudi airmen and had, at that point, a single qualified Saudi Arabian copilot. The ground personnel were largely Saudi Arabian, although there were a few Syrians and Lebanese.

In the early days, SAUDIA was a kind of royal family airline. If members of the King's royal family wanted seats, other passengers were bumped from the flight. A trip thirty years ago could be a circus. Occasionally a Saudi would bring along all his worldly possessions, including livestock. A goat or sheep in the aft cabin section was not unheard of. Sometimes the passengers would cook their own meals on the six-hour flight from Jidda to Riyadh; there weren't any regulations about barbecuing between the seats of a DC-3. It was, however, an operation conducted with a perfect safety record. It wasn't easy flying, either, for while the weather generally was superb, occasional sandstorms were as dangerous as blizzards, and the mountain ranges of the West were unforgiving.

The airline, of course, was a monopoly, although Aramco (Arabian American Oil Company) also ran what amounted to an airline in Saudi Arabia, which made a weekly trip to San Francisco with personnel and high-priority cargo.

SAUDIA today is a thoroughly modern, jet-equipped carrier, with routes stretching from Western Europe to Pakistan. TWA still has a technical-assistance contract (soon to be phased out), with a team of pilots, mechanics, engineers, and computer and other specialists flying for SAUDIA. At the same time, TWA has U.S. route authority to parallel SAUDIA from Western Europe to Saudi Arabia through Dhahran.

Before returning to the United States, I was able to spend a few days in Taif with a detachment of excellent British officers and noncoms training the Saudis in the use of vehicles, small arms, and howitzers. The British commander was hospitable, helpful, and polite—and frankly confided his desire to expand British influence throughout the country. In fact, he expressed large disappointment at his being isolated in the hills behind Jidda. In my report on the Saudi Arabian mission, I warned the State Department that it was not only desirable but also essential to replace the British with an American military technical-assistance group and U.S. equipment. My words eventually were heeded: For some years, the United States has wielded the dominant military influence in this vital area; the Saudi Arabian military forces are largely U.S.-equipped, small but efficient, with Northrop F-5 jet fighters and Raytheon Hawk missiles. They form a kind of pro-American island in the turbulent sea of Arab-Israeli tensions, and we should vigorously help them to defend themselves and their energy resources.

While my civil aviation adviser mission had not been completely successful, I still considered it a worthwhile experience. It gave me great insights into Arab thinking and the mores of Arabia's Bedouin. I loved them and sympathized with them, even though I couldn't see how they could develop on their own a growing, viable transportation system unless they moved toward a profit-oriented merit system of doing business—which they later did.

Back in Washington, I began working on some very highly classified communications intelligence as our Research and Intelligence group became increasingly involved in monitoring and analyzing Soviet activities throughout the world. But in Washington, bureaucratic jobs can change as rapidly as the capital's unpredictable weather, and mine was no exception.

The National Security Act of 1947 establishing a Department of Defense had been signed by President Truman, thus inaugurating the great Armed Forces unification experiment. I had watched these developments with interest but with no sense of forthcoming personal involvement. It came about almost by accident. The first Secretary of Defense was James Forrestal, who happened to be a close friend of Doris's godmother, Mrs. Chase Donaldson, at whose home I had courted my future wife. Elinor Donaldson later married James H. Douglas, who became Secretary of the Air Force and then Deputy Secretary of Defense. Jim and Elinor today are among our closest friends.

Elinor knew Mr. and Mrs. Forrestal quite well; in fact, Jim would drop in occasionally at her home for an afternoon cocktail. In the course of one of his visits to our block, Elinor brought up my name and background to the Secretary of Defense. I don't think he was totally unaware of me, for we lived only a few doors away from the Donaldsons and Jean and Jim La Touche who introduced us to John H. Ohly, one of Forrestal's first and best assistants. The result of all this neighborhood nepotism was an invitation to the Pentagon for an interview, during which time we discussed the possibility of my working at the Defense Department, and in May of 1948 I was hired as his assistant by John H. Ohly, whose responsibilities included international affairs, foreign intelligence, and liaison with the Joint Chiefs of Staff.

Forrestal was one of the most brilliant, dedicated, complex, and tragic figures I have ever known. Working for him and with him, one could feel his objectivity, his driving desire to get things done, his unyielding devotion to the national interest. These were qualities a young government official would want to emulate, and I was no exception. Unfortunately he let these admirable qualities take over his personal life to such an extent that they destroyed him as a husband, father, and in the end as a human being.

The too brief time I spent working for him was one of the most exciting and stimulating periods of my life. For one thing, Forrestal was especially astute in selection of his staff: His principal civilian assistants were Wilfred J. McNeil, Marx Leva, and Jack

Ohly, each an extremely competent and dedicated public official. His choice as director of the Joint Staff and his main link to the Joint Chiefs was General Alfred M. Gruenther, an exceptionally able strategist and administrator.

The biggest cross Forrestal bore was one fashioned by the first Secretary of the Air Force, Stuart Symington, who was regarded by the Defense Secretary as the main challenger of unification of the Armed Forces. Symington was so headstrong about the Air Force that he considered the Army and Navy mere anachronisms. Feeding his total absorption in air power were Generals Hoyt Vandenberg, Curtis LeMay, and other top Air Force officials feeling the full frustrations of the years during which their branch of service had been under the thumb of the War Department. To strong, willful men like LeMay and Vandenberg, unification was fine in theory, but only so long as the Air Force dominated.

Forrestal was the real architect of the National Security Act, and he believed fervently, passionately, in unification as the best means of assuring an efficient defense establishment. He held steadfastly to this conviction in spite of his own Navy background. (He had been a Navy pilot in World War I and had served as Secretary of the Navy.) He knew that the Navy, like the Air Force, wanted to go it alone, and the pressures on him as the first Secretary of Defense not only were unrelenting but—as it turned out—virtually unbearable for anyone with such inner tensions.

He neglected his home life. His wife had become quite frustrated, and he seemed to have only a little comradeship with his two sons. His real home was the Pentagon, where he would start work as early as 7 A.M. and finish as late as 10 P.M. Often he would breakfast with columnist Walter Lippmann, whom he admired and trusted. Forrestal had many friends but he isolated himself from them, mostly because he was afraid friendship might lead to favors. Symington's opposition (Forrestal considered it defection) hurt Forrestal because he liked and enjoyed his fellow "Yalie," the Air Force Secretary.

Forrestal made a fatal mistake during the 1948 campaign between Harry Truman and Thomas Dewey. Forrestal had told several people he thought Dewey was likely to get elected and that he'd be willing to serve in a Republican administration. His remarks got back to Truman, and the President never forgave him. Forrestal already had more enemies than he needed, and adding the President of the United States to the list was the clincher.

The late J. Edgar Hoover was one such enemy, and I unwittingly played a part in turning the FBI chief against the Secretary of Defense. One of my early tasks in the intelligence area was to survey how many agencies were engaged in domestic and foreign intelligence activities. I spent several weeks on this study and handed Forrestal a report that showed there were no less than twenty-three overlapping, conflicting, and friction-producing agencies within the city of Washington, D.C., all busy at various forms of internal-security intelligence aimed at countering the Soviet threat.

"There must be some buckling together," I wrote—deliberately using a phrase Forrestal was fond of.

My recommendation was that an officer be appointed to the President's National Security Council staff whose whole duty would be to eliminate this wasteful duplication of effort and thus reduce some dangerous friction. Along with the report were elaborate charts depicting, as no words could, the maze of bureaucracy that had been allowed to grow into a quarreling, uncontrolled, almost unmanageable mess. Forrestal called me in a few days after I submitted my report and told me he was greatly impressed. Only sent me a note.

"I'm going to arrange for you to see Attorney General Tom Clark and Mr. Hoover," he wrote. "I think you should go over this report with them."

He probably was right, inasmuch as the FBI was right in the middle of this jurisdictional battle over intelligence activities. But in retrospect, letting Forrestal give J. Edgar Hoover my report was either the stupidest or the bravest thing I could have done. The FBI director regarded it as a declaration of war against his department, and he hit the ceiling. Within two weeks, Washington newspapers were carrying stories to the effect that the Pentagon was trying to take over the FBI and that Forrestal was nothing but a power-hungry despot.

The war against the Secretary of Defense was on in earnest. Rumors were spread, for example, that Forrestal was anti-Israel.

These reports were printed just when the new Israeli state was being formed, amid massive Zionist pressure on the White House. The stories suggested that Forrestal was so concerned about oil, the communications network, and the air and naval bases we had in the Middle East that he favored the Arabs over the Israelis. I was told on very good authority that some of the more militant Zionist organizations actually warned President Truman to make sure Forrestal didn't strangle Israel under the guise of strategic military interests.

There was some validity for the Zionist fears in all this; Forrestal *was* deeply worried about Arab-Israeli relations, to such an extent that he asked Mark Ethridge, the highly regarded publisher of the Louisville *Courier-Journal,* to make a study of the impact a major Middle East conflict would have on the availability of oil for America's military machine and the effects on our bases in the area. Ethridge reported back that the military would have very serious problems indeed if the Arabs turned against the United States.

Forrestal was neither pro-Arab nor anti-Semitic; he merely acted and spoke in accordance with his all-consuming commitment to national security, but in this one-dimensional crusade, he left himself terribly vulnerable to attack. And he did, from all available evidence, urge Truman not to alienate the Arabs. On Forrestal's other flanks, virtually the entire upper echelon of the Air Force was against him, and the press pack was in full cry, led by columnist Drew Pearson, who hounded, slandered, and excoriated Forrestal to the day Forrestal died. According to Oliver Pilat's study of Pearson (Drew Pearson, *An Unauthorized Biography,* Harper's Magazine Press, 1973), the Pearson-Forrestal feud began during World War II—in 1944, to be exact—when Forrestal, who was then Under Secretary of the Navy, brought President Roosevelt proof that the columnist had bribed a Navy clerk to obtain some classified information. Pilat relates that FDR merely laughed at the idea of prosecuting Pearson and put the incriminating evidence into an office safe where apparently it just gathered dust.

Pearson really hit Forrestal below the belt when he accused the Defense Secretary of running away, panic-stricken, while four gunmen robbed Mrs. Forrestal of jewels and money. The robbery actually occurred when she was being escorted home from a party by a friend, and Forrestal wasn't anywhere near the scene—a fact that Pearson ignored even though one of his own investigators had told him the Secretary wasn't involved. Forrestal had all the ingredients of a fat libel suit but he never sued, brooding instead as his brilliant mind began to be unbearably overstressed.

Forrestal went into semiretirement at a friend's home in Hobe Sound, Florida, in March 1949, after Truman named Louis A. Johnson the new Secretary of Defense. Pearson continued to bait Forrestal, finally breaking the story of his mental illness, which alleged that Forrestal had run into the street yelling, "The Russians are coming! The Russians are coming!" Forrestal was taken to Bethesda Naval Hospital for psychiatric treatment, and two months after his admission, he jumped from a twelfth-story window to his death.

I have never bought the oft-repeated charge that Pearson's persecution drove Forrestal to suicide. The columnist was cruel, vindictive, and unfair, and there is no doubt that his incessant attacks contributed to Forrestal's breakdown. But Forrestal could have survived even a Drew Pearson were it not for his tragic obsession with work as a total substitute for a normal life. Then too, Pearson wasn't his only enemy; in his last days in the Pentagon, he seemed to have half of official Washington against him, including the President.

I myself learned something from his preoccupation with power, which is that it has a way of totally mesmerizing even the most well-meaning of men. Forrestal was one of those who loved power but deluded himself into believing he always could use it wisely, that he alone could turn power and authority to beneficent purposes for all.

This kind of rationalization is one of the most serious temptations of public service. I suspect there is a bit of dictator in most men of above-average leadership qualities, not in the sense of being a Hitler or a Stalin, but in the belief that achieving something for the public good justifies nearly any use of power. From the exalted, heady position of authority one can easily see what has to be done, and there is an irresistible urge to get it done. In that process, one can quickly lose all sense of both humor and humility. This is what happened to Jim Forrestal; that also is what happened to men like J. Edgar Hoover, Lyndon Johnson, Richard Nixon, and a few other public officials in the postwar years. There was no doubt about their good intentions, but as they gained and used power, they also began to lose human perspective, the ability to laugh at themselves, and the humility that teaches that all men are mortal and, therefore, often mistaken.

I grieved the loss of Forrestal. His successor, it quickly developed, had a far worse malady: megalomania. Louis Johnson, former national commander of the American Legion, came into the Pentagon as the nation's second Secretary of Defense with absolutely no sense of humor, totally devoid of humility, and more obsessed with power the longer he stayed in office. In exercising that power, he almost wrecked the Defense Department and the nation's military security.

It was no secret that Johnson was really running for President from the political base of the Pentagon. His strategy was to cut back on defense spending so he could proclaim he had saved enough money to put the federal government in the black—a theoretically worthwhile achievement and one that he figured could make him a serious presidential candidate in 1952. In retrospect, of course, it appears that Johnson couldn't have beaten Dwight Eisenhower in 1952 if Congress had passed a law requiring all blue-eyed Americans to vote Democratic. But at the time Johnson had truly serious political ambitions, which collided unhappily with the growing belligerence of the Soviet Union. These were the days of the Marshall Plan, the Greek-Turkish Aid Program, embryonic NATO, and other Cold War measures designed to offset the spreading "Red Threat." Louis Johnson emasculated the Armed Forces just when we needed military muscle to keep the Cold War from expanding into world conflict. Only the A-bomb and the H-bomb were beyond his reach.

Johnson was done in by a famous policy paper known as "NSC 68," prepared for the National Security Council by a high-powered group of experts on every phase of the Cold War. Briefly stated, NSC 68 pointed out that the Soviets had the H-bomb and would soon have the ability to build intercontinental ballistic missiles, giving the Soviets enough punch to attempt domination of Europe, the Mediterranean, and even the Pacific. The report urged development of a military capability to deal with the Soviet Union from a position of power. This became the cornerstone of American policy in the 1950–53 era, one forged mainly by the new Secretary of State, Dean Acheson; the President's security adviser, Sidney Souers; and the new chairman of the Joint Chiefs, General Omar Bradley.

Actually, it took our early setbacks in the Korean War to expose the folly of Johnson's Pentagon regime. There hadn't been time enough to implement all of NSC 68's policies, and the initial debacles in Korea not only gave them impetus but also exposed Johnson's ineptness.

I was part of the group that worked almost clandestinely on NSC 68 in the winter of 1949–50. It was a task that also got me involved in the greatest personal crisis of my public life. At the time I was collaborating with Paul Nitze, director of the State Department's Policy Planning Staff, on this vital military, diplomatic blueprint for the nation's future. (NSC 68 was primarily a State Department project.) After Forrestal died, Jack Ohly had moved from the Pentagon to the State Department, under Secretary Acheson. My joining the NSC 68 team was thanks mainly to Ohly's faith in me and his urging that I remain at the Pentagon under Louis Johnson's jurisdiction.

To use a football phrase, we were double-teaming the Secretary of Defense in a sense; for Johnson, without realizing he was allowing a time bomb to be placed under his own policies, had bought a recommendation of mine that an International Security Affairs office be established within the office of the Secretary of Defense. To direct it, Johnson enlisted the services of a retired Army officer, Major General James H. Burns, who had worked with Averell Harriman on the Lend-Lease program during World War II. Johnson knew and trusted Burns completely; the general had been his assistant when Johnson was briefly Assistant Secretary of War under Henry Stimson. What Johnson didn't perceive was that Burns was totally independent, objective, and definitely not a "yes man" when it came to serving the Secretary of Defense.

Because I was the organizer of the International Security Affairs office and by now had served four years in foreign affairs, Burns made me his deputy—together with Major General Lyman Lemnitzer, whom Ohly and Gruenther had brought in to head up the Office of Foreign Military Assistance. We became an anti-Johnson *troika* in charge of all NATO, military assistance, and political/military affairs. We were a trio thoroughly convinced that the Secretary of Defense had to reverse course in his blind plunge toward dangerous economies.

Johnson's megalomania made it impossible for him to listen to views that conflicted with his political ambitions. Those who opposed him were not just opponents, they were also conniving plotters. I'll never forget the day, early in Johnson's Pentagon regime, when the Secretary of Defense heard that reporter Stewart Alsop was upstairs interviewing Air Force Secretary Symington. Johnson's reaction was almost paranoiac; he rushed to his private Pentagon elevator, went up to Symington's floor, and then burst into the Air Force Secretary's office where, without preamble, he launched into a tirade: Symington was plotting against him just as he had plotted against Forrestal . . . this illicit interview was proof . . . he was trying to undermine his authority, etc.

On the surface Johnson showed no particular animosity toward me, even though he knew I had admired Forrestal and was committed to policies aimed at containing the Soviet Union. He was aware, for example, that I had participated in the drafting of the North Atlantic Treaty and the organization of NATO. In fact, he made me his chief staff officer for NATO defense committee activities and appointed me first chairman of the Military Production and Supply Board of NATO. He was even cognizant of the Burns group's attitude toward his defense pruning, and he knew our little *troika* also was working with the State Department on NSC 68.

But apparently Johnson considered himself so powerful that my opposition had less sting than a flea bite; he was secure in the belief that he had President Truman's full backing, never dreaming that the combination of NSC 68 and the outbreak of the Korean War would make Truman realize the mistake he had made putting a politician into the Pentagon.

It developed, however, that Johnson never really trusted his own military diplomat whose wings needed clipping. That began to develop at, of all places, the horse races at Bowie, Maryland.

Johnson's Deputy Secretary of Defense, former White House Press Secretary Stephen Early, went to the races one day with his old friend J. Edgar Hoover. In the course of what Early thought was a relatively inconsequential and unimportant conversation, Hoover happened to mention "that fella Halaby on Johnson's staff."

Early later told me Hoover's exact words: "You'd better watch that Halaby, he'll get you in trouble on the intelligence front." High-impact words from the director of the FBI in the midst of the McCarthy era.

Early passed on Hoover's comment to Johnson, never thinking that the Defense Secretary would take it as anything more serious than a warning that Halaby was the kind of man who rushed in where angels *and* fools fear to tread. Early was stunned when Johnson seized on Hoover's remark as evidence that I might be a "security risk." He swiftly called for a review of my security-clearance file, and from it he presumably deduced that I could be a Communist sympathizer, or at least a threat to him, for in my government security file since 1946 was an admission that I had not only tried to go to the Soviet Union but had also lied in the course of attempting to get a visa for transit of Manchuria in 1939.

The story itself was simple. Just before I started my final year at Yale Law School in the summer of 1939, as the war clouds gathered, I decided to visit Italy, Germany, the Soviet Union, and Japan to see what the threatening dictatorships were all about. My planned route would have taken me across the Soviet Union via the Trans-Siberian Railway through Manchuria and into Japan. Manchuria at that time was known as Manchukuo and had been granted independence by Japan even though it was in Chinese territory. The United States had refused to recognize Manchukuo in the belief that it was nothing but a Japanese-controlled "stooge state" created illegally against the wishes of the Chinese Government. The Manchukuoans reacted by refusing to grant any visas to Americans.

Faced with this impasse, which threatened to spoil my carefully planned itinerary, I sought the advice of Edwin Borchard, professor of international law at Yale Law School and a respected State Department adviser.

"You have to prove to the Manchukuoans you have something

they want," Borchard told me. "That's the only way you'll get a visa."

It sounded easy. Even a third-year law student knew what Manchukuo (and Japan) wanted and needed: scrap iron. So I prepared a letter in which I stated that I was going to Japan for the express purpose of arranging a shipment of scrap iron to Japan. Technically I had some justification, as I really did have an uncle in Colombia who was in the export-import business and who conceivably might have arranged such a shipment. But in truth the letter was nothing but a subterfuge to obtain that visa, which I hoped to pick up either in Rome or Berlin.

It didn't work; I was still refused a visa and later was glad it had been refused, because what I had done was neither proper nor sensible. I had made a mistake stemming from the overzealousness of a young law student seeking to complete a desirable and educational trip.

In 1946, when I was first offered a job in the State Department's Office of Research and Intelligence, I had to undergo a complete top-security clearance check. In the course of that investigation, I had frankly told an FBI interviewer about the visa incident. The FBI and the Secretary of State obviously didn't consider it a serious infraction because I was then given a "Q" clearance, the highest clearance of all, permitting access to nuclear-weapons data and development.

But at the time Johnson was trying to maneuver me out of the government, McCarthyism was beginning to rear its ugly head, and I was worried. That youthful indiscretion was the kind of raw meat on which the senator from Wisconsin fed, and for weeks I dreaded the ring of a telephone bell, fearing it would be a summons before Joe McCarthy's investigating committee.

The call finally came—four years later—although not for the reason I feared. McCarthy was holding hearings on a red-hot issue of the day—whether Greek ships were transporting material to North Korea. My boss, Assistant Secretary Frank Nash, was supposed to testify but was out of the country, and everyone else in my department was scared to death. So was I—wondering if anyone had fed the deceitful part of my file to the senator. I was picked as the patsy, but fortunately my personal background never came up while I testified. Apparently I was not on McCarthy's "kill" list.

I survived the Defense Secretary's vendetta largely through the intervention of Averell Harriman and Dean Acheson, who engineered my transfer from the Pentagon to the Mutual Security Agency. From there I morbidly observed Truman's firing of the ignoble "Colonel Johnson" and later was invited by General George Marshall and Defense Secretary Robert A. Lovett to return to my former job in the Pentagon. I survived not only the Hoover-inspired Johnson attack but also the changeover from a Democratic administration to a Republican one after Dwight Eisenhower was elected to the White House. I stayed on at the Pentagon, serving Charles Wilson as Deputy Assistant Secretary of Defense for International Security Affairs.

The job itself was interesting, but working for "Engine Charlie," the former chairman of General Motors, was not the most ennobling experience. I liked him personally but had little respect for him as an executive and policymaker. In 1953, I was nominated by him and selected by the U. S. Chamber of Commerce to receive the Arthur Flemming Award as the "outstanding young man in federal service." The honor was of sufficient magnitude to keep me working in government probably longer than I wanted to; but my family was growing, we had never really enjoyed financial security, and there were too many times when my presence as a Democrat in the Eisenhower administration made me feel like an unwanted relative.

One day in 1953, I attended a naval reserve officers' meeting at the Navy Yard in Washington and found myself sitting next to Laurance Rockefeller. At the time he was an adviser to the Secretary of the Navy and had been a Navy officer himself during World War II. We hit it off immediately, and I found myself confiding that it was about time for me to leave government service, after seven years.

Rockefeller invited me to visit his New York office at Rockefeller Center to discuss his venture-capital business.

"If you want to return to private life," he said, "I've got some ideas that might interest you."

I could hardly wait to tell Doris that night about my encounter with Rockefeller. The magic of his name, of course, made the prospect of working for him even more intriguing, and a few weeks later I took some time off to pay him that visit. It was an exciting talk; he told me that my aviation background, combined with my government experience, would be very helpful in controlling and monitoring his investments in a variety of technical industries. For example, it was Laurance who gave J. S. McDonnell the seed money to get McDonnell Aircraft going during the early World War II days—an investment that later culminated in McDonnell's absorbing the giant Douglas Aircraft Company.

Rockefeller also was the largest shareholder in Eastern Air Lines and an intimate friend of Captain Eddie Rickenbacker.

The Eastern Air Lines situation, in fact, had made Rockefeller think of me as a possible aide. The airline was a moneymaker but one with a clouded future. National was challenging its supremacy on the New York–Florida route, which had been Eastern's bread-and-butter monopoly for years until the Civil Aeronautics Board allowed National to compete. Rockefeller was troubled by Eastern's reputation for poor service, and Rickenbacker's ultraconservative politics had made his name anathema in Washington, to such an extent that the airline was not only faced with the prospect of increasing competition on its existing routes but also had virtually no chance to get new route awards.

Among other things, Rockefeller told me he needed someone to keep a closer watch on his 10 per cent ownership of Eastern. He was also involved in electronics, a field in which I had little practical knowledge but a great deal of interest. I visited him again in the fall of 1953, and accepted when he offered me a job as more or less of a personal troubleshooter. That status didn't endear me to his associates, some of whom I had met but didn't know very well. I didn't realize that unless they themselves had a hand in choosing a new man, they rather resented a stranger coming in to work for "Mr. Laurance," as everyone called him.

Around the corner from his office was "Mr. Nelson" Rockefeller, a private citizen whose presidential aspirations, if he had any at that time, were kept to himself. The fifty-sixth floor of 30 Rockefeller Plaza was then something of a palace with royal family atmosphere. Since the Rockefeller brothers completely controlled all the activities and did not share with outsiders any of the equities in the family's holdings—for example, there were no stock options for employees—the only way to make any real money was to find an investment and be granted by Laurance some of the original stock offering, usually at an attractively low price. The Rockefeller staff would help put a new company together and then after it matured finance it publicly, the result usually being a hefty markup in the value of the stock. Salaries were reasonable, and all in all I was happy to be associated with this First Family of American business.

One of the things I worked on was a company called Reaction Motors, an early manufacturer of rocket engines. At Laurance's request, I also did a study in 1955 on the use of solar energy. This fascinating project lasted quite a few weeks while I examined the huge costs and limited effectiveness of converting the sun's energy into electric power. Later I was loaned out to New York Mayor Robert Wagner, and along with General Willis Crittenberger and a young bank president named William Kyle, surveyed New York City's civil defense situation, including the question of whether it was possible to evacuate the city in the event of a nuclear attack with only fifteen minutes' warning.

By far my most interesting early assignment for Laurance was a survey of Eastern Air Lines. I've found out since that Rockefeller had a double motive in handing me this chore: He really did want me to take a new look at Eastern's operations, but he also wanted Eastern to take a good look at me. I've been told that over one of his fortnightly luncheons with "the captain," as Laurance called Rickenbacker, I was the prime subject of discussion.

So I finally met the famous Captain Eddie, who was hospitable enough, and I spent several weeks touring Eastern's various facilities in New York, Miami, and elsewhere. My most vivid recollection concerned one of his infamous semiannual management conferences held in the convention hall of a Miami Beach hotel. I use the word "infamous" deliberately, for it was more a cruel fraternity initiation than a business meeting. Rickenbacker and three of his top executives sat like judges and jury on the stage while station managers, supervisors, and vice presidents marched forward to describe current operations and future budget plans, as well as how they were doing in relation to the competition.

Rickenbacker theorized that exposing young executives to the scrutiny of their colleagues would increase their poise and instill a greater sense of responsibility. Maybe it did in some cases, but it also created an atmosphere of cold fear. Some of these very capable young men became so anxious and worried about the allotted five-minute presentation that they got stage fright, nausea, and sometimes a total oral freeze; so choked up they couldn't speak a word.

There was an aura of phony superpatriotism in the big room. The meeting opened with the playing of the National Anthem and the Pledge of Allegiance, and then Captain Eddie dominated the proceedings. He stayed through every session, eight hours a day for four days, asked some very embarrassing questions, and took a number of people to task right in front of their peers. There were some five hundred top supervisors in the room, and if it was tedious and exhausting for me, it must have been triply worse for them. I had never seen a more dictatorial example of centralized management nor such public humiliation of employees, to say nothing of the waste of time.

As far as I could see, Rickenbacker was blaming subordinates for difficulties largely of his own making. His tight-fisted policies had put Eastern far down the list in passenger service: He fought giving away meals and drinks, for example, until the competition forced him into it. His archaic marketing practices were the same ones he had used in the days when Eastern didn't have any competition. His route problems could be traced directly to his open contempt for the regulators in Washington; Eastern's lobbyists had a tough time selling their airline's route aspirations to government officials who didn't like being called a bunch of bureaucrats. And his ego was colossal; years later I was to read in his autobiography that he had correctly predicted the structural problems later to be encountered in three new transports: the Martin 202, the British Comet, and the Lockheed Electra. In the case of the Electra, he claimed to have ordered structural reinforcements before the new prop-jet became involved in two mysterious crashes. Maybe so— but I know that Eastern's Electras went through the same $25 million modification process as everyone else's after the cause for the accidents was ascertained.

Strangely enough, though, he could command loyalty and even affection on the part of his older employees, pilots in particular. He generally got along well with his flight crews, who admired the tough old bird even when they were arguing with him, for to them he was as much a fellow pilot as their boss. They continued to love him even as his leadership brought Eastern to the brink of disaster. Eastern was the last major carrier to hire female cabin attendants and the last to order jets—management decisions typical of Rickenbacker's reactionary thinking. A senior Eastern captain, long since retired, once told me about a meeting Captain Eddie held with a group of pilots. One of them arose and asked point-blank: "Rick, why the hell don't we have stewardesses on our planes?"

"Because," Rickenbacker roared, "you guys are making enough dough to buy your own."

Nothing ever came of my Eastern survey, either as far as the airline or myself was concerned. Certainly I didn't have any desire to work for an autocrat like Rickenbacker, and my rather cursory study of the airline's operations hadn't given me much respect for some of his top subordinates. I suspect that Captain Eddie didn't think much of me, either. In my report to Laurance Rockefeller were recommendations that a No. 2 man be selected to be Eastern's president, with Rickenbacker elevated to chairman of the board, and the airline be decentralized. I suggested that the No. 2 man be given some real authority. Later I learned that the whole thing was something of a charade; Rockefeller wanted to see (1) if Rickenbacker would take to me as a possible successor and (2) whether I'd take to Eastern and the airline business. I had no idea that the so-called survey was primarily an exercise in mutual inspection and, at any rate, I'm glad both Rickenbacker and I flunked our respective inspections. It would have been worse going into Eastern at that time than it was more than twelve years later, when I went into Pan Am. I have no way of knowing whether I would have been Rockefeller's eventual choice to run Eastern, but although I'm proud that he even considered me, I'm damn glad I didn't get the job. It was a can of worms, as Malcolm McIntyre, the lawyer and former Under Secretary of the Air Force who became Eastern's president, was to find out. With Rickenbacker looking over his shoulder, all he could accomplish during his stormy, unhappy tenure was a near merger with American and the birth of Eastern's famed shuttle service. Not until Floyd Hall, a brilliant operations expert at TWA, came to Eastern did the airline start to pull out of its spin, and by that time Captain Eddie wasn't being allowed to look over anyone's shoulder.

Far more interesting than my first inside glimpse of the turbulent airline industry was another Laurance Rockefeller assignment. I was given a short but intensive training course in investment banking at Smith, Barney & Co., one of the better if rather small Wall Street firms. It was headed by the Harding brothers, Charles B. and William B., the latter a marvelous man with a great variety of interests; a probing, far-ranging mind; and a huge heart. Bill Harding was a close personal friend of both Nelson and Laurance Rockefeller; Bill Harding had worked for Nelson during World War II and did special jobs for Laurance, such as the development of New York Airways as a helicopter service for the New York area. One of my first "courses" under Bill Harding's tutelage was to follow the fortunes of New York Airways in its early years, during which time I learned quite a bit about the inefficiencies and political difficulties of operating any kind of transit system in a large urban area.

I worked in each branch of Smith, Barney & Co. for a few days or a few weeks, depending on how much time I needed to grasp the operation. In corporate financing, for example, I participated as a kind of observer/kibitzer in financing for airlines, air-conditioning companies, and others. I worked briefly in the municipal bond department, where I picked up valuable knowledge on the financing of airports and highways. I spent some time in the sales department learning how stocks are bought and sold, and for a few hours I followed a trader around the floor of the New York Stock Exchange.

In Smith, Barney's excellent research branch, I got to know William Grant, one of the nation's outstanding investment research men; he taught me a lot about how stock market analysts looked at the airlines.

But most important, I became good friends with Bill Harding and his wife, Mary, and they entertained Doris and me frequently at their home. Bill saw in me qualities that my associates and competitors in the Rockefeller office did not see, and he spent many hours guiding and advising me on the venture-capital business. It was, in fact, the lack of such supervision that made working for the Rockefeller brothers occasionally difficult for me and frequently wasteful; Bill Harding supplied this training, and it was the equivalent of a master's degree.

Yet I remained most grateful to Laurance and Nelson. Between them, they were to get me involved in a most challenging assignment and one that eventually would lead to my heading a major federal agency. I had written a paper for Laurance in which I noted how little money was being spent on airways and airports in the United States and how the growth in aviation was racing far ahead of adequate federal facilities for coping with such growth. Laurance was impressed to the extent of telling Nelson about the paper and the import of its warnings. The result was a request from Nelson Rockefeller, who was then a White House staff adviser to President Eisenhower, to Bill Harding: Would he head up a small task force to investigate the civil airways and airports system and recommend any necessary actions?

Nelson had to engage in some bloody in-fighting before he could get President Eisenhower's approval of an aviation task force. The record of the Eisenhower administration in civil aviation advancement up to that time had been one of blind parsimony and false economy. The chief villain was Secretary of Commerce Sinclair Weeks, aided and abetted by the director of the Budget Bureau, Maurice Stans. Formerly Weeks had been mayor of Newton, Massachusetts, and he brought small-town New England frugality and vision into his Cabinet post.

The Under Secretary of Commerce was Robert Murray, former chairman of the Pennsylvania Economy League and, like Weeks, a devotee of the theory that economy surgery is best performed by wielding a butcher's cleaver instead of a surgeon's scalpel. At the very moment aviation was taking off in a major expansion, thanks to the technological advances gleaned from two major wars and the economic demands of growing prosperity, the Weeks-Murray

59

team went to work with their cleavers. The Civil Aeronautics Administration's research and development budget was slashed to a mere one million dollars; considering what had to be done to make the airways safer, this was like handing a destitute father with nine children fifty cents for groceries. The CAA's funds for investment in new facilities and safety equipment were cut to eleven million dollars—at a time when nearly all the nation's airline-served airports lacked instrument landing systems.

Weeks and Under Secretary of Commerce Robert Murray were against the Harding task-force proposal from the moment it was first proposed. They might have gotten further with their opposition were it not for a series of bad crashes that focused public and congressional attention on air-safety problems and made their objections untenable. Only Nelson Rockefeller's great influence within the Eisenhower administration overcame Weeks's opposition. Nelson not only had been Under Secretary of Health, Education, and Welfare but also now occupied the far more prestigious position of chairman of President Eisenhower's Committee on Government Organization. When Laurance spoke to his brother personally about the mushrooming aviation crisis and later sent him a memorandum based on my paper, Nelson took the matter over Weeks's head right to Chief of Staff Sherman Adams and then to the President himself. Thus the task force was born, officially titled the Aviation Facilities Study Group. Bill Harding was chairman and I vice chairman, on loan from the Rockefeller office, along with Ted Walkowicz, a very imaginative retired U. S. Air Force colonel. The other members were George Baker, dean of the Harvard Business School; Fred Glass, director of the New York Port Authority's Airports Division; and Jerome Lederer, head of the Flight Safety Foundation.

It was a thoughtful, hard-working group, which labored from May of 1955 to the following December. The President had asked Harding to develop recommendations in three major areas:

1. Should a study of long-range needs for aviation facilities and aids be undertaken?
2. What should be covered in such a study, and particularly what subjects deserved immediate priority?
3. How should the study, if made, be organized and conducted?

Our task was far more complex and vital than the work blue-print implied, largely because we went far beyond those rather vague initial instructions. Bill Harding was strongly convinced that no government study group should exist for the sole purpose of writing a report.

"We have to get our recommendations already approved before filing the report and, if possible, have our recommendations either implemented or about to be implemented before they are made public," he told us.

His wisdom was borne out when it came time to submit our recommendations. Unfortunately, Harding became seriously ill in the last month of our work, and it became my responsibility to do most of the necessary pulling together of the various pieces and composing a final report. But to Bill Harding belonged the majority of the credit, for it was largely his idea to urge on the Eisenhower administration the most far-reaching and controversial recommendation of all: the creation of a special assistant to the President, with offices in the White House itself, who would draw up a plan for organizing a new civil aviation agency. We didn't go so far as to suggest specifically the creation of an independent aviation agency, leaving that up to the man who would be named special assistant on aviation policy.

We didn't recommend just any special assistant. In accordance with Harding's orders to get action rather than words, we picked a specific man for the difficult job. We wanted a man with executive ability, someone who knew something about aviation, and someone who would have Eisenhower's complete confidence. Walkowicz suggested Edward P. Curtis, vice president of Eastman Kodak in Rochester, New York; our reaction was unanimous approval. He was a retired major general in the Air Force and a good friend of the President; Curtis had, in fact, served on Ike's staff in London during World War II. His own company, one of the best-managed firms in U.S. industry, regarded him highly enough to consider making him president. We quickly cleared his name through Sherman Adams and set about convincing Curtis he should take the job.

Curtis was bird-shooting in Georgia with J. H. "Jock" Whitney; "Tooey" Spaatz, the Air Corps hero of World War II; and some other friends the day we contacted him and asked him to fly to

61

Washington. Curtis arrived not really knowing what he was getting into; he wasn't overjoyed at having to break off his Georgia vacation, and it was only the magic of an Eisenhower summons that persuaded him at least to talk to us. In Harding's absence, I was by then the only full-time member of the study group, and it was my job to brief Curtis on our forthcoming report, with its key recommendation. Meeting him for the first time, I was impressed with his immediate grasp of what we were proposing.

Later, Curtis met with Nelson Rockefeller and Adams at the White House, where Curtis would only promise, "I'll consider it." Adams took him down to the White House swimming pool, where the President was enjoying a brief dip. Someone found him bathing trunks, and he joined Eisenhower in the pool. It was a productive swim for the future of American aviation: Curtis accepted the job as special assistant for the reorganization of the airways/airports system.

The work of the Harding Commission was done, and I expected to return to my full-time duties at 30 Rockefeller Plaza, but this was not to be. Curtis said he wanted to make immediate use of our group members and took on several of our top staff people for his own new organization. Apparently Curtis liked me as much as I liked him, because one of his first moves was to recommend that I be named CAA administrator. The former administrator, Frederick Lee, had been fired by Weeks for insubordinate advocacy of higher CAA budgets, and his successor, Charles Lowen, had died of cancer and had been replaced temporarily by James Pyle, who was brought over from the Navy Department on an interim basis.

I was stunned. I knew Curtis thought highly of me, but I knew that he knew of my contempt for many members of the Republican administration. As soon as he was sworn in, he asked me to become his deputy, but I demurred. I said I needed to make more money after my years in the government, that I had a promising position with the Rockefeller brothers, and that, in any case, I was a registered Democrat. Curtis said he understood how I felt and asked me to serve as a consultant, which I did for a number of months.

But Lowen's tragic death and a series of bad crashes convinced

Curtis that he had a crisis on his hands. He called me in and proposed that I succeed Lowen as Civil Aeronautics administrator. He said the so-called Curtis plan, now being formulated, couldn't be put into effect soon enough, and he wanted me to work with him as head of the CAA to get at least some of it into execution before a new agency could be formed. I repeated the arguments I had given him when he asked me to become his deputy, but this time he got Bill Harding to put pressure on me. They both sought my permission to broach the subject to Adams and Weeks.

"Ted," I finally told Curtis, "before we can consider this seriously, you ought to get the President's approval of me on political grounds. I can't see how he could appoint me."

Apparently he could. Curtis approached Adams, and Adams saw the President, who vaguely recalled my work in the Pentagon when we first met and my role in NATO's formation. Adams then informed Curtis that the President felt the CAA job was largely technical and operational and that the political preferences of the administrator were unimportant. This encouraged me to believe that the Eisenhower administration finally was beginning to see the aviation situation as one requiring urgent nonpolitical action. So I agreed to meet with "Sinny" Weeks, as he was known, and was surprised to find him cordial, although he did give me the impression that he might as well be interviewing an applicant for the fire chief's job in Newton, Massachusetts.

He asked a number of questions about my background and my views on aviation problems. Then with somewhat obvious relish, he came to the subject of politics—my politics.

"Tell me, Halaby," he said, "if two men of equal ability were applying for a job as a tower-control chief and one was a Republican while the other was a Democrat, wouldn't you choose the Republican?"

I was so surprised I couldn't believe he had asked the question; I thought he was kidding.

"Mr. Secretary," I finally managed to reply, "I wouldn't know whether they were Republicans or Democrats. I wouldn't even ask."

"Oh you wouldn't?"

"Certainly not. These are Civil Service jobs, and they aren't even allowed to put party affiliation on an application. In any case, I don't see what politics has to do with air traffic control. If you had a tower operator or center controller handling your airplane, Mr. Secretary, I don't think you'd care about the party he belonged to; you'd be more interested in his skill."

"Well, you're a practical fellow, Halaby," he chuckled, "and I'm sure you'd exercise good judgment."

His next question concerned what I'd do about the CAA's budget.

"I can make no commitments except to seek whatever money is necessary to modernize the airways and airports," I said as firmly as possible.

I was told later that Weeks admired my forthrightness but was worried that he'd never be able to control me. In that respect, I agreed with his fears. Certainly I'd be working for a man who didn't want me in the first place; obviously I was being shoved down his throat, although Adams' influence was sufficient to force Weeks into asking me to meet him a second time. The second session, which took place the following week at LaGuardia Airport, where he and his wife were taking off for a vacation, proved as unproductive as the first. I spelled out the conditions under which I would accept the CAA post, and the conditions added up to one word: independence. I wanted freedom of action, an increased budget, and a free hand in any internal reorganization I felt necessary. Weeks's face bore the expression of a man who had just sucked on a lemon after expecting an orange, but he made no specific comment. Apparently he was under considerable White House pressure because Ted Curtis called me and told me Weeks was ready to accept me on my own terms. Doris and I were making plans to move back to Washington when the roof fell in.

A short time before I met Weeks in New York, my wife and I had been invited to spend the Labor Day weekend at the home of some close personal friends in Millbrook, New York. Our hosts also had invited, among others, Mr. and Mrs. John W. Hanes; he was a former Under Secretary of the Treasury, and they were both very active in Republican right-wing politics. In the course of a fairly happy evening, Mrs. Hanes, a handsome woman and a stimulating conversationalist, began talking politics. This led to a discussion of leading GOP officials, such as Secretary of State John Foster Dulles and Defense Secretary Charles Wilson. Fueled with several drinks, I ventured the opinion that history would judge Dean Acheson as one of our greatest Secretaries of State, and that I doubted whether Mr. Dulles' record would ever earn him even a page in U.S. history.

When someone asked me what I thought of "Engine Charlie" Wilson, I said I was grateful to him; he had given me a medal when I left the Pentagon and had recommended me for the Arthur Flemming Award.

"However," I added, "while I'd love to have him as a grandfather, I wouldn't want to have him as Secretary of Defense."

The conversation and the party ended with the atmosphere on the chilly side, but I didn't give the matter any further thought until after I had had the second meeting with Weeks and was getting ready to accept my appointment to the CAA. It turned out I had dug my own grave—or escape tunnel—at that party. Hanes reported what I had said about Dulles and Wilson to Charles F. Willis, an Eisenhower staff member concerned with political appointments. Willis informed Weeks, who informed Adams, who informed both Curtis and Bill Harding that I had committed heresy. Cutting up Charlie Wilson was bad enough, but to criticize Dulles was blasphemous; the President considered him one of history's greatest men, and at that point Eisenhower wouldn't have nominated me for dog catcher.

Curtis and Harding both called me to ask what the hell I had said at Millbrook to make me *persona non grata* with the White House inner circle. I recounted my conversation, and Curtis, after sighing in resignation, said, "I think I can take care of it."

But neither he nor Harding could repair the damage. They sadly reported to me that Adams had decided I was not to be appointed.

"I can keep trying, Jeeb," Curtis said.

"Well, look, that's it," I told him. "I'd like to withdraw my name from further consideration, and let's forget the whole thing."

Subsequently the President named James Pyle to the top CAA job, where he served until the Federal Aviation Agency was created. I went back to the ivory tower at 30 Rockefeller Plaza, where both Nelson and Laurance expressed disappointment at what I had done but also sympathy for my position. Now, however, I was getting restless. The family disliked New York, and it was no place to raise children; our daughter, Lisa, was four; our son, Christian, two; and Doris was expecting a third child. And I was beginning to feel trapped in the job. Yet I hadn't fully examined myself or my alternatives.

Late in 1955, I submitted myself to the Psychological Corporation for three days of attitude and aptitude testing. It cost me a hundred dollars but it was worth it because the battery of tests and two penetrating interviews by industrial psychologists gave me fresh insights into myself.

In effect, I was told I was far more intelligent verbally than I was arithmetically, thus suiting me more for a job as a public administrator, in marketing, or in public relations and promotion than in a business management post requiring mathematical analysis. In other words, I was more idea-oriented than money-oriented.

Considering my rather exalted status as a Rockefeller associate, I refused to accept these conclusions fully, but inwardly I had an idea they were probably correct. When 1956 rolled around, I had a long talk with Laurance, the gist of it being that I was not in the right place at the right time and that while I was grateful for his making possible my transition from government to private industry, I would be happier elsewhere. I stayed with Rockefeller briefly while I let one of the executive headhunting firms know I was looking for other work. I must add, however, that I held and still hold Laurance Rockefeller in the highest regard. I liked him personally and had the same feeling toward his kind, sensitive, and generous wife, Mary; it was my place in his tower that bugged me.

While trolling in the uncertain waters of job seeking, I continued to give Curtis whatever help I could. Ted himself had had enough of the Washington rat race; he was slightly shaken by the abrupt White House 180-degree turn in my own case, and he wanted badly to get back to Eastman Kodak. The President asked him to choose his own successor as special assistant, and he consulted with me, Laurance Rockefeller, and a number of others on various names that were being proposed.

High on the list was a retired Air Force general named Elwood R. Quesada, who had been active in several small electronics companies and who had served briefly as head of Lockheed's embryo space and missiles program in Los Angeles. When Curtis asked me about Quesada, I gave him divided advice: I told him Quesada had exceptional experience in research, development, and operational activities within the Air Force. He was considered a good, rugged administrator; he had a splendid aviation background, having been an active pilot himself, and he had a reputation for honesty and integrity. On the other hand, I advised Ted, Quesada also had a reputation for being temperamental, for provoking controversy, and for not getting along with subordinates.

Curtis eventually recommended Quesada's appointment and went back to private industry, having sown the seeds for the greatest civil-aviation reform in history: the creation of an independent aviation agency. I followed its legislative birth with avid interest, mostly from California. The headhunters came up with several promising job offers, and I finally accepted the executive vice presidency of Servo-Mechanisms, Inc., a $20 million-a-year electronics subsystems manufacturer with plants in Los Angeles and Long Island, New York.

I stayed in touch with aviation somewhat vicariously, reading about Quesada's subsequent troubles and controversies in the FAA and mentally sympathizing with him from the standpoint of one who had escaped the political pressure boilers.

I never dreamed I was going to be pulled right back into those boilers—but on November 8, 1960, John Fitzgerald Kennedy was elected President of the United States.

CHAPTER THREE

The first intimation I had that I was being seriously considered to head the Federal Aviation Agency came shortly after John F. Kennedy was elected.

It was in the form of a telephone call from Carl Christenson in Denver, a veteran United Air Lines pilot and one of the nation's top experts in air safety. Carl, who was a fellow trustee of the Flight Safety Foundation, engaged in a few seconds of small talk and then, without further preamble, remarked that he hoped I'd take over at the FAA because of my work on the Harding Commission and my long interest in air safety.

All I could do was thank him, commenting at the same time, "Nobody's asked me yet, Carl," or words to that effect. After he hung up, I wondered if he had heard something I hadn't heard or whether he was hinting I actually should make a pitch for the job. At any rate, I didn't give it much additional thought until a few days later, when Stuart Tipton, president of the Air Transport Association, phoned to say he was in Los Angeles and would like to have lunch with me.

We agreed to meet at Trader Vic's, and over a pleasant meal, fortified with a few Navy grogs, Tipton conducted a very thorough interview, questioning me closely on my views concerning the major issues of great importance to the airlines. Some of those views were not entirely favorable to the airline/ATA way of thinking, but I tried to be honest with the soft-spoken, easy-sell Tipton, who invariably smoked corncob pipes and always managed to seem calm even in the middle of a raging crisis. He must have admired my frankness if not all my views, because later ATA was to support my nomination. It was obvious Tipton was sounding out Democrats who might be available and qualified for the FAA post —he told me he had already interviewed someone from Chicago who apparently had been recommended by the Air Force, and Harold Stuart of Tulsa, Oklahoma, whom American Airlines was pushing with the support of Oklahoma's two senators, A. S. "Mike" Monroney and Bob Kerr.

Now I had to start thinking seriously about the FAA job, although there still had been no official overtures. I did get calls from two Washington lawyers, James Rowe and Lloyd Cutler, both of whom had been active in JFK's campaign. Each inquired whether I'd be interested in heading the FAA or in some other job in the new Administration. I gave Rowe and Cutler identical answers: I wasn't going to seek any job, because I had just started a profitable, challenging company of my own, American Technology Corp., and had resumed law practice in Los Angeles, and if the President-elect wanted me, he'd have to seek me, and not the other way around. I also told them that if I were going to be drafted back into the federal government, I'd prefer the Pentagon or the CIA, with the FAA only a third choice.

I figured that should end any FAA courtship, but I was wrong. The next "come hither" call was from Francis Fox, who ran all Los Angeles County airports and was easily the most highly respected major-airport manager in the United States. Fox said Kenneth O'Donnell and Dick McGuire on JFK's staff had asked him to see me.

"They're old friends of mine," Francis explained. "I knew them in Worcester, Massachusetts, when I ran the airport and a travel agency there."

Fox, too, sounded me out on the FAA possibility. It was clear the President-elect's staff was putting out lines of inquiry about me through a variety of channels, some of them as unfriendly as the others were friendly. Someone on the staff even leaked a story indicating that I might be appointed administrator of the FAA—a typical trial balloon designed to draw all the critics, enemies, supporters, and friends out of the woodwork. It's a time-honored technique that enables a President or President-elect to get information about individuals that might not be easily obtainable through normal pre-appointment investigation.

The rumors and planted stories about my becoming administrator inevitably reached the ears of a man quite naturally interested in all of this—Pete Quesada, the first and now outgoing head of the Agency. He called me about a month and a half after the election, in my Beverly Hills office, and with typical bluntness asked, "Jeeb, when are you going to get back here and take this job over?"

"I haven't had any word from Senator Kennedy," I replied firmly. "So far there's been nothing but rumors and speculation, but if I do take it on, I'll certainly let you know."

I don't think he believed me—in fact, to this day I'm sure Quesada thinks I sought the job—but outwardly, anyway, he took my word for it, remarking, "Well, I hear you're gonna get this job, and if there's any way I can help you, I'll be happy to do it."

My appointment didn't come until the day before John F. Kennedy took the oath of office. By that time I had a pretty good indication that the FAA job was mine if I wanted it; I knew that Sargent Shriver, the President's brother-in-law, who had been a class behind me at Yale Law School, was pushing my name, and so were two of JFK's chief "talent scouts," Ralph Dungan and Adam Yarmolinsky; I had never met Dungan, but I knew Yarmolinsky slightly from my law school days. For one thing, my supporters had been emphasizing to the President-elect that I had an extensive aviation background, that I had played a role in the various studies leading to the establishment of an independent Federal Aviation Agency, and that I also had enjoyed a reasonably respectable and constructive career in the federal government itself during the Truman administration.

Finally, Kennedy and I had a slight social acquaintance dating back to the days when he was a young congressman. I recalled having seen him several times at Cape Cod when Doris and I were spending summers up there, shortly after he and Jackie were married. Ours was not much more than a nodding acquaintance, however, and my impressions of him as a lawmaker were not very sharp. I was with the Defense Department at the time, and he seemed to be a curious combination of a Boston Irishman and a sophisticated internationalist; he was interested in issues mostly as they affected Massachusetts voters, but he also could get involved in major world issues, such as the Algerian revolution. Yet whatever subject he picked was certainly well researched and drew his wholehearted attention.

Dungan made the first direct move, phoning me to confirm officially that the President-elect wanted me to head the FAA. I told Dungan I wasn't interested in the job unless I had a chance to talk to Kennedy in person about it.

"He has a lot of demands on his time," Dungan reminded me. "Why not accept it now and talk to him later?"

I felt I had to stand my ground. "No, I still want to have an eyeball-to-eyeball understanding with him about the job."

Dungan wasn't happy but said he'd see what could be done. The word came back within a few days: Fly to Washington for a meeting with JFK.

The appointment was set up for late in the morning of January 19, 1961, at Bill Walton's house on P Street, which had become a kind of pre-inaugural command post. Kennedy had decided that his own home on N Street needed some relief from the revolving-door process of interviewing scores of appointees and would-be appointees, and Walton had offered him his own house, where I had visited as a friend of Bill's.

There was a sharp chill in the D.C. air and snow was predicted, with long and steady precipitation. Later it would turn into one of the worst blizzards in the capital's history, but weather wasn't on my mind as I climbed the steps leading to the old red-brick Victorian structure, marched through an iron gate up to the front door, and rang the doorbell.

A thin, quiet woman opened the door, peering at me through her glasses. This, I found out later, was Evelyn Lincoln, Kennedy's personal secretary.

"Najeeb Halaby," I murmured.

"Yes, he's expecting you," she said.

The house was rather dark, but Mrs. Lincoln escorted me to Bill Walton's cozy study, where a coal fire was glowing. Walton was there, and he introduced me to the President-elect; or rather he reintroduced me, because I was pleased to find that Kennedy recalled my face from our few brief social encounters of the past. Ralph Dungan then joined us, and after a few minutes of discussing mutual friends, we got down to the business at hand.

Kennedy said he considered the job of Federal Aviation Administrator to be of particular importance at the time, requiring a calm, experienced, and objective hand. He cited two then current aviation controversies in the headlines—one a recent air tragedy and the other a raging labor fight—as indicative of the problems a new administrator would collide with as soon as he took office. The former was the disastrous midair collision between a United DC-8 and a TWA Constellation over Staten Island, New York, on December 16, 1960, only a month before—an accident that underlined the still prevalent weaknesses of the air-traffic control system. The second was a Pier Six brawl involving airline pilots and flight engineers, their respective unions, and airline managements. Flight engineers had struck Northwest Airlines the previous October, and the dispute by now was about to spread to other carriers. The President-elect made it clear I'd be inheriting a few cans of worms.

"I've considered a number of men for the FAA job," he said, "and I'd like you to take it. Would you be interested?"

This was the opening I had been waiting for. I told Kennedy that I had not sought the job and sincerely believed that the position of FAA chief, like that of Defense Secretary or FBI director and a few others, should be seeking the man rather than the other way around. I assured JFK that he had my full support and we shared many ideals and convictions but that I never could promise that my heading the FAA would bring either of us any kudos.

I cited the Staten Island disaster as evidence of the uncompleted work in making the nation's airspace safe and efficient. I warned him that there would be other midair collisions unless the airways could keep pace with the airplane itself. And I frankly predicted there would be many occasions on which he'd be advised to re-

72

verse my decisions or even fire me at the urging of some lobbyists and Washington pressure artists.

He gave me that wonderful ingratiating, endearing grin of his and quickly assured me he was only too well aware that running the FAA was nothing if not high-pressure.

"I have confidence in you or I wouldn't have asked you to take the job," he said with a quiet smile.

I nodded gratefully and then plunged into the delicate and difficult matter of my relationship with the President. Two days before, Kennedy had named James M. Landis as a special adviser on regulatory agencies. There was immediate speculation that Landis would be a kind of co-ordinator or "czar" for all such agencies, including the FAA, and this bothered me considerably. I could see Landis foisting his own views and recommendations concerning FAA activities on the President. Landis was no aviation neophyte, either; he had been chairman of the Civil Aeronautics Board and had been a lawyer representing a number of airlines.

So I informed Kennedy I'd be interested in being head of the FAA only if it were clearly understood that I'd report directly to the President, take orders from no one else, and have unimpeded access to him if a major aviation issue arose. I didn't want any interference between the FAA administrator and the President. I went so far as to mention Landis by name.

"You'll report only to me," Kennedy assured me, "although you shouldn't hesitate to communicate with Landis on any matter within his limited, temporary consulting field."

My face must have mirrored my continued doubts, because JFK then proposed, as I had previously suggested to Dungan, that I be named his presidential aviation adviser as well as Federal Aviation Administrator. I couldn't have asked for anything more—but I did. I told the President-elect I had heard that Senator Pastore of Rhode Island had been pushing the appointment of Bruce Sundlun, a Washington and Providence attorney who had contributed significantly to Kennedy's own campaign. I informed JFK that Pastore reportedly had organized a group within the Senate Commerce Committee (of which he was a member) that was not only urging him to name Sundlun to the FAA post but that also would be vastly disappointed if the President chose me. The group in-

73

cluded the committee chairman, influential aviation-minded Warren Magnuson of Washington, and Clair Engle, my own senator from California.

Kennedy confessed only slight knowledge of this political power play and asked Dungan if it were true.

"That in fact is the situation, sir," Dungan said. "The delay in naming an FAA chief has made it possible for Pastore to create quite a bit of support in the Senate for Sundlun. I think, however, that if Mr. Halaby goes to see Pastore, Magnuson, and Engle within the next week, the matter will be resolved."

"Of course," Dungan added with a side glance in my direction, "one thing Mr. Halaby could do to ease matters would be to consider Sundlun as deputy administrator."

I already had heard this Sundlun-for-deputy administrator compromise proposal, and I was prepared for it. JFK's eyebrows rose in a kind of "Well?" aimed directly at me and, at this point, I figured I was going to blow the whole appointment. I knew that the post of deputy administrator, in the FAA's brief tradition, should go to a career government official and was not supposed to be a political plum.

"I feel most strongly that I should retain the present career deputy administrator until I know precisely what kind of a man is needed in the job," I said as firmly as possible. "At that time he should be appointed strictly on professional merit. And that's the way the FAA should be run—on merit, not on personalities."

To my great relief—and some surprise—the President-elect said he agreed with me.

"It'll be quite a political problem for you to work on," he warned, "but I'm not going to force you to accept Sundlun as your No. 2 man against your better judgment."

"Then I'd like to make another point," I said. "All appointments to key positions within the FAA will be made on merit, and I can't accept dictation from the Democratic National Committee or your own staff, sir, with regard to these appointments. The Agency by its very nature deals with highly technical and vital safety matter and it's no place in which to dump purely political choices."

"I agree," JFK said with equal firmness.

"Then with that understanding, Mr. President, I'd be most happy to serve you and the country as head of the FAA."

I was now, more or less officially (I still had to be confirmed by the Senate), a member of the New Frontier. We discussed briefly how to announce my appointment, and Walton suggested that we right then and there draft a short statement for the President-elect to read to newsmen outside the house. Walton, Dungan, and I huddled over a desk typewriter pecking out the statement that JFK approved after making a minor pencil change. It was only three sentences long, but for me it marked the start of a brand new career that was to take me into new areas of controversy and challenge—into crosswinds from all points of the compass.

In recounting these personally crucial moments, I have to confess that my meeting with Kennedy was not an uninterrupted session devoted exclusively to the fate of one Najeeb E. Halaby. The gracious and vivacious Marietta Tree had just departed with her appointment as a UN ambassador, raising her and the world's hopes.

Our meeting had lasted about forty-five minutes, the session being sprinkled with occasional interruptions by Evelyn Lincoln, who kept handing Kennedy notes or telephone messages. I was struck by the extraordinary relationship between this fine woman and JFK. And in those forty-five minutes I got my first real inside look at John F. Kennedy. He was a master at understatement, a device he used to both calm and charm an individual who might come to him loaded for bear. It's easy to fight with a big, blustering person, but JFK's soft-spoken, sometimes subtle and understated, approach was vastly effective and also unusual in a political figure.

I also got the impression of a man who was very much relaxed, in full command of himself and others; a man of growing strength and self-confidence. I got the idea he really didn't care too much about administrative formality, organization, and management. But overall, I truly admired him, and it was a proud moment when he accompanied me to the front stoop and read the brief statement on my appointment to the half-frozen group of news media representatives standing around. It read:

"We have looked for the best qualified and professionally competent man. We have found him in Jeeb Halaby of Santa Monica. He reports directly to me and will be my principal aviation adviser and the Administrator of the Federal Aviation Agency."

Late that afternoon, I paid a courtesy call on the man who had headed the FAA since its conception: stocky, pugnacious Elwood R. Quesada. I already knew Pete Quesada and rather liked him for his forcefulness, courage, and total integrity. I had met him initially at the Pentagon in 1949 when he commanded the Joint Task Force (Defense Department and Atomic Energy Commission) that exploded the world's first hydrogen test bomb on Bikini Atoll. Quesada was something of a martinet, hot-tempered and arbitrary at times; he had a military mind, military bearing, and military attitude, all of which made him difficult to work for in a civilian agency. But the infant FAA probably needed a boss of his unyielding, demanding ilk. The new agency had absorbed many of the CAA's former personnel, and Quesada inherited a lot of deadwood, a tradition of unproductivity, and a spirit of lethargy. This was not entirely the fault of the CAA or its people; as part of the Commerce Department, the old CAA had been a starved stepchild, and what administrative and technical talent it did possess had been buried under years of indifference and even hostility toward civil aviation.

I already have recited how the Harding and Curtis groups laid the groundwork for what was to become an independent Federal Aviation Agency. President Eisenhower—in July of 1957—appointed General Quesada to succeed Curtis as his special assistant for aviation affairs with the specific task of implementing what Curtis had recommended—particularly in the field of air-traffic control. One step the report had urged was the establishment of an interim independent Airways Modernization Board, to get something done on the critical airspace problem while a permanent agency with independent status was being created via the tortuous congressional process. Congress did act with unprecedented speed in approving the Airways Modernization Act, which established an Airways Modernization Board. President Eisenhower promptly named Quesada Chairman of the three-man Board, along with a representative from both the Defense and Commerce departments.

The Board didn't have much time to achieve even modest modernization. Fate lit a fire under the glacial congressional pace in the form of two midair collisions between military fighters and airliners. On April 21, 1958, an Air Force F-100F jet collided with a United DC-7 near Las Vegas; forty-two passengers and five crew members aboard the transport perished along with both military pilots. One month later a Maryland Air National Guard jet smacked into a Capitol Viscount over Brunswick, Maryland; this time the jet pilot survived by parachuting, but there were no survivors on the airliner.

The twin tragedies starkly illuminated the dangers of letting two air-traffic control systems, one military and the other civilian, allocate the same airspace. They also galvanized Congress into passing the Federal Aviation Act, as recommended by Eisenhower, shortly after the Brunswick tragedy. The legislation itself was mostly the product of the Senate Aviation Subcommittee headed by able A. S. "Mike" Monroney, one of the relatively few lawmakers who really understood and loved aviation. There was some opposition to the measure, mostly from the Bureau of the Budget, which wanted a Department of Transportation of which the FAA would be only a part. The Budget Bureau, a few years ahead of its time, could generate little support, and on August 23, 1958, the President signed the Federal Aviation Act into law—only two months after the White House had asked for its passage.

One of its main provisions called for giving control of all airspace to the FAA. A somewhat more controversial provision specifically declared that the administrator of the new agency had to be a civilian—this was included for the express purpose of further reducing military influence over airspace control, but it had the side effect of apparently eliminating Quesada from the post even though he was the President's open and avowed choice. Pete wanted the job but technically he was ineligible; he was a lieutenant general on the retired list of the regular Air Force, and the only way Eisenhower could get him into the top FAA slot was to have him resign his commission and forfeit a sizable pension.

Fortunately Quesada was a man of means; he had married a Pulitzer and he had proved himself a capable entrepreneur in private industry after he left active military duty. He didn't mind giv-

77

ing up his Air Force pension, but the President felt a lot more strongly than he did.

"The fact that a man of Mr. Quesada's qualifications is obliged to resign his retired status in the regular Air Force to comply with the letter of the law so he can again serve his country," declared Eisenhower, "does not, in my opinion, seem logical or desirable."

The President did more than merely object. He asked Congress to pass a law exempting Quesada from the civilian-only provision, and this was done in the form of a bill that allowed the general to resume his retired Air Force status after he left the FAA. Quesada, in turn, resigned his commission "for the duration" so to speak, and this paved the way for his confirmation as FAA administrator. His major opposition came from Senator Clair Engle of California who didn't like the idea of a general filling what was supposed to be a civilian post—Quesada's resignation from the Air Force notwithstanding.

Engle also expressed doubts that Quesada would treat all airspace users impartially; he thought Pete was prejudiced against private pilots and general aviation overall, a charge that Quesada denied. The Californian feared that Quesada's new agency would try to solve the air traffic control problem with a lot of fancy electronic military hardware priced way beyond the means of general aviation, and that such expensive gadgetry would be used solely to "chaperone the airline and military pilots through thousands of miles of bare airspace."

Finally, Engle didn't think much of Quesada's attitude toward airport construction; he considered him too gung-ho about building new or improved airport facilities exclusively for airline use, while thousands of private pilots were left with their wheels up.

Engle's fight against Quesada's confirmation earned him Pete's unrelenting enmity. One of Quesada's final acts as administrator was to march right into Engle's office on Capitol Hill, a few days before Kennedy's inauguration, for a face-to-face confrontation. They had been exchanging increasingly angry correspondence over Quesada's alleged bias against general aviation and Engle's alleged status as a kind of "mouthpiece" for the Aircraft Owners and Pilots Association, the trade organization representing the majority of private pilots.

On this particular occasion, Quesada had alerted a few newspapermen, who trailed behind him into the Senator's office where Pete personally handed him his final letter—a bitter harangue in which Quesada, in effect, called Engle a demagogue and a liar. Engle, in turn, was infuriated over the general's invasion with a squadron of newsmen who went along at Quesada's personal invitation. He never forgave Pete, either, as I was to find out myself in the near future.

Quesada and I spent almost an entire afternoon listening to the taped ground-air communications in the Staten Island UAL/TWA collision which had occurred just six weeks before. Quesada was understandably sensitive about the disaster. Only a month before it had occurred he had proudly told the National Press Club that jets were being monitored by radar "from takeoff to touchdown." The tape showed only too plainly that radar coverage wasn't that good; in fact, there was one damning bit of dialogue showing that ATC terminated radar control of the United flight just before the two planes hit, at a time when the UAL DC-8 was eleven miles beyond the position its crew was reporting. Why the system never spotted this deadly discrepancy was never really ascertained, but the failure was to become the basis for expensive litigation against the FAA after I took over.

I listened to the grim but fascinating tapes without much comment. We talked rather briefly about the administrator's job itself before we both decided we should head home—the storm was getting worse, and the nation's capital traditionally fears snow worse than San Francisco fears earthquakes. Quesada suggested that he take a taxi and that I should use his official car, a handsome, black Lincoln Continental.

"You might as well use it from now on, Jeeb," he said generously. "This job's yours now."

"I appreciate that," I said, "but I haven't been confirmed or sworn in yet. I'll stick to taxis until it's official."

We compromised by my accepting his suggestion that his chauffeur drop him off at his house and then take me to Georgetown, where Doris and I were staying with friends. It would have been a twenty- or thirty-minute trip under normal circumstances, but the snow had snarled traffic hopelessly. The drive took well

79

over three hours, and in the course of that time I heard the story of Pete Quesada's whole life—including the time when, as commander of the Ninth Air Force in Europe, he had taken a fellow general named Eisenhower for a piggyback ride in a single-seater fighter and was royally chewed out by the Pentagon. Or the day he was trying to start the balky engine on a Grumman amphibian after a forced landing in the ocean near the coast of Ecuador. The ignition switch didn't work and he couldn't get it started with a hand crank. So he resorted to an old pilot's superstition: He wet the tail. The engine started.

But mostly we talked, or rather *he* talked, about the two years he had spent as head of the FAA. It was more denunciation than discussion. He was intensely bitter over the various pressure groups that had feuded with him almost from the day he took over. He was proud of his overall record in air safety, mentioning in particular the FAA's "takeover of more than two thousand military air-traffic control facilities throughout the world—a major step in restoring ATC to civilian hands."

Quesada sincerely and deeply felt that his obligation as FAA chief was not to airlines, pilots, manufacturers, or even Congress, but to the public. I could not and still cannot quarrel with such dedication, but being for the public safety is like taking a stalwart stand against sin; in Quesada's case, it was difficult and even impossible to question, challenge, or fight his decisions. If anyone tried, he was put into the untenable position of being against safety, and this was the primary source of the bitterness he had aroused throughout civil aviation.

The snow lasted all night and did not stop until just before JFK left for the White House and the ceremonial ride to the inauguration ritual at the Capitol. I don't know who had arranged it, but Doris and I had special places reserved for us just behind the inaugural platform. It was pure exhilaration, knowing we were following John F. Kennedy into his struggle for a better America, and his inaugural address lifted our hearts and spirits even higher. It was a fresh approach to age-old problems, in the sense of recognizing mountainous obstacles, deep chasms, and arid areas to be tackled with vigor, with open, inquiring minds that would be satisfied only with active, creative solutions.

But before I could become an official New Frontiersman, I had to face the ordeal of confirmation—and in my case, I didn't think the word "ordeal" was any exaggeration. Not having sought the job, I had made little effort to enlist influential support where it counted: in the Senate, and particularly within the Senate Commerce Committee, where the confirmation hearings would be held. I hadn't bothered to woo the Democratic senator from California, Clair Engle, and when my appointment was first rumored, the Los Angeles *Times* asked Engle to comment.

"Halaby?" he asked. "Who's he? I never heard of him."

I had two strikes against me right from the start: The senator was miffed because he hadn't been consulted by the Kennedy staff before a Californian was nominated, and he also felt let down because Democratic officials in California hadn't cleared my appointment with him.

I decided to have a meeting with Engle. I walked into his office, where I introduced myself to his wife, an intelligent, activist woman who had achieved the status of almost an assistant senator. Engle himself was small and ferocious; he reminded me of a belligerent bullpup, and he wasted no time in cross-examining me on my aviation policy views, particularly as they applied to general aviation and private flying.

Engle had been one of the first politicians in history to use his own small plane as a campaign tool, and while running for office he had flown into the most remote areas of California. His deep interest in general aviation and his own flying experiences had led him to become the private pilot's spokesman and the Aircraft Owners and Pilots Association's own champion. Just as Quesada had unloaded his anti-Engle, anti-AOPA spleen on me, so did Engle regale me with his dislike of the first FAA boss.

He told me Quesada's trouble was that he used a military approach to civil aviation, that he ordered private pilots around instead of persuading and educating them. He regarded the FAA's establishment of more stringent medical regulations and examinations for general-aviation airmen as an invasion of privacy.

"A private pilot wants to use his airplane like he does his private automobile," Engle argued. He waved a stack of letters from protesting pilots who had written the senator that the stiffer FAA rules meant increased flying costs and were making it almost impossible to operate their airplanes.

"He hasn't been promoting aviation as is required under the Federal Aviation Act," Engle declared. "He's been handicapping it."

I did more listening than arguing or discussing, and in the end Engle said that while he would not oppose my nomination, he would find it difficult to support it in view of his pledge to Senator Pastore.

"What you should do is try to get Pastore to release all those who pledged to support Sundlun," Engle advised.

"I don't think that's possible, Senator," I replied. "The price is my naming Sundlun my deputy administrator, and I'm not about to do that. I'll consider him, but that's as far as I can go."

Engle didn't belabor the issue and ended our two-hour meeting by handing me a stack of letters about two feet high, which he asked me to go through when I had the time. They were all epistles from private pilots, the hundreds who had written Engle, at AOPA's suggestion, with their ideas for helping general aviation. I agreed to do this, and eventually I did cull from this correspondence some good points. But as far as Engle and my confirmation were concerned, about all our session had accomplished was his neutralization.

I did get some encouraging support from Senator Monroney and Representative Oren Harris of Arkansas, Monroney's aviation counterpart in the House. And now it seemed only fair to fulfill my promise to Senator Magnuson and at least meet with Bruce Sundlun. I made the arrangements through a friend of mine who had just been elected junior senator from Rhode Island, Claiborne Pell, who also happened to be a good friend of Sundlun. Pell set up a luncheon meeting in the Senate dining room and was with the Rhode Island attorney when I joined them for what turned out to be a rather long and taut affair.

Nothing that transpired at the luncheon changed my original conviction that Sundlun would never be satisfied or happy with the No. 2 slot. Furthermore, his legal and aviation background was too much like my own, and thus he could not offer counterbalancing assets.

I knew that if I caved in from the pro-Sundlun pressure, I'd be going against my determination to run the FAA myself; I wanted to be independent, answerable only to the President and the Congress; naming Sundlun as my chief assistant would be a major abdication of independence.

And that was that. In a brief meeting with President Kennedy I told him I had decided not to accept Sundlun. Kennedy was openly reluctant to alienate Senators Pastore and Pell but said that he'd go along with me. In subsequent months, a number of people who knew both Bruce and myself said that my decision had been wise.

I contacted the senators who had committed themselves to backing Sundlun, explaining my reasons for rejecting him and emphasizing that the President had concurred. All except Pastore seemed satisfied, although Pell wasn't exactly overjoyed. But at least I had cleared the air somewhat and, at this point, Magnuson agreed to hold hearings on my confirmation—hearings that reportedly had been delayed at Pastore's request while he made a last-ditch effort to replace me with Sundlun. And what helped immensely was a sudden switch to my side by Engle. Relieved of his commitment to Sundlun, and wanting very badly to have a fellow Californian heading the FAA, he became my champion along with Mr. Aviation of the United States Senate, Mike Monroney.

The education of a new public servant is miserably inadequate. Seldom does he grasp easily the subtle, constantly shifting balance of powers—legislative, executive, and judicial—that must be kept in mind from the moment of nomination to the farewells of resignation. But I had already served in the Executive branch as a civil servant, and unlike some neophytes facing a confirmation hearing, I had learned one sharp and very important lesson: Congressmen and senators are elected by the people and, next to God, the source of all power in our republic is the people.

Thus I regarded myself not as a man elected to office on his own merits and experience but as merely an appointive official serving temporarily at the will of an elected President, with the advice and consent of senators elected by the people. The appointee who pictures himself as the people's choice, who misconstrues his nomination as a kind of election, is in for trouble. It is that kind of man who walks into a confirmation hearing with a large chip on his shoulder and stands a pretty good chance of getting it and his head knocked off.

Another lesson for the nominee is that his critics and opponents all regard the hearing as an opportunity for revenge. Anything and anyone from the nominee's past are liable to be brought up at the hearing. Even sectional rivalries, social suspicions, professional prejudice, and personal piques emerge once the questioning starts. If you've had previous public-service experience, your adversaries are furnished additional ammunition. And if you've ever written a book in which you've taken a stand or made comments on certain issues, the pages will be tossed right back in your face.

I found out very quickly that the President expected me to get myself confirmed with no assistance from the White House. First of all, he was too busy getting his Administration under way to worry about a single nominee. Second, the White House "hands off" policy was traditional; only when an appointee gets into such serious trouble in the course of confirmation that it may embarrass the President does anyone from the White House staff lift a hand. At least that was the case with JFK.

So I went about the task of getting confirmed in a systematic way. I now had Engle on my side, but I made sure of support from the other California senator, Republican Thomas Kuchel. My wife had friends and relatives contact Senator Bartlett of Alaska, where her family had lived for two generations. He turned out to be the friendliest questioner at the hearing.

Having lined up some backing, I next tried to anticipate the line of questioning and potential attacks. One possible source of trouble, I figured, might be my association with the Aerospace Corporation, which I had helped found, as its first secretary-treasurer under its chairman William C. Foster, my former boss at the Mutual Security Administration, who had been asked to organize the new nonprofit company. The Air Force in 1948 had begun forming a number of nonprofit corporations to assist them in analysis and planning of its space and missiles programs. They recognized that under the Civil Service system, it was impossible to find and maintain the kind of intellectual and technical talent required for these tasks; the nonprofit corporations were organized as a device to find and buy such talent.

So I expected that the Senate committee would be firing questions regarding my formation of another nonprofit corporation, the salaries and fees paid, and probably what fees had been paid to me as the incorporating lawyer. A few questions were asked on the subject; I met them with an all-out defense of the need for buying technical talent in the absence of radically revising the Civil Service regulations.

I also was prepared to undergo a searching inquiry into my personal finances and relationships, a galling experience for any nominee and one of unbelievable irony. It amounted to two standards of ethics: one for the senators interrogating you and the other for the nominee, who may have been dragged into the job by White House pleading. I had already purged myself in following the usual technique of listing everything I owned, actual or potential, and recording all connections, however minor. Then I sat down with the general counsel and procurement officers of the Agency to determine whether there would be any possible business or financial ties that might conflict with the forthcoming government work.

For example, I had been on the Board of Governors of the Flight Safety Foundation, a nonprofit organization dedicated to the same goals as the FAA itself. But I was advised that at some point the Foundation might need to be critical of the FAA or enter into a contractual agreement involving an air-safety project or survey. So with considerable reluctance I resigned from the Board of Governors.

I had to sell my one hundred shares of American Telephone and Telegraph stock, even though the idea that I could influence contracts in favor of a company in which I held about one zillionth of its total stock was fantastic. I also had to dispose of stock in Texas Instruments Corporation because, I was told, the FAA would soon be considering a bid for a radar contract with this company.

I disclosed these divestments at the hearing, refraining from voicing my opinion that presidential nominees too often were getting the proverbial shaft. The truth was that I, like so many men

85

and women willing to brave the jungles of public service, had to pay dearly for the privilege. Before President Kennedy named me to the FAA, my gross annual income amounted to some $70,000 in legal fees and compensation from various Southern California companies in aviation, electronics, and real estate in which I served as an officer or director.

My yearly salary with the FAA: $22,500.

The "fringe benefits" in private industry, such as life and health insurance and a retirement fund, had been much greater than what the government was offering at the time. I had enjoyed a few expense accounts, which added up to around $10,000 a year. There is no expense account in government, except for a ridiculously low per-diem rate paid for room and board on trips outside of Washington. To make matters worse, I was amazed to learn that the federal government didn't pay one cent for the cost of relocating one's home and family.

I must admit the family took my decision to go back into the federal service with a mixture of excitement and concern. Doris was secretly pleased because she had more close friends in Washington than in the Los Angeles area. My wife had always hated what she considered to be California's superficiality, a preoccupation with what you owned rather than what you thought. And the kids were quite pleased with all the excitement about my appointment. As for myself, I had always considered California my home and wasn't as sanguine as my wife about returning to Washington, where we had been married and spent our first ten years. The early intoxication of appointment to a forty-three-thousand-employee Agency diminished noticeably under the cold water of a few unpleasant financial facts, the strains of getting confirmed and the crisis-to-crisis life of a federal regulator.

Much of that strain involved the then current controversy over the Lockheed Electra, a new transport plane that had suffered two fatal crashes that at first were totally unexplainable mysteries. I knew I faced some possibly rough questioning on whether the airplane was really safe; the Electra had generated such an emotional and technical rhubarb that at one point Pete Quesada's job was at stake because he had refused to ground the prop-jet.

The Electra crash had occurred on September 29, 1959. A

Braniff Electra flying from Houston to New York via Dallas and Washington had lost a wing somewhere over the small town of Buffalo, Texas, at an altitude of fifteen thousand feet in perfect weather, and crashed. For 5½ months, the Civil Aeronautics Board (which investigated major air accidents at that time) conducted a painstaking investigation but failed to find out why a wing came off a brand-new, thoroughly tested airliner flying in clear weather.

The Buffalo crash was still under investigation, and still a complete mystery, when on March 17, 1960, a second Electra also lost a wing in clear weather and went down with all sixty-three persons aboard near the small town of Tell City, Indiana. A total of ninety-seven passengers and crew members had lost their lives to a new airliner that was supposedly the finest product American aeronautical engineering skill could create.

Quesada knew only too well that there was something wrong with the airplane—a brand-new transport doesn't lose a wing in clear weather without some major fault. But acting on the advice of his own technical experts within the FAA as well as those from Lockheed and the airlines concerned, he merely ordered that the speedy Electra be operated at lower cruising speeds until the cause of the two crashes could be determined. The pressure from a few but highly vocal lawmakers for more drastic action—outright grounding—was both relentless and bitter. I learned later that one of Quesada's own subordinates remarked at the time, "If another one goes down, Pete might as well be aboard." He was only too right. Quesada's decision not to ground the Electra put his public career right on the line; a third unexplained crash probably would have forced his resignation.

When it became known that certain elements within the CAB itself favored mandatory grounding, the pressure became even greater. There was one tense, dramatic, and totally secret meeting held at the FAA in the midst of the crisis, with Quesada presiding, involving the heads of all airlines operating the big prop-jet. One of them, Donald Nyrop of Northwest, stood up and announced that he was ordering all his Electras taken out of service that very day. It was mainly Quesada who convinced Nyrop that the plane was safe under the new speed restrictions, pending solution of the

87

mystery, and Pete's firm stand saved the Electra from the shattering humiliation of mandatory grounding. If he hadn't talked Nyrop out of it, the other airlines would have been forced to go along with Northwest.

It was on May 5, 1960, that technicians announced they had found the answer to two of commercial aviation's most puzzling catastrophes—after, incidentally, an unprecedented display of government/industry co-operation that had even Lockheed's two major rivals, Boeing and Douglas, supplying their competitor with technical aid and advice.

"Whirl mode" was the verdict—a form of vibrating motion inherent in any piece of rotating machinery such as oil drills, table fans, and automobile drive shafts; or, in the case of the airplane, the propeller.

A propeller has gyroscopic tendencies; in other words, it will stay in a smooth plane of rotation unless it is displaced by some strong external force, as a spinning top can be made to wobble if a finger is placed against it. The moment such a force is applied to a propeller, it reacts in the opposite direction. Suppose the force drives the propeller upward. The stiffness that is part of its structure promptly resists the force and pitches the prop forward. Each succeeding upward force is met by a protesting downward motion, and the battle of vibration (whirl mode) progresses—the propeller continues to rotate in one direction while the rapidly developing whirl mode is vibrating in the opposite direction. If the mode is not checked, the result is a wildly wobbling gyroscope that eventually begins to transmit its violent motion to a natural outlet—the wing.

Normally, propeller whirl mode inevitably encounters the stiffness of the entire engine/nacelle structure and is damped before it can spread to the wing. But in the case of the Electra, engineers found an Achilles heel—the nacelles themselves, the outboard ones in particular. If they were weakened or damaged by turbulence or a hard landing, for example, they were incapable of stopping whirl mode before the deadly, ever-increasing vibration reached the wing.

The spinning turbines and propellers in the Electra's engine/nacelle package are nothing but a giant gyroscope. Any severe jolt, such as extreme turbulence (the Northwest plane apparently encountered clear-air turbulence just before the wing came off), was a giant finger reaching out to touch this smoothly whirling mass, causing it to break stride and wobble.

As the agitated engine began to wobble, so did the propeller, with its normal plane of rotation disturbed. And as the prop wobbled, its violently uneven motion was transmitted to the wing, which also began to flex and flutter. This, in turn, sent additional discordant forces back to the engine/prop structure, which now wobbled ever more wildly. Whirl mode was now under way, unchecked, each cycle feeding new and destructive energy into the succeeding cycles.

The next step in this chain reaction was the tendency of uncontrolled whirl mode to slow down in frequency even as it increased in violence. The frequency would be about five cycles per second at the start, but lessening to three cycles per second as the vibration continued. Three cycles per second happened to be maximum frequency at which the Electra's wing could flutter. The moment the two vibration frequencies touched the same level, the effect was that of a sustained high note eventually breaking a glass tuned to the same vibration level. Scientists estimated that the elapsed time between the jolt that excited the nacelle, causing whirl mode to start, and the inevitable separation of the wing was only thirty seconds.

Once the cause of the two crashes was known, it then cost Lockheed some $25 million to beef up both the nacelle and wing structures so that whirl mode, even if it began, could never attain a force capable of breaking the wing spars. By the time I had been nominated to the FAA, Lockheed's drastic modification program was in full swing, and grueling flight tests had demonstrated the effectiveness of the "fix." But while the engineers were satisfied, there wasn't much doubt that the public, after weeks of spectacular headlines, still had to be sold on the airplane; even after the solution was announced and corrective action was under way, passengers in disturbing numbers were still avoiding Electra flights. I felt as the incoming FAA chief that I had to do something to help restore confidence in the process of assuring airworthiness in what I was convinced was a fine airplane.

That "something" was a personal conviction that I should test-fly a modified Electra myself, and I went to James Pyle for advice. Pyle had been named Acting Administrator after Quesada left and would serve in that capacity until I was confirmed. A Navy pilot and an aviation official for seven years and a considerate, co-operative person, he already had been of immense help in getting me oriented toward Agency problems. He was high on my list to be deputy administrator, but he told me he was doubtful that he wanted to stay on. He had a large family to support, he had spent a decade as deputy and briefly as the administrator of the old CAA, and finally two years under the Quesada regime. He was rather tired of government work.

On balance, he thought my "see for myself" idea on the Electra was a good one, although he pointed out some drawbacks. Pyle reasoned that the test flight probably would draw publicity, and he thought the much-maligned airplane had received enough of a bad press. Second, he feared that I might be accused of doing it strictly for the publicity. As a matter of fact, I heard later that Pete Quesada thought exactly that and thus took a dim view of my test proposal. He told a mutual friend I was "headline hunting."

Actually, I not only wasn't thinking about publicity but, in fact, already had decided to make the test flight in absolute secrecy—revealing my findings only if asked about the Electra at any confirmation hearing. Armed with Pyle's mixed blessing, I got in touch with Robert Gross, president of Lockheed, and told him what I wanted to do. He was naturally reluctant at first, feeling that any more attention drawn to the Electra's problems could do the airplane no good and, perhaps, might inflict further harm as far as public confidence was concerned.

"Let me talk it over with my staff and I'll call you back," he promised.

When he did call back, he said he appreciated what I was trying to do—namely, restore confidence—and that everyone at Lockheed thought it could be accomplished in a constructive manner.

"But that's going to be up to you," he added.

"All I have in mind is to establish two points," I assured him. "First, that the Electra is a sound airplane and second, that the FAA and I are going to be damned sure before we give it a final seal of approval."

"You've got a deal," Gross said.

Arrangements were made for me to fly to Burbank in the FAA's Gulfstream—and I had no qualms about using an official government airplane. For the interim period preceding confirmation, I had been given the status of a consultant to the agency, and the self-assignment fitted in that category. In Burbank I was reunited with two old flying friends from my test-pilot days at Lockheed—Tony Levier and Herman (Fish) Salmon who, along with Roy Wimmer, had done much of the Electra's post-crash testing. It had been rugged flying, too; they had flown a heavily instrumented Electra into the Sierra wave, a California mountain-area air mass known for violent, almost perpetual turbulence, where updrafts and downdrafts were like miniature tornados. This was before whirl mode was tagged as a killer, and their early flights had disclosed that the outboard nacelle structures, under extremely heavy motion loads, were taking more of a beating than anyone had thought possible. This was the first clue that unstable whirl mode might have caused the two crashes.

Later, Lockheed's test pilots flew a modified Electra into the Sierra wave to test the stronger nacelle-and-wing combination. The final step was a cliff-hanger—Salmon and Wimmer penetrated the Sierra wave again, but this time in an Electra whose engine mounts had been weakened deliberately to induce whirl mode. The pilots were ordered to wear parachutes, because in effect they were re-enacting both accidents; their Electra was equipped with special tiltable vanes to excite flutter. Fortunately they didn't have to use the chutes—despite the weakened engine mounts, the stiffer nacelle/wing combination dampened whirl mode almost as soon as it began its deadly vibrations.

Salmon and Levier were assigned to ride with me on my own test flight, a two-hour ordeal that in most respects duplicated the crucial flights that proved the efficiency of the "fix." Riding with us were an FAA pilot and also an engineer from the Agency plus some Lockheed technicians. We took off from Burbank and headed for the familiar testing ground over the desert near Mojave and Palmdale, where I had spent so many exciting hours instructing and testing from 1940 to 1943. It was an airborne homecoming, but I didn't have much time to waste on sentiment.

The goal was to simulate the worst conditions of turbulence and stress that the Braniff and Northwest planes had encountered before disintegrating. We climbed to twenty-two thousand feet, went through some routine tests for stability and control, and then dove the airplane fifty miles an hour beyond the maximum permissible speed. We induced yaw and roll during other high-speed dives, and I was amazed at the Electra's controllability and overall performance. No wonder airline pilots loved that bird; it was a dream to fly, almost as responsive as a fighter, and possessing tremendous reserve power.

After finishing the high-altitude phase, we pointed the Electra's snout toward the Sierra wave at the maximum allowable speed, and once we entered the turbulent area, it was like suddenly leaving a smooth superhighway and ramming into a washboard country road without slackening speed. I was vastly impressed after the two-hour flight ended, and after I also had gone over all the data of previous static flight tests.

The FAA already had lifted the Electra's speed restrictions, the order going out fifteen days before JFK was inaugurated. But anti-Electra prejudice still existed, and toward the ending of my confirmation hearing, I dropped my own personal bombshell. It was Senator Vance Hartke of Indiana, an avowed critic of both Quesada and the Electra, who sprang the question—asking me what I thought of the airplane in a tone from which I inferred that he, personally, wouldn't have flown in it from Newark to La-Guardia.

I then revealed that I had test-flown the Electra myself, recounted the details of that flight, and expressed my firm conviction that the aircraft was not only safe but also that I considered it an extremely fine machine. I gathered that if I had suddenly confessed membership in the Communist Party, Hartke couldn't have been more surprised—not only at my defense of the Electra but also at what I had done to help clear its name.

"But you aren't going to do this for all aircraft?" he asked incredulously.

"Senator," I replied, "I intend to do just that for all new major aircraft. I will personally fly them after my people have done their own certification testing."

I am not egotistical enough to believe that this revelation of personal involvement with a controversial airplane tipped the confirmation scales toward me. In truth, many of those who knew of my test-flight plans in advance had advised me against doing it, arguing that I was identifying myself with the Electra and would be held responsible if anything further happened to its already marred safety record. But I had been certain that Hartke would grill me about the plane—he literally had reviled Quesada over the issue—and I saw in all this one of the first tests on how I would deal with the most important aspect of the administratorship: safety. My test flight would not be the last "find out for yourself" approach to my job. At any rate, I was confirmed, and on March 3, 1961, I was sworn in at a ceremony held in President Kennedy's office.

There was a residue of disappointment, however: My wife and children couldn't come from California to witness the swearing-in ceremony in the Oval Office simply because we couldn't afford it. But a certain Laura Wilkins Halaby, who could, was present at the invitation of the President of the United States—who had no way of knowing that my mother, raised a Texas Democrat, had been voting Republican since the days of Franklin Roosevelt. She had voted for Richard Nixon and against Kennedy, in fact; she regarded JFK as an upstart who was probably under control of the Pope, labor unions, and left-wingers. She informed me that if the President asked for her opinion, she was going to warn him against his would-be captors—a prospect that gave me considerable anxiety.

But to my great delight and fervent relief, JFK charmed her right off her feet. He rushed forward when she entered his office to be introduced, and she never really got a chance to tell him what she thought. Whatever she intended to say was drowned under Kennedy's boyish, disarming personality. Instead of unloading on him, she turned typical mother and gushed effusively about what a marvelous man he had acquired in her son. All the President could do was politely agree—although he murmured something to the effect that he'd learn more about me as time wore on.

A few minutes later, I was sworn in as the second administrator of the Federal Aviation Agency.

CHAPTER FOUR

It would have been exciting for my family to be present at the swearing-in ceremony, even more so during my first six months at the FAA and the first hundred days of the New Frontier, but it was not to be.

They were treated to one thrill, however, after it was decided that I stay in Washington alone until the following summer. I had cleaned up my California affairs during a brief visit following the inauguration and was informed that the Chamber of Commerce of Los Angeles and the Aero Club of Southern California wanted to give me a little farewell party—a civic luncheon at the famed Cocoanut Grove in the Ambassador Hotel. They couldn't have picked a more apt location: The restaurant had been the scene of a few romantic moments during my college days.

Our hosts weren't satisfied with a prosaic means of getting us from our house in Santa Monica to the hotel. Bruce McNeil, who headed a brand-new helicopter taxi company, sent one of his choppers to our home to pick us up, fly us downtown, and deposit the whole family on the Ambassador's lawn. I am reluctantly convinced that this gave my children a bigger kick than my appointment had provided.

The FAA maintained a large regional office in Los Angeles, and

I knew this would give me a legitimate excuse to see my family on at least a few occasions. It was a poor substitute for actually having them with me, but I also was well aware that even if they had come to Washington, they wouldn't have seen much of me. Not even the much-appreciated and helpful advance briefings Quesada and his staff provided me precluded the inevitable tough break-in period after I assumed the administrator's post.

Those briefings by Quesada's staff had been thorough. One, for example, provided guidelines on the confirmation process, which I devoured prior to the hearings. On one occasion, Daggett Howard and his assistant, Nate Goodrich, came to the home of outgoing Deputy Secretary of Defense James H. Douglas, where I was staying prior to taking office. With them they had a full biographical sketch of each member of the Senate Commerce Committee, his attitudes toward the FAA, and the Agency's current experience with him.

Howard and Goodrich also provided me with detailed information on the Federal Aviation Act, along with the various amendments that had been added since its original passage. Next, Quesada placed in my hands a thick looseleaf binder containing biographical data on the top dozen or so FAA executives, their photographs so I would gain some instant visual recognition, and an outline of their service experience and accomplishments since they had been with the Agency. Finally, the career staff compiled status reports on every major issue then before the FAA—some of them more than a hundred pages in length.

All this, plus that two-foot stack of private-pilot letters Senator Engle had given me, gave me several days and nights of homework, which I actually welcomed—it kept me busy at a time when I hated to appear that I had taken over the Agency before actual confirmation. In fact, I deliberately stayed away from the old building on New York Avenue, feeling it would have been presumptuous to assume authority before the Senate gave me a green light. But Jim Pyle told me bluntly I was being foolish and that my physical presence at the Agency was part of my preparing for the job.

The FAA's headquarters in the ancient Emergency Hospital were no exception to the axiom that most federal buildings must have been designed by an architect with ulcers, a dyspeptic disposition, and the friendly personality of a robot. Being in a former hospital, the FAA was even worse than most—it was purely makeshift and incredibly inefficient in layout. It also was too small, capable of handling only a fraction of the FAA's Washington personnel. As a result, FAA employees were scattered among no less than thirteen separate buildings, some of them dating back to World War I. Eventually, during my tenure at the FAA, we were to have a new, carefully planned, well-designed FAA building housing all key Washington employees. But until it was erected we had to put up with one of the ugliest and most outmoded structures in the capital.

My living quarters were considerably more attractive than where I worked. I had intended to stay in the Douglas home only until after I took office, but Elinor and Jim Douglas insisted that I might as well live there pending my family's arrival six months hence. It was an imposition on them, but it was salvation for me. Their lovely Georgetown home was vastly preferable to a coldly impersonal hotel room or a rented apartment. I worked at the FAA for a solid ten or eleven hours before going home at from eight to nine at night. When the dilapidated FAA building was almost empty was my most productive time—there was no one around to bother me with new problems and new papers, and I could not only catch up on the day's "in box" but also get a running start on the next day's chores.

Those first six months prior to the family's arrival had passed quickly. The early weeks, naturally, were spent in my getting adjusted to the Agency and its top personnel and in their getting adjusted to me. The first day the new head of an agency enters the "Washington Cockpit," he finds everything set for him—his secretary, assistant secretaries, special assistants, deputies, etc. They're all eager to please and also to continue as they have been doing. The result is a superficial appearance of great stability and smooth transition, but underneath there has to be anxiety on everyone's part, including that of the new pilot in command. I was fortunate in having Quesada as a predecessor; in his military career he had turned over many commands to fellow officers, and he had learned what both a clean desk and cleaned-up problems can mean to a successor.

The heavy reliance Pete had placed on the FAA's legal staff was immediately apparent, and I concluded right from the start that it was time to put the Agency's lawyers back to practicing law rather than making aviation policy. I could understand why Quesada had given almost *carte blanche* to the legal staff; as an Air Force General setting up and manning a new agency, he had been conscious of the limitations on his authority, and he naturally leaned on the staff's advice. But it seemed to me that Pete had gone far beyond what was necessary—putting the lawyers into positions of undue and even pre-emptive strength. Admittedly they happened to be the most intelligent and ingenious men within the Agency, but it was not right that they should be so far up in the operating chain of command—in many ways, unofficial rulers of the FAA.

I didn't go behind anyone's back in ordering some changes. I knew Bud Howard from my law school days, and I had served with Nate Goodrich at the Defense Department. While they were briefing me on the history of the FAA and its regulatory powers before I was sworn in, I frankly explained to them that things were going to be different—they would have plenty of voice in the definition of policy but not any in the direction of the Agency or the execution of any policy. As a fellow lawyer, I expected some disappointment, although I never sensed any strong resentment, a fact much to their credit.

My job clearly was to pick out the best of the CAA career people and try to integrate them with the new men Quesada had brought in and with the new blood I wanted to bring in myself. My predecessor had recruited 136 officers from the Air Force, Navy, Army, and Marine Corps. No one could fault this military transfusion; the Federal Aviation Act's chief and most pressing goal was to erect a common air-traffic control system serving both civil and military aviation.

The difficulty, however, was that some of the military officers were unsuited for working with civilians in what was primarily a civilian agency. A few were outright incompetent, and the superior ones felt they had been sidetracked from their military careers. I frankly was surprised at the poor relations between the FAA and the Defense Department officers assigned to the new Agency. There was virtual war between the Navy and the FAA. Air Force-FAA relations were only slightly better, and Army/Marines-FAA the best of all, although not in the category of joyous, perpetual harmony. Underlying this uneasy military-civilian alliance was the former's long-smoldering resentment of the old CAA's ponderous, almost primitive approach to modernizing air-traffic control. The Air Force in particular had always considered the FAA's predecessor agency a kind of bureaucratic dinosaur and, at the time I took over, felt that the new Agency was just as prone to procrastination. The Air Force, for example, was not enamored of the FAA's research and development program, headed by a bright young engineer named James Anast. The Air Force believed, and with justification, that the FAA's R and D was always looking for supersophisticated hardware to be used in a futuristic Air Traffic Control System (ATC), instead of grabbing available improvements right off the shelf and doing something about immediate problems. The Air Force contended that R and D invariably kept looking for something better, unwilling to adopt equipment that may not have been the last word but that at least was usable immediately. Badly needed ATC reforms seemed to be always just around the corner without ever reaching fruition.

As more or less of an old Washington hand, I already had some personal rules in mind the first day I sat down at my new desk. Anyone who enters the jungle along the Potomac had better set up a kind of *modus operandi* for Agency chiefs or he'll be eaten alive. The Halaby formula for survival was simple:

Get and keep the initiative.

Distinguish between action and activity.

Don't play favorites and don't be afraid to make decisions.

Let no one come between you and your boss, namely the President of the United States; and on major issues, see him eyeball-to-eyeball.

Don't get into more than one fight at a time; in other words, keep your flanks and rear protected before launching a frontal attack.

Get your facts first, and know the bias and weaknesses of the source providing alleged facts.

Maintain an independent, policy-minded staff, with some sense of history, around you.

Always have a home base of political support and nurture it.

Remember that the press and Congress have no predictable code of ethics or standards and are not accountable for their transgressions except in subscriptions and elections.

Recognize at the outset that in any argument with the Pentagon, the dice are loaded against you; it's too hard to fight national security, $50 billion a year, and 2.5 million people on the payroll.

I knew all these rules when I took the FAA job, but I also knew it was inevitable I would have to bend or break some of them either deliberately or inadvertently. For example, in an agency of the FAA's size and with the scope of its authority, it was impossible to limit myself to one fight at a time. Controversy and crisis became a way of life and tended to overlap in occurrence—the fire under the administrator's padded chair was never allowed to simmer or go out.

Quesada's greatest manpower legacy to me was a superb administrative officer in Alan Dean, who had never really been given a chance to show that he could economize as well as expand.

I gladly gave him that chance, and with his guidance I reversed the FAA's course toward management centralization. I took the position that the Agency and its employees had to concentrate their efforts in the field, not in Washington. Field staffers had to work at the roots of the various problems—on the grass strips of small airports, in the factories, in airline operations offices. My first major decision was to put regional administrators into the field, giving them all the responsibility and authority they could bear. Seven regions were established and, interestingly enough, Quesada publicly declared that I was making a great mistake. Halaby, he said, was creating eight FAAs—one in Washington and the other seven in the field.

Another king-sized management problem was that for many years the FAA's specialists had been allowed to congregate in functional groups. The Agency thus became compartmentalized instead of unified. So we began the task of crossing flight-safety specialists with air-traffic specialists, airport specialists with installation specialists, and so on.

My final and probably least popular personnel edict involved transfer of some key people from Washington to the field and vice versa. I found that too many on the Washington staff had served in the capital for years and had acquired an overload of bureaucratic barnacles. Some of them had been at the FAA or the CAA headquarters for as long as seventeen years. When they were transferred to the field, there was a lot of grumbling, and I must admit there was considerable turbulence within the Agency during the first year.

Doctors Robert Snowden and Robert Glazer, consulting psychologists, helped me shape up a new team, completely turning over the old civil servants, decentralizing the organization, and either promoting or inducing early retirement for most of the key people. Snowden in particular enjoyed this work very much; I think he felt he was playing an important part in influencing public safety, and it also was giving him the chance to analyze the use of public power by private men.

While better management was tops on my priority list, I suppose what might be termed public relations was next—not in the sense of publicity, but in repairing at least a portion of the ruffled feelings, deflated egos, and bloody butts left in the wake of Quesada's personality and policies. This is not to say that he had been more often wrong than right in administering his verbal and legal spankings, but I did judge that there was room for improving relations between the FAA and the various segments of the aviation community. Therefore, as soon as I could arrange it and clear his appointment with the White House, I hired as my special assistant and press officer Phil Swatek, the Washington correspondent of the Cincinnati *Enquirer,* who was to give the people five years of devoted service with me and to rise to other top jobs in the FAA. This mending of fences began with the Air Line Pilots Association, then headed by personable, articulate Clarence (Clancy)

Sayen, who was to be killed in a tragic air crash shortly after he left office a few years later. Clancy had quarreled bitterly with Quesada, exchanging more epithets than reasonable points of view. Their battle began when Quesada issued a ruling that forbade any pilot to leave the cockpit except to answer a call of nature or some cabin emergency. When FAA inspectors were seen holding stopwatches on flight crews parked in the traditional "blue room," and filing violation notices if they stayed away from the cockpit over five minutes, Sayen went into verbal orbit.

He wasn't really on very solid ground—there *had* been too many cases of loose cockpit discipline, and the unforgiving jet didn't allow such formerly approved practices as captains spending rather long periods in the cabin chatting with passengers. In the old piston-engine days, that made for excellent public relations, but the jet cockpit demanded constant attention and alertness. Quesada also was only too cognizant that pilots under the CAA had become rather spoiled, complacent, and underregulated; Pete loved to quote what a veteran CAA inspector said when someone asked him why he didn't crack down more on flight crews.

"How the hell do you spank a Greek god?" he replied plaintively.

Yet I also knew that airline pilots had never really been given sufficient credit for their own contributions to air safety. Too often in the past, I had to admit, ALPA had been ahead of both the airline industry and the federal government in urging and/or developing major safety advances. Standardization of cockpit instruments, reversible props, wing lights that flashed on and off instead of remaining static, weather radar for all airliners, better approach and runway lighting—all these improvements were ALPA-urged before the airlines and government got around to adopting them. It was an American Airlines pilot who perfected center-line runway lighting to make night landings safer; he successfully demonstrated his system thirteen years before the FAA finally approved it for general installation.

During my own tenure at the FAA, I relied heavily on two fine airline captains, Paul Soderlind of Northwest and Robert Buck of TWA, for advice in critical safety areas. Soderlind's work on the behavior of swept-wing aircraft in turbulence and his recommendations for combating so-called turbulence upsets did much to eliminate a previously unsuspected hazard. Buck did a brilliant survey of the FAA's efforts in the vital field of bad-weather operations. Utilizing the skills and knowledge of these dedicated pilots was just one by-product of my determination to make the FAA and the pilot part of the same community instead of constant adversaries. And the intelligent, reasonable Sayen was of no small help in this achievement.

Right from the start I found him eager to co-operate in improving FAA-ALPA relations. We agreed to have me meet with regional pilot groups throughout the country, and Sayen himself brought all his regional chairmen into Washington for a frank discussion with me on the issues that had divided the Agency and the pilots' union so bitterly. I, for one, found that the chairmen—all line captains—were not the "pampered prima donnas" Quesada was fond of labeling airline pilots. And I think these men went away from this first large session with me feeling that I was one of them—namely a pilot like themselves, who had an open mind and was willing to listen to pilot views before making key decisions affecting airline operations. Many of ALPA's difficulties with both the FAA and the airline industry were the result of the union's own split personality. ALPA was not one organization but two. It was a highly professional group of airmen with a tremendous amount to contribute toward our mutual goals of greater safety. It also was a labor union, which too often masked purely economic demands under the guise of safety. Sometimes it was hard to tell which organization was making a certain proposal. Typical was the "fourth man in the cockpit" donnybrook, which erupted a few months before I took office.

ALPA put pressure on the airlines to man every four-engined jetliner with a four-man crew—three pilots and a flight engineer. A few of the carriers succumbed: Eastern, American, and Pan Am, each headed, interestingly enough, by one of the industry's giants who apparently was more interested in avoiding a strike by agreeing to a crowded cockpit than standing for efficiency. The pilots argued that a four-man crew enhanced safety, claiming that the bigger and more complex jets required a quartet of airmen in the cockpit. (From the beginning it seemed to me to be "featherbirding.") The FAA's own regulations merely required a three-man crew for large jets—two pilots and a flight engineer. United had solved the controversy in a sensible fashion, by requiring that its flight engineers be qualified pilots.

When United decided to give all of its flight engineers pilot training, several other airlines went along. The majority of engineers were in favor of this solution with the exception of the small but aggressive Flight Engineers International Association (FEIA). FEIA knew it was being backed against the wall: As its members became full-fledged, qualified pilots, they would have to join ALPA, and retaining membership in both unions would be senseless. When Quesada gave the United plan his official blessing, FEIA's very existence was threatened, and it blew the whistle. On October 11, 1960, Northwest's flight engineers struck in a walkout that by the following February had spread to seven other carriers.

At the heart of the issue were the qualifications of the flight engineer himself. His job had been created in the late thirties and forties, when the airlines began operating DC-6's, Constellations, and Boeing Stratocruisers—all pressurized aircraft. Their greater complexity required the presence in the cockpit of a man who had to be a "Mr. Fixit," trained to solve accessible in-flight mechanical problems and aid the two pilots in fuel management, cabin pressurization, monitoring engine instruments, and other cockpit chores that really did lessen the pilot's workload. Most of the first flight engineers, in fact, were ex-airline mechanics, and their cockpit training was predicated on these skills. They were experts on the innards of an airplane and thus were extremely valuable in that role.

But when the jets came along, the need for mechanics on the flight deck diminished. The flight engineer, for all practical purposes, was more of a third pilot than a mechanic. The jets didn't require the old specialization skills, and in fact the first two-engine jets—the DC-9 and BAC-111—went into service with only a two-man crew. ALPA logically insisted that the bigger jets needed three pilots, mostly in the event of incapacitation, but this demand could have only one of two results: "The third man" in the cockpit either had to be pilot-trained or there had to be a four-man crew. And when it became apparent that the four-man concept was an economic monstrosity, United's plan won increasing support—and touched off the ALPA-FEIA jurisdictional brawl.

It was easy for me to sympathize with the FEIA's dilemma, but it also was obvious that based solely on the question of safety, theirs was a lost cause. It was not just a jurisdictional dispute as far as the FAA was concerned, but a safety matter—it was safer to have that third man in the cockpit capable of flying the airplane, and that was the stand I took and that earned me the undying enmity of the FEIA and its president, a former Douglas and National Airlines mechanic named Ronald Brown.

The flight engineers' strike came at a time when President Kennedy had his hands full trying to organize his new Administration. He put the dispute into the hands of a special commission headed by the very capable dean of the University of Wisconsin Law School, Nathan Feinsinger. The first task, however, was to get the struck airlines operating again while the Feinsinger Commission worked out a solution. This brought me into the act with both feet.

Under the existing regulations, a mechanic-trained man had an inside track to the flight engineer's seat. The rules actually were written virtually to eliminate a pilot from the job unless he also had mechanics' training. It was my firm conviction, supported by my technical experts, that there was no measurable difference between a well-trained flight engineer who had started as a pilot and a well-trained flight engineer who had started as a mechanic. Either skill offered an adequate basis for qualifying for an FAA flight engineer's certificate.

Therefore I had the FAA legal staff draft a new regulation that in effect said the airlines could put pilots into the flight engineer's seat. The proposal also was discussed with key individuals in the airline industry, and I also briefed Labor Secretary Arthur Goldberg on what I was prepared to do.

When the proposed new rule was made public, the FEIA attacked me bitterly, claiming that only a mechanic could read instruments, record the data, adjust engine controls, conduct walk-around inspections before flights, and make in-flight repairs. From Clancy Sayen of ALPA came the rebuttal that pilots had been doing the walk-around for years, that the jets made it less and less necessary for a flight engineer to have much mechanical training, and that automation and easily removable components had all but eliminated the possibility of repairing something in the air. Ronald Brown of FEIA came back with the claim that there should be an independent man in the cockpit—in other words, a crew member from a union other than the ALPA so there could be a check and a balance on crew performance.

Feinsinger's group came up with a temporary formula for ending the crippling strike: The engineers should go back to work and start negotiating with both the pilots and management, while the Commission would continue to work on the complex, emotion-ridden dispute. All the airlines except one agreed to this; the holdout was Western, headed by crusty Terrell C. Drinkwater.

Goldberg called Drinkwater personally and asked him to let Western flight engineers return to work while everyone concerned tried to reach a long-range solution. But Drinkwater, who had already fired his flight engineers, refused to take them back and they, in turn, went on a violent picketing rampage during which cars were overturned and other Western employees physically threatened. A stubborn and petulant man, Drinkwater was determined to crush Western's FEIA chapter. He got Western back into operation using younger pilots already qualified or quickly trained as flight engineers. His stand, in direct defiance of the new President of the United States, had the effect of prolonging the strikes on the other airlines for a brief time.

Goldberg had concluded wisely that this was primarily a political and economic rather than technical-safety issue. To get the warring parties to sit down peacefully, he could not tolerate violence and confrontation, and hence his call to Drinkwater "to be reasonable." His personal plea having failed, he had Evelyn Lincoln place a call for JFK to Drinkwater at the latter's office in Los Angeles. I was told later that Drinkwater refused to take the call, knowing what the President wanted. The word of Drinkwater's affront to the President spread throughout the Administration, and he became *persona non grata* in one hell of a hurry. Coincidentally, Drinkwater was a guest at the luncheon in my honor at the Cocoanut Grove, and I spent fifteen minutes before the affair got under way telling him rather vividly what the White House reaction had been to his actions.

Drinkwater himself was to claim later that a heavy fine subsequently levied by the FAA against Western for alleged violations of maintenance regulations represented the Administration's revenge. I've been given to understand that he blamed me personally for what he considered a punitive measure, but this I categorically denied. It was true, however, that Drinkwater's unpopularity with the Kennedy administration hurt his airline in obtaining a Hawaiian route, which, on the face of all the evidence, Western actually deserved a lot sooner than it was eventually received.

It took the Feinsinger Commission eighteen months to arrive at a final formula: Flight engineers displaced by pilots were to be given severance pay of at least ten thousand dollars or offered training as pilots so they could qualify as the third crew member. The recommendation ignited more angry recriminations from the FEIA, and for a while I feared a continuation of the fight. It was TWA's flight engineers' local, headed by an able and persuasive flight engineer named Harry Dietrich, that pulled the rug from under the union's feet. When TWA's flight engineers accepted the Feinsinger decision, FEIA members on other carriers fell in line and the war was over, the last skirmish being an unsuccessful strike by Eastern's flight engineers in the summer of 1962. This occurred when Eastern and the other airlines, which had gone for the four-man-crew concept, reverted to three men—two pilots and a pilot-qualified flight engineer. The FEIA struck Eastern for a month, demanding that it rather than ALPA must represent the third man, but when the shooting was over the Feinsinger formula prevailed.

Crisis, I learned to my sorrow in my first sixty days, was a way of life for whoever headed the big aviation Agency. Even well-meant actions and decisions supposedly noncontroversial seemed to have explosive fuses attached to them. On one occasion, shortly before I took office, I innocently accepted an invitation to attend a special meeting of the Air Traffic Controllers Association—a professional group of about seven thousand controllers, most of whom worked for the FAA and were Civil Service employees. (Subsequently this Association gave way to a more militant, union-type outfit called the Professional Air Traffic Controllers Organization [PATCO].)

106

The opening question there was whether I thought the ATCA should become a labor union.

The second, coming before I had a chance to answer the first, was whether the ATCA should retain its present executive director, Frank McDermott, who wasn't present at this session.

"I can't give you any advice on either count," I responded, "either as a private person or a public official. You'll have to decide these matters by yourselves. I will say, however, that I hope working conditions in the agency will be so attractive that there will be no need for the formation of an aggressive association to obtain improvements."

A few minutes after I left the meeting, the ATCA executive council voted to terminate McDermott's contract. The only part I played in that decision was simply to duck the question completely, yet I heard in the ensuing months that McDermott believed I was responsible for his dismissal.

I seemed to be picking up enemies even as I tried to make friends. Not until one starts making decisions and taking stands on issues does the shooting start, and while I was getting set at the Agency, all was more or less sweetness and light. Even the anti-FAA, anti-Quesada groups that made up the general aviation community were offering—rather gingerly and tentatively, it must be added—hands of friendship and promises of co-operation. Virtually all aviation organizations had written me or called after my appointment was announced—including, I remember, the Flying Funeral Directors of America. I couldn't resist writing them in return that I wasn't sure whether they were in favor of flying funerals or whether they were funeral directors who flew their own airplanes.

Once in office, however, I knew the honeymoon had to end, and I turned my fence-mending activities toward general aviation. A target for a small gesture was the powerful, very vocal Aircraft Owners and Pilots Association, which had regarded Quesada as a Hitler and the FAA as his Gestapo. I phoned the AOPA president, J. B. Hartranft, Jr., and said I'd like to visit AOPA's headquarters in Bethesda, Maryland, for a little chat. Hartranft was surprised but delighted, and our talk evolved into a most interesting discussion on the problems of private flying. Admittedly, we didn't see eye-to-eye on many issues, but at least the ice was broken and, as had been the case with the ALPA, Hartranft at least was aware that my mind was open and that I'd accept good advice.

I, in turn, was impressed not only by Hartranft's defense of the private pilot but also by his firm conviction that the general-aviation airman, long ignored by the FAA, had a great deal to contribute. With that in mind, I drafted a form letter that was sent to every licensed pilot in the United States—approximately 287,000 of them. The letter simply invited their comments, criticisms, and suggestions on all aviation matters.

I had opened a Pandora's box. My subordinates tabulated the first one thousand or so replies, with a few accompanying snickers and quite a few raised eyebrows. There were really no startling new proposals; what the form letter had produced, instead, was an outpouring of rather personal beefs and gripes, not all of them concerning aviation.

We got seventeen letters demanding mandatory instrument training for private pilots and fourteen letters denouncing such training. One pilot called my attention to the Los Angeles smog situation. (Many letters were devoted solely to local problems in the writer's hometown.) An embarrassing number of pilots replied with complaints that they were still waiting for the FAA to answer previous letters. No less than forty suggested that we correct our mailing list.

If I needed any confirmation of the individualism rampant among aviators, this was it. The ultimate and inevitable response came from one pilot who said I was wasting taxpayer money by mailing the "Dear Airman" letters in the first place. He may have been right, although it seemed like a good idea when we thought of it, and it was good to hear the *vox populi*. The responses indicated greatest emotional reaction to the FAA—mostly fear—in the South and the Southwest, and this introduced more practical and productive good-will gestures, a grass-roots campaign aimed at instilling respect instead of resentment for the FAA among private pilots. I decided to get out in the field, so to speak, and hold personal meetings—"Hangar Flying Sessions" was one name we gave to the campaign, and "Air Share Meetings" was another. We ran the program exactly as we would have run a political campaign. An FAA advance man would go out and select an area where there were a large number of private and commercial pilots, fixed-base operators, and manufacturing and sales representatives. The advance man would talk some local sponsor into arranging a meeting in a hangar at a convenient hub airport, and I'd fly out there to talk, answer questions, and meet these brother airmen in person. The results of these hangar sessions, by their very nature, had to be somewhat intangible, but I sincerely believed they did some good and at the very least diminished some of the anti-FAA feeling.

They also enabled me to meet the FAA men and women in the field who had never before "pressed the flesh" with a live administrator and, perhaps more important, to bring them face to face with those whom they regulated; to issue information rather than citations; to impress, not arrest.

Admittedly, I never did achieve the rapport with general-aviation groups that I managed with the ALPA. Part of the latter was due to the mutual respect Clancy Sayen and I had. Not that Clancy and I didn't have disagreements. It used to infuriate me that it was so hard to get the ALPA to take a stand on any issue that the union hadn't instigated. There were times when I wished the ALPA had been a little more aggressive, a typical case being what might be termed the "hanky-panky" battle.

This was an aftermath of the flight engineers' dispute. Some FEIA members, still smarting over the ALPA's jurisdictional victory, began taking pictures in the darkened cockpits, using infrared film. They also made sure the pictures received widespread publicity. The pilots depicted in the photographs obviously were unaware that their pictures were being taken: They were shown napping at the controls, holding stewardesses on their laps and, in one instance, apparently letting a stewardess fly the airplane.

A congressional committee promptly scheduled hearings on what was described as a serious cockpit discipline situation. I didn't think the hearings were necessary nor even wise—the FAA already had taken corrective and punitive action, fining thirteen pilots up to six hundred dollars each and warning both the airlines and their flight crews that cockpit discipline in the jet age was just as important as keeping the wings intact. Neither the carriers nor the crews really needed that warning, but it was issued anyway just to make sure everyone knew the FAA was alert to the problem. And I knew the hearings would produce a lot of smoke, fire, and black headlines over a situation that was really past history.

My fears were justified. The hearings, held under the chairmanship of Representative Jack Brooks of Texas, produced much sensational testimony—mostly from admittedly biased flight engineers and ex-stewardesses, one of whom was married to a flight engineer and whose objectivity was suspect. They drew a picture of a disciplinary breakdown in the cockpit that was widespread, not just rare or even occasional. They insisted that the incidents depicted in the photographs were typical, and the news media played up their charges for all they were worth.

It was only too apparent that the whole affair was aimed squarely at discrediting the ALPA and its members. I was asked to testify and I agreed, but I fully expected the ALPA to put up its own witnesses. Much to my surprise and disappointment, the ALPA's officialdom decided against it—apparently on the lofty theory that the accusations weren't worthy of an answer.

I told the committee that the overwhelming majority of airline pilots were not guilty of any cockpit shenanigans, the charges stemmed largely from the bitterness of the ALPA-FEIA labor dispute, and the pictures all involved flights made at least three years previously. Actually I might have made a stronger case if I had had all the facts about those photographs. Not until months later did I find out that many of them were taken on the ground and didn't involve in-flight breaches of cockpit decorum. In any event, the hearings blew the controversy way out of proportion, and the committee didn't help matters a few months later when it issued a report implying that pilot laxity still existed. Mr. Brooks and his colleagues were beating a dead horse; the incidents the FEIA had brought up all occurred between 1957 and 1961, and no cockpit-discipline violation had been reported to the FAA since early 1961—a year before the hearings were held and a report issued.

As I look back over the FAA years, I'm surprised to realize how much I did or tried to do in behalf of the airline pilot. (Come to think of it, perhaps that's why a group of them were promoting me as their president in 1964.)

But as the airman's regulator, I had to regulate. To bring objectivity, one of my first actions at the Agency was to appoint a group of consultants to examine the FAA's rulemaking and enforcement procedures. Headed by Lloyd C. Cutler, one of the ablest and wisest of Washington's "superlawyers," the study was known as Project Tightrope, and its findings confirmed much of the criticism that had been directed at Quesada's "I am the law" philosophy. The task force conceded that the FAA's enforcement procedures were the product of the air disasters that had brought the new Agency into being, infecting its first administrator with a sense of "desperate urgency," as Cutler's group phrased it. But, the task force added, while that motivation may have explained the strict enforcement policies, it didn't entirely justify them—not when so many procedures were frequently unfair, inefficient, and disorderly.

Project Tightrope was aptly named. It reflected my realization that the FAA administrator had to walk a very high and taut wire if he was to do justice to the individual and simultaneously protect a public totally dependent on that individual as part of a system of safety and convenience. It was no minor balancing act, and Cutler's group did a masterful job in helping me achieve badly needed enforcement reforms that did not weaken the cause of safety. I still regard the work in this area as one of the most important accomplishments of my administration.

We not only created a system of investigation, prosecution, and appeals that worked and restored confidence in the process but we also boiled down thirty years of regulations into a single Code of Federal Air Regulations, which were far more intelligible, simple, and effective. We phrased our rules and regulations in simple high school English and eliminated a lot of fine print that nobody could understand—including those who composed it. Finally, we launched a nationwide program to explain to the entire aviation community what we meant to do in the way of enforcing the new Code, emphasizing that we weren't going to be soft about the laws of the air but also that we wanted to be fair even when we were being firm. We frankly appealed for mutual respect between the men who lived under our regulations and the Agency that promulgated them.

111

That program led to a few gags about the FAA's new philosophy: We were dubbed the "Friendly Aviation Agency," a sobriquet that stuck throughout my FAA years and one that I wholeheartedly preferred over the "Fierce Aviation Agency" that somebody else tagged on us. But overall, I believe we did much in that first year to replace fear with respect toward the FAA. While that "Friendly" contained an element of sarcasm, we really did change the general attitude. For one thing, pilots found out I wasn't just mouthing words when I promised to listen to their problems and do something about them if possible. For example, in the meetings I had held with the ALPA's regional chairmen, an oft-voiced complaint was that too many FAA flight inspectors weren't qualified on the very airplanes on which they were conducting check rides.

"I had one telling me what I was doing wrong in a Viscount," a captain told me, "and the son-of-a-bitch had never flown a Viscount."

My response was to sign contracts with several airlines for the purpose of training our inspectors on the same type of aircraft flown by the men whose performance they were checking. This little reform did more than just improve the quality of FAA's inspectors, it also led to better relations between the inspectors and line pilots, who began to acquire some respect for one another. I suppose there always will be a few below-par, arbitrary, or nitpicking inspectors, just as there always will be some hard-nose airline captains who simply resent any authority in the form of a government employee. But, in the main, the training program that Quesada and I pursued raised the professionalism of the inspector corps and definitely improved safety.

I did not revoke Quesada's most controversial rule—the mandatory grounding of airline pilots at age sixty. The ALPA's pressure to scrap the retirement rule was constant and heavy. I conferred at length with the FAA's Medical Advisory Panel, a group of about twenty leading doctors we had brought in from around the country. We also looked at voluminous medical research data from the National Institutes of Health and compared notes with a number of European airlines and their medical staffs. I was influenced to some extent by the fact that many of these airlines in welfare states overseas required their pilots to retire at fifty-five, and I was influenced a great deal more by the data on incidents of cardiac problems, which definitely showed a sharp rise in the possibility of incapacitating attacks after sixty.

Yet I also had to agree with the ALPA that many pilots at sixty are healthier than much younger men—and better captains, too. There was a great need, I felt, to find a way of determining physiological age as opposed to chronological age. Eventually I reaffirmed the rule but had the Agency conduct some in-depth research on the geriatrics of flying—in other words, the aging of pilots. I had high hopes that this program might come up with a method that would allow us to dictate retirement on an individual rather than an arbitrary basis.

Unfortunately it didn't work out that way. Georgetown University's fine staff tried hard but never did come up with the necessary accurate yardstick, although much valuable information was obtained for possible future research into this intriguing problem. Establishment of the Georgetown program at least had the effect of temporarily reducing the ALPA's scrap-the-rule pressure, the union being convinced I was trying anyway.

The only chuckle I ever got from the retirement controversy involved a Washington aviation reporter who wanted to do a story on the Georgetown research program. He was a licensed pilot, and the best approach, he decided, was to go through the pilot aging tests himself. When he finished, he was advised to quit flying until his health improved, and for a while he lived in mortal fear that the FAA would find out about the results and lift his license.

My attitude toward controllers was a carbon copy of how I felt about pilots: tremendous respect for the vast majority of them, sympathy toward their problems, and an intense awareness of their dedication and devotion to their duties. Along with national defense, there is no more important federal job than that of the air-traffic controller. Human lives depend on him. National security rides with him. The economy of the airlines depends on him. And this reliance is a constant, twenty-four-hour-a-day business that can only be described as crucial. It's important to have FAA personnel issuing pilot licenses, check-riding, monitoring maintenance procedures, and all the other aspects of regulating the air transportation system in an operational sense. But none of these have the immediacy, the unrelenting pressures, the never-ending responsibilities of a controller's job.

The controllers' biggest beef was that there had been a hell of a lot of money spent by the FAA research and development branch but little practical, readily available, and usable hardware to make their jobs easier and more efficient.

One of the first things I did was to look at all the R and D programs and projects on which the Eisenhower-Quesada regime had spent millions. The controllers kept hearing about all the wonderful technical improvements just over the horizon, but they never saw any actually being put into service. I visited shifts at the busy New York center, for example, and was shocked at their dingy, overcrowded, and almost primitive working conditions. They were using World War II radar to handle six-hundred-mile-an-hour jet traffic. They were keeping track of flights with the old "shrimp boats"—tiny pieces of wood identifying planes full of people—that dated back to DC-3 days, and this was their primary bookkeeping tool at a time when computers and other electronic devices were being used routinely throughout American industry and government—including the airline industry itself.

But while there was merit in controller complaints about the job environment, it wasn't as bad as some of the more zealous gripers claimed. It is only too true that in major towers at peak periods, controllers are under great stress. But as FAA chief, I found surprisingly few cases where it was possible to diagnose and verify a physical ailment resulting from the strains of the occupation. I tried hard to produce evidence to the contrary, accurate medical data for ammunition to use when I went to the Civil Service Commission and later to Congress on behalf of the controllers. I wanted to justify their demands for pay increases, early retirement with full benefits, as FBI employees enjoyed (the FBI force had the best deal of all federal employees), and additional controllers if they were needed to reduce work overloads. The trouble was that we just couldn't produce such evidence, not in any conclusive proportions. I did have some medical studies done, for review by the Civil Service Commission, and the studies confirmed to some extent that compared to the average government employee, controllers did have more ulcers, more cardiological problems, and more mental health difficulties. On the other hand, the studies also showed the FAA controllers were no more prone to health troubles than their military brethren performing identical duties; the latter, in fact, seemed to be subject to even more stress than a civilian traffic specialist.

There wasn't any doubt that controller workload could be excessive in peak hours at major centers. But just adding more manpower, which many controllers regarded as the ideal panacea, didn't solve the problem one bit. We found that in too many instances the extra men just got in each other's way. Frequently the increased work force resulted in more handoffs from one controller to another, and this increased the risk of human error. Finally, adding controllers was the least productive step we could have taken.

The more moderate controllers, I felt, had legitimate beefs, and we tried to correct them. We launched a retraining program, for example, sending many men back to the FAA training center in Oklahoma City. Complaints about "no new stuff coming in" were curable by sending selected individuals to our research and development facilities in Atlantic City to examine what was in the pipeline and what might be coming out soon. We did get three pay raises for them during the time I was in office, an accomplishment of which I was very proud. And despite some doubts as to the capability of additional manpower to provide an effective solution, we did hire a number of new controllers. Inevitably almost any action we took prompted some opposition or criticism, sometimes from controllers themselves. A case in point was my decision to discontinue hiring during my last year at the FAA and shift on-the-job training to the individual centers. This training was not only just as good as it was in Oklahoma City, but in many ways even better—more practical, faster, and more economical. The move actually enhanced safety, but I was accused of endangering air-traffic control by reducing the Oklahoma City operations, most of the shouting coming from local politicians and a few FAA supervisors who resented having fewer people to supervise and less justification for promotion and higher-grade jobs.

One has to have some historical perspective truly to understand the controller and his problems. He always has been somewhat neglected, and occasionally cruelly neglected. In the early days, he had no real part in the guidance of air traffic. He was more like a bookkeeper who took down each flight plan and forwarded it to the next station, almost in the manner of a railroad dispatcher. Until World War II ended, air-traffic control was not much more demanding than it had been prior to 1936, the year that the federal government took over the ATC system from the airlines.

ATC itself dates back to 1934, when Glen A. Gilbert, generally regarded as the "father of air-traffic control," instituted a flight-following system for American Airlines' planes. Gilbert, who worked for American as a radio operator at the time, conceived this system for all American flights approaching Chicago from a radius of about a hundred miles. Other airlines serving Chicago, such as United, TWA, and Northwest, gradually came into Gilbert's primitive but effective communications network. It worked well enough for a similar system to be established at Newark, then the nation's busiest airport. From this modest beginning evolved the first airway-traffic control centers, operated by the principal airlines serving Newark and Chicago. The initial center started at Newark, followed by Chicago and then Cleveland, and their controllers were absorbed into the new federal service on July 6, 1936.

The military really ran ATC during World War II, and the controllers didn't come into their own until the postwar years. Hampered by inadequate equipment, official indifference, and congressional stinginess, ATC was thousands of light-years behind other government operations of a technical nature. It took a few serious crashes to bring the system's inadequacies to the attention of Congress, and appropriations began to increase. Just about the time the resources became more readily available, air traffic itself suddenly started booming, and the old CAA's management wasn't ready to hire and train the manpower needed for handling the air-travel explosion. By the time ATC had gotten around to meeting the challenges of the fifties, the jet age was upon us, and the cycle of inadequacy began all over again. Traffic kept soaring, and it piled not only more workload but also a workload of an increasingly complex, high-speed, and demanding nature, all on people who were trained in a DC-3 world and found themselves trying to cope with the jet world of the 707 and the DC-8.

The Air Traffic Control Association (ATCA), founded and developed as a professional organization by the early CAA men, eventually brought into its ranks younger controllers who quickly became fed up with all the inequality and disparity. Gradually they moved the ATCA closer and closer to a collective bargaining group. And they found an important ally in Labor Secretary Goldberg, who convinced President Kennedy that federal employees, with certain exceptions, should be allowed to bargain collectively. This culminated in JFK's issuing famed Executive Order 10998, authorizing the creation of federal employee unions. The ATCA by this time had become much more militant and greeted that Executive Order like the controllers' Magna Carta.

All agency heads were, of course, briefed and consulted before the Order was issued. I was not only surprised but also shocked to learn that the Secretary of Labor was planning to include controllers among the employees authorized to unionize. For the great mass of federal employees I could see the logic, but for the FAA, the FBI, and Coast Guard personnel, I felt exceptions should be made. I fought this not only with Goldberg but also with Civil Service chairman John Macy and, finally, with Attorney General Robert Kennedy. I went to Kennedy as a last resort, knowing he wielded immense influence with JFK, and pleaded that controllers be exempt, as were members of the Armed Forces, the CIA, and a few other agencies primarily in national defense or dealing with matters of national security.

But Kennedy declined to support me. Almost in desperation, I handed Goldberg an alternate suggestion—special status for controllers in what would be known as the Federal Aviation Service. Within the FAA, we even debated giving them uniforms. Along with this special status would go early retirement benefits, exemption from the military draft, and a number of other fringe and pay benefits then enjoyed by the Coast Guard, the FBI, and the Secret Service.

There were all kinds in this body of some seventeen thousand men in all fifty states—and I still regard most of them as professionals occasionally led astray by a handful of hotheads whose loyalty to the public has an alarmingly lower priority than their loyalty to themselves and their own interests.

My concern about unionism among the controllers turned out to be justified. The ATCA and its cadre of older controllers wasn't militant enough for some of the younger men, and they formed a splinter group known as the Professional Air Traffic Controllers Organization (PATCO).

Eventually the ATCA faded, and it was the PATCO that pulled the horrendous slowdowns and work stoppages that almost brought civil air transportation to a halt in the summer of 1968. Counseled by famed trial lawyer F. Lee Bailey, the controllers mobilized their frustrations and caused a partial collapse of the ATC system.

Actually, the number of controllers involved was relatively small, but in so complex a system, a platoon of dissidents amounts to a whole division. Airline on-time performance dropped from over 90 per cent to less than 50 per cent, due solely to air-traffic delays. On a single afternoon at O'Hare in Chicago, there were sixty planes lined up awaiting takeoff clearance.

I had already gone with Pan Am by this time, and I was relieved not to have to deal with that kind of militant action. I'm afraid I would have been even tougher about the PATCO than Transportation Secretary John Volpe and FAA Administrator Jack Shaffer were. I believe the job of controller is a calling so high that he must sacrifice some of the normal rights of a private citizen in the area of collective bargaining and unionization. But I also believe that the controller is owed a special set of benefits—prerogatives, if you will—for "taking the cloth" as he commits himself to the public service.

I sure as hell tried to achieve the latter for these men, and to some extent I succeeded. We built sixteen new ATC centers, with the personnel literally going from shacks to the most modern industrial structures. Instead of badly ventilated, poorly lit cubbyholes, they got air conditioning, indirect lighting, and even snack bars. I think we did a tremendous amount to improve working conditions, along with the pay raises mentioned earlier.

We added a considerable number of bright display radars to replace the outmoded World War II models. We further improved the radar network by adding transponders to the system, both ground and airborne—a transponder being an electronic device to aid target identification on radarscopes. Transponders themselves were really Chapter One in a program to automate ATC under a system known as Alpha Numerics, a program started but unfortunately not finished during my regime. All these and other improvements allowed us to expand "area positive control" within the continental United States. Positive control involves long-range radar-monitoring protection for high-flying jets. Airspace under such control cannot be entered without permission, and aircraft using it must operate under instrument flight rules and be equipped with transponders. This protected airspace was expanded to include all flights operating above twenty-four thousand feet, and subsequently the positive-control floor was lowered to eighteen thousand feet.

I tried hard not to wait for a major disaster before taking corrective action. For example, there were several near collisions between civilian planes and military interceptors that were flying practice missions on federal airways without ATC knowledge of their presence. This led to the FAA taking over certain phases of the Air Defense Command's interceptor missions, putting these lightning-fast fighters under ATC control, with their movements monitored by FAA radar.

I must admit that we didn't solve all the problems. In fact, we fell woefully short in some areas. When I left office in 1965 my greatest regret was that I had not been able to modernize the airways system more rapidly than we had. My intentions were good. But in my four years as administrator, we still didn't make enough progress to satisfy either myself or the controllers, who had to run what we gave them.

The FAA wasn't unique. The Air Force, Army, Navy, and Marines have the same conflict between advancing technology and the problem of trying to run a war concurrently with the introduction of new weapons. As in the case with rules enforcement, I went outside for help and advice—appointing a task force of excellent professional engineers, scientists, and operators to come in and take a good, hard look at R and D. It was called Project Beacon, and it was under the leadership of Richard Hough, Princeton,

MIT, Bell Labs, top systems engineer and active private pilot, later executive vice president of AT&T.

The Beacon experts spent several months digging into what had been done and what remained to be done in modernizing the combined civil and military airspace system. Their final report was a blueprint for what basically was implemented over the ensuing decade and is still being implemented.

I read with great interest a book by a former FAA procurement specialist named Philip Ryther called *Who's Watching the Airways?* (Doubleday, 1972). It indicted the FAA for its procurement policies, which Ryther regarded as criminally inefficient. Like most books of this kind, it was overcooked, with steam obscuring some of its valid points. I agreed with a lot of what the author said, including some of his criticism of my own administration. But what Ryther found unpalatable at the FAA was true not just of the FAA bureaucracy but also of all bureaucracy. Yes, we goofed at times, underspent, overspent, procrastinated on some problems, and acted prematurely on others. But there were no multimillion-dollar bloopers when I was with the FAA—not of the C5A or TFX variety, for example, which marred Robert McNamara's Pentagon tenure. There was no scandal that came to my attention or that of the press or numerous critics eager to blow up the muck of Washington. There were no charges of favoritism or corruption of any kind. There were delays and all kinds of bureaucratic obstacles, but we never had to write off an entire program and start all over again.

Much of the criticism directed against the FAA when I headed it, in fact, was aimed more at me personally than at the Agency in general. I heard frequent charges that I "showboated," for example—that accusation first made when I insisted on test-flying the Electra and repeated testing on all new models throughout my administration. When sky diving mushroomed in popularity, we began getting complaints from airline captains that the divers were jumping through the airways. We decided that the growth of this sport required a few regulations to protect the divers themselves as well as the public.

I didn't know a damned thing about sky diving, and neither did anyone else at the Agency. I figured maybe I'd better learn something about sports parachuting, so I arranged to go up to Orange, Massachusetts, where Jacques Istel ran reputedly the best parachuting school in the country. I did a couple of jumps after the proper instructions, and while sky diving didn't turn out to be a permanent pastime, I at least got a feel for what made people love it. When we did issue regulations prohibiting jumps down through airways and under certain wind conditions, we relieved the public and got very few objections from the various sky-diving clubs. Maybe I had been guilty of "showboating," but I think we earned quick acceptance of the new rules simply because we hadn't shoved them down throats without first talking to the people who would be the most affected and sharing their experience.

The "showboating" tag also was applied to my propensity for responding like a fire marshal to almost every major air crash. I was accused of horning in on the CAB's Bureau of Safety, of trying to interfere with the CAB investigators, of trying to imply that the FAA and not the CAB was in charge of crash probes, and of grabbing headlines for both the FAA and myself.

Before explaining why I dashed to crash sites, let me give some background on CAB-FAA relations. The seeds of what was to become a bitter feud between the two sister aviation agencies were planted within the Federal Aviation Act, which created the FAA. The FAA not only was given the same independent status that the CAB had enjoyed for years but also assumed some of the CAB's regulatory functions in the safety field. While the FAA had no specific authority to investigate and officially determine the probable cause of crashes, it had full authority to put new safety rules into effect—many of them based on what was learned from accidents. Under the new law, all the CAB could do was *recommend* safety measures; it was the FAA's job to decide if they were really necessary and to implement them or not. The CAB's role was purely investigation—the determination of the probable cause.

Quesada openly called on Congress to amend the Federal Aviation Act to give the FAA total authority over accident investigation. Quesada's undisguised hostility toward the CAB in general and its Bureau of Safety specifically led him into violent conflict with the fellow Republican who was CAB chairman, James Durfee. Their feud was climaxed by a shouting, angry, face-to-face

121

confrontation at the site of the Staten Island TWA-United collision—a regrettable incident that did the public image of neither agency any good. They were brawling at a time when the deaths of 135 persons and the pulverized remains of two great airplanes brought silent prayers for co-operation among all concerned to make sure it would not happen again.

I think Durfee and the CAB's watchdog PR man, Ed Slattery, lost sight of the necessity of ascertaining whether any immediate corrective measures could be taken. That was not the CAB's job but the FAA's, and that was the primary reason I later insisted on going to major accidents before the wreckage stopped burning. I wanted to make sure, if humanly possible, that the same accident wouldn't recur one hour later. I wasn't trying to butt into the CAB's province; I was there to assure that the FAA would perform its own function of instituting emergency corrective or preventative measures based on whatever the CAB could tell us or we could ascertain—*and to do it on the spot when necessary.*

Quesada and Bud Howard had tried to push me into seeking legislation that would eliminate the CAB's investigative powers, limit the Board to purely economic regulation, and turn crash investigation over to the FAA. I held my peace on this latter point because, having been trained as a lawyer—as were Durfee and Alan Boyd, his superb successor—I considered it questionable that any bureaucracy should have the authority to investigate itself. The Staten Island tragedy was a perfect example of why the FAA should not be given such powers—it was obvious right from the start that weaknesses in ATC at least contributed to the collision; I had to doubt whether such weaknesses would have been detailed in a probable-cause finding written by the FAA.

I wasn't at all sure that accident investigation belonged in the CAB, but definitely the Agency responsible for an operation like air-traffic control should not be responsible for investigating and judging it. So instead of fighting the CAB's authority, I sought means of creating a new spirit of co-operation and mutual goals on the part of both aviation agencies. The opening came when Durfee resigned, giving me a chance to urge the appointment of a new chairman with whom I could work harmoniously. My candidate was Alan Boyd of Florida. When the Senate confirmed Boyd's eventual nomination, we had a long talk about the FAA-CAB feud. It helped no little that we personally liked each other. I have always considered this tall, soft-spoken, but very tough Floridian possibly the best chairman the Board ever had. (And that's not casting aspersions on anyone who preceded or followed him.)

I told Alan that I had approached the CAB-FAA conflict from a lawyer's viewpoint. Congress, in establishing the FAA, had left an area of overlap—making the FAA administrator operationally responsible for safety and then making the CAB chairman responsible investigatorially. This left the CAB powerless to do anything about what it learned in the course of a crash probe, whereas I had all the latter authority, the resources, and the responsibility.

"You can make the investigation and come up with a finding," I told Boyd, "but no one really cares about the finding except for punitive purposes. What seems important to me is to put all our resources together not just to find the cause but also to put the cure into effect as soon as possible. I don't feel I'm interfering with you when I go to a crash. Rather, I think I'm carrying out my responsibility to prevent recurrence. I'll probably make mistakes, but I'd rather err on the side of personal intervention than just wait for the bureaucratic process to grind its wheels for several months."

Happily, Boyd was fully in favor of co-operation between the sister agencies. One of the things he understood about my stand was my own background as a test pilot and occasional trial lawyer —I simply did not trust all the conflicting interests that were at work during every accident investigation. He and I worked out a fairly detailed system of accident-investigation co-operation—visiting sites together, close staff exchange, organizing a joint school for investigators, etc.—and, with the exception of a few diehards, resentment on the part of CAB personnel lessened to a marked degree. I'd be a liar if I said the feud was ended at all levels; frankly, while Boyd and I got along fine, all was not warm fellowship in the lower echelons. But I felt strongly about the FAA's role in air safety, and that's why my presence at a crash scene became standard procedure.

There were two accidents at which I probably should have missed making an appearance, one major and the other minor.

123

The first involved the crash of a Continental Air Lines 707 on May 22, 1962. Heading from Chicago to Los Angeles via Kansas City, the plane vanished off radar, and the wreckage was found in a field near the small town of Centerville, Iowa. I had been at the Ames Laboratory in California, NASA's research center, getting briefed on various new aeronautical experiments involving aerodynamically supercritical wing shapes that produced lower drag. While at Ames, I was notified of the crash and immediately boarded the FAA N-1 plane, which I flew all night to get to the accident site at dawn. What happened resulted from a combination of my own fatigue and something I saw—I remember lifting up a metal piece of the top of the cockpit in the hole the cabin had bored into the ground, and there was the open skull of the captain with the red-warm, almost live brains draining out.

I almost threw up; I was terribly shaken—a vivid nightmare even now—not only by what I had seen in that pulverized cockpit but also by the whole tragic scene. Along with the human tragedy, the logic and symmetry of a beautiful airplane had been destroyed; the pilot in me felt immense sadness, and the public official in me felt intense anger that it had happened. Someone filled me in on what was known about the flight up to the time of the crash—it had been reported flying in an area of severe thunderstorms. Later, when I was talking to some newsmen at the accident site, I made some remark about the storm area that permitted the press quote, "That's what happens when you fly through thunderstorms."

It was a stupid, unfair, and—as it turned out later—totally inaccurate remark. The investigation soon disclosed that a bomb placed in a rear lavatory had blown off the 707's tail, and it also proved that the pilot already had circumnavigated the storm area. Continental officials were furious with me and they had a right to be, for I had inadvertently raised a doubt about the judgment of a dead pilot with a senseless snap comment of my own. I lamely explained to them I merely had been speculating, which was true, except that I shouldn't have been doing any speculating out loud, and particularly not in the presence of newspapermen wired for headlining quotes. While I can't defend what I did, I must re-emphasize how strongly I felt about the FAA's role in preventing recurrence of an accident even as the CAB probed its cause or causes. As wrong as that remark about flying through thunderstorms had been, I suspect it was a subconscious reaction to a problem just beginning to raise an ugly thunderhead: the unpredictable behavior of swept-wing aircraft in severe turbulence.

There had never been a jet crash blamed on turbulence, but the FAA had received reports on numerous turbulence incidents in which passengers and crew members were injured. At the time of the Continental tragedy, we were beginning to worry about thunderstorm-penetration techniques, and I believe they were in the back of my mind while I was inspecting that wreckage. Our vague fears were confirmed less than nine months later, when a Northwest 720B disintegrated in a Florida thunderstorm.

That one accident was one of the most tragic yet important in aviation history, because out of it came reforms that made jet travel far safer. We learned from the flight recorder tape, for example, that the Northwest plane didn't come apart as a result of turbulence-generated stresses but rather from the methods the crew used to overcome their control difficulties. Their procedures were in perfect accordance with the book, but the book was incorrect. We knew there must be something wrong with that technique, but at first we weren't sure what.

I recall I was criticized sharply in some quarters for calling a secret meeting in Seattle to discuss the jet-upset problem. Boeing wasn't happy, because the meeting tended to focus attention on the airplane instead of the operator. All planemakers—their lawyers, their propagandists, as well as their engineers—are very, very sensitive about any intimation of fault, and Boeing is probably the touchiest of all, with the most planes in the sky. Bob Twiss of the Seattle *Times,* a very aggressive aviation reporter directly plugged into Boeing at all times, found out about the meeting and lambasted me for interfering with the investigation process. Twiss was pro-Boeing, and I wished he could have been there to hear my opening remarks to a room of about fifty experts from the FAA, Boeing, the CAB, NASA, the Air Force, and the airlines.

"I wanted to get everybody into one room, everybody who has anything to do with this upset business, and the best place to do it is right where most of the airplanes are built and where you can go

125

out and conduct tests immediately based on what we learn here," I said.

The Twiss criticism stung, but that was the risk I took being an activist administrator, and I must say that we accomplished a lot during this rather stormy but frank session. Later it was Paul Soderlind of Northwest, working closely with Boeing, who confirmed what we had suspected about the book being wrong. In what was almost a personal crusade for this exceptionally dedicated pilot, he wrote a widely distributed safety publication unrivaled in aviation history, a discourse on jet behavior during turbulence and how to combat control problems caused by abnormal buffeting and bucking. He even toured the country, spreading his new gospel to flight crews: Stop fighting turbulence and holding altitude, and just concentrate on keeping the aircraft level at a safe speed.

Before the Florida crash, jet pilots had been penetrating thunderstorms with the same technique they had employed in straight-wing piston airplanes: Slow down to prevent structural damage. Soderlind, with the help of Boeing flight tests, proved they were slowing down too much, creating the possibility of high-altitude stalls. They also were trying too hard to maintain airspeed during severe updrafts and downdrafts instead of maintaining level flight. Soderlind's advice was to increase penetration speeds slightly, thus eliminating the stall possibility. He reasoned that the jets were structurally strong enough to withstand the stresses of higher penetration speeds, and preventing stalls was vastly more important. He also urged pilots caught in a turbulence snare not to worry so much about such pressure instruments as airspeed and altimeter indicators. In turbulence, he reminded his fellow airmen, those instruments often are unreadable anyway, and trying to "chase" them can lead to loss of control.

This was probably what had happened to the Northwest crew. They followed the procedures prescribed at the time for flying through turbulence. Caught in a violent updraft and fearing an imminent stall, the captain trimmed the nose down and dove. Just as he took this step, the plane was nailed by an equally violent downdraft—with the controls set in a dive position. The dive became steeper, so steep that elevator control was reduced. And as he

126

tried to control the nose, the stresses exceeded the design strength of the stabilizer-elevator section, which resulted in structural failure. The final mistake was to use an electric trim switch; Soderlind's recommendation was to use the manual elevator control in turbulent situations.

The FAA put Soderlind's new procedures blueprint into immediate effect—never had the FAA embraced an airline captain's expertise so fully—and I was delighted when the ALPA later awarded him its annual Air Safety Award. I was equally pleased over the final outcome of the upset problem, for it offered a perfect example of industry-government co-operation in solving a major safety crisis and, I think, justification for my "activist administrator" role. But there was another occasion when I should have been more administrative and less activist.

At about 5 A.M. on November 9, 1961, our communications center woke me up to advise that a Constellation operated by a nonscheduled airline had crashed at Richmond, Virginia. I immediately phoned CAB Chairman Alan Boyd who, under our new collaborative procedures, already had been alerted by my people, and agreed to meet him at National Airport.

"We'll fly down in the FAA Gulfstream," I told him. "What do you know about the accident?"

"Just that there were about seventy new Army draftees on board and, apparently, there were no survivors," Boyd informed me.

The young soldiers were on their way to basic training when the crash occurred. By the time I met Boyd at Hangar 14, where the FAA keeps its Washington-based aircraft, a few more details were available. All seventy-four passengers were dead and so were the stewardesses, a student flight engineer, and the copilot. The flight engineer and captain had survived. It was not only a tragic accident but also, apparently, a spectacularly nasty one. The flight was en route from Baltimore to Columbia, South Carolina, when two engines failed as a result of fuel mismanagement, it later developed. The crew attempted an emergency landing at Richmond, but then mismanaged the hydraulic system and had to go around, at which point one of the two remaining engines was overboosted and also failed. With only one engine left, the second landing attempt failed, and the old "Connie" crashed short of the runway threshold.

At that time many of the nonskeds were shabbily run outfits with a horrendous safety record that already had drawn FAA attention. The operator in this case was Imperial Airlines, headquartered in Miami Springs, Florida. In the past Imperial had been the target of FAA inspections because of a history of substandard maintenance procedures. A fresh investigation was in fact in progress when the crash occurred. The crash raised the question of whether Imperial should have been put out of business by the FAA long before November 8, as it had already been caught making nonstandard repairs adversely affecting airworthiness and failing to report in-flight mechanical discrepancies on aircraft flight logs.

Understandably, I was in a hurry to get to the crash scene. The FAA's own regulatory procrastination seemed to be involved, and I was not only impatient but also angry as we boarded our Grumman Gulfstream I, a turboprop I had flown frequently. Almost instinctively, I climbed into the left seat, with a qualified FAA captain occupying the copilot's seat. We expected immediate takeoff clearance—at 6 A.M.!—being an emergency accident-investigation mission, but for some reason the tower held us behind a United Viscount, which was on the run-up block at the head of Runway 15. We completed our own engine run-up, but United was still going through that process, so I asked the tower for permission to taxi around the Viscount.

Cleared, I started a right turn. It looked close but I thought my left wingtip would clear United's right wingtip. I did brake the Gulfstream momentarily while both my copilot and I checked the wing clearance. The Viscount's copilot was watching us, expressionless, so I figured my early-morning depth perception must be good enough. It wasn't. As I moved forward slowly, our respective wingtip lights grazed, both of them breaking.

Red-faced, I taxied back to the ramp area with United waddling behind and apologized to the UAL captain for aborting his flight.

The Gulfstream flight had been scrubbed too, so we climbed into an old DC-3 that had been CAA property for years and took off for Richmond. On the way down, I sat back in the cabin with

Boyd and the CAB investigation team, where I should have been on the Gulfstream. It was the start of a miserable day: The Constellation accident was the most unnecessary, stupid, and grisly I had ever seen or probably will ever see, and the memory of my own boner was sitting sour in my belly. The fate of those helpless young recruits, of course, was far more important than my transgression. They literally had been barbecued in their seats, unable to evacuate the burning airplane. But in another sense they were victims of bad airline management and the inadequate federal regulations governing nonsked or supplemental-airline operations.

When I returned to Washington that night at the end of the worst day in my official life, I was greeted by headlines in the Washington *Star,* something to the effect that FAA CHIEF HALABY IN COLLISION AT NATIONAL.

I wasn't sure whether the collision belonged in the category of an accident or an incident, but I knew I had to make a formal report. (Fortunately, the CAB doesn't investigate such insignificant incidents, but if they wanted the probable cause, he was within instant reach!) National Airport was in the FAA's Eastern Region, with headquarters in New York and with a district office in Washington. I made my report to the local district safety officer, and so did the United captain. Both were forwarded to Regional Administrator Oscar Bakke in New York, who reviewed the case with his flight standards director.

After waiting several weeks without hearing from Bakke or anyone else, I sent someone up to New York to find out what was happening. He reported back that it looked as if they were going to send me a simple letter of reprimand.

"They'll probably just tell you not to let it happen again," my informant predicted.

"That would be a very unsatisfactory enforcement action," I retorted. "We not only have to be even-handed and fair but, if anything, set an example for other pilots."

My opinion was duly dispatched to Bakke, one of the most competent and highly regarded men in the FAA and an acknowledged air-safety expert of the finest reputation. But Oscar in this case seemed reluctant to lower the boom on his boss, and he also resented my questioning the leniency he had displayed. After some palavering between Bakke and the general counsel, I received the following letter:

FEDERAL AVIATION AGENCY
EASTERN REGION
Federal Building
New York International Airport
Jamaica, New York

December 18, 1961

Mr. N. E. Halaby
1711 New York Avenue
Washington 25, D.C.

Dear Mr. Halaby:

This office has received a report disclosing that on November 9, 1961, you, the holder of Commercial Pilot Certificate No. 69841-41, while piloting public aircraft bearing identification No. N-1 (Gulfstream) on takeoff from Runway 15, at Washington National Airport, neglected to provide adequate clearance from a United Air Lines' Viscount standing in the run-up area for Runway 15, awaiting takeoff clearance, and that you permitted the left wingtip of N-1 to contact the right wingtip of the Viscount, thus causing damage to both wingtips. The foregoing indicates that you failed to exercise the care and caution required of the holder of a pilot certificate and consequently, that your operation was contrary to Section 60.16 of the Civil Air Regulations and Section 610 (A) of the Federal Aviation Act of 1958 (72 Stat. 780).

By reason of the above violation, pursuant to Section 901 of the said Act, you are subject to a civil penalty of not to exceed $1,000. This office is authorized to accept a lesser amount in compromise of such penalty. In accordance with usual procedures, we have evaluated the incident to determine what sanction, if any, should be imposed. We note that you have acknowledged full responsibility; that safety of flight operations was not compromised and that in your previous twenty-eight years of flying, you have not been involved in any accident or cited for violation of safety regulations.

Upon full consideration of the foregoing, we have determined that an offer of $50.00 in full settlement of the civil penalty incurred would be acceptable. Enclosed is an explanation of the compromise process.

Sincerely yours,

MARTIN J. WHITE
Regional Counsel

It was probably the most widely publicized fifty-dollar fine in aviation history. The reaction was twofold: I either was loudly praised for being a bureaucrat willing to fine himself or I was accused of being handled too leniently. The former view seemed to be more prevalent, but in any case it was the end to the most exaggerated incident that occurred while I was in office. I don't think, however, that Bakke was favoring me; he honestly felt the incident was too minor to warrant a monetary penalty.

Of far greater import to me than the wingtip incident was the reason I was rushing to Richmond in the first place. Both Boyd and I were shaken by what we had seen and heard concerning the reliability of the supplemental airlines. The Imperial crash led to hearings not only into the operating standards and records of the nonskeds but also into the manner in which the CAB had certificated them and how the FAA had regulated them. About six of these carriers were grounded almost immediately. The requirements for supplementals obtaining certification were strengthened, and the FAA rules and regulatory enforcement were tightened drastically. Significantly, once we began to police this segment of commercial aviation, the supplemental-carrier industry did a 180-degree turn in safety and corporate responsibility. Their safety

131

record in the past decade has been as good as that of the scheduled airlines; the survivors of our purge learned their lessons well.

In the years I spent at the FAA, I dreaded a fatal crash far more than I did personal criticism and crisis, of course. There was always the fear that some of our own policies or decisions might have contributed directly or indirectly. Safety, after all, was the FAA's major business, primary goal, and first priority, and virtually every accident challenged our responsibility.

One crash that got me embroiled in a donnybrook with both the media and certain personnel at the CAB involved an American Airlines Boeing 707 that took off from Idlewild on March 1, 1962. Only eight seconds later, it lurched to the left in a sharp bank, continued an almost graceful roll until it was on its back, and then fell nose down into the waters of Jamaica Bay. All eighty-seven passengers and eight crew members died in what was and, in my mind, still remains an unexplainable accident.

I went to that crash scene, too—a visit that, despite my excellent relations with CAB Chairman Boyd, was still resented by several CAB people. In the course of the investigation, some of our FAA experts handed me a report that amounted to a theoretical solution. A bolt inadvertently installed upside down, it said, may have fallen out of the hydraulic system, ramming unwanted fluid into one side of the elevator control system and causing a hard-over shove that locked the controls in a turn. Flight Standards informed me that such a bolt displacement could very well have forced the 707 onto its back and, acting on this warning, we issued an Airworthiness Directive (AWD) calling the attention of all 707 operators to this possibility and ordering immediate inspection of the bolt assembly in question.

AWDs are open to daily inspection by the press, and I didn't want this one to sneak into print, promoting wild speculation that the FAA had solved the mysterious Jamaica Bay accident. I talked it over with Phil Swatek, my press officer, and we agreed to hold a news conference explaining why we had issued the AWD. At the conference I emphasized that the whole action was precautionary, that the CAB investigation still was in progress, and that even in the event our theory didn't turn out to be the actual cause, we thought it necessary to plug a potentially deadly loophole without waiting for final causal determination.

Unfortunately certain CAB officials regarded the FAA announcement as blatant interference with their investigation. Several months passed, and then *The Saturday Evening Post* came out with an article on the Jamaica Bay accident, attributing the cause to a short circuit in the wiring of a small motor that activated the hydraulic boost system for the rudder. The electrical malfunction, the *Post* author wrote, had sent the wrong voltage throughout the circuit, kicking the rudder over hard. This time we at the FAA were infuriated.

First, the article went beyond disclosure of a casual theory—it gave the crossed-wires explanation as the CAB's actual probable-cause finding—and it did so before the CAB issued its final report. It was only too obvious that someone at the CAB had leaked to the *Post* what was supposed to be kept confidential until the official verdict was released. And from the tone of the article, it was obvious why those findings had been leaked. The *Post* tore into the FAA's loose-bolt conjecture, assailed the FAA for even proposing it, castigated me for holding that news conference, accused me of butting into the CAB's business for personal-publicity reasons, and last but not least ran a separate editorial calling for my dismissal.

I was angry enough to have Phil Swatek issue a point-by-point rebuttal of the article's claims, insofar as the FAA's actions were concerned. From the vantage point of hindsight and the calming effect of ensuing years, I suppose I may have overreacted. But I regarded the article as a piece of dirty journalism, not just because of its slanderous aspects but also because we had invited the writer to talk to us before it was published. Swatek had been tipped it was being prepared; he had been told by someone who had seen a draft of the article that it was extremely critical of Boeing and the 707's subcontractors, of the FAA for certificating the airplane, and of me for making visits to crash sites but not doing enough to prevent such accidents. We did try to provide the author with the FAA's side of the story, but his final version virtually ignored everything we had told him. It was a one-sided hatchet job for which

I blamed not so much the guy who wrote it as the editors of the *Post.*

There is a certain amount of infighting during the course of every accident probe, and Jamaica Bay was no exception. The ALPA was trying to show that recently adopted noise-abatement procedures contributed to the crash, claiming that if the pilot hadn't been forced to make a noise-abatement turn under reduced power, he might have overcome whatever malfunction occurred. Boeing naturally would have preferred to remove any onus from the airplane and have the blame cast on the crew or some subcontracted component like the autopilot. Pratt & Whitney would have resisted any attempt to indict the engines. American would and did try to prove that it had no liability in this accident. The FAA's control of the flight might have been suspect and, of course, there was the CAB's Bureau of Safety, with its knife out to protect the "safety" of its investigative process.

All of these forces are at work on a crash probe. I might add that a number of aeronautical engineers never bought the CAB's probable cause for the Jamaica Bay crash. Boeing didn't, for one, with some of its experts still suspecting an autopilot malfunction, and neither did American. And the FAA to this day remains dubious, with good reason. We ran flight tests on an FAA Boeing in which that rudder-control short circuit was simulated. The aircraft began to roll, as the American 707 had, but recovery was made in only two seconds by shifting from hydraulic to manual controls. True, our pilots expected the maneuver, whereas the American crew had no warning; they probably were still trying to diagnose the problem even as they rolled, and didn't have the luxury of advance warning, as our test pilots had. Officially the accident was solved, but doubt remains.

That business with *The Saturday Evening Post* was my worst experience with the press. I never did attain honeymoon status with the news media. I certainly never tried to hide anything from the news media to cover up mistakes or failures. I recall one occasion when a controller mistakenly gave a small private plane a wrong turn, vectoring him right into a mountain while he was approaching Los Angeles International Airport. My regional administrator at the time was Joe Tippetts, a beloved and wonderful man who had spent a lifetime in aviation. Tippetts and I talked it over and agreed to admit publicly that ATC was responsible for the deaths of the pilot and his three passengers. When our lawyers heard we were going to concede culpability, they went into orbit. They told us flatly that we could not admit liability because the United States Government would be sued, and in large amounts. So we did the next-best thing: We leaked the story anyway.

To me the credibility of any federal agency is terribly important —perhaps more so at the FAA, where one runs the daily risk of human error. As far as I know we never deliberately withheld the truth, tried to mislead either press or public, or attempted to duck responsibility. Some of my strongest supporters might challenge that last claim, citing the case of the Staten Island UAL-TWA collision in which I fought hard to keep the FAA from assuming any financial responsibility in the litigation that followed one of aviation's worst disasters.

An aviation writer whose views I respected once told me bluntly: "Jeeb, I always thought that was the worst mistake you made while you were administrator—trying to sweep FAA's role in that collision under the rug when you knew damned well a controller goofed and that weaknesses in the ATC system were a contributing factor."

There was some merit in his criticism. Without any doubt the FAA *was* partially responsible, as was demonstrated in the numerous ATC reforms that followed the collision. A few days after the Staten Island collision, where an overspeeding DC-8 jet overran its clearance—several months before I was appointed—the FAA drastically reduced speed limits for planes entering terminal areas. It began assigning extra controllers at high-density traffic centers with the specific duty of watching radarscopes for any planes straying from terminal-area clearances and holding patterns. The Agency also improved radar "hand-off" protection, the process under which one ATC center hands off traffic to the next jurisdiction. And finally, I ordered mandatory installation of two new navigation aids for all jetliners—Position Fixing Radar transponders and Distance Measuring Equipment (DME) for more precise navigation in the overcast.

All these actions were taken to correct the deficiencies

135

unmasked by that terrible accident. Furthermore, there was the undeniable evidence that proper manned radar should have spotted United's plane eleven miles beyond where its crew thought they were. So for some time I debated defending the Agency. The controllers were positively vehement in their belief that the collision occurred primarily because the United jet figuratively had run an aerial red light, had failed to report an accurate position, and that they were trying in violation of FAA regulations to navigate with only one of their VORs operative.

Eventually they convinced me that the FAA's responsibility was only indirect and in a sense conjectural—that is, wasn't it possible that the collision would have occurred even if some of the subsequent reforms had been in effect?

No less than 115 damage suits were filed against United, TWA, and the FAA. Hearings before a federal judge consumed more than five months of testimony that filled some 14,000 pages. At stake were claims totaling at least $77 million. To end the legal wrangling and speed up settlement of the claims, United, TWA, and the Justice Department agreed to share the lawsuit costs in what amounted to varying degrees of liability. United would pay 60 per cent, TWA 15 per cent, and the federal government 25 per cent.

I couldn't swallow that compromise settlement. First, it would be slapping our controllers in their faces. Maybe it was a case of sentiment overriding judgment, but I didn't want our men to carry the stigma of implied guilt when they were so sure in their own minds that they weren't guilty. I knew of controllers who had to be placed under psychiatric care when flights they were handling were involved in a fatal crash, even though their own actions played no part in causing the accident. To admit that the FAA was 25 per cent responsible for the Staten Island collision could sentence every controller remotely involved to a lifetime of brutal self-recriminations and doubts.

Second, and perhaps most important, I thought the compromise ignored the true role of the controller. The term "controller" implies authority to dictate to flights. But a controller doesn't really control; he *co-operates*. A pilot, on the other hand, can cancel a flight plan at any time. He can ignore advisories and warnings, as the TWA crew did when ATC warned them that the radar had spotted approaching, high-speed traffic. The Constellation pilots acknowledged the warning but apparently never spotted the converging DC-8—since they were flying in the overcast—and continued their course.

Third, and this was purely a bureaucratic reaction, I didn't relish having our budget nicked by millions of dollars that would be better spent on ATC improvements.

So I decided to fight the settlement deal, and I went as high as Attorney General Robert Kennedy in my opposition. I told him that if anything we should continue litigation in the case, and if we lost—if it was found that FAA personnel and rules were a primary cause of the collision—then we'd pay for whatever sins we were judged to have committed.

"If it isn't litigated," I warned, "and we admit liability by default in this partial settlement, we'll always carry the stigma. I don't want to let down those controllers and the men who work for me."

Kennedy was unyielding, and in the end the FAA had to pay its share. I'll never know whether my stand was the right one, but I do know that thousands of controllers were grateful.

The United-TWA tragedy and the subsequent legal battle was just one of the carryover problems. One immediate problem was something Quesada had inherited himself, and that was the FAA's ancient headquarters building. We won congressional approval for funds with which to erect a new FAA building capable of housing all the Agency's various departments.

Maybe it was an extension of my old dreams of becoming an architect, but I took a personal interest in the planning. I had long admired Eero Saarinen, one of the world's outstanding architects, whom Quesada had selected to design the terminal building at Dulles International Airport. Saarinen died shortly after completing the airport plan, but his influence indirectly went into our new headquarters structure at 800 Independence Avenue. His wife, Aline, had been married previously to a good friend of mine, and I used this old connection to convince her, along with Bill Walton and several top architects and designers, to serve on the FAA's Design Committee, which I created and which was organized in high style by Mrs. Jane Wheeler Suydam who was an early activist for art in federal architecture.

I informed the officials on the building project that all plans for structure and landscaping had to be approved by the Design Committee. Later I heard that this decision was greatly admired by both the President and Mrs. Kennedy, for what we achieved was something of a revolution in the General Services Administration, the agency entrusted with all federal building projects. We were able to design the interior of the new FAA building without any substantial increases in cost, yet achieved good industrial design elements: modern furnishings, lighting, mobile paneling, and a functional quality that didn't sacrifice beauty. It was a proud moment when we moved into our new quarters—almost as proud as the day we dedicated the new Dulles Airport, which had proved to be a more difficult and controversial task.

The new Washington International Airport dated back to 1950, when President Truman signed a bill authorizing the construction of a second airport to serve the capital area, at a cost not to exceed $14 million. The vision was more realistic than the price estimate. The revised cost estimate for the new airport was $60 million—a figure that Quesada confessed to me before I took office was an underestimate. He sadly reported that not only was the $60 million figure too low, but so also was the planned time of construction. The overages were not Quesada's fault, and he deserves the lion's share of credit that Dulles eventually became one of the world's finest and safest airports. It was Pete who chose Eero Saarinen as the chief architect and who fought hard for the major (and most controversial) Saarinen concept: an airport where the terminal was brought to the planes instead of the planes having to go to the terminal. This was the so-called mobile-lounge innovation, which the airlines fiercely resisted on the grounds that it represented an unnecessary expense to them (they would be charged for every lounge trip to and from the aircraft ramp area a mile away from the terminal building). As it turned out, the lounges proved to be overwhelmingly successful and actually saved the airlines money because they reduced high fuel-priced taxiing costs and modifications required each time a new model such as Concorde came along.

I regretted not having been able to work with the brilliant Saarinen right from the start of the mammoth project. He was a beloved man with a rumpled charm and a great imagination which far transcended the magnificent terminal building he designed. He insisted on a single-purpose access road which, as it developed, resulted in cutting the travel time between downtown Washington and the airport substantially, despite the nearly thirty miles a bus or car had to cover. He also was adamant about the government obtaining a total of 10,000 acres instead of the originally planned 4,500. Saarinen kept warning that Dulles would turn into a noise nuisance, as had such airports as Los Angeles International and New York's Idlewild, unless sufficient land was purchased to prevent residential encroachment.

I regret even more that Saarinen died before the airport was dedicated. But I did get a chance to work with him briefly during the planning and construction stages and treasured his warm words of gratitude for my going ahead with a project in the face of noisy criticism, demands for cancellation, and warnings that it would be nothing but a gigantic white elephant.

It wasn't easy to fight for Dulles. When I came on the scene, the runways were finished and the terminal foundation was being laid. Quesada had informed me that the cost at that point was $30 million over the original estimate. I called in the managers of the New York, Chicago, and Los Angeles airports and asked them to examine what had been done, what remained to be done, and to give me an educated guess at what the whole thing would cost in the end. Their guess: at least $110 million! They turned out to be nearly correct.

Most of the battling over the lounge concept was waged in private meetings between industry officials and the FAA. This was not the case with another major dispute I had with the airlines, which involved our plan to conduct public crash tests at Phoenix, Arizona, in conjunction with the Flight Safety Foundation. The carriers didn't object to the tests themselves, for they agreed there was much to be learned and done in the area of crash survival, emergency evacuations, and so forth. But they did register strong protests over our decision to permit news media coverage of the experiments, including motion pictures that were later released to television.

The real industry fireworks were ignited after the first test crash of a former United DC-7 crammed with impact-measuring instruments, dummies, experimental crash-survival equipment, and cameras to record what was happening in the cabin interior both during and after impact. We sent the old DC-7 down a specially prepared runway that was nothing but a deadly obstacle course. Telephone poles were placed where they would smack into the wings, and even small mounds of earth were built to simulate a takeoff accident. To make sure the unmanned DC-7 wouldn't run amok, we installed a steel track down the center of the runway. The plane's nosewheel was removed and replaced by a "shoe" fitting onto the track. A remote-control device released the brakes and advanced the throttles for the old aircraft's last takeoff—or so we hoped.

Everything went as planned except for one unexpected development: Just as the DC-7 started its roll down the booby-trapped runway, a last-second tailwind increased the impact speed around twenty miles above what our engineers had set. The result was considerably more damage than anyone expected, along with some startling movie shots. Shown later on television, they gave viewers an uncomfortably realistic look at what it was like to be involved in a crash: dummies in the cabin being tossed around wildly and crushed by collapsing seats; a telephone pole crunching into the wing like a hot knife slicing into soft butter. I'll never forget the most spectacular shot of all—the cockpit disintegrating as the nose plowed into a small hill—all in color and in slow motion.

It was easily the most thoroughly covered and widely publicized air-safety experiment ever conducted, and the airline industry's reaction was wild. Before there was any official protest, I heard from several airline executives who said the films in particular had set air travel back twenty years. Then Stuart Tipton, president of the Air Transport Association, wrote me a letter along the same lines. I replied that the public had a right to know what the FAA was doing about improving the chances for survival in a landing or takeoff accident.

In a second letter, Tipton said the industry wasn't objecting to press coverage of the crash tests but rather the propriety and discretion of a federal agency handing out gruesome pictures that could only "scare the daylights" out of people already afraid to fly. Tipton tartly reminded me that the FAA by law is charged with contributing to the advancement of commercial aviation and that scaring people was a questionable advancement. But I also felt that the airlines too often gave the impression that even discussing air-safety problems is bad for business; a sort of an "if we don't talk about it, the problem may go away" attitude.

I also thought the airlines were being oversensitive. The public already had been conditioned to the fact that the Phoenix crash was a scientific experiment in crash survival, involving an obsolete aircraft. I'm convinced that even the most shocking pictures were accepted in that spirit. More important, the overall effect of the publicity was one of reassurance, not fright—by making the public aware of how much effort was going into the task of making air travel safer.

Sure, the films may have "scared the hell out of some people"—and maybe that in itself was beneficial. One of our chief problems when I headed the FAA is still very much with us, and that's passenger apathy toward pretakeoff safety briefings, oxygen mask demonstrations, and those seldom read seatback cards. I'm willing to bet that anyone who saw the Phoenix films was more aware of the nearest emergency-exit location the next time he or she took a flight.

I took a pasting from the industry's leaders because of those pictures, but there was a significant exception. W. A. Patterson of United broke with his colleagues and publicly praised our tests and the attendant publicity. The tests, he said, contributed to flight safety, and publicizing them helped people realize how much was being done by both government and industry. We both remembered United's survivable accident at Denver's Stapleton Airport, when seventeen souls perished needlessly in the fatal confusion among passengers and crew after the emergency landing.

The second and final crash test in Arizona involved an old ex-TWA Constellation, which we rolled down an inclined ramp to simulate a landing accident. This time there was no tailwind problem, much less ire, not nearly as much damage—and the news coverage was correspondingly duller and definitely less controversial.

We learned a lot from the two tests, although not as much as we hoped. I was grateful for Patterson's defense of our good intentions.

I don't mean to imply that United had any monopoly on its attitude about safety. Individually the carriers all had a great sense of responsibility toward their passengers and were devoted to our mutual goal of improving air safety. Collectively they were represented by their trade association, the Air Transport Association (ATA), which had a greater blind spot toward safety than some of its individual members. While I didn't agree with or like the ATA's occasional ostrich attitude on safety issues, I had to admire the organization's professionalism. Its staff was manned with specialists in airline operations, and they were well informed, intelligent people. Unfortunately they operated under a policy of having to speak for the least common denominator among the ATA's members. For example, if a single airline balked at spending money on weather radar, that opposition tended to become ATA policy, or lack thereof. The Association, composed of highly individualistic and intensely competitive airlines, was seldom in a position to take any imaginative initiative. The ATA's initial reaction to virtually any air-safety proposal was negative, particularly if it involved spending airline money. On the other hand, we welcomed the considerable technical aid its experts were able to provide, and I at least understood its consistently foot-dragging attitude. In an industry that quarrels over everything from fares to the permissible size of sandwiches, it was too much to expect unity on safety matters.

If we made impressive strides in safety during my tenure, much of it was a matter of government-industry co-operation. I'm proud of what we accomplished in those five years. Our joint civil-military program doubled radar coverage of en route traffic. We upgraded the proficiency of our flight inspectors, introduced new tools to help our controllers, renewed the Aid to Airports Act, hacked away at the age-old problem of air-to-ground communications, set up a system of inspection for airport operators, clamped down on falsification of aviation records, and rolled back the first wave of skyjacking. We joined with the CAB in setting up a new accident-investigation school, improved regulations governing emergency evacuations, stepped up medical investigations of general-aviation accidents, and ended turbulence upset as a major safety hazard. We enlarged the area of positive air-traffic control to cover virtually the entire country, developed better approach and runway lighting, began experiments on the use of parallel runways (now in use at a number of large airports), increased our VOR coverage 17 per cent, and added fifty-eight new instrument-landing systems to carrier-served airports.

One set of statistics speaks for itself. Between 1957 and 1961, the United States scheduled airlines averaged .48 passenger death for every 100 million miles flown. In the five-year period covering 1962-66, the rate was .22 per 100 million miles. Government and industry didn't accomplish this with mirrors or the power of prayer.

One of our prosafety efforts got me into the most heated and unhappy brawl of my government career—a decision to reduce the number of air-route traffic-control centers, which provided en route control over regions of the nation's airspace. The primary motive was economy through higher productivity, but an important by-product was increased safety: By contracting the number of centers, we reduced the number of handoffs required for flights passing from one center's jurisdiction to another's—and thus cut the chances for human error. Our goal was to eliminate eight of the twenty-nine then-existing centers. I went directly to President Kennedy with the plan.

I warned him there would be political repercussions. We already had experienced early static when we reduced the number of centers from thirty-five to twenty-nine, and I now wanted to cut more. From the standpoint of both economy and safety, the further reductions had been made possible by our expanding network of long-range radar, along with more efficient communications facilities and increased computer capability. Further, due to rapidly rising costs of new computer and display technology, each center would cost more each year.

Southern airspace between Phoenix and Memphis was one of those affected; between these two cities we had centers at El Paso, San Antonio, Fort Worth, and New Orleans. My own experts told me that the centers at El Paso, San Antonio, and New Orleans

143

were not needed and that the Fort Worth center would be adequate for handling all traffic between Memphis and Phoenix.

With the backing of the Budget Bureau and JFK, I began the long, laborious, and delicate process of advising the congressmen and senators whose constituencies were included in the cities to be affected. One of them was a newly elected Democratic representative from San Antonio, Henry Gonzales, who had won his seat in a district that had been heavily Republican and unusually dependent on federal largesse at defense facilities, veterans' hospitals, and homes for retirees. I didn't know it at the time, but Gonzales was very close to Vice President Lyndon Johnson, who had recently campaigned for him on the streets of San Antonio.

I tried to get an appointment with Gonzales to discuss the closing of the San Antonio facility, which employed some two hundred people. Gonzales hemmed and hawed about seeing me but finally suggested I have lunch with him. When I arrived for lunch, he had a colorful newswoman, Sarah McClendon, and another woman with him.

"I'm sorry," he said, "but we'll have to have lunch another time."

I was nettled. I had called him, my staff talked to his, our San Antonio controllers had protested to him, and I was up against deadlines. I had telegrams in my pocket announcing the eight closures and pulled out the one involving San Antonio.

"This is going out tonight, Mr. Congressman," I told him, "and you and I have had little discussion about it."

"Well, discuss it with my assistant," he replied.

I made one last effort, knowing that what seemed to be outright rudeness or indifference may have been the natural excitement and disorder of being a newly elected solon.

"I'll be happy to go down to San Antonio and make a public statement of your opposition to this closure and the fact that I just had to go ahead and do it," I offered.

Gonzales again murmured something to the effect that I should see his assistant, so I gave up. I already had decided to visit each of the affected centers personally, explaining to the FAA employees why they were being moved to other cities and the plans we had for making the shift as painless as possible. New Orleans was the first stop, and everything went off well. However, at San Antonio, as soon as we landed I was faced with a mob scene of civic protesters. One would have had the impression that the closure order had thrown two hundred thousand people out of work instead of causing two hundred to change job location.

I had expected a few newsmen to meet me, but I never anticipated that crowd of shoving, shouting citizenry. It had never dawned on me or my political-affairs adviser, William Schulte, that the closing of any federal facility in San Antonio, a city with a rather large federal payroll, was regarded as a major threat to its survival. After I was mobbed when I got off the plane, the Republican mayor showed me an Associated Press dispatch datelined Washington that said that Gonzales had asked the General Accounting Office to investigate "Halaby's illegal and improper closure of the San Antonio center."

I turned to one of my assistants and muttered, I thought unheard, "Boy, he's acting like a freshman congressman, isn't he?"

Both the mayor and the Chamber of Commerce officials overheard me, and they promptly quoted me—only too accurately—to the news media. That offhand remark hit the headlines and the newscasts, and from that moment on, Gonzales was an indefatigable enemy not only of me but also of the FAA. He began anti-Halaby, anti-FAA speeches and statements, claiming that I was playing "Russian roulette with the lives of people in the skies over Texas" by closing that center.

Gonzales went much farther than issuing mimeographed accusations about my bureaucratic incompetence; he actually tried to get me fired. He first went to Walter Jenkins, one of LBJ's assistants, and bluntly told him, "Halaby has to go." He complained bitterly about me to his friend and mentor, Vice President Lyndon Johnson. Finally he wrote the President himself a vituperative letter that claimed I was tampering with human lives and that I had been rude to him. That letter prompted a call to me from the White House.

"What on earth did you do to Henry Gonzales?" JFK asked mildly.

I told him the whole story of the offhand/overheard remark that had gotten me into hot water. The President chuckled.

145

"Well, Henry has a very hot temper," he observed, and said no more on the subject at that time.

Gonzales kept up his attacks, and eventually I got a call from the Vice President, who suggested I drop in and see him about "the Gonzales matter." I went over and told him the same story I had given the President.

"That's the damndest thing I ever heard of," Johnson said.

"What can I do to help him?" I asked. "As I understand it, he's a liberal, he has a good sense of humor, and he represents a neglected part of our society [Gonzales was one of the first if not *the* first Mexican American elected to Congress]. The last thing in the world I would want to do is hurt him. That's why I went down to San Antonio, not just to see my own people at the center but also to tell everyone how much he had opposed the closure."

"Well," LBJ drawled, "you sure fouled it up."

"I sure as hell did," I admitted. "I'm going to write him a personal, handwritten note of apology."

Johnson allowed that this would be a good idea, and I wrote Gonzales what may have been too humble contriteness. He never answered but instead continued to blast me—hardly a day passed without a fresh attack in the Congressional Record or a statement handed the press assailing me and/or the Agency for our alleged sins. Any aviation incident, regardless of the casual circumstances, prompted a Gonzales charge that the FAA was to blame, directly or indirectly. Between his blind bias and someone's fertile typewriter, he came up with some incredibly off-base charges. I remember two incidents in particular in which Gonzales achieved the apogee of unfairness.

One concerned the crash of a Pan Am 707 near Elkton, Maryland, which was in a holding pattern awaiting approach clearance to Philadelphia Airport when it was seen going down on fire. Investigators quickly determined that the jet had been struck by lightning and that an explosion had occurred in the wing area hit by the bolt. There were thunderstorms in the vicinity, but communications transcripts showed that the Pan Am flight was clear of turbulence. Both these facts already had been made public when Gonzales apparently decided that he couldn't blame Halaby for a freak lightning strike.

146

"Although the probable cause of the Elkton crash will not be determined until the Civil Aeronautics Board has completed its investigation," he proclaimed in a press statement, "it is reasonable to assume that turbulence played some part in this tragedy. Why did not the FAA controller instruct the Boeing 707 to fly in a 'holding pattern' outside or away from a turbulence area?"

The second incident involved the crash of an Eastern DC-7 near Kennedy International Airport. The DC-7 had just taken off when its crew took violent evasive action to avoid an incoming Pan Am jet, which they believed was on a collision course. The Eastern maneuver was so sharp that the pilots lost control.

Almost immediately, Gonzales was out with a statement charging the FAA with failure to provide proper separation. We denied this, and he promptly accused us of lying. Nineteen months later, long after I had left office, the CAB issued a final report exonerating ATC and blaming the accident on an illusion: The Eastern crew, flying into a darkened sky with no visual horizon reference, misjudged the jet's altitude and tried to avoid a collision danger that didn't exist. I was curious to see if Gonzales would issue a statement admitting he had been wrong.

He didn't.

CHAPTER FIVE

Henry Gonzales was not the only Capitol Hill cross I had to carry at the FAA, but he certainly was the most persistent critic around. After sending President Kennedy that first letter, he wrote a second along the same lines. I learned that JFK discussed it with Johnson; they were counting on the young Texan's support on a number of crucial bills, and they didn't want to alienate him. Kennedy sent one of his congressional liaison men up to the Hill to talk to Gonzales, without getting anywhere; he was adamant in his opposition to me. When I heard that the peace mission had failed, I began to get worried.

The next time I saw the President, I asked him if there was anything I could do about Gonzales.

"Don't worry about it," JFK advised. "Lyndon will help you out and it will pass."

It did, in the sense that Gonzales proved to be loyal to the Kennedy administration in most respects, even though he never ceased going after me. I've always regretted Gonzales' antagonism because he was admirable in so many ways. He represented his constituents forcefully, he was unquestionably courageous, and he personified the American Dream, as a man who overcame ethnic bigotry to become a United States congressman. It finally came to light that the ex-ATCA director McDermott was the acid penman behind the congressman's desk.

Another tormentor (as well as a genial friend) was John Bell Williams, the chairman of the House Commerce Committee's Subcommittee on Aviation. A one-armed former Air Corps pilot, this witty Mississippi Democrat (and later governor) was a kind of Mr. Aviation in the House of Representatives.

At President Kennedy's insistence, we had included in the Federal Aid to Airports Act a provision that permitted a ban on federal funding for any airport practicing segregation in rest rooms or restaurants. One of the cities seeking federal help under the act was Jackson, Mississippi, right smack in John Bell's district. We already had won desegregation fights at New Orleans, Tallahassee, and Montgomery airports. But the Jackson situation was something else. For one thing, we were dealing not just with a dedicated Southerner but also a lawmaker whose influence on aviation matters was considerable. John Bell Williams also was a firm aviation supporter who had helped us immeasurably in his subcommittee.

My conscience gave me no choice. I went to the President and informed him I was going to get into trouble with Williams over our insistence that the new Jackson airport be desegregated.

"It's up to you," JFK said. "You'll have to make a deal with him on your own. I'm not going to take up your battles for you with John Bell Williams."

I already had skirmished with Williams when the Airports Aid Bill was going through the legislative mill, and John Bell was trying to keep the antidiscrimination clause out of the Act. He did a lot of sniping at committee hearings, he wrote some nasty letters, and he tossed quite a few barbs at me at public dinners and luncheons—once introducing me as the "head of the FAACP"! But he somehow got the idea I merely was following Bobby Kennedy's orders in trying to desegregate airports.

"I know you don't really believe in this—it's that so-and-so Bobby," Williams would say.

On more than one occasion, I'd tell Williams that airport desegregation was not merely Administration policy but also my own, because I sincerely believed in civil rights. Williams would grin knowingly and cheerfully reiterate, "Yeah, I know, Jeeb—it's that Bobby Kennedy."

We had to get Williams overruled in full committee before the antidiscrimination clause went through, but he was aviation-minded enough to vote for the bill even with that provision. I made sure he was invited to the signing ceremony when the bill became law and I think he appreciated the gesture. But when Jackson was chosen as the first real airport desegregation test case, he found antidiscrimination not just a noble-sounding policy but also a matter of federal muscle. Jackson was a tough nut for more reasons than its location in John Bell's district. The black population there was not very aggressive, and the feeling of racism was extremely high. The President wouldn't brook undue delay or opposition to administering the Airports Act, but he also recognized that Williams was a key to many of our aviation programs and plans. He and Bobby—well advised by Burke Marshall, assistant attorney general for civil rights—therefore gave us permission to work out an agreement with the mayor of Jackson so there wouldn't have to be any crackdown and public threats and possible violence.

We conducted informal, unpublicized negotiations with the mayor, who knew we had that federal grant aid as a lever. We had virtually concluded a pact with him—with Williams' knowledge—to desegregate Jackson's new airport quietly and without fanfare, when the Civil Rights Commission suddenly got into the act. Its chairman, Dr. John Hannah, decided to select the FAA's federal assistance to airports in Mississippi as an example of how the government should not help states and communities practicing segregation.

Hannah's aides had drafted a report threatening to cut off Mississippi's airport funds, including those already promised for the Jackson airport, unless segregation was ended. No one quarreled with Hannah's intent, but his timing was atrocious. When Hannah informed the White House of the proposed draft, aides quickly told the President that our efforts to settle the Jackson situation without verbal bloodshed were about to be torpedoed. JFK called me and authorized me to explain to Hannah what we were doing—but Hannah refused to change the draft, and our negotiations with the Jackson mayor blew up. Eventually we got the terminal at Jackson desegregated and I suppose Dr. Hannah felt his public blast was largely instrumental. I thought it was more detrimental than helpful and actually delayed what we both wanted. In fact, I said as much to Beryl Bernhard, Hannah's executive director.

"It seems to me you guys are more interested in activity than action," I said with some bitterness.

This was not the only occasion on which I felt civil rights advocates regarded publicity as more important than achievement. There were too many instances where the efforts of both JFK and his brother Bobby to advance the cause of civil rights with a minimum of controversy were "overkilled" by the Civil Rights Commission and its highly aggressive and well-publicized policies. The President never ducked a fight, but he also wanted to minimize bloodletting as far as possible.

Typical was a decision he made in a situation that arose after he ordered the Justice Department to assure James Meredith's entrance into the University of Mississippi as a student. To back up the order, JFK dispatched federal troops to Oxford, and the FAA co-operated by flying U.S. marshals there, as well as sending extra controllers to the university's tiny airport.

The White House was advised that Mississippi Governor Barnett had announced his intentions of flying to Oxford in a gesture of defiance toward the federal troops. I was en route to Capitol Hill that morning when JFK reached me on my mobile telephone.

"You know about Barnett's flying to Oxford?" he asked without preamble.

"Yes, sir."

"Do you have any means of preventing that flight?"

"Well, some limited means."

"Exercise all of them," he ordered, in a tone he didn't employ often.

I called my office and issued orders to have the airspace over the Oxford airport declared restricted airspace, citing military air-traffic congestion as the reason. Next I called the director of the Mississippi State Aeronautics Commission, whose friendship I had cultivated through Representative Williams over the previous two years. I warned him that if he or anyone else flew a state-owned airplane into Oxford, they would be violating restricted airspace. Tension was very high, I reminded him, and we would have to meet and arrest anyone who flew in illegally.

He said he understood, and apparently he passed the word to the governor. Barnett canceled his plans to fly to Oxford—and I have no doubt that if he had showed up, the rioting would have been even worse.

One of the most remarkable things about my relationship with John F. Kennedy was that he seldom issued a direct order without first ascertaining whether it could be carried out or if there were alternatives. It was usually "Can you do something . . . what are the alternatives?" And then, in a rather gentle but very clear tone, he'd ask me to do it. That technique simply engendered an even greater desire to do what he wanted you to do. It was a kind of understatement, of underdirection, that was both wonderful and extremely effective.

I remember a grim day in August 1961 when we were notified that a Continental Air Lines 707 had been hijacked—Flight 54 from Los Angeles to Houston via Phoenix, El Paso, and San Antonio. The hijackers were two men, an ex-convict named Leon Beardon and his son, Cody; they had boarded at Phoenix, and thirty minutes after leaving Phoenix, the father had pulled a gun on one of the stewardesses. The pilots were told to fly to Cuba, but the gunman agreed to let the plane land at El Paso for refueling.

At El Paso, considerable stalling on the part of both the flight crew and ground personnel delayed the fueling process long enough for some countermeasures to be put into effect. The El Paso airport was crawling with law-enforcement officials, including FBI agents, but nothing could be done with those guns pointing at crew members' heads. One shot was fired into the floor of the 707, in fact, although whether deliberately to scare the pilots or accidentally was never learned.

Continental's president, Bob Six, was en route to the scene in a CAL Viscount and authorized a deal by which a Continental DC-7 would be flown to El Paso from Houston to take the hijackers to Cuba along with a few hostages. The Beardons refused to accept this switch of planes and insisted that the 707 be used. They did, however, agree to let all the passengers off the plane, retaining as hostages four passengers who volunteered to stay.

The wave of Havana-bound hijackings already had started, but this was the first hijacking of a jetliner. Because of this, and because Cuba was involved, I notified the President.

"What do you think we ought to do?" he asked.

"I don't think we should let that plane leave the ground," I advised.

Presidential adviser McGeorge Bundy, who was in the Oval Office with JFK at the time, came on the line and agreed with me.

"We can't let them get away with it," he said to both JFK and me. "We're taking an awful risk of injury or death to some of those passengers, but we have to preserve law and order. If they can get away with this kind of thing, it'll spread all over."

"I think you're right," Kennedy said. "Jeeb, keep me informed, and take any action necessary to make sure that plane doesn't leave El Paso."

While talking to the White House, I got J. Edgar Hoover's office on another phone and relayed the President's orders. To my surprise, the FBI was reluctant to take aggressive action. But when I also notified the El Paso tower and local authorities of JFK's decision, on behalf of the President we directed the FBI to take whatever action was required to block a takeoff. The FBI contacted Six by radio and told him the 707 was not to be allowed to take off. It was a real dilemma for the FBI because the agent in charge, Francis Crosby, knew the jet could be stopped if its tires were shot up or by blocking it with a couple of fire trucks or fuel trucks. But this wouldn't have prevented the Beardons from threatening to kill one or more of the hostages unless the trucks were moved or the tires replaced. Unknown to me or anyone else in Washington, Crosby asked Six if he had any ideas.

"Wait until the last minute and then shoot out the tires when the plane starts taxiing," Six suggested.

Texas Ranger sharpshooters did just that, and the Beardons, infuriated but confused, finally surrendered. It was a happy ending to an extremely explosive situation, and I was pleased the next day to receive a handwritten note of thanks from JFK.

In the course of apprehending the father-and-son skyjacking

team, an interesting thing happened in the 707's cabin. The younger Beardon had been fed champagne by the stewardesses as he threatened them with a gun and was feeling no particular pain toward the end of the action. The son let down his guard to a passenger named Leonard Gilman, who happened to be a Border Patrol regional director in California. Gilman hit Cody Beardon so hard on the jaw that he broke his hand. When Gilman appeared beside me about two weeks later before the Senate Commerce Subcommittee on Aviation, he still had a large cast around his hand, wrist, and arm.

He and I appeared together at the hearing because immediately after the incident, I had gone to my tough new friend, Senator Engle, with a draft bill to make aerial hijacking a federal crime. He had introduced it and called hearings immediately; in what must be a record for legislating a federal felony, there were hearings in the Senate and House, the bill passed both houses of Congress, and was signed by the President—all in less than sixty days.

With Cuba only 90 miles off the Florida coast, and a Castro who was all but inviting this kind of humiliating and disruptive activity, skyjacking was a serious problem. It appealed not only to the handful of revolutionaries seeking a dramatic escape from the United States but also to persons whose imagination would be excited into action by the tremendous amount of newspaper and electronic journalism on these sky spectaculars. We therefore were determined to set up a very strict surveillance enforcement system to nip this activity at an early stage. In particular, we trained and swore in as FAA inspectors a large number of Border Patrolmen and a few fully qualified FAA inspectors who were deputized by federal agencies to act as police as well as inspectors—"sky marshals" we christened them, with a heavy spray of hyperbole.

This tough approach won the general approval of the public but was also met by two very strong sources of opposition. The first came from airline crews who were concerned that we were going to make the cockpit a battleground and who were particularly worried about "trigger-happy Border Patrolmen and unqualified FAA tigers in the cabin and cockpit." To my amazement, most airline captains adopted the policy of "do what the man says" to avoid trouble rather than the attitude of a captain of a ship who was sternly in command of everything on board, and particularly ready to quell or prevent piracy.

The other source of opposition was the airlines themselves, who grumbled about "overkill" since, with the exception of Eastern and National, which flew to Florida so frequently and so near to Cuba, most of them did not at first take the threat of skyjacking very seriously. The other carriers grumbled about having to pay for the "sky marshals" flying and eating on board their aircraft. In any case, we recognized that we could cover only a few flights, but we felt that the premeditating criminal would have to take this into account as a deterrent.

Finally, we studied all of the hijackings in aviation history to try to determine a few common denominators in the motivation and the profile of the type of criminal. This profile later became the basis for the "thicket theory," a notion I developed after looking over all of the available psychological profiles of skyjackers, most of whom had previously been motivated by the desire to make money on insurance policies (unlike the current crop, who were more politically motivated). I conceptualized in early 1962 that there was no way we could surely identify in advance and apprehend a skyjacker—there were too many passengers every day. What we could do was to create a thicket where passengers could be observed from the time they entered the terminal, went to the life insurance vending machines, came to the ticket counters, and finally boarded the airplane. I proposed that airports be staffed with specially trained airport terminal security personnel and airline ticket-counter and passenger-service boarding personnel who were educated and alerted to the profile. After I left the FAA, this became the standard procedure, to be eventually supplemented by the purchase of the detection equipment and the hiring of many guards. We moved very rapidly toward law and order in the sky in the early sixties as a result of this tough stand, and I think it's fair to say that from the time of the Continental skyjacking in El Paso until I left office in June of 1965, domestic skyjacking declined sharply—at least until more stringent measures had to be taken when skyjackings by political terrorists and extortionists proliferated in the late sixties.

At times of crisis, JFK was great to work with. I appreciated almost more than JFK's personal thoughtfulness his willingness to let me run the FAA without White House intrusion. For me his lack of interest in details of administration was a blessing.

From my own standpoint, he gave me more than just *carte blanche* in running the FAA since he had made me his "principal aviation adviser." I was invited by his very able naval aide, Captain Tazewell Sheppard, to be a member of the White House Staff Mess, which let me mingle more frequently and freely with the President's close associates than any of the other regulatory agency heads. This gave me an unusual opportunity to participate in White House life. I suppose it may have been a reflection of his own operating style, but my earliest impression of JFK's White House operations was a lot of people running around and bumping into one another, without rigid organization but with plenty of ideas germinating and great *esprit de corps.*

I always kept the President informed of aviation policy developments or crises, particularly those involving some controversy that eventually might be tossed on his lap for a decision. There were times when his decision went contrary to my advice, such as in the fight over the preservation of Mitchell Field on Long Island. There had been strong pressure to close it down and turn it into a shopping center, but I publicly urged that it be retained as a general-aviation facility because it reduced the load of nonairline traffic on LaGuardia.

My stand didn't please "Sissie" Patterson Guggenheim, publisher of the Long Island *Newsday,* who had been waging a strong editorial campaign against the airport as a noise nuisance. Quesada, an old friend of hers, had also lined up noisily against the FAA regional administrator, Oscar Bakke, at a public hearing. She had supported Kennedy, and she went right to the White House with her demands that Mitchell be closed. I received a call at lunch one day and, as usual, JFK didn't waste time on pleasantries.

"Jeeb, what are you doing up in Long Island? Mrs. Guggenheim is here and she tells me it doesn't make any sense for us to fight for that airport. Do you think you can relax on that?"

I mentally consigned this fine lady to whatever purgatory is reserved for those who forget in how many instances airports were there before real-estate developers moved in, thus creating noise problems that never would have arisen if proper zoning had been applied. But I wasn't about to challenge John Kennedy over the issue of keeping a small airport open—especially since it was clearly a losing battle in the community.

"Well, Mr. President," I said, "I think we ought to try to save it, but if you feel otherwise, we can relax our stand."

"I think you should," JFK said—and that was that. I didn't resent his pulling the rug out from under me; he didn't do it often to anyone, and when he did, it was only when he felt the goal wasn't too important. This was never more apparent than in a fight over international air policy, one in which I got directly involved because I was the instigator of a full-scale review of such policy. With world air travel not just expanding but exploding, I thought we should take a close look at the increasing foreign competition, the bilateral air agreements we had been making with other nations, and the belief in some quarters that we should have a single U.S.-flag carrier performing all overseas operations. The President approved my recommendation and designated me chairman for the study, but in doing so we opened the doors for some intensive lobbying.

Most of it came from Juan Trippe, founder and chief of Pan American World Airways, who at times seemed to have a key to the White House back door. This wasn't surprising, for Trippe was a prominent member of the President's Business Advisory Council. So Trippe had above-average access to Kennedy who, in turn, held a warm feeling of respect for the old titan—although once or twice he referred to him as "that pirate."

Trippe's chief dream, goal, and obsession was that "chosen instrument" concept—one U.S.-flag carrier for all U.S. international routes, and that carrier, of course, would be Pan Am, which had pioneered overseas air transportation for its country. His efforts in the past had been combined with those of Jim Landis, who had been a close colleague of the President's father, Joseph P. Kennedy, and who had represented Pan Am's interests on a number of occasions.

Normally, Pan Am would have had stiff opposition to its chosen

157

instrument goal from its chief North Atlantic competitor, TWA. But at the time that we were wrestling with the international air-policy issue, TWA and Pan Am were groping with each other in serious merger negotiations, so that TWA momentarily could not openly oppose the chosen instrument plan. It was no secret that the study I had instigated was veering not only against the chosen instrument but also was generally expansionist instead of restrictive. Both Pan Am and TWA, especially the former, did everything they could to get our policy statement watered down to a vague statement that really took no stand on the single-carrier issue. We had a formidable platoon working against us, what with the President's father and Landis on the Pan Am side and working constantly through Pan Am's ALPA chapter, and other unions working on Bobby Kennedy and White House aides Kenneth O'Donnell and Mike Feldman.

Their efforts did result in JFK's referring the statement back to us for changes in the wording, but he never asked us to alter the main thrust. The significant thing was that it finally came out against a chosen-instrument airline and urged a policy for our international routes of carefully balanced and limited competition instead of contraction or open skies.

Amid all the chosen-instrument fireworks, I also became convinced that we had to try to end the constant bickering between the CAB and the State Department over U.S. route authorizations for foreign carriers, most of whom were either nationalized or heavily subsidized by their respective governments. The CAB was more prone to protect U.S. airlines, while the State Department, with broader international relations at stake, tended to sympathize with the foreign competition. With Mike Feldman's support, I developed two alternatives: either have the Secretary of State name a full-time director of international aviation affairs, or make me a co-ordinator between State and the CAB—a kind of arbitrator or umpire for the State-CAB quarrels, which would have formalized what Feldman and I had been doing informally.

This touched off an interagency free-for-all. Secretary of Commerce Luther Hodges insisted that it was only logical for him to be the co-ordinator for international aviation affairs. Secretary of State Dean Rusk recommended Secretary of State Dean Rusk, while the CAB urged Kennedy to give the Board the job. No one of the President's staff wanted the task, and my volunteering—figuring as the President's chief aviation adviser, I also was a logical choice—fell on deaf ears.

It finally wound up in that classic decision that is more of a compromise than a solution: an interdepartmental committee was formed under the chairmanship of the Secretary of State, who was authorized to choose a co-ordinator; this, in effect, kept the job under the State Department's jurisdiction. Rusk's choice was Averell Harriman, who recruited an aviation expert as his deputy. I welcomed working again with my old boss in the Mutual Security Program, but "government by committee" didn't thrill me at all. In the absence of someone better, I had been willing to take on the job in order to see that our new policy initiative was faithfully carried out; I was a little disappointed that JFK named a committee instead of me, but I understood the need for central conduct of foreign affairs, of which international aviation problems and policies are only a small part. In fact I even offered to become an assistant to Dean Rusk, which would have meant my wearing three hats—FAA, White House adviser, and State—and this was considered briefly until Rusk opposed it. JFK did offer some solace by naming me vice chairman of Harriman's interdepartmental committee, which, while it soon atrophied, was at least better than having no medium for anticipating and settling quarrels before they had to be dumped on JFK's desk.

I was en route to Tullahoma, Tennessee, the day that JFK started that fateful motorcade through Dallas. Representative Joe Evins of Tennessee was with me in the FAA's Gulfstream; he wanted me to inspect the facilities of the Arnold Engineering and Development Company in Tullahoma, which were reported to have the finest wind-tunnel installations in the world. Evins, who was No. 3 Democrat on the House Appropriations Subcommittee for Federal Aviation, was anxious to obtain for Arnold an FAA contract in conjunction with the supersonic transport program.

Over the aircraft radio we got word that the President had been shot. When we landed, we stayed glued to a television set at the

159

airport. An hour later, Kennedy's death was confirmed. I headed right back to Washington—inspecting a wind-tunnel facility seemed of monumental unimportance. I was stunned, sick at heart, and suddenly unsure. As for most of the New Frontiersmen, for me working for JFK had become a way of life; helping him fulfill his dreams of a better and greater America dwarfed the petty annoyances and frustrations of bureaucracy. Most of us didn't just like and/or respect JFK, we also tended to idolize him.

I had brought the tears under control by the time I landed the Gulfstream at Washington National and stepped down the stairs to the stillness of the shocked capital. Big, grimy mechanics were standing there sobbing, doubting that it could really have happened. Numbness, doubt, anger, guilt that we could have produced an assassin of our President—our brother and leader gone. Several days would pass before the cruel loss could be accepted, and I guess the exalting example of Jackie, Bobby, and the Kennedy family, and the deference and dignity of the new President, sustained us all. Never, ever, will we forget little John-John's salute before the flag-draped caisson carrying his father to the final rites with all of us marching behind in black.

It was only too obvious that life under LBJ, compared to serving under JFK, would mean more than just a change of initials. I had come to know Lyndon Johnson quite well before the tragedy at Dallas, and I admired him in several ways. For one thing, he was about as air-minded as a President could be. It was Johnson who subsequently gave me the valuable backing I desperately needed to get a supersonic transport program launched. It was Johnson who dispatched me to the Soviet Union on a kind of reassuring mission just after JFK's death—the main object being to determine whether a bilateral air agreement that had been drawn up but never signed was still acceptable. To Johnson, this gesture was a small but hopeful signal to the Soviet Union that his new Administration was not slamming any doors on improved relationships.

Johnson's Texas earthiness could be colorful and frequently apropos, even if it didn't produce a lot of harmony and affection. Salty language notwithstanding, LBJ was smart, shrewd, basically well-intentioned, and in some ways a better administrator than JFK. He didn't have John Kennedy's intellect, appreciation of policy and strategy, or his style and rapier wit, but he was great at ramming JFK's ideas into legislation. As a Southerner he had enough color blindness and sense of justice mixed with guilt to press forward the fight for civil rights. He ruled through a combination of favors and fears and painful arm-twisting, but he had a quality of courage of his own, and he could get things done—some of them wise things.

For example, when JFK died, we were heading toward a sort of crisis in congestion in all forms of transportation—airways, airports, railways, highways, and especially urban transit. A group of us led by Alan Boyd had concluded in the early sixties—and had started to convince President Kennedy—that we needed a long-range transportation policy that would recognize the growing interdependence of the various transportation interests, a policy that would curb the worsening competition among the airlines, railroads, highway contractors, truckers, and maritime interests for the public dollar. The greedy, ungovernable maritime labor unions were a special problem—their rapacious demands and dictatorial power had reduced our once-proud maritime industry to a collection of whiners utterly dependent on federal handouts. The numerous railway unions had filled the trains with feather beds. Static and cynical managements had failed to modernize and fulfill the needs of the shippers and passengers, who had become victims rather than beneficiaries of a century of federal subsidies.

As FAA administrator, I saw only too clearly how all phases of the transportation industry had developed narrow, parochial, special interests—each doing his thing, his speciality, without consideration for others. Yet in this complex technological society of ours, there could be no dominant transportation branch, for no single one could endure and prosper alone. There was no sense, for example, in spending millions on a new airport facility twenty miles from the urban area it was supposed to serve, and doing nothing about the antiquated roads or railways leading to that airport.

I can cite the cases of the Los Angeles and JFK airports, where we wanted to reroute the access freeways so they would be directly under the runway approach paths. This could have blocked the planned building of residential dwellings directly under the ap-

161

proach airways later causing enormous noise-generated political problems. I found that neither state nor federal highway authorities gave a damn about the airways; we couldn't get as much as a mile of rerouting, even though it would have saved the local, state, and federal governments a lot of money and later trouble.

There were other gross deficiencies stemming from the lack of an integrated policy. We regulated airmen very stringently, but nobody really regulated car drivers. We were spending millions to police a relative handful of pilots while tolerating over fifty thousand automobile deaths annually; it was no wonder that the favorite remark of airline captains was, "The most dangerous part of my day is the drive to the airport."

The transportation system was allowed to grow at random, the individual segments highly regulated but with no overall co-ordination or co-operation. The regulatory organization itself contributed to the chaos—the Bureau of Public Roads was in the Commerce Department; the CAB governed the airlines; the FAA financed airports and engineered airways; the ICC handled rails, trucks, and interstate buses; and the Maritime Commission regulated sea commerce. Each segment had its own interests, its own lobby, and its own form of blind provincialism.

Just before leaving the FAA, I prepared a memo for the President—suggesting that there be a full-fledged Department of Transportation, whose chief officer would have Cabinet status. Such an agency, of course, would end the FAA's coveted independent status—something for which we had fought so hard. But I also pointed out to LBJ that the various independent agencies had more than two hundred persons reporting to the President, and this had to be a hopeless administrative situation. A professional transportation leader in the Cabinet itself, I felt, would give the proposed Department of Transportation—and the FAA—some badly needed clout; in theory, and many times in practice, a Cabinet officer not only has the biggest word but also the last word. I guess I was a rarity—an independent agency head proposing to become less independent.

The Department of Transportation became a reality after I returned to private life, pushed through Congress by LBJ himself, although not without stiff opposition from such aviation zealots as

Mike Monroney. Mike feared that aviation would get buried in a Department of Transportation just as it had been in the old CAA days under Commerce, and it was largely through his efforts that the FAA retained at least some of its autonomy. To a certain extent, Monroney's concern was justified, and a lot of people have criticized me for supporting the new Department. I testified as a private citizen urging legislation prescribing and preserving the FAA's full operating autonomy. Yet I still believe that basically Congress made a sound decision; while the Department of Transportation has tended to be surface-oriented, sometimes at the expense of aviation, we airmen must realize that the whole purpose of creating the Department was to integrate *all* transportation through policy planning that took a broad, long-range view.

Aviation-minded Alan Boyd was President Johnson's choice to become our first Secretary of Transportation, and he couldn't have made a better selection. But Boyd's two Republican successors, first John Volpe and then Claude Brinegar, were anything but respectful of the legislative history designed to assure the independence and integrity of an agency entrusted with enhancement of air safety. It does not seem coincidental that from the very start of the Nixon administration, morale and efficiency within the FAA began to deteriorate sharply—to such a point that the FAA became a prime target for congressional and news media criticism, mainly on the grounds it was procrastinating on badly needed safety reforms and losing its early dynamism.

When I left the FAA, it was an agency with tremendous power for public good, occasionally arrogant in its independence, but with zeal, enthusiasm, and initiative unusual in a bureaucracy. But instead of maturing, it seems to have just grown old, elephantine in its awareness and reactions. When it lost its independence, it apparently lost much of its spark. Significantly, it isn't even a real voice in aviation policy anymore; the Department of Transportation does most of the planning and speaking on policy matters.

This is in stark contrast to the major role it used to play, exemplified by Lyndon Johnson's sending me to the Soviet Union on a trip that involved everything from technological discussions to diplomatic negotiations. The United States and the Soviet

163

Union had been talking since the last year of the Eisenhower administration about exchanging nonstop rights between New York and Moscow. A tentative agreement was reached under which Aeroflot, the Soviet state airline, would operate one round-trip flight a week between the Soviet capital and New York, while Pan Am would have similar once-a-week authority. Early in the new Kennedy administration, I suggested that Jim Landis continue the negotiations and obtain a specific bilateral agreement.

Ambassador Llewelyn Thompson went to the Soviet Union under instructions that the agreement include some restrictions—namely that we didn't want Aeroflot operating flights into the interior of the United States or beyond to other Western Hemisphere cities in addition to Havana. The Soviet Union, naturally, was equally insistent that Pan Am not venture beyond Moscow. The negotiations were friendly and an agreement was initialed in 1962 by both governments, followed by a supplementary intercarrier agreement between Pan Am and Aeroflot.

But at about the time for actual signing of the bilateral air pact, the Soviets put up the Berlin Wall, and the agreement was shelved. Later, in 1962, the Soviets frequently and fairly insistently kept bringing it up; they made it quite clear they wanted very much to sign officially. We were reconsidering our stand when the Soviets began emplacing missiles in Cuba and the President confronted Khrushchev, who blinked, and the agreement was shelved again.

Kennedy was beset by conflicting advice. Late in 1963, shortly before he went to Dallas and under Ambassador Kohler's prodding, he held a high-level conference on the matter. Mac Bundy gave me the consensus of that meeting: I was to visit the Soviet Union with a small party of technical experts, to probe the situation further, and keep the unsigned bilateral agreement alive. I was instructed to discuss with the Soviets the technical details of the operation so there would be no hitches or misunderstandings in the event the political decision was made to go ahead.

That was the understanding when JFK was murdered, and within a few days after the Dallas assassination Johnson called me into his office. There was my respected friend, Mac Bundy, whose role had greatly increased and who at that moment was coaching the new occupant of the Oval Room. LBJ told me to visit the

Soviet Union as planned. I knew Kennedy eventually would have approved the agreement if he had lived, believing as he did that it was an opportunity simultaneously to open up the Soviet Union to our own people and introduce the liberalizing aspects of American society to the Soviets. The only question was the timing, and this wound up as LBJ's chief problem, too; he would have signed the air pact much sooner were it not for continuing Soviet belligerency —including shooting down some of our unarmed aircraft over East Germany.

These trigger-happy manifestations hadn't occurred when I left Washington for Moscow aboard the FAA's Lockheed Jetstar. We included my wife in the official party, a decision that drew some press and congressional criticism—which I had expected and didn't give a damn about. Doris had never been to the Soviet Union, and with her interest in internationalism and peace equal to my own, it would have been cruelty to leave her behind. We were a hopeful, excited group. Also aboard were George Prill, the FAA's director of flight standards; Ray Maloy, chief of the Agency's International Affairs Division; Tex Melugin and George Orenge, two of the FAA's finest pilots; flight engineer Isaac Newton Ebbs; navigator Romney Patterson, and a young, able Soviet specialist from the State Department.

Before departure, I met with some experts on the Soviet Union at the CIA to find out if there was anything we should be looking for—not in the sense of spying, but with the thought that we might inadvertently pick up some information of value to our intelligence boys. Their only advice was to watch the patterns that appeared on our weather radar after we crossed the Soviet border.

"If it looks like something Picasso or Dali might have painted," one of them said, "you'll know they're jamming your radar."

We also read all the available information on Soviet civil aviation—and what there was would have fitted comfortably into a condensed version of the *Reader's Digest*. The best book ever written on the subject unfortunately was published three years after our flight to the Soviet Union—John Stroud's amazingly thorough *Soviet Transport Aircraft Since 1945,* originally published in England. I wish the voluminous data and material gathered by this fine British aviation expert had been available to us when we were planning our trip. As it was, I found it incredible how little the West knew about Soviet commercial aviation—thanks entirely to the Soviet penchant for secrecy.

We reached Moscow in stages, by way of Goose Bay, Keflavik, London, Berlin, and Stockholm. At the latter stop we dropped off navigator Patterson and picked up a Soviet navigator and Soviet radio operator to aid us on the two-hour flight to the Soviet capital. They were pleasant enough fellows but they didn't speak much English; mostly they'd nod and smile while indicating a course-change direction, left or right so many degrees. The course numbers were about all we could get out of them.

Before leaving Stockholm, we had made a point of talking to some Swedish aviation officials about the problems of flying into the Soviet Union. The Swedes probably had compiled more experience in this area than anyone else, and they told us some hair-raising tales of Soviet air-traffic control. Soviet air maps (the counterparts of our fine Jeppesen airway charts), we were warned, were out of date. They had Instrument Landing Systems (ILS) but they hadn't been put into commission yet, according to our Swedish friends. And not even the Swedish pilots had been able to learn whether the Soviets were using any navigation aid other than the pre-World War II nondirectional beacons. We learned that if the weather was bad at Moscow, we'd be brought in by Ground Controlled Approach (GCA)—a system dating back to World War II. (With GCA, an approaching aircraft is monitored by ground radar; the controller tells the pilot the direction and altitude to fly, if he's lined up with the assigned runway, and whether his glide slope path is too high or too low.)

I had no objections to a GCA-guided landing, but our non-English-speaking "crew members" posed a problem bordering on the hazardous. In a GCA landing, a pilot literally is "talked down" to his assigned runway, and we had a definite language barrier in our Jetstar cockpit. Our advisers had assured us that the English deficiencies of our new navigator and radio operator wouldn't make any difference because the Soviet ATC personnel would communicate with us in English. Unfortunately, as soon as we crossed the Soviet border, all we heard was Russian.

We asked the radio operator, in effect, "Where the hell are all the English-speaking controllers?" Both he and the navigator, through our diplomat-on-board interpreter, kept reassuring us that we'd be getting instructions in English as we approached closer to the Moscow airport. We never did; the first English we heard was from the American Embassy personnel who greeted us after we landed. And the landing itself may have been unique in aviation history; God knows, it was about the slowest, most prolonged approach I had ever made, and in this case I guess "unique" is synonymous with "hairy."

When we realized that all the promises of English-speaking controllers were about as accurate as Russia's claim to have invented the airplane, we had to take rather drastic action. The weather was overcast, with a six-hundred-foot ceiling—nothing to worry about under normal conditions but sufficiently poor to warrant a GCA approach. And this called for voluminous dialogue in Russian. We summoned our debonair Foreign Service officer to the cockpit, where I was in the left seat and Tex was acting as my copilot. This put five people into a cockpit designed to carry two. All we could do was turn up the volume of our radio receiver and hope that the GCA controller's instructions, complete gibberish to Tex and me, could be strained through the Soviet radio operator/U.S. diplomat combination fast enough to keep us from landing atop the Kremlin. I still remember the way Tex and I were shaking our heads as we made our final approach—in what seemed to be slow motion.

I went to Moscow with some specific goals. First, I wanted to exchange information, particularly in the area of safety, and I was fully prepared to tell the Soviets anything they wanted to know. Unhappily, my intentions weren't reciprocated, and it was their very reluctance to discuss the subject that convinced me their safety record wasn't as bright as they claimed.

I wanted to move forward to a possible exchange of air service between our two countries under the tentative bilateral agreement already on the books. Some progress was made but not enough to let me return to Washington with glowing optimism.

The same was true for another goal—to lay the groundwork for the Soviet Union's entry into the International Civil Aviation Organization (ICAO) by helping them with technical standardization. If they were to join the international aviation family someday, they would have to comply with its established standards in such areas as navigation aids. I also wanted to sound them out on the possibility of setting mutual U.S. and Soviet airworthiness standards, looking ahead to the day when Soviet airliners would have to comply with certain American regulations and our transports with theirs.

This was a touchy field. The Soviets felt that even talking about the subject was a reflection on their airworthiness criteria. They saw no reason to adopt our standards because they were convinced that in many ways their airworthiness requirements were tougher than ours. In the physical aspects, they were right; I found that Soviet-built and Soviet-designed airliners were built like tanks, with far more structural redundancy than in U.S. transports. This didn't mean they were safer, as I tried to point out; in fact, their undue emphasis on strength made their aircraft overweight, uneconomical to operate, and harder to fly. Some of their planes, for example, had cast-iron toilets, with the virtue of great durability but the bigger liability of a weight penalty. Incidentally, the few Aeroflot stewardesses we saw were built like the planes they worked on—some of them could have played defensive tackle for the Washington Redskins. Aeroflot subsequently adopted more of the West's pulchritudinous standards for flight attendants, but at the time of our visit they were being chosen for their ability to lift heavy weights and handle unruly passengers, male or female. In truth, they were not just stewardesses but also a part of state security.

I wanted badly to find out anything I could on two new airliners the Soviets were rumored to be developing. One was the Soviet SST, the TU-144. Our hosts obviously were not about to make me privy to any confidential information, but they did indicate they were working on a supersonic transport and expressed enough pride and confidence to convince me they'd be flying one by the early 1970s—and they met that deadline with margin to spare. They were almost as coy about the second transport on my "shopping list"—the IL-62, which turned out to be almost a carbon copy of Britain's fine VC-10. The two planes, each with four aft-mounted engines, looked like twins at first glance, but there was no doubt that the VC-10, at that stage, was the superior aircraft.

While I was not allowed to see even a sketch of the TU-144, Soviet aviation officials did condescend to let me give the IL-62 a cursory inspection. The one I saw had some noticeable scratches and dents on the aft fuselage; apparently it had been involved in a hard landing or perhaps a minor accident. Outwardly it was an impressive piece of machinery, but we heard reports that its stall characteristics were giving the Soviets headaches. They didn't seem too confident about the plane and absolutely refused to let me fly it.

I went as high as I could with this request, short of appealing to the Soviet Premier himself. After being turned down on lower levels, I brought up the subject of an IL-62 test flight with my Soviet counterpart, Minister of Civil Aviation Yevgenyi Loginov, a dashing, personable fellow who enjoyed his vodka and his flying.

"Comrade," I announced, "I'd sure like to fly that airplane."

"Mr. Halaby's a frustrated test pilot," Ray Maloy explained eagerly.

Loginov wouldn't have let Lyndon Johnson aboard the IL-62 at that stage, not with all its teething troubles. But he did grant me permission to fly the transport that hopefully would be flying a route to the United States—the giant, four-engine TU-114, which was the largest propeller-driven airplane ever built. It is a prop-jet carrying up to 224 passengers, its most unusual feature being counterrotating props hitched to turbine engines. From all I could ascertain, this dual-prop arrangement was necessitated by the aircraft's great weight—until the Boeing 747 came along, the TU-114 was the world's heaviest as well as largest airliner. (The Germans had tried counterprops on a World War II bomber and had nothing but misery with the design.)

Most Soviet Union transports come from one of two lineages: They're either a copy of Western—usually United States or United Kingdom—airplanes or they're modified versions of Soviet-designed military planes. The Soviets have, for example, two transports almost identical to the DC-3 and Convair 240. But their first operational jetliner, the TU-104, is a civil version of a medium-range Soviet bomber. Likewise the TU-114 had a military predecessor, the TU-20 long-range bomber.

I truly appreciated the chance to fly what was then the queen of

Aeroflot's fleet, but the plane itself was a huge disappointment. It seemed to be a structural engineer's dream—heavy and enormously strong—but a pilot's nightmare. Control forces were extremely heavy, and there was no doubt the plane was overweight—our takeoff roll seemed to last forever on this ground-loving beast, and we were flying almost empty, at that. It handled like a Mack truck.

Instrumentation seemed good, better than I had expected; I had been told that air-transport instrumentation was noticeably inferior on Soviet airliners, but that wasn't the case with the TU-114. I didn't get a chance to put the weather radar into operation, but reportedly Soviet radar—usually "chin-mounted" under the aircraft's nose—had superior definition to our own sets.

The flight engineer had a unique position: he sat in a literal hole, on a level just below that of the cockpit, and faced rearward, toward the cabin. He controlled the power—all prop and thrust levers—a duty apparently dictated by the TU-114's stiff handling characteristics. The pilots had to keep both hands on the control yokes and left the throttles to the flight engineer—giving him the correct settings orally!

For all its immense size, the TU-114 overall was primitive by American standards in many respects. Obviously the Soviets could have done better if they hadn't been concentrating so much on military aircraft, missiles, and space. They proved this with their SST, brought out about the same time as the British-French Concorde. And their latest transports, I find from recent visits, are much like ours in flight characteristics, cabin decor, and structural design—which even before the Soviet Union joined the ICAO was beginning to coincide with Western standards. The days of the cast-iron toilet seem over.

But at the time of my visit Soviet civil aviation was just starting a reform movement. When I arranged a meeting with Ivan Dementiev, Minister of Aviation Production, he made it clear he didn't want airline officials interfering with transport design or production. This attitude would have been heresy in the United States, where most of the great airliners had been designed and built in accordance with FAA air carrier specifications; not until Aeroflot itself began a modernization program did the "go away and don't bother me" philosophy of their designers change. Dementiev, incidentally, told me that the Soviet aircraft industry could turn out as good a product as Boeing or Douglas anytime it wanted to—a boast that the TU-144 may show was not completely empty. From what I observed at that time of Soviet transport planes, their SST represented a quantum leap in technology—but thirteen years later it still is not operating on the world's airways.

We were interested in meeting Soviet aviation people as well as seeing and flying their aircraft. Perhaps to assuage our disappointment over the IL-62 refusal, they did finally consent to let us talk to some pilots and controllers. In the course of meeting the latter we visited a control center where we got additional evidence of how far behind the Soviets were in so many civil aviation aspects. The controllers seemed highly competent, but the tools with which they had to work would have sent their U.S. counterparts nightly to a bar. Some of their communications were being sent via Morse code by hand-operated transmitter!

I was surprised at the relatively lofty social position Aeroflot pilots enjoyed. Many of them had cars, for example—a privilege only a few Soviet citizens were accorded. We interviewed some of the pilots at the airport, and while we never did visit them at home, we were told they had far above-average living quarters. When I asked one of them how he rated an automobile, he replied blandly: "Well, we have to get to and from the airport, you know."

From all indications, their training was most adequate and similar to that given to Western airline crews in at least one respect— they started out on smaller equipment and graduated to larger aircraft as they gained experience and seniority. Their required rest periods and on-duty hours were comparable to our own regulations. Aeroflot's veterans all are ex-military, but airline officials told us that many of the younger pilots were 100 per cent civilian-trained.

Aeroflot itself is easily the world's most unusual airline in that it is not just an air carrier but also the national aviation system. Its airline activities are just one facet of its many activities—crop dusting, general aviation, helicopter operations, weather research, and aerial ambulance service. In brief, in Soviet aviation, if it isn't a military operation, it's Aeroflot. It was said in 1963 to have more than a thousand planes in its air-carrier division and some three thousand overall. Reportedly it carried about fifty million passengers a year, a fourth of U.S. traffic volume in a fleet half the size of all U.S. airlines combined. As a state-owned airline, Aeroflot is under the direct control of the Ministry of Civil Aviation (the Minister is also its chief executive); the only analogy I can draw to emphasize the scope of this huge organizational setup is a situation wherein all U.S. scheduled carriers, general aviation, supplementals, FAA, CAB, and NTSB were under a single federal departmental official.

On my 1968 visit to Moscow, some changes in attitude already had occurred. We had been seven years without implementation of the bilateral pact, and such Cold War stresses as the Cuban crisis and the Berlin blockade were history. Pan Am's Juan Trippe was anxious to start reciprocal service between the United States and the Soviet Union, and the Soviets seemed just as anxious. We had intensive talks with Loginov, dangling some attractive bait in the form of an offer to help the Soviets build modern hotels—poor hotels being one of their major drawbacks in attracting tourists. Loginov's interest in this was the best indication of the altered atmosphere. An American-designed hotel in Moscow was discussed, although I suggested that Leningrad was a more logical first choice; I couldn't see the Soviets allowing an American-created hotel to be erected in their own capital. Despite Loginov's interest, however, this bait was never grabbed. Intourist, the Soviet tourist organization that controlled the Soviet hotel business, would have no part of aid from Pan Am's Inter·Continental Hotels Division, and Loginov, for all his influence, got nowhere with his own hotel people or the Kremlin.

The improved cordiality notwithstanding, we found we still had a long way to go. When Trippe suggested that Pan Am and Aeroflot pool their planes for the proposed service, he got a flat rejection. Loginov, on his part, evidenced great interest in obtaining more than just landing rights in New York—he thought it would be an admirable idea to let Aeroflot also come into Washington and fly across the United States to West Coast cities and maybe even to inland points. We knew this would have been totally unacceptable not just to the State and Defense departments but also to practically the entire congressional membership. We already suspected that the Soviets couldn't resist trying a little espionage on what was supposed to be a strictly commercial venture; TU-114's flying from Murmansk over Canada and then down the U.S. East Coast to Havana had been observed "straying" into U.S. territory —we always assumed with surveillance gear on board.

But some progress was made in that 1968 trip, enough to pave the way for eventual implementation of the bilateral agreement. Even as I write this, Aeroflot not only is flying into New York but also is supposed to begin service to Washington. This, along with Red China's purchase of Boeing 707s and joint U.S.-Soviet talks on mutual aviation problems, shows how far we have come with Communist civil aviation since that 1963 trip when we really didn't get much more out of the Soviets than free tickets to the Bolshoi.

It was around the time of my first trip to the Soviet Union that I began thinking of my own future. I didn't want to, nor could I, stay in government service forever; in fact, when I took the FAA job, I had in my mind only committed myself to JFK for a four-year stint, although I suppose I would have stayed through a Kennedy second term if he had asked it of me. His death seemed to have taken some of the drive and dedication out of the New Frontiersmen. Furthermore, I was getting tired, and I sure wasn't getting any richer.

In December of 1964, after Lyndon Johnson buried Barry Goldwater in a Democratic landslide and won the presidency in his own right, I was called down to the ranch for a budget meeting. I managed to get LBJ alone for a few moments and confided my desire to leave the FAA. I told him I had accomplished in four years almost all of what I had promised Kennedy I would try to accomplish; four years was enough, I said, and I felt I had done my duty.

"I won't hear of it, Jeeb," Johnson drawled. "We won't even talk about it."

After the first of the year, I wrote him a letter requesting that he accept my resignation sometime in the spring, leaving it up to him to fix the date. It took him several weeks to answer, and his reply was the same as he had given me at the ranch. I finally had to tell Jack Valenti, one of LBJ's most trusted aides, that I was deadly

173

serious about leaving and wanted to see the President personally to discuss it. Jack asked me why I wanted out.

"Well, one of the reasons is that I need to make some money," I confessed, "and I've had some quite attractive overtures. I want my resignation on the record so that there can be no criticism."

This was true. Early in 1965 I had organized a conference at the FAA called the "Annual Shareholders Meeting of the Aviation Community"—a kind of formalized bull session about mutual aviation problems. Among those attending was Harold Gray, newly elected President of Pan American World Airways. Gray was impressed by the meeting, sufficiently so, he later told me, that he returned to New York and told Juan Trippe I had done an excellent job of bringing the aviation community together—the right people at the right time and at the right place. Gray suggested I might be considered for an executive post at Pan Am, and Trippe was intrigued. Trippe was still smarting over the loss of an able lieutenant, Roger Lewis, who had left Pan Am to take over General Dynamics. The old Pan Am chieftain felt he had a gap in the organization that should be filled, and he must have sensed that his political luck in Washington had run out.

He began to woo me, calling me frequently during those early months of 1965 on some flimsy excuse and coming down to Washington on several occasions to have breakfast or lunch with me at the famed (or infamous) Suite 1040 at the Statler Hilton, a room that Pan Am kept permanently and that was the site of many closed-door sessions. Trippe was at his charming, most persuasive best. At first he insisted he just wanted to talk about various aviation matters, such as air-traffic control, Soviet relations, and the supersonic transport, in which we had a strong common interest. But then he began to indicate he had something more serious in mind—namely, my employment.

Even though I had indicated publicly that I intended to resign at the end of four years, I was worried about even discussing a job with Pan Am while I was still running the FAA and also, literally, still regulating Trippe's own airline. I never committed myself and, in fact, kept steering our conversation into safer channels. Moreover, other opportunities needed to be explored.

Only my wife and my executive secretary, Mary Alexander,

174

knew of these confidential meetings with Trippe. Because of my own insistence on keeping everything above board and not wanting to get committed, Trippe did not make a job offer—he merely let me know there would be something more definite as soon as I was willing to talk about it. From the first meeting with Trippe, I saw to it that my deputy, General Grant, handled all FAA matters involving Pan Am. And that was the situation when I told Valenti I wanted to see the President about resigning.

LBJ took his own sweet time about agreeing to meet with me. Typically, he growled to Jack that he couldn't understand why I was in such an all-fired hurry to leave his Administration. He became very irritated at and suspicious of any Kennedy appointee trying to resign. Yet when he finally gave Valenti a green light for my appointment, he couldn't have been friendlier. It was one of those rather flattering arm-twisting sessions for which Johnson was so famous. He said he didn't want me to leave his Administration and that he never held it against me for ruffling Gonzales' feathers.

"You've done a fabulous job, you know more about airplanes than anyone else, the SST is just getting started, and I want you to keep going on that," he said earnestly. "And remember, you've got good support on the Hill—Senator Magnuson, Representative Thomas, and quite a few others. You've got to stay, Jeeb."

We were alone in his inner office and I can't remember how long he actually talked, in a one-sided but touching whirlwind of arguments.

"Well, Mr. President," I finally managed to say, "I'll certainly think it over again, but I do need to get out. I'm tired, I'm running out of dough, and I hope I'll have some opportunities outside."

"Do you have any now?" LBJ asked quickly.

"I've been told by a couple of people that when I leave the FAA, they want to talk to me. One of them is Juan Trippe."

"I've heard about that," the President snapped. "You think it over."

I did, but in two weeks I saw him again and told him I had to go. I had been warned by some of his intimates that if I stuck to my guns after all the effort he had made to keep me, I was not going to be classed as a beloved ex-colleague. They were right, and this is what made my last months at the FAA rather bitter and unhappy. My relations with the President weren't helped by his difficulty in finding a replacement for me. Once the word was out that I was leaving, various congressmen were pressuring the White House with their own appointee ideas—Senator Mike Monroney, for example, was backing Bill Schulte, one of my own top deputies. I had recommended Alan Boyd for the FAA post, but this was stymied at the time Johnson decided to name him Under Secretary of Commerce for Transportation. I urged Boyd for Under Secretary post, but I would rather have seen him get the FAA job, because I hoped that from there he might go on to become the first Secretary of Transportation, which he did. I had boomed and groomed Boyd for the FAA job, in effect, keeping him informed of every major Agency development and having him attend frequent meetings with key FAA officials.

All the congressional pressure irritated LBJ, who thought the FAA appointment was taking up too much of his time and wasting political energy. Gonzales didn't help much, either; *Life* printed an article in which Gonzales quoted the President to the effect that he was getting rid of me because of how I had treated the Texas congressman, and LBJ never bothered to deny the story. Gonzales had absolutely nothing to do with my leaving the FAA. I was mad enough to ask Valenti and a few other White House insiders to either have the President issue a denial of the Gonzales story or make some comment as to its untruth when I officially turned the FAA over to my successor.

The business of choosing and nominating a successor got downright touchy. Boyd was out of the running—maybe because he was my personal choice, and hell had no fury like an irritated LBJ. Schulte was the most active and open candidate, but I didn't think he was qualified for the job, and I kept having to tell this to the President's inner staff every time his name came up. Eventually Johnson turned for advice to a man he admired and trusted implicitly—Defense Secretary Robert McNamara, whom he had consulted on many nondefense matters previously. McNamara suggested Air Force General William F. McKee, known to all as "Bozo" McKee.

Officially, McKee's appointment was recommended by John W. Macy, Sr., chairman of the Civil Service Commission and the President's chief executive recruiter. But there was no doubt that McNamara had a heavy hand in the appointment. Macy's private memorandum submitted to Johnson, one that urged the naming of McKee as my successor, included this from the Secretary of Defense:

"In my twenty-two years of general association with General McKee, in a variety of roles, I have considered him to be one of the strongest managers in the service of his country."

I hadn't even heard McKee was being considered, largely because I never expected another military man to get the FAA post. I knew Bozo to be an exceptionally capable administrator and an expert on procurement. Although he was the only Air Force general who never learned how to fly, he was highly regarded for his administrative abilities. My own choice, after Boyd, was Francis Fox, general manager of the Los Angeles County system, who I thought would have made an exceptional FAA chief. He was a proven aviation executive knowledgeable in virtually every phase of aviation, and a progressive Democrat.

By coincidence, I was with Fox at the time McKee's appointment was announced—to my great surprise. Fox happened to be president of the American Association of Airport Executives and had invited me to address the group's annual meeting in Fort Worth. Francis knew I had recommended him for my job and was hoping for such an announcement when I flew into Fort Worth. As was the custom, there was an informal reception for the administrator in a hotel suite, and we were having some quiet drinks when we got word the President was holding a news conference and would make some announcements.

We turned on a television set and saw six men seated in a row behind the President—Boyd, McKee, and four others whose names I can't remember. LBJ introduced each one, and while I mentally cheered Boyd's appointment as Under Secretary of Commerce for Transportation, I was stunned when the President announced McKee as my successor. Obviously I hadn't been very influential in the choice, and I was further embarrassed at not knowing that McKee even was in the running.

I recall mumbling something to Fox when the telephone rang

177

and someone told me the White House was calling. It was Valenti's secretary.

"Mr. Halaby, the President is going to name General McKee as your successor and asked me to call you and tell you that," she said.

"Thanks very much," I replied. "I just saw it on television."

We went downstairs and at the end of my speech I announced McKee's appointment—after which I received a standing ovation from an audience which, with a few exceptions, never realized how embarrassing the transition had been for me. I had an appointment in Mexico City that same night and by chance our routing took us over the LBJ ranch. I called in from thirty thousand feet, got Valenti, and asked him to give the President a message: I would co-operate in every way to make the succession effective. I was greatly relieved to be returning to private life, and I was most grateful that a new administrator had been named.

I had resigned of my own accord, but apparently under un-friendly circumstances, and I really didn't have a firm idea of what I was really going to do. Furthermore, I dreaded the ceremonial change of command when I would have to be present to see my successor sworn in. It bothered me that the President hadn't acknowledged my resignation with the traditional letter, accepting it with "greatest regret," or "personal regret," depending on the President's attitude toward an individual's departure. Maybe I was lucky I didn't get the letter, but I was disappointed—I had done my best for more than four years in a difficult job, and I didn't consider myself disloyal to LBJ for quitting.

I wasn't even sure I'd be invited to McKee's July 1, 1965, swearing-in ceremony scheduled for the Cabinet Room. That I was, I suspect, was due to the intervention of Valenti and two other White House aides, Howard Busby and Bill Moyers. They had not only urged the President to invite me but also suggested that he acknowledge publicly in some way that I had done a reasonably good job and wasn't being fired because Gonzales had forced him to do it. I sometimes doubt whether LBJ's heart was in it, but he was gracious and cordial to me. And he read with apparent feeling and sincerity a statement that Valenti and Busby had prepared for him:

178

"This is a ceremony of more than usual significance," LBJ began with a wisp of a smile on his lips. "It is one of the relatively rare occasions when a native of the state of Texas is leaving the government voluntarily. I hope that none will regard that as an ominous link in an ominous chain."

There were some chuckles from the House and Senate leaders present in the Cabinet Room. The President continued:

"Jeeb Halaby gave up the quiet, everyday pleasures of being a test pilot to face the perils and dangers of bureaucratic life in Washington. But every passenger who flies across the country in a plane owes him a deep debt of personal gratitude. In four years of dedicated, tireless service he has done much to assure public confidence in the safety of air travel. By the inspiration of his vigorous leadership, he has greatly advanced the performance of the fine Agency that he has headed."

Now there was more than just the trace of a smile.

"And certainly," Johnson drawled, "Mr. Halaby has won a place in history as the first regulator—in my memory—to fine himself for violating one of his own regulations."

Loud laughter, in which I joined ruefully.

"I am grateful to him," LBJ concluded, "for his willingness to serve his country by remaining at his post at great personal sacrifice, and I wish him every success ahead."

I appreciated those words. But I appreciated even more a couple of other events that occurred in my last days in office. At the instigation of Jerry Hannifin, *Time*'s very able aviation expert, a group of Washington aviation writers had gotten together to throw me a small bash at the National Aviation Club. Not one of them was earning a hell of a lot of money, but they all chipped in for a sumptuous dinner and a satisfactory quantity of booze—none of which, I'm reasonably sure, ever appeared on their expense accounts. It was a gesture of respect and maybe even friendship, and I was touched. In fact I was on the verge of tears when, toward the end of the evening, Hannifin handed me a beautifully gift-wrapped box and intoned a few solemn words to the effect that the news media didn't want me to leave office without an expression of its goodwill and high regard. I tore open the wrappings with trembling fingers, groped through the many layers of tissue paper, and came up with their expression of goodwill and high regard.

It was a model of a United Viscount, with the right wingtip very slightly but only too visibly damaged!

A few days later, just before relinquishing the reins to Bozo McKee, I was flying to Washington from Los Angeles, where I had just presented a medal to Captain Charles Kimes of Pan Am; he had safely landed a 707 with one third of a wing torn off by a fire and explosion, a masterful job of airmanship. I couldn't have picked a better occasion for my last official act.

We flew back in N-1, the FAA's Lockheed Jetstar, and all the way across the country the various centers were giving me personal messages. I had only to ask for a frequency change or some kind of clearance, and some unseen, metallic voice would tell me good-bye. . . .

"You sure gave it a try, chief." . . . "Thanks for all you did for us, Jeeb." . . . "Good luck and God bless you, Jeeb."

And God bless those great guys, too. I *had* tried to do something for them and for all aviation. But I also knew much had been left undone. As Quesada had thoroughly briefed and prepared me for the takeover, I had given McKee the same courtesy—knowing there could be no transition without inheritance of some unsolved problems.

And one of the unfinished tasks I left behind was the controversial supersonic transport program.

180

CHAPTER SIX

I was working for Laurance Rockefeller when I saw my first supersonic transport plane, or rather a sketch of one.

That was in the spring of 1955. With a group of Eastern Air Lines officials and stockholders I visited Lockheed prior to Eastern's purchase of the prop-jet Electra. Rockefeller was there and so was Captain Eddie Rickenbacker. Included on the agenda was a stop at Lockheed's design center, Kelly Johnson's famed "skunk works," where Rickenbacker got curious.

"Kelly," he asked with a grin, "what have you got for the future on that drawing board of yours?"

Johnson reached under a stack of specifications for the Electra and pulled out a penciled sketch, which he passed around.

"The supersonic transport," he explained as the group examined the drawing. When it was handed to me, I whistled. An incredibly beautiful, arrow-shaped plane, very futuristic and almost of the Buck Rogers variety, yet somehow conveying the impression that it wasn't just a wild dream.

"Captain," Kelly remarked to Rickenbacker, "we'll have one of these before long, and you ought to be the first one to order it."

"I'm having enough trouble making up my mind whether to buy

the Electra," Rickenbacker snorted, "so don't bother me with the year 2000."

As I write this, we're still twenty-three years away from the year 2000, and the supersonic transport is a technical reality. The British-French Concorde is carrying passengers on scheduled flights, and the Soviets are hoping shortly to do the same with their SST. Our own supersonic transport program is stalled, the victim of many factors, ranging from an ecology uprising to poor selection and timing. As one who helped lead the fight for the project, I can only say that I'm not sorry I got into the scrap, and yet I'm also not deeply sorry we lost. Considering the current economic state of international air operations, an American SST would have been a financial disaster for all concerned: manufacturer, government, and airlines alike. The long-haul, world-girdling carriers like Pan Am and TWA, whose overseas routes are ideal for SST operations, would have been the least able among the airlines to afford to buy them. In 1977, they would be even less able to pay the fuel bill.

But at the time I got involved in the supersonic transport project, it really looked like the airplane of the future—in fact the inevitable airplane of the immediate future. It was a logical expression of faith in aviation's progress—the faith of the airman himself. In 1945, when I flew that YP-80 across the country at speeds of 450 miles per hour, the queen of the U.S. commercial air fleet was a 180-mile-an-hour DC-3. A modern jetliner goes coast-to-coast in less than five hours at 550, but in 1963 I had flown an Air Force SR-71, which could at 2,000 miles per hour traverse the continent in an hour and fifteen minutes. To the airman, progress and speed had been synonymous; growth and compressed time, identical. The airman saw progress and growth as inevitable; the economist and the politician did not. The airman regarded swifter transportation as a logical goal; economics and politics perceived it as merely complex, costly, and difficult. To me in 1961, a man of aviation, the supersonic transport was just as sensible as the DC-6 and Constellation replacing the DC-3, and then being supplanted by the 707 and DC-8. Until 1970, civil aviation always had used speed as its primary yardstick of achievement, and in fact so had the public.

The U.S. supersonic program dates back to the fifties on National Advisory Committee on Aeronautics (NACA) later to become NASA, North American, and Lockheed drawing boards, and to 1959, when Pete Quesada proposed that the government spend $2 million out of civil and military funds for research on and development of an SST—the technology to foal from the mammoth B-70 supersonic bomber. Quesada's plan never got off the ground, thanks to the almost total indifference of the Eisenhower administration and opposition by Secretary of Defense Thomas Gates and Budget Director Maurice Stans. But there was no such indifference on the part of President Kennedy, whose interest in a supersonic transport undoubtedly stemmed from the knowledge that both the British and French—and probably the Soviets—had begun preliminary design studies that might be far ahead of anything on our own drawing boards.

I know that when we presented the program to the President and Budget Director David Bell in the spring of 1961, Kennedy was taken with the dynamism of exploring this incredibly complex endeavor. Bell was receptive too, impressed by the fact that the SST was no Buck Rogersish flight into fancy but a definite, technical possibility already based on solid military experience in the realm of supersonic flight. My recommendation to JFK was that we seek from Congress $13 million for preliminary design work on a steel-and-titanium SST capable of cruising at Mach 2.5 (roughly 1,700 miles per hour) and carrying between 150 and 175 passengers. It would have transoceanic nonstop capability—New York–Paris/ London, and West Coast–Hawaii. It would have to be designed to use existing major airports and generate no more noise than conventional jets.

Its climb after takeoff would be steep and fast; it would fly at subsonic speeds up to thirty-five thousand feet and then accelerate to supersonic levels as it reached cruising altitudes that would range between sixty-five thousand and seventy-five thousand feet. Landing speeds would have to be only slightly higher than for regular jetliners—again, so the SST could operate in the conventional-airport environment. Such an aircraft should be able, noise permitting, to cross the United States in just under two hours.

On the basis of our optimism and twenty years of research that had been going on at the National Advisory Committee for Aeronautics and Wright Aero-Development Laboratories, plus considerable work from North American on the B-70 and Boeing, Lockheed, Douglas, Convair, Pratt & Whitney, and General Electric, Congress decided in principle that we should proceed with a $20 million appropriation for the first phase of the SST program, but not without some static from lawmakers with heavy Air Force leanings. They went along with the Air Force's contention that a civilian supersonic plane should await full development of the B-70 supersonic bomber, just as the original 707 was a fallout from a jet tanker designed for the Air Force. Their attitude was understandable; President Eisenhower had canceled the B-70 development program for economy reasons, and they figured the only way President Kennedy might be persuaded to revive the B-70 project was to declare the dividend of a commercial application for an SST.

Opposition also was voiced by several high-ranking aviation executives and ex-officials who felt that an SST was strictly a private-industry baby; they objected strongly to any federal financing in the development and "production" of commercial aircraft. In fact, Quesada shared this philosophy—he did not seek to go beyond federal funding of basic research and did not fight very hard for that.

The Pentagon's position could charitably be labeled lukewarm—Department of Defense brass could find no military requirement for a high-speed *transport* and thus were indifferent toward the SST project.

There even was considerable divergence of views among those who supported SST development. In the early stages, NASA felt that having done a lot of basic research, it should develop the "research" airplane on its own through the prototype stage, much as it had designed and test-flown the experimental X-15. The result was a loose and friendly compromise arrangement to "proceed in formation":—The FAA would provide program leadership and financial support, the Defense Department would contribute technical and administrative support, and NASA would give us research and overall technical help. Having achieved a treaty among these great tribes, it was left to me to carry the lobbying ball for the first four years of the SST program—in the 1961–65 period. The highest Air Force officials favored the SST only pro forma, giving the B-70 a far higher priority. I could count only on my old friend Deputy Secretary of Defense Roswell Gilpatrick, who furnished me with a letter generally supporting the SST program.

I recall one incident that occurred during the dedication ceremonies at Dulles Airport. I was sitting with President Kennedy, former President Eisenhower, and General Curtis LeMay, and was startled to hear JFK ask LeMay, "General, what do you think of Halaby's SST?"

LeMay chomped down hard on the cigar invariably jutting belligerently from his mouth.

"Well, Mr. President," he growled, "I think it's a good idea, but I don't think we should do anything about it until we've got a fleet of B-70s flying."

JFK chuckled, only too cognizant of the pressure being generated by the Air Force, industry, and a large segment of Congress for him to go all-out on B-70 production.

"Why don't you take on the SST project?" he asked LeMay.

"Mr. President, I'll be glad to after we have all the B-70s we need in our inventory."

End of conversation.

So it was clear we were virtually alone. In fact, all I had at this starting point was the President's tentative approval in principle to a staff of not more than eight men, an uneasy alliance with DOD and NASA, and some rather grudgingly appropriated funds. What we sought at this stage were some answers to major questions: Could a supersonic transport be built that met all standards of safety, ecology, and profitability? If we got affirmative answers out of the first phase—namely, a comprehensive study of these three key areas—we could proceed in two other areas—get the prototype development going, and engender public and industry support for the project.

The indispensable parties to this experimental study partnership had to be the companies who would make and those who would operate the supersonic transport. I already had met personally with the heads of the major airlines, getting their comments and advice on what the SST program should entail. From these early discussions, I was able to tell the President that the airlines were supporting the project but were not overly enthusiastic about buying the SST until they had absorbed the enormous costs of transitioning to subsonic jets. I also informed JFK that the manufacturers were willing to share the financial burden of research but not take on the whole funding responsibility. They left no doubt that under no circumstances would they undertake the technical and financial risks of building an SST alone or in combination; they insisted on heavy federal commitments, and that was that. I urged them repeatedly but to no avail that several companies pool their efforts; I even offered to get a Justice Department ruling that would exempt them from antitrust liability, but they all insisted it was too big a job for private industry to tackle on its own. William M. Allen, the lawyer-chief of Boeing, was particularly adamant on this point.

The group that General Cook and I put together was a dedicated, experienced, and penetrating team. Most of the men serving were old and trusted colleagues of both Cook and myself, such as Ted Wright, former CAA administrator and president of Cornell Aeronautical Laboratories; John Stack, former director of supersonic research at the National Advisory Committee on Aeronautics and later NASA's director of aeronautical research; Jim Mitchell, vice president of Chase Manhattan Bank and an expert on aviation financing; Bill Harding, whose role as chairman of the White House Aviation Facilities Study Group already has been described; Charles Froesch, vice president of engineering for Eastern Air Lines; Captain Robert Buck, one of TWA's top technical experts and a superb regular-line captain as well; Al White, chief B-70 test pilot who was one of my students in World War II; and finally Francis Fox, director of airports for the city of Los Angeles.

This was, indeed, a knowledgeable and skilled cross section of virtually every phase of aviation. A distinguished advisory group was formed, and they listened to the sonic-boom phenomenon, got the views and advice of all the trunk airlines as well as those of the aircraft and engine manufacturers, had talks with British and French SST experts, and held many discussions with various banking and technical groups.

After all this groundwork, the group's verdict was pro-SST. These air-minded men concluded that the United States should

186

proceed with a supersonic transport development program that would cost between $1 billion and $1.5 billion, emphasizing that despite this enormous price tag, it would be worthwhile. They did express serious doubts whether the airlines would be able to pay royalties to the government on the purchase price—a proposal I advanced early in the game to make the SST project more reasonable to Congress and the public, which might have understandable misgivings of Uncle Sam's financing development of a commercial transport for the first time in history. The group didn't think much of the idea because it estimated the direct operating cost of the supersonic transport it had in mind at a substantially higher level than that of the then current subsonic jets.

Having succeeded in obtaining presidential, congressional, and some public support, I recognized that the next step was to strengthen management of the program. I knew I couldn't take on that task myself and run the FAA. The man who had been doing all the preliminary staff work, Lucian Rochte, was an exceptionally able Air Force officer, but he lacked any airline experience and was virtually unknown to the carrier management corps who would be the eventual customers. So I began a quiet but determined search for a program manager.

My instinctive choice was an engineer-manager from the aerospace industry, like Lockheed's Willis Hawkins or Douglas's Robert Hage. But offsetting their ability as the best design engineers and managers around was the obvious conflict of interest; they were certain to get into the airframe competition.

We canvassed the airlines but struck out; they had no men who were both suited for the SST job and also willing to leave their own industry for what had to be a turbulent and controversial role as a political executive. And, as the program began to gain momentum, accompanied by not unfavorable publicity (in those days), more and more Administration officials took increasing interest. A major manifestation of that interest came one day when Ed Welch, executive secretary of the National Aeronautics and Space Council, whose Chairman was Vice President Johnson, called me.

"The Vice President wants to have a presentation of the SST program at the next meeting of the Council," he informed me. "They haven't dealt with any aeronautical matters up to now but

187

the SST seems to be within our charter and I don't think we can neglect this area any longer."

I agreed to make the presentation but with mixed feelings. I welcomed LBJ's support, but I wondered if I should be letting the Council get into the act. I went ahead with the meeting, however, and was pleased to find Johnson highly interested. He listened very carefully to what I said and made several valuable suggestions as to certain additional work that could be done. After the meeting I spent a few moments alone with him, at which time he offered to help in any way he could, both on the Hill and within the Administration.

Fears of LBJ's intervention were expressed not only by Defense Secretary Robert McNamara and NASA chief James Webb but also within the White House itself. One day I was telling a presidential special assistant about the Space Council meeting I had attended and how interested and helpful the Vice President had been.

"My God," he exclaimed, "what's Lyndon Johnson doing getting into that program of yours? I want to tell the boss about this—we don't want him getting involved in any more big projects."

I recognized that reaction as indicative of the suspicion JFK's intimates had about Johnson, fearing his assuming any role other than the traditional—and hoary—Alexander Throttlebottom version of the vice presidency. Yet I also was convinced that the President himself did not share this view. On January 21, 1963, in fact, I received a memorandum from John Kennedy, with copies going to Secretary Rusk; Bob McNamara; Secretary of Commerce Luther Hodges; NASA chief Webb; CAB chairman Boyd; Director Jerome Wiesner of the Office of Science and Technology; new Budget Director Kermit Gordon, who had succeeded David Bell, and Chairman Walter Heller of the Council of Economic Advisers. The memo—which was stimulated by the rapid technical progress and political momentum our program had achieved and by the concern that Ted Sorensen and a few others around the President felt about the rising cost estimates and the true social value of the SST as compared with the other New Frontier programs—made it clear that the President *wanted* a comprehensive interdepartmental review of all SST matters so that major decisions concerning the

188

project would be made "only after the most thorough evaluation of all the probable benefits and costs to the government and to the national economy."

About a month later he sent LBJ a memo assigning him the job of co-ordinating an interdepartmental review of what had been accomplished and what still needed to be done through a special task force.

"If you are agreeable, it would be most helpful to me if you would take the leadership in co-ordinating the recommendations on this matter [those of the various departments and agency heads regarding the SST]. I attach considerable significance to this report and hope that this study can be completed as early as possible," the President requested.

Johnson accepted this challenge immediately, asking me to forward to him and all fourteen members of the committee he set up the results of the study JFK had urged and my own recommendations based on what the study developed. In mid-May I handed Johnson this verdict: The United States should proceed with an SST prototype development program, looking to a potential market of up to 250 airplanes. The Vice President relayed this recommendation to the White House with the task force's endorsement.

The design, speed, and type of structural material to be used—titanium vs. aluminum—would be decided upon completion of a detailed design competition by leading manufacturers. The tentative goal was an SST with a 4,000-mile range, a payload of at least 150 passengers, and a minimum service life of 45,000 hours (about 15 years). It should be operable within existing major airports at costs comparable to subsonic jets and produce sonic booms from a cruising altitude of not more than 1.5 pounds per square foot—the equivalent of a light clap of thunder. I also recommended that an SST Development Authority be established within the FAA, headed by a director to be appointed by the President and confirmed by the Senate. The first project phase would be the design competition and, if successful, the second the construction of a prototype, followed by flight tests.

One thing the Johnson group scrapped was a proposed U.S./Britain/France joint SST program. The British, even before I

189

became head of the FAA, had expressed great interest in possible intergovernmental supersonic collaboration. Their first approach to the United States had been by Peter Thorneycroft, their Minister of Aviation, when he visited Quesada and explored the possibilities for a joint U.S.-U.K. program. Quesada had indicated in late 1960 that the Eisenhower administration was not prepared to proceed with even a study of the supersonic transport at that time, and he therefore saw little basis for American-British collaboration. He also pointed out the very wide gap in technical approach between the British Mach 2 aluminum concept and the American Mach 3 steel-and-titanium concept.

Soon after I came into office, Thorneycroft corresponded with me and then authorized Sir George Edwards, managing director of British Aircraft Corporation, to visit me in Washington. I explained to Edwards that I was always eager to collaborate with the British, as my record prior to World War II and in the Department of Defense on NATO had shown, but that I saw grave difficulties in it for the same reasons Quesada had already cited, and also because of the problem that the United States Government would have in selecting from among several fierce competitors a single engine manufacturer and airplane manufacturer to collaborate with the British concerns. A wonderfully direct, vigorously honest man, Sir George confirmed that the British were only thinking of one engine manufacturer: the Bristol Company, which built the Olympus engine to be used in the British TSR-2 bomber. I said we could not accept that engine outright and would want GE, Pratt & Whitney, Rolls-Royce, and Bristol all to compete in any kind of new engine development program. Edwards felt that this was neither necessary nor financially feasible. I pointed out to him the quite different relationship that British industry bears to the British Government as compared to American industry's relationship to the United States Government. Not only did the British Government control BOAC, the national airline that would buy the transport, but also it was the predominant owner and controller of the entire British airframe and engine-manufacturing industries. The best I could offer was my personal encouragement that he at least discuss with Lockheed, Boeing, and Douglas, plus Pratt & Whitney and General Electric, the chances for possible co-operation with their British competitors. Edwards never got off the ground with them, except to receive assurances that the U.S. firms would share certain technological findings, principally as they related to safety and the sonic-boom problem. Aside from this, I was impressed by Edwards' enthusiasm and determination for supersonic flight; that first meeting with him eventually developed into a friendship based on our mutually high priority for safety in whatever SST would be built.

Later I spoke along the same lines to Georges Hereil, president of France's Sud Aviation. At that time, early in 1961, our view of the embryonic British/French SST program was rather vague. There had been no truly active efforts to marry the British and French projects, but Hereil already was on record urging an international developmental program. He had taken a leaf from the book of KLM's Otto Plesemann, who had first urged a multinational SST at a conference in The Hague in 1959. Plesemann was very strong for the United States of Europe concept, and he was sincerely convinced that not only because of the enormous costs and technical problems needing solution but also for political reasons, the SST should be a joint project of the Western world.

Hereil like Plesemann was articulate, candid, and simultaneously partly idealistic and partly pragmatic. I liked him and his ebullience, and I gave him the same advice: Go talk to Lockheed, Boeing, and Douglas. He did, and like Edwards he found that the American manufacturers preferred to go beyond the conventional aluminum construction planned for the Concorde, into the far more complex and expensive, yet potentially more profitable steel-and-titanium SST—one that would be much faster, longer-ranged, and more durable. Further, both Hereil and Edwards were told politely but bluntly by the U.S. manufacturers that all of them really wanted a new engine developed specifically for commercial SST operations and were opposed to either a U.S. military engine or the Olympus power plant, which had been developed for a British bomber.

Nor were the American companies particularly anxious to divide the market. They considered their concept more competitive in the long run, and this adverse American attitude made the

191

British/French consortium not only more attractive but also essential to those two governments.

First, the physical proximity of the countries made sense out of collaboration and, second, the British had an SST engine, whereas the French did not. Once they failed to find receptivity to a joint program in the United States, they exchanged marriage vows on January 19, 1963. French President Charles DeGaulle announced that while France was opposed to British entry into the Common Market, the French were welcoming its neighbor across the Channel into partnership on the Concorde project.

Since the early 1961 talks we had been following the British and French designers closely. In the spring of 1963, when we were considering the alternative-design concepts for an American prototype, the Concorde shaped up as an aircraft carrying 110 passengers in a rather narrow, cramped cabin with a range of just under 4,000 statute miles. What both impressed and concerned us was the speed of their development work; they literally were cutting metal while we were still scribbling on paper. True, the Concorde appeared to be a relatively limited airplane that was more of an interim SST than the ultimate revolutionary transport we envisioned. The Concorde's Mach 2 capability; its aluminum construction, which put an apparent ceiling on growth possibilities; and its rather high airport noise and sonic-boom-intensity projections all appeared to be major liabilities and definite obstacles to potential viability. Its cruising speed of about 1,200 miles an hour, for example, had to be compared to our own goal of an 1,800-mph aircraft that would carry a greater payload over long distances.

Yet, it was still a real design, not a paper concept. And, when DeGaulle embraced the joint Concorde project, it seemed to trigger competitiveness in John Fitzgerald Kennedy. In fact I think JFK associated the Concorde most with DeGaulle; on more than one occasion, he said, "We'll beat that bastard DeGaulle." Kennedy resented the Frenchman's simultaneous support of the British/French SST and his rejection of the British from the Common Market. Every time I saw the President, from the day DeGaulle made his announcement, he would press me on how our studies were going—and how the British and French were doing, not to mention the Soviets.

192

The former seemed to be doing very well. Concorde project officials were confidently predicting the first test flights by 1967 and the start of scheduled SST commercial service by early 1970. They were indicating a purchase price of a relatively modest $10 million per aircraft, less than half of what we had been projecting for an American SST, although that price tag obviously excluded the massive developmental costs, which were to be absorbed by the British and French governments.

We had scant information on Soviet supersonic transport progress. We had a pretty good idea that they were at least blueprinting an SST, and there was some speculation that it would be a civil adoption of a Soviet supersonic bomber—a usual Soviet format for producing civil transports. We even heard rumors that the Soviets were going to convert a supersonic bomber into a small SST that would speed Khrushchev and other top officials on some spectacular foreign mission. All we knew for sure, however, was that the Soviet Union wanted badly to get into the SST picture, and eventually we were to learn that there were at least two design teams working on two different models, one of which would become the TU-144.

Johnson's own strong support for the SST had been preceded by some bloody infighting within the task force he headed. McNamara made no bones about his opposition to what he regarded as a strictly "commercial project" with no advantages to the military. Kennedy's new budget director, Kermit Gordon, also was against the SST. And a third no-man suddenly surfaced—Under Secretary of Commerce G. Daniel Martin—who picked up a Douglas Aircraft proposal for a five-hundred-passenger transport plane contemplated by the Air Force as a heavy logistics transport. It had the double appeal of joint military/civil application and the prospect of cut-rate air fares in such areas as the transatlantic and transcontinental markets. Douglas, in fact, was talking about the capability of an aircraft this size to reduce one-way transcontinental fares to as low as fifty dollars—in stark contrast to the SST, which at this stage was being talked about as an all-first-class or surcharge plane, as the jets were at first.

Averell Harriman, representing the State Department, was an SST supporter, and so were Dillon of Treasury, Dr. Jerome

Wiesner, the President's science adviser, and the CAB's Alan Boyd—although Boyd said he'd break ranks if the supersonic transport wound up requiring a new federal subsidy or would result in the airlines going back on subsidy. Johnson, I might add, was very much in command of the task-force meetings, open in his personal support of the SST, and emphasizing that his goal was a program on which everyone could agree.

On the eve of the committee's deliberations, I finally settled on a man to head the SST program within the FAA. My choice was a tough, abrupt, no-nonsense guy with considerable airline background—Gordon Bain, who had been my assistant administrator for appraisal for several months. Bain brought a fresh, strong mind into the picture. He had been a top executive with both Slick Airlines and Northwest Airlines as well as a CAB staff member. His government experience also had included a stint with the Budget Bureau as an analyst.

Throughout the course of the task force's meetings and discussions, the Vice President gave Bain and myself every opportunity to present the case for the SST. We initially prepared a two-hundred-page report fully laced with charts, graphs, and statistics. Our strategy was to play down the threat of the Concorde, emphasizing instead the need to advance aviation technology and American prestige to enhance the balance-of-payments situation and to supply new jobs for American industry—the latter a goal that won the late support of the Secretary of Labor, who became convinced the SST would provide about fifty thousand jobs a year for the next decade.

McNamara at our very first session left no doubt that he would be our most formidable opponent. He expressed great reluctance about the SST, arguing that the government should not proceed with the controversial airplane until we had more experience with supersonic flight—a questionable point, I thought, because as of early 1963 we already had compiled thousands of hours in the realm of supersonic military operations. (Even I had a few supersonic flights logged—in the B-58, the F-4, and later the SR-71.) He also advised delaying the SST until the airlines and manufacturers gave us unmistakable assurances that they really wanted the airplane built. McNamara saw no military fallout advantages from

194

development of a civil supersonic aircraft; he held that as a commercial project it should meet all the tests of profitability and yield applied to any business venture. He also informed us that not enough staff work had been done and suggested several additional studies. All this added up to delays, delays, and more delays.

Administrator Webb of NASA was a sleeper at this meeting. He came out strongly for the SST, but in a rather cute way he made it clear that his agency would have to conduct years of basic aeronautical research before a prototype could be built and test-flown—another delay. He also left the door wide open for reassignment of the project from the FAA to NASA, hinting that the SST was more of a research than a developmental project and that NASA could do the job better.

After the session, LBJ called me aside.

"You can see what your problem is," he said. "You may have convinced Gilpatric, but you haven't convinced McNamara."

I cited the letter I had received from Gilpatric only the day before expressing his support, and said this indicated we'd have the Defense Department's co-operation.

"Yep," Johnson chuckled, "but you know that's a one-man show over at the Pentagon. The Budget Bureau's against the SST and so is the Commerce Department. You'd better get all your fresh data together and make it convincing for the next meeting."

The President's own reaction to the first meeting was to agree with McNamara that some further studies would be helpful. He asked Treasury and Commerce to verify our claims as to the effects of a successful American SST program on the balance of payments, and told the State Department and the CIA to thoroughly examine the effects of our being outrun by the British and French with their Concorde.

To understand McNamara, who is a strong-minded, highly rational man, we must realize that at that very moment he was failing to perform the technical *tour de force* of the TFX, namely, requiring the U. S. Air Force and the U. S. Navy to agree upon a common fighter for both ground-based and carrier-based operations. We must also remember that he was facing strenuous obstacles and oppositions to his favorite project—a very large military air transport known as the C5A. Finally we should note now what we could not discuss then—that the supersecret Lockheed strategic reconnaissance Model 71 (SR-71) was in the advance stages of development and flight testing and, since he had struggled with numerous power plant and stability/control difficulties plus cost overruns, he was more impressed with the SST's problems than its prospects.

The other side of this coin, however, was the SR-71 itself, which Kelly Johnson had designed in his "skunk works." It was an all-titanium airplane that worked very well and flew at speeds in excess of Mach 3 at eighty thousand feet. In fact, despite its teething troubles, it was a tremendous accomplishment, giving me confidence that in the five years ahead we would not only have considerably more supersonic experience with higher speeds at higher altitudes but also that Lockheed and Pratt & Whitney (the power-plant manufacturer) would have had ample time to improve the technology, reduce the cost, and solve some of the safety problems that would be encountered.

Far from making me more skeptical, the large body of experience with this very exceptional airplane—known to only a handful of people—seemed to me to give us not only a leg but also an arm up on the British, French, and Soviet programs as far as civil supersonic flight problems were concerned. I felt so strongly about it that I persuaded Mac Bundy that we should take the British into our confidence and show them the SR-71 at the secret Lockheed hangar in the desert near Muroc. (My 50-minute flight the previous year at 60,000 feet faster than Mach 3.0 had been the "hottest" of my life.) My aim was to give them concrete evidence of our own progress beyond Mach 3.0 and the use of titanium, and perhaps dissuade them from spending too much money on the already obsolete Concorde.

Mac Bundy agreed with me, and with the President's approval I invited Julian Amery, Minister of Aviation, and Sir Solly Zuckerman, the British Prime Minister's scientific adviser, to accompany me in the Jetstar to Muroc. They were duly impressed with these airplanes that were already flying at speeds higher than Mach 3 and, I must add, never leaked a word about this project, as some had feared they might. I never regarded it as irrational that McNamara opposed our plans for the SST largely because of his doubts about this triplesonic aircraft. But what he apparently interpreted as unacceptable technical difficulties, I regarded as inevitably to be overcome in the development of any radically new plane. His jaundiced views of the SR-71 (which was built for the CIA), plus his conviction that commercial transports should be developed and financed by private industry, were understandable for a man who had his craw full of technical and budgetary obstacles. Thus he sought first to stop the SST program and then to place severe constraints on it. It is with more sadness than anger that I have to credit—or blame—him for the long delays and high costs in the developmental program that we undertook. But, was he right?

McNamara failed to scuttle the project at this point, but his influence was such that the Johnson Supersonic Advisory Committee bought the controversial "75-25" formula of which the Secretary of Defense was the chief author. This called for an overall developmental cost of $1 billion, the Government paying $750 million of this amount and private industry the remaining $250 million. Both Bain and I were widely criticized for this cost-sharing formula, but neither of us had much to do with it except to try to reduce it to 90-10 because we knew no private company would risk more. We were merely carrying out the policy of the task force that evolved it and, in truth, my own feeling was that it was unworkable, unreasonable, and unwise—as was borne out later when industry convinced Congress in no uncertain terms that it couldn't afford to spend $250 million on an airplane that had to involve such unprecedented technical and economic risks.

Competition from the Concorde seemed to be a greater concern for Kennedy than any financing hassle. When it became apparent in the spring of 1963 that the British and French were moving ahead more rapidly than we first thought possible, JFK's interest in the SST quickened accordingly. Then came the day when I had to give him some surprising and bad news: namely, that Pan American was discussing the purchase of the Concorde and Juan Trippe already had been in London and Paris for some serious negotiating.

"Keep me informed and make sure Trippe doesn't decide on any Concorde order before we make our own decision on the SST," he told me.

Kennedy had before him the Johnson report recommending a go-ahead. On the weekend of Memorial Day 1963, he took the papers and data supporting the Vice President's recommendations to Camp David. While he was studying the material that weekend, I received word that Trippe was about to sign a contract for six Concordes and that an official announcement was about ready to be made. I called Trippe, told him the President was on the verge of deciding whether to build an American SST, and added that we would appreciate his deferring any announcement regarding the Concorde. Trippe agreed, or at least that was my understanding at the end of our telephone conversation.

The President phoned me several times from Camp David, not only on the forthcoming Pan Am decision but also with several questions on our own program. I believe he also talked to Johnson and others as well; JFK obviously was wrestling with the SST problem, and the extent and probability of the Concorde's success had to be a key factor. By Monday I had not been advised whether he had made up his mind, but the roof fell in when I landed at LaGuardia, en route to a meeting in New York. A report of the Pan Am order had been made out of Paris, and the first person to greet me when I landed was a New York *Times* reporter asking for comment.

I didn't have any, and it probably was just as well in view of a phone call I got a few minutes later—from a very irate John F. Kennedy, who in vivid and purple prose demanded to know why I had failed to delay the Pan American order announcement. I explained my understanding with Trippe and was ordered to go immediately to the Pan Am office building for a confrontation with the Pan Am chief.

I hadn't been at Pan Am long enough to get into Trippe's inner sanctum when a secretary informed me the White House was calling. It was the President again, still furious at both me and Trippe. He had no sooner hung up when Lyndon Johnson phoned, expressing the same sentiments in even saltier language. Quite obviously, both Kennedy and Johnson felt that Trippe had, in a sense, forced the President's hand. By the time I was ushered into Trippe's office, their resentment had spilled over onto my own emotions and I angrily accused him of double-crossing us.

"I didn't announce the contract," he defended himself. "It was given out by the French prematurely."

"As soon as you signed the contract, there was a danger of a leak," I retorted. "You never told us you were going through with the signing—you promised to postpone any action."

We had quite an oral battle over this point. In his presence, I called the President and related what Trippe had told me. JFK's Harvard-Boston accent failed to keep the venom from seeping through.

"Well, you tell Mr. Trippe we will not forget this," Kennedy growled.

Needless to say, Trippe himself was chagrined. He spent the succeeding months trying to get back in the President's good graces, explaining—I'm told—that I had misunderstood his original promise and that the French, in any case, had jumped the gun.

It was shortly after this that Kennedy was scheduled to deliver the Commencement address at the Air Force Academy's graduation ceremonies in Colorado. I had not seen a draft of the talk but had considered the occasion a good one for an SST announcement, a draft paragraph for which Bain and I had provided. Either because of a delay in his decision or the problems of getting the revised text reproduced, the supersonic-transport decision was interpolated at the last minute and came somewhat as a surprise to a lot of people.

The date was June 5, 1963. The words were simple but dramatic as the President read from a freshly typed page. It began:

As a testament to our strong faith in the future of airpower, and the manned airplane, I am announcing today that the United States will commit itself to an important new program in civilian aviation. Civilian aviation, long both the beneficiary and the benefactor of military aviation, is of necessity equally dynamic.

Neither the economics nor the politics of international air competition permit us to stand still in this area. Today the challenging new frontier in commercial aviation and in military aviation is a frontier already crossed by the military-supersonic flight. . . .

199

The essential paragraphs were:

Having reviewed their recommendations, it is my judgment that this government should immediately commence a new program in partnership with private industry to develop at the earliest practical date the prototype of a commercially successful supersonic transport superior to that being built in any other country of the world.

An open preliminary design competition will be initiated immediately among American airframe and power-plant manufacturers, with a more detailed phase to follow.

If these initial phases do not produce an aircraft capable of transporting people and goods safely, swiftly, and at prices the traveler can afford and the airlines find profitable, we shall not go further.

But if we can build the best operational plane of this type, and I believe we can, then the Congress and the country should be prepared to invest the funds and efforts necessary to maintain this nation's lead in long-range aircraft, a lead which we have held since the end of the Second World War, a lead we should make every responsible effort to maintain. . . .

It was immediately and widely speculated that Pan Am's Concorde decision had pushed the President off the fence. Such speculation was natural but inaccurate. Actually, JFK was well aware of Trippe's option for six Concordes before he had me trying to pry that promise out of the Pan Am boss. And I firmly believe the President had made up his mind in favor of the SST announcement for the Air Force Academy speech; Ted Sorenson says it was ready before JFK went to Colorado Springs; it was released at this time because the occasion seemed most appropriate, and not because Trippe ordered the Concorde. It may be that the latter event resulted in a somewhat faster revelation of the SST decision, but it was by no means the key factor.

Once we had the green light, however, all we saw were yellow caution signals flashing. McNamara and Gordon insisted that the "75-25" formula had to be followed and went beyond this by demanding that private industry also pick up all development costs in excess of the $750 million federal contribution. In vain did I argue that the question of excess development costs should be made a subject for future negotiation and not an inviolate rule. Neither McNamara nor Gordon would send anything to the President unless their stringent conditions were met, and I finally went along reluctantly, believing that Congress would restore balance to the program.

Once Congress rejected the "75-25" formula, as I expected, the result was another controversy as to how much private industry *should* chip in. It was my old friend Ros Gilpatric, a man close to the airframe industry, who proposed that Eugene Black be brought in as a special adviser to the President on SST financing. Black, former head of the World Bank, accepted, but only on the condition that Stanley Osborne, a New York investment banker, also be brought in. I told Kennedy that appointment of special financial advisers merely diffused responsibility for the program and that I had to question the selection of these two men—Black was an officer and director of the Chase Manhattan Bank, a huge lender to the airline industry, and Osborne was an Eastern Air Lines director; I thought there was a possible conflict of interest.

Both McNamara and Gilpatric strongly favored them, however, and convinced the President to name them over my opposition. Black and Osborne wound up recommending that the government pay 90 per cent of development costs, a much more palatable ratio but one still not to industry's liking. They issued their report shortly after Kennedy was assassinated, and it was left to the new Johnson administration to continue the SST fight.

Three airframe manufacturers—Lockheed, Boeing, and North American—entered the design competition, with GE, Pratt & Whitney, and Curtiss-Wright submitting engine proposals. Douglas never did get into the act; it was having financial troubles and considered the SST project too much of a financial risk. Those deciding to compete submitted their designs to a 210-man government evaluation group, which had large NASA and military representation; the airlines themselves established their own evaluation committee, at my request turning their recommendations over to the federal group. In retrospect, the task we gave these dedicated men was too great to be accomplished in the hoped-for time span.

Both evaluation committees, government and airline, were unable to come up with selection of a clearly superior airframe and engine combination, and a second phase of competition was necessary: this one boiled down to Lockheed vs. Boeing on the airframe and GE vs. Pratt & Whitney on the engines.

Significantly, however, the groups agreed that a viable and safe American SST could and should be built. In a novel approach to the airline managements, Bain and I offered to sell "delivery positions"—serial numbers of a paper model of a nonexistent assembly line at an unknown date—and TWA's Floyd Hall immediately led a parade (to Juan Trippe's chagrin) to the FAA "sales" window. The world's airlines provided a welcome show of faith by reserving more than one hundred delivery positions, with a one-hundred-thousand-dollar down payment for each position. The Concorde, far ahead in development, could muster less than sixty optional orders. More than twenty airlines "ordered" the U.S. supersonic transport sight unseen; twelve placed orders for the Concorde.

I had long since left the FAA and gone with Pan American when the second competitive phase was completed by Secretary McNamara and General McKee, Boeing winning the airframe decision with its "swing wing" design, and General Electric being picked for the power plants. The selections were made on the basis of 32,000 pages of technical data, bound in some 280 separate volumes, and they were made in good faith. Unfortunately, in my judgment, the airframe choice not only was wrong but also delayed the SST program even more; further research revealed that Boeing's pivot-wing concept would result in too heavy an airplane, and Boeing's revised SST version wound up closely resembling what Lockheed had proposed in the first place. Moreover, the company with the greatest experience and the best supersonic development team—Lockheed—was passed over. These revisions cost us another two years in the building of a prototype; incidentally, I remember telling Bozo McKee in my only "second guess" that the wrong airplane and the right engine had been picked. He was not especially appreciative. But in hindsight I think it may have saved Lockheed from bankruptcy.

The "swing wing" was an intriguing, ingenious design, conceived and advanced by John Stack, Robert Gilruth, and other "aerogodamycists," old friends of mine at NACA, Langley Field, Virginia. It permitted Boeing's paper SST to take off, land, descend, and climb with its wings extended at a normal angle from the fuselage; in other words, at lower altitudes it was a conventional airplane, with no particular handling idiosyncrasies and with none of the low-speed disadvantages of a highly swept-wing aircraft. What was especially attractive about this design was that the variable wing resulted in less takeoff, landing, and approach noise and speed.

I suspect this virtue of quietness was largely responsible for the choice of Boeing; Lockheed's fixed delta-wing design made for a noisier airplane in the vicinity of the airports. The Boeing wing folded back sharply into a delta configuration at higher altitudes, but this versatility carried a far greater weight penalty than anyone expected—including NASA's experts, who had always been gung-ho for the variable-wing concept. (NACA had become NASA and Stack had moved up to hypersonic technology in the space team.)

My own thinking about the supersonic transport has changed somewhat throughout the years. I still think we're going to have regular supersonic travel—in fact, the Concorde entered service in early 1976—but not in an American SST until a new, cheaper, quieter fuel/engine cycle is developed. And I still think we were right in trying to get the SST program started when we did. In fact I'll go one step farther: I think if we had followed the original timetable set up during the Kennedy administration, we would have had a prototype flying—and defining and solving our technical, economic, and ecological problems involved in supersonic flight in time for introduction of regular SST schedules when the airlines and the traveling public are really ready for this revolution before the end of the century.

Those of us who fought for the SST never said we were for it regardless of cost or regardless of ecology or without full assurance of economical operation. We said it would be acceptable only if it proved viable, safe, and environmentally compatible. In the words of JFK's announcement (which we helped draft) that we would build a prototype: "If these initial phases do not produce an aircraft capable of transporting people and goods safely,

203

swiftly, and at prices the traveler can afford and the airlines find profitable, we shall not go further."

My emphasis was and is on safety and regularity in scheduled passenger service—that's paramount in view of the radically higher speeds, temperatures, and altitudes in which the SST will operate. In some areas, we were overoptimistic about our ability to conquer all technological problems as fast as we thought possible. In the even touchier area of ecology, we underestimated public concern, fear, and involvement. The rapidly cumulative effects on technical and industrial trespasses on the quality of life were not yet in focus. Looking back on those Kennedy years, I guess we felt too readily that we could do everything, anywhere—and immediately. We gave the SST a priority it didn't deserve simply because it was such a dramatic, challenging step forward in aviation progress— shrinking the globe to less than half its time size. We allowed ourselves to worship speed per se, ignoring the fact that the public— for the first time in aviation history—is giving spacious comfort a rating equal to or even greater than speed. The success of the wide-bodied jets offers irrefutable evidence of this new dimension in passenger taste. I believe that when we do build an American SST or HST (hypersonic transport) it will have to be wide-bodied (with bigger engines than we planned); I don't think the extremely narrow fuselage of the Concorde or the nearly as confined cabin of what would have been our initial American SST design is going to win wide acceptance by a public accustomed to the 747s, DC-10s, and L-1011s.

I used to argue with Charles Lindbergh about the SST, which he vehemently opposed almost from the start.

"All we're asking for, Slim," I'd say, "is a prototype for testing. And you know more than anyone else what we can learn from a prototype."

"It's wrong environmentally," he'd reply, "and it consumes too much energy per pound of payload." He spoke those words long before the fuel crisis made the SST, like the 747, the right airplane at the wrong time. Lindbergh, of course, wouldn't have agreed that the supersonic transport would have been right at any time. I remember one occasion in 1969 when I had arranged for the Pan Am directors to go to Kennedy International in a bus to see the

747 coming in on its first visit to New York. Trippe, Gray, and Bill Allen of Boeing were in the group, along with Lindbergh, who happened to be sitting next to Cyrus Vance, my old Yale Law School contemporary.

I sat close enough to them to overhear what Slim was telling Cyrus, and coming from a man who symbolized aviation progress, what Lindbergh said was a surprise to me as well as Vance. He confessed that he was now of two minds on whether the airplane had been a boon or a bane on man's existence. He expressed great concern over its use in wartime—a means of destroying cities, cultures, and hundreds of thousands of people. But he was even more worried about the possible impact of the SST and large numbers of huge airplanes on the environment. Lindbergh felt that technology had become excessive and that the airplane—one of the most useful devices to save time—had perhaps become overused by too many people to too little purpose.

The noise, pollution, and commotion of air travel had begun to disturb him. The gist of what he was telling Vance was that unless travel has some purpose, such as to improve pleasurability, creativity, or productivity, it could become just a kind of mechanical "going and coming" in the sense of being rather aimless. To Slim, the availability of air travel at low cost could develop into another mode of indulgence and a waste of energy, rather than conserving time for a good purpose—merely millions of people rushing back and forth without accomplishing anything.

The airman in me could never entirely agree with this heresy, but otherwise I found deep truth in what he said and—as applied to the supersonic transport—I came to realize that he had a point.

When Lindbergh finally came out in public unequivocally against any SST, it was no small factor in killing the project I had helped start—and by that time I wasn't too unhappy about the defeat. It wasn't just Lindbergh's opposition, of course. Those of us who fought for the unwanted bird were guilty of some misjudgments, particularly in the way we tried to win the public over to the SST's side.

For example, we underestimated the sentiment for noise- and air-pollution abatement. Moreover, none of us had any way of knowing that the entire airline industry would be so troubled and weakened by the time the Concorde became a technological reality. Maybe we should have known. The RAND Corporation, at my request, did a study for the FAA when the SST project was in relative infancy—a "sensitivity study" projecting what effects certain abnormal conditions would have on the supersonic transport program. One such condition was an unexpected and massive rise in the cost of fuel, and RAND predicted that this would be catastrophic to the SST. The study also forecast that development costs would far exceed Gordon Bain's estimates. I'm afraid we reacted to this dire crystal-ball warning by consigning them to a false-pessimism category. The late Steve Enke, SST project study manager at RAND, always felt we had hired them to do a job and then ignored all the danger signals—and to some extent he was right.

Another reason for the SST's defeat was, to put it bluntly, dirty pool on the part of some opponents. They issued scare stories, fed public and press with a lot of unproven scientific mumbo jumbo, and succeeded only too well in frightening the hell out of a lot of people who had no scientific basis for judging the truth of what they were being told. Hardly a day went by without the news media disseminating some new SST horror story—the plane would destroy the mating habits of minks, kill all the fish in the ocean with sonic booms, shatter millions of windows on every transcontinental flight, give every third person in the United States skin cancer, and so on *ad infinitum*.

We didn't need a more effective propaganda machine, however, as much as we did an effective testing bed for answering questions that the supersonic transport raised—namely, a flying machine. We could have had one without committing ourselves to actual production and around-the-corner scheduled service. It cost us more to terminate the SST program than it would have cost to finish the prototype we hoped to put into the air, and we should have been so far along in this project that it would have been obviously foolhardy to halt it. For this I have to blame the procrastination of the Johnson administration—ironically, because nobody fought harder for the SST than Lyndon Johnson and Bozo McKee.

Ironic, also, was the "paralysis by analysis" that occurred in the later days of the Johnson administration as inspiration yielded to calculation. The greatest calculator of them all was Bob McNamara, and with a very bright, aggressively analytical Joe Califano at his side, he had maximum authority and minimum responsibility for diagnosis and dissection of the SST program. Not only was he reacting to some of his own unfortunate experiences in military aircraft development, but also he was beginning quite rightly to be concerned with the number and incredible cost of "Great Society" programs that LBJ was spawning like a salmon going upstream.

Of course, McNamara knew far more about the strategic position of the United States and the President's total program because at times he really acted as Executive Vice President of the United States, due to LBJ's almost total confidence in the man with the "stickum on his hair." He could even have vetoed, if he had wanted to, the start of the 747 program in 1966 when the jumbo jet program's start coincided with shortages in steel and machine tools and anxieties about inflation. Boeing's Bill Allen and Juan Trippe came to Washington to get the President's blessing on the 747 program. He immediately turned their case over to McNamara, who came back with a favorable answer. These were the days when there was magic in "parametric analysis," "cost-effectiveness studies," and man's nearly infinite ability to apply systematic logic to any of his problems.

Perhaps the greatest irony of them all was that at the very moment we were going through years of analysis and resultant paralysis of the political and financial impetus of the SST program, there was built and operating in total secrecy an extremely successful supersonic aircraft—the SR-71. In moments of deep frustration, Bain and I longed for the opportunity that the CIA and the Air Force had to hire Kelly Johnson and his small, highly productive Lockheed staff, with its capability for designing, building, and testing the most advanced powered aircraft in history.

The day I relinquished command of the FAA, at McKee's swearing-in ceremony, the President gave every indication that he was as strongly committed to the supersonic transport as he ever had been. He made it clear, in fact, that he had picked McKee to succeed me largely because he believed the general could finish what he had started. LBJ ended his remarks with this paragraph:

"So given the ability of industry, the government, and the peo-

207

ple all working together, I have not the slightest doubt that under the predicate laid and the preliminary work done through the years by men like Jeeb Halaby and carried through under the direction of Bozo McKee, America will proudly reach her goal in due time and on time."

I was amazed that Johnson had placed the supersonic transport above all other FAA projects, duties, and responsibilities to be undertaken by the new administrator. Perhaps, I mused, this resetting of priorities by the President six months after his landslide victory is the Great Society itself. The President left the podium, shook hands with General and Mrs. McKee and their son, and with Doris and myself, and left the room. I remember wondering then if McKee really could get the bird off the ground—the whole awesome, controversy-ridden program was the chief legacy I left him. Yet I also sensed that McKee was in for more trouble than the President's pro-SST words implied; a hint of potential delay; a touch of wavering support; a slight, almost imperceptible tinge of doubt.

"The Committee members have recommended a plan of action to move the program forward *at the fastest possible rate consistent with the attainment of those goals that I have outlined* [italics mine]," LBJ had said. I found out later that his remarks had been prepared by none other than Bob McNamara—and they amounted to a kiss of death. I was still trying to figure out why the word "paradox" kept sprinting through my mind when Senator Magnuson interrupted my thoughts.

"Jeeb, you did a great job," he said warmly. "We're going to miss you."

Maybe I was wrong. Magnuson seemed elated at what the President had said, and Magnuson was about as pro-SST as any lawmaker on Capitol Hill—the biggest employer in his home state of Washington was Boeing.

Then Chairman Oren Harris of the House Commerce Committee approached and shook hands. "Congratulations, Jeeb," he smiled. "It looks like the President has bought your SST program."

It turned out he really hadn't. His next move was to request that $140 million appropriation from Congress for the eighteen-month interim research and development program he had just announced. But he didn't send the request to the Hill until August, six weeks later—and it was made under rather confusing circumstances. After it was announced, White House aide Bill Moyers held a press briefing at the White House. A reporter asked:

"This means there will be a decision at the end of this eighteen-month phase as to which airframe and which engine will be selected, or go ahead on a dual basis?"

Moyers sidestepped the question and turned it over to Joseph Califano, who he explained had been working for Secretary McNamara and had been closely associated with the Supersonic Transport Committee. Califano, now promoted to special assistant to the President, replied:

"You could go any way. You could have four manufacturers, two manufacturers, or you could even have three manufacturers."

The newsman seemed puzzled. "There might or might not be an engine or airframe selection?"

"That is correct," Califano said tersely.

In other words, it was left completely up in the air by this spokesman for the President whether the United States would ever build an SST prototype. The only interpretation I could place on Califano's statement was that the decision would not be made for approximately another two years. In mid 1963 Johnson had avowed his support for a decision to proceed with the construction and testing of an actual airplane by the end of 1965. That timetable obviously had been scrapped.

I should have seen it coming, especially when the Black-Osborne report reached the White House after the Kennedy assassination. It went beyond recommending a new financing plan in that it also expressed some pessimism as to the eventual cost of the program. The report so worried Johnson and his staff that the President, by Executive Order, established the second interdepartmental committee under McNamara's chairmanship. That was in April of 1964. I never really grasped the delaying mood most of the members were in. I knew that, like all interdepartmental committees, this one was expert in diffusing responsibility and deferring action. Maybe it was because I was too concerned about my own future to realize what McNamara and his friends could do to

209

the SST program, or maybe I leaned too heavily on what I believed was Lyndon Johnson's unyielding support. At any rate, the McNamara-inspired delays were deadly to the supersonic transport. They postponed a decision on the building of a prototype so long that the SST was a sitting duck for the far more vocal, efficiently organized, and emotionally motivated opponents.

But on the day I left office a year later, I was only too happy to hand the hot brick over to Bozo McKee. I had a decision of my own to reach—how to leave the jungles of Washington for the equally savage world of private industry.

CHAPTER SEVEN

That same night after I turned the FAA over to a new administrator, Juan Trippe called me at home.

"I've prepared a definite offer of employment as a senior officer of Pan Am and I'm putting it in the mail," he said.

It arrived a few days later, but I was in no mood to respond. First I wanted to decelerate to a more human velocity and to take a star sight or two. Then I wanted to try to rediscover myself and my family before entering another wringer—whether it be Pan Am or some other.

In addition, press speculation about my future had pricked my conscience about regulating one day and being regulated the next. My public ethic and image were troubling me, especially after reading a speculative piece by David Hoffman, the very able aviation editor of the New York *Herald Tribune,* which reported, among other things:

> Najeeb Elias Halaby, durable Administrator of the Federal Aviation Agency, will resign this month to become Vice President of a large U.S. airline, according to high Administration sources.
>
> Mr. Halaby, a lawyer and former test pilot, is believed

ready to join the staff of Pan American World Airways as an Executive Vice President earning in excess of $60,000. He would be based in New York.

Reached by telephone, Mr. Halaby acknowledged that he had recently offered his resignation to President Johnson. But he denied that he had made a firm commitment to join any company in the aerospace field.

"I serve at the convenience of the President," Mr. Halaby said, "and should he accept my resignation, I have no commitments whatsoever except to Doubleday (publishing company) to write a book on my experiences in Washington."

An appointee of the late President Kennedy, "Jeeb" Halaby stayed at the FAA's helm for more than four years, twice as long as any predecessor. The previous endurance record was set in 1933 when the FAA was little more than an office in the Department of Commerce.

Mr. Halaby reportedly accepted the Pan Am post last month while skiing in New England. [I didn't even have an offer much less accept it.] Airline sources said the offer was extended by Juan Trippe, Chairman of Pan Am's Board. [He never skied in his life.]

Money is believed behind Mr. Halaby's decision to resign. His tastes are by no means spartan and with three school-age children, the 49-year-old Administrator apparently felt the time had come to fatten the estate. During his four years with the FAA, Mr. Halaby earned an average of $30,000 a year.

Appointment as head of the FAA forced Mr. Halaby to divest himself of extensive airline stock holdings. [I had never owned a single one—too risky!] His shares were sold early in 1961—a time when the airlines were in deep financial trouble. Mr. Halaby, however, was not then connected with Pan American.

Under Mr. Halaby, the FAA got the supersonic transport project off the ground [It was still taxiing!]. His task force conceived a plan to automate the air traffic control system [the first hardware is now being tested], but the Budget Bureau withheld adequate funding. Mr. Halaby also decentralized the FAA, transforming it from a monolith with 40,000 employees [I reduced it from 46,000] into a network of semi-autonomous regional offices.

Furthermore, in addition to my sensitivity to public relations, I was quite disappointed in Trippe's offer. It was legalistic and rather unpromising, so much so that after mulling it over I called Trippe and told him I would need the summer to think about it but that first I wanted to get some rest up in Vermont. I also tried to be completely fair and open with him; I told Trippe he should be aware of some of the problems I had had with Johnson in recent weeks—a deterioration of relationships that might make me far less valuable to Pan Am than Trippe assumed.

"You should make your own independent inquiries as to whether I left with the President's illwill or goodwill," I suggested, knowing how vindictive LBJ could be.

Trippe scoffed at this presenting any serious problems but said he would look into the matter. Whether he did or not, I never found out. But he did come back a few days later and insisted that I come down to his estate at East Hampton, Long Island, for some golf. So I spent a long weekend with him discussing both the nature of my leaving the FAA and the nature of possible employment by Pan Am.

The July heat was getting me down and the family and I finally holed up in a Vermont farm rented from my old boss, Jack Ohly. It wasn't entirely a rest-and-rehabilitation stint, however—I was trying to write the book for which I had signed a contract with Doubleday & Company. I wasn't totally enamored by the project, but it gave me time and reason to reflect, and it appeared that the book would be my only source of income until I took up new work.

It was a dry, hot summer in Vermont, and the family had a pretty good time, marred only by my knowledge that when summer faded into autumn, I had to be gainfully employed. Doubleday's advance on the book was for only three thousand dollars (obviously, they didn't expect any smash best seller), and the writing was a new kind of torture for me. About all I did was scratch out some chapters on my early years in aviation, outline some of the events during the FAA years, and worry about Juan Trippe.

He kept calling me—his persistence was a legend in New York

213

and Washington—and I made a few trips to Long Island and the beautiful Maidstone Golf Club near his estate, with no decision made. I had two choices at this point: going to work for Pan Am or trying to make it on my own either in law or in what had intrigued me when I was with Laurance Rockefeller—venture capital. One of the men I consulted for advice based on hard and related experience was Roger Lewis, the former Pan Am executive who had left to head General Dynamics.

Our careers had been similar. Roger's background had included Stanford, Lockheed, and wartime service in the Air Force. I had supported Under Secretary James Douglas' idea in 1953 that Lewis be named Assistant Secretary of the Air Force under Harold Talbott, and Lewis was holding this post when Trippe lured him into the Pan Am hierarchy, under circumstances not much different from my own. We had two long sessions together, during which Roger gave me some very frank pros and cons about working for Trippe.

He told me there were a number of very fine professional airline people in Pan Am, men who had built a good operating system despite Trippe's eccentricities. Lewis had great respect for Trippe's courage and creativity, but he felt that Pan Am's founder had wandered too far afield in various diversifications such as hotels and aerospace-support projects. He warned me about the absolute disregard for personal and family considerations that characterized Trippe's dealings with senior officers—Howard Hughes had nothing on Juan Trippe when it came to making business phone calls in the wee hours. And finally Lewis expressed concern about the "court atmosphere" around Pan Am—with some of the senior executives playing the role of courtiers who gathered around the king in fawning obeisance while simultaneously getting embroiled in rivalries and jealousies.

But Roger also had the feeling that I stood a fairly good chance of becoming Pan Am's president and chief executive officer eventually. Many of Pan Am's top officers, he noted, were nearing retirement age, and he didn't expect Gray to last in the presidency very long. Lewis thought Gray was as good an operations man as there was in the whole airline industry, but Roger also felt that

Gray was too preoccupied with statistics and engineering really to run Pan Am as it should be run.

It was during this same period of indecision and vacillation that I turned to fellow pilots for advice. One was Captain Olaf Abrahamsen, a highly respected senior Pan Am captain and a veteran of the transatlantic schedules. He truly loved Pan Am, but in the course of an hour's conversation he expressed concern about his airline's labor relations. Abrahamsen thought the company's rather hard, callous industrial-relations policies had created an atmosphere of mutual distrust and dislike between management and the various unions, and Abrahamsen definitely was more pro-management than pro-union. He also worried about a lack of service competitiveness and poor communications between Pan Am's marketing men and operations personnel—which had to result in a reputation for poor service.

I even went to an "opposition pilot" for advice—my old friend Captain Bob Buck of TWA, who arranged a meeting with a particular buddy of his, another senior Pan Am captain. The latter was much more bitter about Pan Am management than Abrahamsen, and both he and Buck agreed that Pan Am, in the many years it had operated as the single U.S. international flag carrier, had grown flabby. TWA was overtaking Trippe's airline in the transatlantic market, United was threatening Pan Am as No. 1 between the mainland and Hawaii, Northwest was proving alarmingly competitive in the Far East, and Braniff was coming up fast in Latin America. Pan Am, indeed, seemed like an old and tired fighter getting punched around by younger, faster opponents.

In brief Pan Am, during the time it enjoyed a virtual monopoly in international markets, had allowed itself to get soft to the point where it couldn't face fresh, agressive competition. It proudly described itself as "The World's Most Experienced Airline," but the one area in which it had never had much experience was competition. The opposite was true for an airline like TWA, which for decades had butted heads against American and United, point-to-point in the most competitive arena of all, the U.S. market.

Buck's friend bemoaned the fact that the addition of competitors to Pan Am's routes, in itself a supposed external stimulation, had failed to stir up his airline internally. I absorbed what he had

215

to say just as I had listened carefully to Abrahamsen's analysis of Pan Am. Pilots, after all, are on the front line of everything that happens, from the purchase of an airplane to the failure of marketing officials to bring aboard passengers in a pleasantly expectant mood. Most of all, the airmen are the victims of union vs. management competition; the union may protect them from management abuses but also compresses them into restrictive work rules that stifle initiative and make the pilots captives of the system.

Trippe had been talking with me about my going with Pan Am as a senior vice president. But I wanted more than a vice presidency, and I told him so. Everything bad, alarming, or disturbing I had heard about that great old airline had instilled within me a desire to do something at once to restore its former stature—to prevent the approaching stall. It may have been conceit, ambition, or pure self-confidence, but in any case I made it clear to Trippe that I wanted to be chief executive officer at the earliest opportunity; meanwhile answerable only to Trippe, who at the time served as Board chairman and chief executive officer while Gray was president.

Trippe was quite candid when I revealed my real goal at Pan Am. At the outset he didn't think Gray would take kindly to me as his superior, and besides Gray deserved a shot at the corporate left seat. He said there was a possibility I wouldn't have to wait for Gray to retire, but added that he felt an obligation to Gray for many years of loyalty and devotion to Pan Am.

Away from Trippe, in moments of introspection, I myself wondered about my desire to run a major airline. Before and during the FAA years I never had such an inclination. In fact after observing a number of industry chiefs at close hand, I had even less of a desire to be in their shoes. After four years as a regulator I was convinced that the airlines were the most regulated industry of all. From the inside I had seen how carrier executives were whipsawed back and forth by the multiplicity of agencies in Washington—not just the FAA and the CAB but also the Department of Commerce, Treasury, Labor, IRS, SEC, NLRB, the State Department, and even the White House, which had life-or-death powers over the granting of international routes.

Yet I also told myself that Pan Am was more of a national institution than an airline. From its very inception, it was devoted to increasing communication among the world's peoples, to worldwide mobility, to giving all nations a portrait of a company excelling in safety and technical ability. It was a great educator, as well; it had become the technical adviser to a number of foreign carriers, which ironically used Pan Am's know-how to become capable competitors. Further, Pan Am's diversification fascinated me—it was now a hotel system with some forty hotels in operation and an Air Force support unit performing the missile and space-base maintenance operations at Patrick Air Force Base, Florida. It ran a downrange system of ships and radars. It was virtually the aviation system of Liberia and had a number of affiliations with foreign carriers—at one time as many as twenty-five or thirty, mostly in Latin America. It even operated airports around the world.

Most important from a sentimental point of view, Pan Am was truly an aviation pioneer. Domestic airlines, when granted a new international route, merely have to start flying it in Pan Am's wake. Pan Am's new overseas routes had to be preceded by survey flights to test feasibility, equipment, and facilities. It had been far ahead of other carriers, by the very nature of its route system, in developing long-range operations. It definitely was the pioneer in the introduction of long-range aircraft, particularly the giant Sikorsky, Martin, and Boeing flying boats, whose luxury was not equaled until the wide-bodied jets came along. It was the first American carrier to fly pure jets, putting the 707 into service months ahead of everyone else. In short, from almost every standpoint, Pan Am appeared to my eyes as a tremendous challenge—it was an airman's airline with a tradition going back as far as the swift clipper ships that showed the American flag in the harbors of the world.

That primarily was why I was interested in not just an executive's job but instead the top job itself. Trippe and I talked about a variety of routes I might take in achieving this, and one idea I presented to him was to make me vice chairman of the Board of Directors, putting me in charge of everything but the airline until Trippe retired and the Board elected the next chief executive. I reasoned that being vice chairman would give me clear preeminence over any other possible contender for the chief executive spot. (Not that there seemed to be many contenders, a strange situation for a company approaching its fortieth anniversary with a host of fine, able men who had been in its ranks.) One would assume Trippe would have a number of potential successors in the wings, from all parts of the company, but this was one of the old pioneer's chief weaknesses—he was unable to select, cultivate, and keep top-flight personnel, largely because of his own domineering and sometimes difficult personality.

Both Trippe and I decided to scrap the vice chairmanship brainstorm I had suggested; for one thing, we knew Gray wouldn't buy it because I'd outrank him. We talked about my becoming executive vice president to Gray, but that would establish beyond any recall a line of succession that didn't fit in with my presidential/chief executive officer ambition. One key factor in all this, of course, was the question of Trippe's relinquishing the reins. The word around the whole airline industry, let alone just Pan Am, was that Trippe's retirement would have to be in a coffin. I was told by more than one person that Trippe would never retire voluntarily and that anyone with dreams of succeeding him had to face the risk of standing around waiting for Trippe to die.

Yet when I pressed Trippe about his intentions, he denied wanting to stay at the helm indefinitely.

"I'm absolutely determined to retire in a year or so," he said, emphasizing that he felt his main job was to choose and train a successor who would take over in another eighteen months or two years. He was quite convincing, and this was one of the main reasons I finally decided to go with Pan Am. What I didn't know was how he and the Board of Directors related to each other, how little independence the Board really had, and how unwilling they would be to push Trippe into or even accept his retirement.

I discussed the Pan Am situation with my family. Typically and perhaps inevitably, my mother and my wife had diverse opinions. Mother thought it was a great opportunity and told me flatly to take the job. Doris, however, was quite concerned over all the pitfalls and problems and was most unhappy at having to move back to New York, where we hadn't been too happy in the mid-fifties, but knew we couldn't afford any more time in Washington. The kids were again mainly worried about leaving their schools and their friends in Washington, a world to which they had adjusted after only four years. They found it hard to imagine, much less enjoy, the prospect of entering new schools in an alien city and with no immediate friends.

Between the doubts of my children and my wife and the rosy predictions of my mother, I was torn anew by indecision, but not for long. Over the Labor Day weekend, at Trippe's invitation, Doris and I joined him and Bettie Trippe, and Harold and Exa Belle Gray—ostensibly a social occasion but one in which the Trippe powers of persuasion were never better; our meeting might as well have been located on Ulysses' Island of the Sirens.

I finally swallowed hard, said "I'll do it," and we then rehashed and agreed on a letter of employment, before announcing on September 13 that I was joining Pan Am as a senior vice president. During the final week prior to announcing the new role, I informed Jack Valenti, one of LBJ's special assistants, what had happened, and I also tipped a trusted reporter that an announcement might be forthcoming soon. I had made firm promises to each of them to notify them in advance of any publicity release. I thought it was only fair to keep the White House advised, so that if questioned they could reply truthfully, and I also wanted to end all the speculation that had been going on since it was first rumored I was leaving the Johnson administration.

Trippe wanted me very badly, but he also wanted to keep open his option, later to select Gray or me as his successor—chief executive officer. Gray wanted that spot and expected me to come aboard his Clipper as a subordinate. I came aboard expecting an equal shot at the chief executive officer job with Gray and believing Trippe would really retire in eighteen months, as he said he would.

Just prior to the announcement, a reporter called me and said he had learned from his own sources that Trippe had hired me.

"Is it true?" he asked with typical journalistic directness.

"Yes," I admitted, "but for God's sake hold off writing anything until the thirteenth—a lot of people at Pan Am don't know anything about it yet."

He promised, but apparently the temptation of a scoop was too much. He did more than merely run the story prior to the official announcement; he included the flat statement that I was going to be Trippe's heir apparent. Thus my name became anathema among certain Pan Am executives even before I climbed aboard the corporate Clipper. He also wrote that until I actually took over for Trippe, I was going to run the airline's hotel subsidiary, and this sent John Gates, head of Pan Am's Inter·Continental Hotels system, roaring into Trippe's office and threatening to resign. The "royal court" was in a tizzy, and I didn't blame them. Roger Lewis already had warned me that any pre-employment speculation and publicity were going to make unenjoyable reading for a number of officials, making it twice as hard to fit into the organization when and if I did actually accept the job.

The combination of the rumors, that one really damaging story, and what had to be an anticlimactic announcement of my employment by Willis Player, Pan Am's vice president for public relations, all added up to poor timing and not very astute management on anyone's part, including my own. Gray and many others suspected me of planting that "heir apparent" bit, and even Trippe was suspicious—he accepted my explanation but for about a month he was rather cool.

The Directors welcomed me warmly but I can't say the same of most of the executives, particularly those close to Gray, who considered me more of a threat than a wingman in the Pan Am squadron. I'll never forget that uncomfortable, inhospitable day I attended the traditional executives' "Monday lunch" at the Sky Club, my first in the Pan Am Building because all other meetings with Trippe had been in East Hampton or Washington. Trippe, as usual, presided, with all the knights-errant present. As the new boy, I was seated at the end of a long, rectangular table in accordance with seniority, and there was a decided chill in the air—introductions were perfunctory, and I sensed a "We'll show this publicity-seeking bastard what kind of an initiation he deserves into this fraternity" attitude. Juan had prepared my way with his Directors but not with his management colleagues. With his penchant for secrecy, freedom of action, and surprise, he had forced them "to read it in the papers."

The newcomer was supposed to listen and not speak. This corporate equivalent of children-should-be-seen-and-not-heard nonsense, combined with some hostility, suspicion, and resentment, didn't improve my own state of confidence. Maybe I was being unfair, but from the very start I felt this was largely a tired, heavy-handed group of reactionaries leading Pan Am, and that impression stayed with me for a long time.

I tried to map out with Trippe and Gray some sort of an orientation program that would give me a chance to learn a little about a lot of the company's operations. But I quickly got the idea that the court had decided to keep me out of the airline end entirely. It wasn't quite a total freeze, but there wasn't much doubt that the word had been passed that I was to be limited to the miscellaneous nonairline activities of Pan Am, and that I was not to be in the operating line of command. I hadn't expected such an exclusion, but there it was—a fact of life to be tolerated if not appreciated.

A second shock for my confidence came when Trippe began to coerce me into visits to Washington on his behalf—in other words, lobbying. From the outset of my employment negotiations, I had told Trippe I was unwilling to have my Washington associations exploited, and that I had no intention of switching suddenly from regulator to lobbyist. The missions on which he wanted to send me should have been undertaken by Trippe himself or Gray. I began to suspect that Trippe knew he was running out of influence and muscle in Washington and had hired me for what he assumed was my clout with my fellow Democrats.

At first his requests were rather innocuous, and even innocent— "Would you mind going down and seeing so-and-so about such-and-such?" I threatened to resign as these chores became outright lobbying, but Trippe blocked me by saying he hadn't previously anticipated Pan Am going into a crisis period that involved the airline's very survival, and that he intended to do more of this politicking personally as soon as he got a chance. I'm afraid he conned me along to the point where I was doing a lot of lobbying while simultaneously not learning a hell of a lot about the airline business.

Yet I must admit that even with these early drawbacks and frustrations, it was exciting to be working with this globe-girdling giant of an airline. For all of his faults and personal idiosyncrasies, Juan Trippe was a true pioneer to whom the nation still owes a tremendous debt. Like many of his style, he was also something of a buc-

221

caneer who parlayed shrewdness, ruthlessness, and a gift for opportunist intrigue into one of the world's greatest air carriers. The story of Pan American World Airways has to be the story of Juan Terry Trippe.

Trippe was the son of Charles Walter Trippe, a Manhattan investment banker. It was his mother's idea to christen him Juan Terry, after a favorite aunt named Juanita Terry, and she may have been blessed with clairvoyance; for years everyone, including a number of Latin American officials, assumed Trippe had Spanish blood in his veins, and this supposition unquestionably did him no harm when he spread Pan Am's wings throughout the Latin world —Spain, Portugal, the Caribbean, and South America. Actually he was no more Spanish than Winston Churchill, but for obvious reasons he never denied the rumors of Castillian forebears.

His ancestry had a decided strain of the sea. A schooner named the *John C. Trippe* fought in the battle of Lake Erie in 1813, and subsequently there were several U. S. Navy ships bearing the Trippe name. Love of the sea came naturally to this man who founded an airline that conquered oceans; it was no advertising gimmick that made the word "Clipper" a Pan Am symbol. It was Trippe's own idea to link his airline's operations with the proud traditions of those fast, graceful Clipper sailing ships that carried the American flag into international commerce. Some of his Maryland ancestors had sailed the Clippers out of Baltimore Harbor.

He entered Yale in 1916, a solidly built, rather reserved youngster according to classmates, who played guard on the football team but never really achieved big-man-on-campus status—not when his classmates included such dashing future luminaries as Henry Luce, Cornelius Vanderbilt, C. V. "Sonny" Whitney, and John Hay "Jock" Whitney. Trippe left Yale in 1917 to join the Naval Reserve Flying Corps, winning his wings and an ensign's commission but not in time to see combat. By this time, however, he was wearing those wings in his heart—he had caught the flying bug in fatal proportions, and when he returned to college, he organized the Yale Flying Club with Sonny and Bill Vanderbilt. Both were close associates during the Pan Am years. After graduation Trippe tried his father's business for a brief spell but with no great enthusiasm. In 1923, a year out of college, he heard that the

Navy was selling surplus seaplanes. He bought nine of them for five hundred dollars apiece and he was in the airline business.

He named this primitive, shoestring operation Long Island Airways, although it was more of a charter airline. In the warmer weather it carried passengers to the New Jersey resort areas, and Trippe occasionally was lucky enough to latch onto someone wanting a charter flight to Florida or a Canadian fishing ground. Long Island Airways ostensibly had six pilots on the payroll at the peak of its existence, but like so many airmen of that day, they were notoriously unreliable. At overfrequent intervals, Trippe would have business lined up only to find his birdmen AWOL—either on binges, barnstorming missions, or so hungover that they couldn't have flown twenty feet. On such occasions Trippe had to do the flying himself, and this raised havoc with his sales efforts. To make matters worse, the old seaplanes were even less reliable than the pilots; the personnel, financial, and maintenance problems finally sank Long Island Airways into the slough of insolvency.

Trippe, according to the legend, was heartbroken but undaunted. His friends unanimously urged him to forget the crazy airline business and return to the safer and saner world of Wall Street, advice that he rejected with all the confident aplomb of a man holding four aces in draw poker. Actually he did have a few hidden cards up the proverbial sleeves—in the form of an inheritance from his father, who died while Juan was trying to run Long Island Airways. Some of the money went down the drain with the airline, but Trippe had salvaged some twenty-five thousand dollars, which he promptly poured into a new aviation venture. This time, however, he had some well-heeled partners; he talked a dozen college-day friends into placing bets on the new venture—principally Bill Vanderbilt and Sonny Whitney from the old Yale Flying Club, and Baltimore banker John Hambleton, whose money and faith in Trippe far offset the fact that he had gone to Harvard. With about a hundred thousand dollars' capitalization, they organized Eastern Air Transport and bid for the New York–Boston airmail route. The company was formed just about the time Congress passed the Kelly Act of 1926, which turned over all but one of the nation's airmail routes to private contractors.

Bidding against Eastern (which had no connection, lineage or otherwise, with what was to become Eastern Air Lines) was Colonial Airways—with twice the capitalization and some seasoned businessmen behind it. Trippe, apparently, had a hunch he couldn't win that bidding war, but he came out with the route anyway—he merely convinced Colonial to join forces, after agreeing to get a mature president. The choice was General John F. O'Ryan, a World War I hero, who some incorrectly considered would become purely a figurehead for the real chief, Juan Trippe.

Aggressive, ambitious, and unafraid of arguing with men by far his senior, Trippe was at constant odds with Colonial's Board of Directors. He had to fight the Board to bid for the New York–Chicago route, a bid that failed in Trippe's eyes because of the Directors' procrastination. An even more bitter battle ensued when Trippe tried to win Board approval to purchase two new Fokker F-7 trimotors; always the visionary, he foresaw the day when an airline could make money carrying passengers as well as mail. He also recognized that the Boston–New York mail route —or CAM-1, as it was known—was too short for much profit potential. He wanted the Fokkers not so much for Colonial's miniscule system but for the expansion he envisioned—for example, southward to Florida and the Caribbean.

The Board, however, was looking at only one item: the thirty-seven-thousand-dollar price tag on a Fokker. It turned down Trippe's request, and the angry young man, figuratively speaking, took his football and went home. He and his original associates sold their Colonial stock back to the Directors and went shopping for another airline. They organized the Aviation Corporation of Americas, perhaps the most pretentious corporate title in history. There have been other grandiose examples, such as National Airlines for a carrier originally operating between St. Petersburg and Daytona Beach, and Continental Air Lines, which flew between El Paso and Denver. But Aviation Corporation of Americas, a name that hinted at a multithousand-mile route covering an entire hemisphere, ran a few charter flights between New York and Atlantic City under the subsidiary name of New York Airways.

In truth, however, the name wasn't as outlandish as it seemed, for Trippe's ambitions were of the Think Big variety. In mid-1927 he was tipped off that the Post Office Department was about to

224

award a contract for a Key West–Havana airmail route. Two companies, one an already established airline, had bid for the route, but that didn't deter Trippe, who flew to Florida with John Hambleton and assessed the situation—which on the surface looked hopeless.

One competitor was Florida Airways, then operating between Miami and Atlanta. Ostensibly in the lead for the Cuban route because it was an operating carrier, Florida Airways was having financial problems. Of greater concern to Trippe was Pan American Airways, Inc., to be headed by a relatively obscure Army Air Corps major who was to become famous in World War II—H. H. "Hap" Arnold. Hap's motives were as much patriotic as financial; like many military men, he had become increasingly worried over the rising influence of German interests in South America. For example, SCADTA (Sociedad Colombo-Alemana de Transportes Aéreos)—a Colombian carrier started with German-Austrian financial backing—was South America's first successful airline and one with international-route ambitions. Its developer, in 1920, was Dr. Peter Paul Von Bauer, who as early as 1926 had petitioned for landing rights in Central America and Panama, and who openly sought a U.S. gateway through Florida.

Arnold viewed SCADTA as a covert military threat, although there was no evidence that the well-run airline was anything except a profitable, extremely efficient commercial venture. He organized Pan American Airways, Inc., with the aid of two other Army pilots, Carl Spaatz and Jack Jouett; an ex-Navy airman named John Montgomery, and two wealthy aviation enthusiasts recruited by the boss, Montgomery—Richard Bevier and Grant Mason. With experienced aviation men and solid money support, Pan American Airways, Inc., loomed as the biggest threat to Trippe's expansion dreams. Florida Airways, in fact, dropped out of the running quickly. It lost two of its three planes in crashes, the third was seized by a sheriff, and the airline went into receivership.

Montgomery, Arnold et al. had fired the first shot by negotiating a contract with the Cuban Government to carry mail from Havana to Key West—just about the time that Trippe and Hambleton arrived on the scene. They promptly flew to Havana and met with Cuban dictator Gerardo Machado. What happened was pure

225

Trippe—he emerged from Machado's office with rights in Cuba for the Aviation Corporation of America, thus making Pan American's mail contract about as valuable as stock in a company manufacturing stage coaches. He had the operating and financial nucleus of a fine airline, but Trippe had those rights. Impasse.

Not for long, however. It was at this time that General Billy Mitchell was court-martialed; both Arnold and Spaatz, completely loyal to the embattled Mitchell, decided to stay in the service and fight for the general's goal of a separate, independent Air Force. It would have been interesting to speculate on what would have happened if Arnold, who was president of Pan American, hadn't been so devoted to Mitchell's cause. Trippe probably would have ended up working for him, because Hap Arnold, in his own way, was just as tough and independent as Trippe.

With Arnold and Spaatz out of the picture, and Florida Airways virtually bankrupt, Richard Hoyt, Sonny Whitney, and Trippe were now able to merge the three competitors for the U.S. airmail contract. It was more of an acquisition than a merger; Aviation Corporation of America simply absorbed both Pan American and Florida Airways. Dick Hoyt of Florida Airways became chairman of the Board, while Trippe was named president of Pan American Airways, Inc., a newly formed subsidiary of Aviation Corporation. Thus was Pan Am born—with patriotism as the father, with Machado, a canny backdoor dealer, as the mother, and with Juan Trippe's ceiling-unlimited aspirations furnishing the genes.

Hoyt and Trippe ran the show; Hambleton was Trippe's right-hand man and Andre Priester, a crack operations specialist who had been running New York Airways for Trippe while the Florida negotiations were in progress, came down to organize Pan American into a working airline—hiring pilots and mechanics for the three Fokker F-7 trimotors Trippe had ordered. Unfortunately the Key West airport was not operable for larger planes by October 19, 1927—the day Pan American was to fly the first load of mail from Key West to Havana under the Post Office Department agreement. Trippe was in Washington trying frantically for an extension of the inaugural deadline, but to no avail. His manager in Key West was J. E. Whitbeck, who from early dawn had been anxiously scanning the skies.

According to folklore, Whitbeck breathed a momentary sigh of relief when he spotted an approaching plane, but his hopes sagged as it came closer and landed—a small, single-engine Fairchild seaplane piloted by a colorful barnstormer named Cy Caldwell. Whitbeck had no choice: He offered Caldwell $175 to fly a round trip to Havana with Pan Am's first mail. For $175 Caldwell might have tried flying all the way to Paris, and he accepted quickly. He refueled, took off at 8:25 A.M., and covered the ninety miles between Key West and Havana in one hour—aided by a tailwind. There were seven bags of mail aboard the little Fairchild—an inauspicious but audacious beginning for what was to become a global airline.

The improvised inaugural, however, was somewhat deceptive. It smacked of a haphazard, slapdash operation that did not bode well for the future. Yet Pan Am in its early years was far from the shoestring status of so many of its contemporary carriers. For one thing it was unusually well financed. Trippe, it was true, worked for some time without salary, taking compensation in the form of additional stock in accordance with an agreement he had made with his principal backers. While Pan Am was capitalized for only two hundred thousand dollars, its seventeen original Directors boasted a combined wealth of nearly a billion dollars. If Trippe was unable to meet a payroll or pay large, outstanding bills, almost any one of those Directors could sign a personal note until additional revenue cash was available.

This financial security was rather rare in the infant airline industry. On other small airlines of the late twenties, most backers expected quick returns on their investments. Trippe didn't have to worry about turning a profit immediately; free of money worries, he could afford to indulge in long-range planning. And to him that ninety-mile midget route from Key West to Havana was more of a ninety-mile laboratory. As Charles J. Kelly, Jr., wrote in his history of U.S. airlines (*The Sky's the Limit,* Coward-McCann, Inc., 1963):

In competition with crack express steamers, the short flight was of little importance. But Havana was the gateway to South America. Already, European lines were working their way upward from South America to the United States. Aeropostale, the predecessor of Air France, and various German lines were operating in Brazil, Argentina, Chile and Colombia. These lines were heavily subsidized by their Governments. Similarly, Trippe saw Pan American as the expression of United States foreign economic policy. Almost from the first, he conceived of the line as the "chosen instrument" of the United States, thus infusing his private business with a sense of national purpose.

On such a dream, such a philosophy, such a simple yet massive goal, was Pan American built. The airline cut its teeth on the Key West–Havana mail route (later it became Miami–Havana), using it as a testing ground for Trippe's expansionist moves. Those moves, of course, involved a combination of acquiring routes by acquiring airplanes, by developing technical competence with diplomatic maneuvering. The latter was Trippe's forte; he simply acted while the competition was still planning. When other U.S. airlines jumped into the bidding for South American mail routes, they were handed the disconcerting news that Pan American already had negotiated landing rights with the countries to be served. And Trippe had support in the State Department and a formidable if unofficial ally in Postmaster General Walter Folger Brown, who is reported to have admired Trippe's imaginative zeal. Brown, from all accounts, was not so much interested in favoring Pan American as he was in opening up South America to U.S. civil aviation. It so happened that this desire coincided neatly with the fact that Trippe's airline was rapidly acquiring a reputation for efficiency and, more important, already had its figurative foot in the Southern Hemisphere doorways. Pan American had the know-how that Brown respected, to such an extent that when the Foreign Air Mail Act was written (and Brown was its principal author), authorizing the Postmaster General to issue South American mail route contracts, it contained a key provision that allowed Brown to award them to "the lowest *responsible bidders that can satisfactorily perform the service required to the best advantage of the government*" (italics mine).

Pan American seldom was the lowest bidder. But that one generalized phrase was a large loophole through which Brown poured out contracts to Juan Trippe. And Pan American *was* the most experienced, qualified, and responsible bidder. It did more than just fly airplanes; it also carefully surveyed the routes over which it intended to operate, built its own airports, and hacked out emergency landing strips in veritable jungles. Nor was Trippe satisfied with any hand-me-down airplanes; from its very inception, Pan American operated brand-new planes, almost always multi-engined for safety reasons.

Trippe, in fact, ordered the original three multi-engined Fokkers because he knew aircraft engines of that day were notoriously unreliable, and he was well aware of the hazards of a forced-water landing in a land-based aircraft. That, in fact, was the motivation behind Pan American's first acquisition of big amphibians capable of landing and taking off either on land or water. And many of the airline's early routes not only were over the ocean, but the cities served were also ports.

With typical astuteness and his inherent flare for publicity, Trippe also acquired something of even greater import than good airplanes: the technical services of Charles Lindbergh. He hired the Lone Eagle early in 1929, shortly after Lindy had helped organize and survey routes for the newly formed Transcontinental Air Transport, which later became TWA and that for some years was called the "Lindbergh Line." When he went to work for Juan Trippe, he began a relationship with Pan American that lasted to the day he died. If there was one thing I had in common with Trippe, it was admiration for Lindbergh as an airman.

Trippe was nothing if not loyal and grateful to his early associates, yet while loyalty and gratitude are noble attributes, in Trippe they could be a weakness as well as a strength. Bluntly stated, his affection for old friends and colleagues in later years would result in a lot of corporate deadwood—"faded aristocrats," as one of my brash new people tagged some of Trippe's cronies who never challenged Trippe and who gave him unquestioned subservience at times when honest opposition would have done more good. One had to admire Trippe's feelings toward those who helped him in Pan Am's formative years, but at times he carried his gratitude too far, and in the long run he usually hurt those he thought he was trying to help.

Admittedly his imperiousness, his single-mindedness, his mania for always wanting to be first—from a new route to a new airplane —were what Pan American needed to achieve greatness. He didn't merely battle competition; he destroyed it. When he began spreading Pan American's wings throughout the Caribbean and South America, he had competitors in Grace Airways, owned by the giant W. R. Grace shipping combine, and New York, Rio, and Buenos Aires Line, Inc., otherwise known as NYRBA. He coveted Lima and Santiago so, true to form, Mr. Trippe solved the conflict by a marriage of convenience and compromise. The result was a Pan American-Grace merger—Panagra, as it became known.

In the post World War II proliferation of international air competition, Braniff was to invade Pan American's and Panagra's territory, with Trippe eventually selling Panagra to Braniff in 1967. But that 1929 merger secured Pan American's position on South America's West Coast and left him free to handle even tougher opponents than Grace.

The second U.S.-based competitor, NYRBA, was no pushover even for the resourceful Trippe. Its backers were impressive, including James Rand of Remington-Rand; W. B. Mayo of the Ford Motor Company; F. C. Munson of the big Munson Steamship Lines; Reuben H. Fleet, who founded Consolidated Aircraft; and Lewis Pierson of Irving Trust Company. Also on NYRBA's Board were Richard Bevier and John Montgomery, Hap Arnold's former associates when he organized the original Pan American Airways; both had been squeezed out when Aviation Corporation absorbed Pan American, and neither had any love for Trippe.

NYRBA was further fortified by the presence of Ralph O'Neill, a prominent and resourceful pilot who had been selling Boeing airplanes in South America and knew the countries as well as anyone. O'Neill, who spoke fluent Spanish, flew around South America trying to find some place that Pan American hadn't already staked out and finally got lucky in Argentina—he obtained an exclusive mail contract from the Argentine Government, which included rights at Buenos Aires. Then he got even luckier: He added Santiago, Chile, to NYRBA's proposed system, thus parking his airline smack on the doorstep of Pan American-Panagra's southernmost point on the West Coast.

Thanks to Fleet, NYRBA also had something that Trippe had to envy: a new Consolidated flying boat originally designed for long-range Navy reconnaissance. It fitted in beautifully with NYRBA's ambitious route plans—Santiago to Buenos Aires via Ford trimotor, and then connecting Buenos Aires to Rio de Janeiro with the long-legged Consolidated Commodores easily capable of flying the twelve-hundred-mile route nonstop. It had a long range and carried up to thirty-two passengers; by early 1930, NYRBA was operating four Commodores over a nine-thousand-mile route—at the time the longest in the world flown by one company.

Stung by NYRBA's success, Trippe tried to buy out its backers but got nowhere—at first. NYRBA sowed the seeds of its own destruction by undercutting Pan American's mail rates, charging half of what Trippe had established for South America. It was a bargain-basement operation that kept Pan American at bay but that eventually disillusioned even NYRBA's wealthy partners. Faced with mounting losses, they sold out to Trippe in a deal that included NYRBA's fine Commodores and left Pan American dominant in the Caribbean and South America except for some foreign competition. And Trippe took care of *that* situation in a hurry.

His target was Bauer's SCADTA, which now found itself virtually surrounded by Pan American's fast-growing system. Bauer had something Trippe wanted: points directly south of the Panama Canal. Trippe had something Bauer wanted: cash. In secret negotiations, Bauer sold SCADTA to Pan American for $1.1 million; because of the Colombian law requiring SCADTA to be owned by Colombian citizens (all the airline's officials had obtained the required citizenship), Bauer was retained as president. He actually ran SCADTA for Pan American, too, for Trippe respected his considerable airline experience.

Juan Trippe's march to the South was brilliantly conceived and executed. He established a Latin aerial empire in the incredibly short span of only five years, utilizing a strategy that could be ruthless or persuasive, relentless to be sure, depending on what the occasion called for. No military operation was better planned or implemented so smoothly; the military analogy is apt, for quite a few people called Trippe "Napoleon" behind his back—but it was more of a grudging compliment than an insult.

He deliberately maintained a low profile. He had a kind of quiet charm that camouflaged his strength, as a velvet glove can hide an iron fist. He could look absolutely benign, smoking a pipe or one of his imported cigars, but underneath they say you could sense the steel of his will and the scope of his ambition. Curiously enough, that ambition was directed almost totally toward Pan American and not in the sense of seeking personal aggrandizement. He married wealth—his wife was a Stettinius—and his social and business associates usually were men of affluence, but Trippe seemed to give his own financial welfare a comparatively low priority. At the very apogee of Pan American's success and influence, in the 1940s, when it actually was America's chosen instrument in international air commerce, Trippe's salary was a modest twenty-three thousand dollars.

The climb to that exalted height was fueled largely by Trippe—his domineering personality, his methods, his persistent determination, his foresight, and his faith in aviation's future. In 1929, only two years after Lindbergh crossed the Atlantic, Trippe was talking to the British about setting up a jointly owned subsidiary, Pan American-Imperial Airways Corporation, to operate a North Atlantic service as soon as the right plane or planes could be developed. At the same time he was talking to a French airline, Aeropostale, about co-operating in the establishment of a more southerly route between the United States and Europe via the Azores and Lisbon. He actually negotiated a secret agreement with both the British and French in which those countries would share 50 per cent of the southern-route traffic while Pan American took the other half—provided that service was started simultaneously by all three.

Trippe was blocked temporarily by the growing superiority of the U.S. aircraft manufacturing industry, which by the early thirties had begun to far surpass foreign planemakers in almost every phase, from airframes to power plants. Pan American had ordered new long-range Sikorsky flying boats fully capable of transatlantic operations, but neither the British nor the French had anything to match them. National pride reared its provincial head and both Britain and France refused to let Trippe get the Atlantic service under way until they had comparable aircraft.

Thwarted on both the northern and southern routes, Trippe decided on an aerial end run. He dispatched Lindbergh on another survey flight—this time in a specially equipped Lockheed Sirius over the Great Circle route from New York to Denmark via a refueling stop at Newfoundland. Lindbergh, accompanied by his wife, made the flight and returned with sufficient data and advice to convince Trippe that the Great Circle route was feasible for the new flying boats. The British either had to accept Pan American service to England or be bypassed entirely by Trippe's planes flying the Great Circle to inland Europe. As it turned out the British didn't have to make this unhappy choice; a political upheaval in Newfoundland overthrew the government from whom Trippe had obtained landing rights (Newfoundland did not become part of Canada until 1949). Nor could he turn to the southern route, for the French had lost the exclusive franchise that permitted them to serve Lisbon and the Azores. Trippe wanted to fly the route in conjunction with the British, who now enjoyed an alliance with Portugal, but London still held fast to that "nobody starts service without the other" agreement.

With negotiations at a standstill—so the story goes—the U. S. State Department finally got into the act by informing all parties, including Trippe, that such a delicate matter as transatlantic air rights must be handled henceforth through official diplomatic channels rather than a private company. So Trippe put aside his transatlantic dreams and turned to the Pacific, where in typical fashion he already had been doing some advance planning. In 1931, a year before the survey flight to Europe, he had dispatched the Lindberghs on a Great Circle flight in the other direction—from Alaska to Siberia, Japan, and China via the Aleutians and the Bering Strait. The Lone Eagle's verdict: This route could be flown safely and was about fifteen hundred miles shorter than a transpacific crossing via Hawaii.

Again with his uncanny foresight, Trippe bought two small Alaskan carriers—for the express purpose of gaining operational experience in Arctic flying. He purchased a faltering American-operated airline system that had been operating in China since 1930, reorganizing it to give the Nationalist Government of China nominal stock control but retaining for Pan American control of its finances and operations. And in 1935 only the State Department kept him from reaching an agreement with the Soviets for landing rights associated with survey flights across the Bering Strait, on the grounds that the Soviet Union might demand reciprocal rights.

The State Department also convinced Trippe that a Great Circle route to Japan was out of the question because of mounting tension between Tokyo and Washington. Trippe shifted his attention to the mid-Pacific, and by the summer of 1935, a Pan American Sikorsky was surveying routes that would establish an aerial highway from San Francisco to Manila via Hawaii, Midway, Wake, and Guam. From Manila, Pan American would head northwest to Shanghai, connecting with its Chinese affiliate, or west to Hong Kong and Singapore.

There were serious stumbling blocks to this grandiose plan. China balked at giving Pan American and all other applicants any Chinese port of entry, to keep the Japanese out, even though its state airline was a Trippe blood relative. Hong Kong appeared to be the only logical gateway to China, but this was British-owned and the British weren't about to let Juan Trippe in through that Union Jack door. Like the gambler he was, however, Trippe had the proverbial ace up his sleeve—he pulled another one of his patented end runs and convinced Portugal to give him landing rights at the tiny Portuguese colony of Macao, only a few miles from Hong Kong and less than seventy miles from the major Chinese port of Canton.

It was a masterful stroke, because British and Chinese merchants in Hong Kong immediately began pressuring the British Government to reverse its anti-Pan American decision. They viewed the Macao port of entry as a threat to their own welfare, and Whitehall caved in. Instead of one gateway, Trippe's outflanking maneuver had given him two—and without the necessity of giving reciprocal rights to foreign airlines. It was no wonder he didn't want the State Department doing his negotiating; he could win more on his own, and avoid competition at the same time. But more important, he had established in Washington's collective mind the image of Pan American as this nation's most effective chosen instrument for international air travel. Significantly, when President Roosevelt canceled the U.S. airlines' airmail contracts in 1934, Pan American (which was not part of the domestic "cartel") was the only carrier allowed to keep flying the mail. And Trippe to all intents and purposes had planned it that way; Pan American had the only aircraft and know-how capable of transporting international mail—always at a substantial subsidy from Uncle Sam.

Also by this time he had established an image for the airline itself, one in perfect harmony with that chosen-instrument status and its overseas route structure. It was one with decided nautical overtones. Pan American was the first airline to call the aircraft commander "captain," the copilot "first officer," and the mechanic-trained third flight-deck member as "engineer." It was the first U.S. carrier to outfit its flight crews in identical uniforms—and the uniforms themselves were of naval style, topped off by white officers' caps. For years, time aboard Pan American planes was designated by bells, and progress was measured not in miles but in knots. The cockpit was "the bridge."

And the planes, too, followed this nautical theme. They became "Clippers" starting in 1931, along with a Trippe-created tradition of having the current First Lady christen every new type of Pan American aircraft put into service. Mrs. Calvin Coolidge was the first presidential spouse to be accorded that honor. I read in the *Christian Science Monitor* while attending Leelanau School that in November 1931 she broke a bottle of Caribbean water (Prohibition eliminated the traditional champagne) over the bow of a Sikorsky S-40 with the words: "I christen thee *American Clipper.*" Trippe had a penchant for making political hay out of christening ceremonies; he not only enlisted the prestige of the White House for such occasions, but also paid off political debts with the process—one of his Fokker F-7s, for example, was named *General Machado* after the Cuban dictator who had given Trippe that exclusive landing franchise. (Later, Trippe was to give him far more than a ceremonial honor; a chartered Pan American Sikorsky flew

235

Machado and members of his government out of Havana after Fulgencio Batista's successful revolution.)

No inaugural flight in civil aviation history matched the start of Pan American's scheduled Pacific operations for sheer drama. It was an event staged with Hollywood-like atmosphere, complete with exciting dialogue. The date was Friday, November 22, 1935, while I was at Stanford, when a crowd estimated at some twenty-five thousand jammed Pan American's terminal area at Alameda, California. The publicity-wise Trippe milked it for all it was worth. Present was Postmaster General James A. Farley. The governor of California had proclaimed November 22 as "Pan American Day." And the departure of the inaugural flight was covered extensively by radio newsmen as well as the newspapers—one of the latter ran a headline on the front page for that day reading: "SAVE THIS NEWSPAPER. IT RECORDS REALLY IMPORTANT HIS-TORY MADE HERE TODAY."

The real star of the show was Pan American's newest and at the time greatest airplane—the huge Martin flying boat officially desig-nated the M-130, or the Martin Ocean Transport. Powered by four engines and with a cantilever internal-wing structure replacing the old Sikorsky external-strut design, the Martin was the last word in air transportation. The one used on the 1935 Pacific inau-gural was the last of three Trippe had ordered; the first was named *Hawaii Clipper,* the second *Philippine Clipper,* and the third *China Clipper.* The big flying boats were not the most efficient aircraft flying, because 80 per cent of their load went for fuel (compared to 30 per cent for one of Donald Douglas's new DC-3s). But no landplane could match their range nor their luxury; not until the 747 came along did any commercial transport equal the spa-ciousness, comfort, and decor of the Pan American flying boats. The Martins carried thirty-two passengers in all this airborne ele-gance, which included a lounge or living-room area.

Another star of the show was the *China Clipper*'s commander, the famed Edwin Musick, who was flying for Sesquicentennial Air-lines when Pan American absorbed it. Musick exemplified the pro-fessionalism of Pan American flight crews. Pan American's chief pilot and a cool, competent, no-nonsense veteran of ocean flying, he became one of the most famous airline pilots in aviation history

236

and a major asset to Pan American from both a technical and public-relations viewpoint. A few years later, he was to be killed in the crash of a Sikorsky S-42 off Pago Pago while on a survey flight (the accident, while never officially solved, was believed to have been caused by an in-flight explosion in the course of dumping fuel prior to an emergency landing). But on this dramatic day, Ed Musick *was* Pan American.

Just before the scheduled takeoff at 3:28 P.M. PST, Trippe asked Musick:

"*China Clipper,* are you ready?"

"Pan American Airways *China Clipper,* Captain Musick, standing by for orders, sir."

"Stand by, Captain Musick, for station reports."

One by one, the radio stations operated by Pan American along the Clipper's route checked in—Honolulu, Midway, Wake, Guam, and, finally, Manila.

"Stand by all stations," Trippe said tersely. Then, turning to Farley, he declared:

"Postmaster General Farley, I have the honor to report, sir, that the transpacific airway is ready to inaugurate airmail service of the United States Post Office from the mainland across the Pacific to the Philippines, by way of Hawaii, Midway, Wake, and Guam islands."

"Mr. Trippe," Farley said, "it is an honor and a privilege for me, as Postmaster General of the United States of America, to hereby order the inauguration of the first scheduled service on Foreign Air Mail Route No. 14 at 3:28 P.M., Pacific Standard Time, on this day, which will forever mark a new chapter in the glorious history of our nation, a new era in world transportation, a new and binding bond that will link, for the first time in history, the peoples of the East and the West."

Trippe nodded with a tight smile, then addressed the crew: "Captain Musick, you have your sailing orders. Cast off and depart for Manila in accordance therewith."

With transocean flights now so routine and commonplace, all

237

that verbiage, including the heavy nautical terminology, sounds corny. But even today I get a thrill reading such dialogue, which is more than mere words in black print. The first flight of the *China Clipper* symbolized Pan American in the days of its greatest glory —when it truly became an American institution instead of just an airline. Farley's presence surely reflected the government's attitude toward Pan American—not merely a benign eye but also an admiring one. Trippe's somewhat stilted, almost archaic orders to Musick somehow smacked of smooth professionalism rather than empty ritual. And the Martin Clipper itself was far more than an example of American aeronautical engineering progress; it also was a portent of the future. Its streamlined beauty contrasted sharply with the struts and wires of the older Sikorskys—which Lindbergh once dubbed "the flying forest." Yet while the layman could look at the Martin and gape, an airman sensed that admiration would last only until an even bigger and better aircraft came along. And that was Trippe's philosophy too; only three months after the *China Clipper* flew its trail-blazing way across the Pacific, he was asking Boeing if it could build a flying boat larger, faster, and longer-ranged than the Martin.

It was typical of Trippe that he named the most famous of the Martins *China Clipper,* a full year ahead of his grabbing landing rights at Macao and Hong Kong. He was ever optimistic—the tougher the challenge, the more impossible the task, the harder his agile mind schemed. Nobody gave him a chance to stretch Pan American's Pacific routes as far as Australia, but less than two years after starting San Francisco–Manila service, a Pan American Clipper, flown by Musick, was landing at Auckland, New Zealand —only five hours by air from Australia itself. New Zealand wanted Pan American but Australia didn't want Pan American, Britain's Imperial Airways didn't want Pan American, and Australia's Queensland and Northern Territory Aerial Services (now familiarly known as Qantas) didn't want Pan American. So how did Juan Trippe get his foot into *that* door?

Since 1934, he had on Pan American's payroll as a technical adviser Harold Gatty, Wiley Post's navigator on their 1931 world flight. Gatty, a true expert in the field of air navigation, was Australian-born and something of a hero in his mother country. Gatty became Pan American's ambassador to the "down under" countries and played a major role in securing landing rights at Auckland—Imperial and Qantas notwithstanding.

Now the Pacific was Trippe's domain, and having conquered one ocean, he returned to another—the potentially rich traffic market of the Atlantic. This time the State Department did his negotiating with the British, who went along with a fifteen-year bilateral agreement calling for twice-a-week service for each between the United States and Britain, Pan American operating two and Imperial two. But the British insisted on the same provision that had hamstrung previous Atlantic accord: No airline could start service unless the other was ready. Pan American and Imperial Airways did run joint survey flights early in 1937, but significantly Pan American used one of its regular Clippers while Imperial employed a converted bomber; the British airline still didn't have any multi-engine equipment capable of conducting a transatlantic operation, although Short Brothers, a British manufacturer, was developing some promising models.

The Short flying boats, however, were too far in the future for the service Trippe was ready to start almost immediately. He hated to alienate the British; he knew he might want to use British bases throughout the world, and he also was aware that nearly 50 per cent of Atlantic traffic originated in Great Britain. But as Imperial hemmed and hawed for nearly two years, he got impatient enough to pull off another of his secretly negotiated pacts—this time with Portugal, which gave Pan American an exclusive twenty-five-year landing-rights agreement at Lisbon and the Azores, with no reciprocal clause.

Pan American was stymied—temporarily, naturally—by Britain's petulant refusal to let the Clippers refuel at Bermuda on westbound flights. The Martins and Sikorskys could make the eastbound flights nonstop but not in the other direction because of the prevailing winds. This obstacle didn't deter Trippe. At the then staggering cost of $4 million, he ordered six new Boeing 314 flying boats capable of flying the Atlantic nonstop in either direction. On March 3, 1939, while I was in New Haven at Yale Law School, Mrs. Franklin D. Roosevelt christened one of them *Yankee Clipper,* and on June 28 the same plane made the first scheduled passenger flight from the United States to Britain via the Azores. Two of the new Boeings went into Pan American's Pacific service, and the remaining four were assigned to the Atlantic crossings. Inevitably, the British sued for peace in the air by insisting on getting three 314s for Imperial Airways from Boeing, with Pan Am's concurrence. The Boeings, incidentally, were the last flying boats Pan American was to operate; when World War II ended, Trippe began operating land-based aircraft exclusively, and with some regret: There was really nothing nautical about a DC-4 or its successors. Despite their size, passenger capacity on the flying boats was relatively limited by the excessive fuel requirements, and they simply had become too uneconomical to fly, not to mention too slow.

At this point in history, as Europe's war clouds darkened, Pan American was supreme in its two-ocean domain. So, to all appearances, was Juan Terry Trippe—but not really, because his highhandedness had provoked an internal revolt against his one-man domination of the airline. The instigator was Sonny Whitney, one of Pan American's original founders, who, it is said, resented Trippe's failure to consult with him or seek his judgment. Whitney, in fact, complained that he never heard of Trippe's expansion plans, back-door agreements, or aircraft purchases until they already had become established. He packed sufficient influence on the Board of Directors to oust Trippe partially from control. There were enough uninformed, unhappy Directors to vote Whitney in as Board chairman and chief executive officer, leaving Trippe with the sole title of president. According to reports the atmosphere around Pan American's headquarters would have made Siberia seem warm—Trippe and Whitney weren't speaking to each other, and Trippe on his part made no effort to educate his highly unwelcome new superior on the problems of running an airline. Inasmuch as Trippe carried his office around in his head, Whitney was trying to make decisions based on a lack of knowledge and few facts.

The outcome was inevitable: The Directors did a 180-degree turn and restored the Board chairman and chief executive officer titles to Trippe. With World War II just over the horizon and Pan American's entire route structure threatened with extinction, they had no choice but to give the airline back to the man who had founded and raised it to maturity. The Directors had no way of knowing that by allowing Trippe to overcome the only real challenge he ever faced to his one-man regime, they had approved a blueprint for future trouble. The very things that had generated Whitney's rebellion—JTT's towering willfulness, major decisions made without consultation, failure to keep executives informed, indifference toward accountability of subordinates—were someday to plague Pan American when it eventually collided with the one enemy Trippe couldn't secretly negotiate out of existence: able competition with the added element of government instigation and support.

Pan American performed brilliantly and patriotically throughout the war years. Even before Pearl Harbor, the government had enlisted the airline's help; Trippe was asked to set up at Pan American's Miami base a school to train Army Air Corps pilots in long-distance flying, based on what the airline's own crews had learned and perfected over the years of ocean operations. The school was established and turned out thousands of airmen—more than three hundred of them earning decorations of bravery and extraordinary service. Pan American also took over the operations of SCADTA and other South American airlines whose governments, at U.S. request, had ousted all German officials working for those carriers.

The War Department came to Trippe with another mission: establishment of bases throughout South America to help protect the Panama Canal and the South Atlantic line of communications. Technically the United States still was neutral at the time and couldn't ask its southern neighbors for such bases, but Pan American already was operating at some of the desired points. Trippe was asked in a secret contract to expand these and build new ones, a task he assigned primarily to his old Yale pal Samuel Pryor, who by December 7, 1941, had brilliantly completed the desired bases, which were used throughout the war—particularly as part of the South Atlantic ferrying and transport operations.

Another prewar Pan American contribution came about at the direct request of President Roosevelt, that was inspired by Winston Churchill. The P.M. called Trippe, who was in London, to

241

give a paper to the Royal Aeronautical Society, and confided that the British probably couldn't hold Egypt without U.S. help. What FDR wanted was an airlift across the South Atlantic and Africa to the Nile, run by an airline with long-haul experience. Pan American had the operation going only sixty-one days after Trippe saw the President, and during the war the route was expanded from Miami to India via Africa and the Arabian Sea.

A large chunk of Pan American's fleet went into the Air Transport Command or the Naval Air Transport Service, including its new Boeing Stratoliners—the world's first pressurized airliners. All Pan Am stations automatically became U.S. bases with the outbreak of war, and the airline virtually abandoned its civil operations to transport personnel, cargo, and aircraft to the combat zones.

So, of course, did other U.S. carriers. Previously limited to domestic routes, they got their first taste of overseas operations—and liked it. The pressures of wartime ended Pan American's monopoly in long-haul ocean flying experience and planted some highly fertile competitive seeds throughout the industry—TWA, Northwest, and American in particular began sprouting some postwar hopes that were to be translated into the first real competition Trippe had ever faced.

Both he and Pan American, when the war ended, were ill equipped for such competition. What had been Pan American's greatest strength—Trippe's chosen-instrument concept with its monopolistic structure—now became a major weakness once the airline had to compete against other carriers.

Competition began hitting Pan American almost as soon as the war ended. With the blessing of the Civil Aeronautics Board, one by one the giants of U.S. civil aviation moved into Pan American's international domain: TWA and American Overseas Airlines (an American Airlines subsidiary) across the Atlantic; United from the mainland to Hawaii; Braniff and later Delta into South America; Eastern into the Caribbean. One of the bitterest pills Trippe had to swallow was the CAB's awarding Northwest a Great Circle route to Asia—the very route Pan American had pioneered with survey flights, a route that was never operated because of State Department objections. It was Northwest's wartime experience, operating an airlift to Canada, Alaska, and the Aleutians, that qualified them for the award—a typical case in which the war proved to be a hidden blessing for hitherto small carriers with little or no long-haul experience.

And no longer could Trippe operate as a one-man, unofficial State Department; now it was the United States Government negotiating all the bilateral air agreements that allowed the proliferating foreign airlines to serve the United States, most of them in direct competition with Pan American. Compounding Trippe's widening difficulties was his failure to obtain domestic routes even as the once-landlocked domestic carriers were granted overseas rights. In vain did he argue, with considerable justification, that if the CAB was going to demolish the chosen-instrument concept internationally, it should at least allow Pan American to compete domestically. TWA, Northwest, Braniff, and American had a network of domestic routes to feed traffic into and out of their newly won international awards; by contrast, Pan Am literally had to stop at the nation's borders. It was a round-the-world airline with one huge vacant gap—the continental United States. "An airline without a country," as I later dubbed it in a zoom of rhetoric.

Much of Pan American's troubles and its almost inevitable downfall did not surface immediately. In my first full year at Pan American, 1966, the airline posted a record net profit of $86 million on revenues moving toward $1 billion—$841 million, to be exact. It continued to make money, although not as much, until 1969—just about the time I was placed, not unwillingly although unprepared, in the figurative left seat. Its track record, in face of all its built-in, unavoidable, and massive handicaps, blinded a lot of people, including myself. One reason, of course, was the apparently unlimited traffic growth enjoyed by the entire industry in the sixties, at the astounding overall rate of 15 per cent annually—internationally it was going up 25 per cent annually! By the mid 1960s the jet had taken over more than 90 per cent of international travel. Under those conditions even competitively flabby Pan American could turn a profit.

And despite the added element of competition and Pan American's reputation for indifferent service, it retained enough of its pioneering reputation ("World's Most Experienced Airline" was not an inaccurate slogan) to attract passengers. Trippe certainly didn't lose overnight the foresight that had made his airline a global institution. Pan American was the first U.S. carrier to order jets, and it was a Pan American 707 that inaugurated U.S. jet service in October of 1958—an occasion as historic as the first flight of the old *China Clipper*. Being *first* apparently made up for at least some of Pan Am's service deficiencies.

Trippe's first really major miscalculation—failure to foresee that if traffic didn't maintain a steady growth rate, Pan American was headed for trouble—wasn't just a mistake on his part alone. Quite a few of his colleagues were overly sanguine, and so were a lot of aviation economists. The general optimism around Pan Am, however, amounted to viewing some serious basic weaknesses through rose-colored glasses. The service superiority of its competitors was just one. Another was and still is the inordinate amount of seasonal traffic over such vital routes as the then lucrative Atlantic, where 75 per cent of the passengers travel for pleasure; by comparison, the business-vs.-pleasure ratio domestically comes close to a 50-50 split. The seasonal, discretionary aspect of pleasure travel is murder when it is applied to Pan Am's widely dispersed system —it means heavy summer traffic with a drastic decline in the winter, leaving Pan American with an equipment surplus and too many unproductive employees through no fault of their own. A third ailment is Pan Am's unbalanced route structure; it flies to a lot of cities with heavy traffic but to a lot more where traffic is miniscule. One can make money New York–London but you'd need an incredibly low break-even load factor to produce black ink on a Hawaii–Pago Pago run. And finally, Pan American had consistently overstaffed many of its most money-losing stations; I discovered one that had thirty ground employees to handle a single daily flight. This kind of management indifference to cost cutting was catastrophic, considering the fact that one third of the airline's stations handle just one flight a day.

All these weaknesses might have been lived with to some extent if it were not for the overwhelming competition. An airline that once enjoyed a virtual monopoly over most of its routes now battled scheduled competition from thirteen airlines in the Pacific, twenty-three in Central and South America, and an unbelievable twenty-nine over the Atlantic. Add the traffic inroads made by seven U.S. supplemental airlines and fourteen European charter carriers and it's easy to understand (1) what I was going to inherit and (2) that it wasn't all Juan Trippe's fault—the flaws in his personality, policies, and philosophy notwithstanding.

Competition, to be sure, emerged gradually and with relative slowness—another explanation for Pan Am's complacency. In the immediate postwar years, Pan Am actually had a semimonopolistic position from which any carrier providing any kind of service could take advantage of the rapidly growing prosperity of individual American travelers, who comprised some 65 per cent of the world's international air traffic. At first only TWA on a few Atlantic and European routes and Northwest with a rather small Pacific operation could give Pan Am any kind of opposition. And the foreign carriers, which eventually were to be pitted against Pan American, were off to tortuous starts. In the wake of a devastating, costly world war, the United States was the only nation capable of resuming with surprising speed its commercial air operations. German, Japanese, and Italian civil aviation had to begin virtually from scratch, and even victorious Britain and France were in no position quickly to challenge Pan American seriously.

Trippe couldn't have done much about foreign competition anyway, but he fought hard to keep his U.S. compatriots out of his backyard. Even before World War II ended, he reportedly had masterminded a scheme to make permanent the chosen-instrument concept, although it was given a different name and was camouflaged slightly to avoid a Pan American label. "The All-American Flag Line Bill" it was called by the lawmaker who introduced appropriate legislation in Congress—Senator Pat McCarran of Nevada. Briefly, it would have allowed all the airlines to purchase stock in a co-operative venture—namely, a single U.S.-flag carrier for international operations. But in the collective minds of the airline industry, there was little doubt that Pan Am would be running the show.

The only carrier outside of Pan American to support McCarran's bill was United. The others lined up solidly against any chosen-instrument policy, going so far as to organize the "Airlines Committee for United States Air Policy," more popularly known

245

as the "Seventeen Airlines Committee." The United/Pan American alliance was somewhat ironic because it was based largely on a pessimistic appraisal of the North Atlantic's traffic potential by two of the industry's leading optimists—Patterson of UAL and Trippe himself.

Two Congresses, the Seventy-eighth and Seventy-ninth, debated the All-American Flag Line Bill without reaching a decision. The final verdict was handed down not by Capitol Hill but by the CAB. On June 14, 1944, the Board announced it would entertain applications for international-route certificates, and the chosen-instrument issue was dead in Congress. The CAB divided the points to be served into five areas: North and South Atlantic, and North, Central, and South Pacific. The North Atlantic, where Pan American already held a permanent certificate, was the biggest plum because of its greater traffic potential. Trippe asked the CAB to let it retain its exclusive franchise, but knowing the Board wasn't likely to grant him that mountain-sized favor, he favored the application of American Export Airlines, owned by the American Export shipping firm. He apparently figured that a brand-new carrier run by a seagoing outfit wouldn't give him as much trouble as an established airline such as TWA.

For once his political astuteness failed him. The CAB ruled that under the Civil Aeronautics Act of 1938, no shipping company could own an airline, so American Export Airlines fell into the willing arms of American Airlines via the merger route, becoming American Overseas Airlines as a separate division of the parent carrier. The final CAB decision gave both TWA and American North Atlantic certificates for a seven-year period. When Pan Am protested, the Board held that the traditional division between domestic and international carriers based on the vast differences between flying boats and land planes no longer held true.

Trippe also got the shaft from President Truman when he approved CAB decisions to give Pan American competition in both the Pacific and Latin America—two areas where Pan Am had pioneered air travel. The embattled Trippe, his political-influence wings decidedly clipped, fought back with one of his patented weapons: superior equipment. He bought twenty new Boeing Stratocruisers, an unusually luxurious airliner still remembered fondly by passengers in the same way they used to recall nostalgically the great Martin and Boeing flying boats. For the airlines that operated them—Northwest, American Overseas, British Overseas Airways (Imperial's successor), and United in addition to Pan Am—the Stratocruiser was a plumber's nightmare to maintain and expensive to fly; the engines never seemed to jell with the airframe. But it was a passenger's dream, with its lower-deck cocktail lounge and wide, comfortable cabin. The airplane offset to a great extent Pan Am's poor-service reputation and kept it competitive for a long while.

It was ironic that Harry Truman, who had treated Pan American so cruelly, finally came to Trippe's rescue. American's C. R. Smith had never been overly enchanted with his international division and finally in 1948 agreed to merge American Overseas with Pan American. When the CAB rejected the merger application in 1950, Truman reversed the decision in what was one of the last major favors Juan Trippe was to get from Washington.

Now for the first time he began serious efforts to obtain domestic routes, and met with persistent refusals. A damaging regulatory blow came in the 1969 Transpacific Case decision, giving TWA and Flying Tiger new Pacific authority and permitting American to serve the South Pacific points of Australia, New Zealand, Fiji, and American Samoa—another area where Pan American had pioneered. In the rich mainland Hawaii market, which Pan Am had shared only with United since 1946, the CAB shoved in a platoon of new competitors—Braniff, American, Northwest, Continental, and Western, albeit with certain service restrictions but each with the one advantage Pan American lacked: the ability to draw single-carrier traffic from domestic routes.

I think Alan Boyd, when he headed the CAB, always tried to give Pan American a fair shake. But his immediate successors, first Charles Murphy and then John Crooker, seemed to be anti-Pan Am (or maybe just anti-Trippe), and by the time I became an airline executive, Trippe's influence in official Washington had eroded to the vanishing point. I'd be the first to admit that my reluctant lobbying activities were only marginally effective, but Trippe had no reason to expect success; why he thought a Kennedy Democrat could compete against the C. R. Smiths, Harding

247

Lawrences, Bob Sixes, and Bob Prescotts I'll never understand. C.R., for example, was a close personal friend of Lyndon Johnson and later served as his Secretary of Commerce briefly. Lawrence had powerful Texas influence behind him, and Six was the personification of political ambidexterity—a lifelong Democrat, he got along just as well with Republicans, serving, for example, as chairman of California Democrats for Nixon.

It also escapes me how anyone at Pan Am thought the airline could get anything out of either the Johnson or Nixon administrations—the two greediest since World War II—without Pan Am officers and Directors making personal political or financial contributions. Trippe wouldn't and other top officers didn't, for personal reasons. But it sure as hell cramped Pan Am's Washington style and, more important, while I was knocking on various Washington back doors, front doors, and even roofs, I could have been and should have been learning the airline business.

It wasn't that I had nothing to do, although I wasn't as busy as I should have been. Officially I was a senior vice president in direct charge of Pan Am's Guided Missiles Range Division (later changed to Aerospace Services Division), which under a $100 million Air Force contract operated all the downrange missile-testing stations from Patrick Air Force Base to Bermuda, Antigua, South America, and East Africa—a system involving not only ground radar installations but ships as well. Also under my jurisdiction was the Business Jet Division, whereby we joined in partnership with the French Avions Marcel Dassault Company, manufacturer of the Falcon, a sleek executive jet known in France as the Mystère 20, which would be marketed in the Western Hemisphere by Pan Am. The airline had a large interest in New York Airways, a scheduled helicopter service, and this, too, fell into my lap, along with a pet Trippe project for STOL (Short Takeoff and Landing) operations in the busy northeastern corridor and the operation of Teterboro Airport and the East Side Metroport for helicopters. If one wanted to give me an unofficial title, I was senior vice president in charge of diversification, *sans* the hotel organization, although I did get into this area somewhat in later years.

But back to the jumbo—as far as I know, Trippe took only three Pan Am executives fully into his confidence concerning his $525 million order on April 13, 1966, for twenty-five Boeing 747s—the largest single purchase for one type of aircraft in the history of commercial aviation. Yet only a handful of men knew Trippe was even talking to Boeing about a transport that was not just a new plane but also an aeronautical revolution. Not a single marketing or sales official, to the best of my knowledge, was told that Trippe was considering the huge plane until the decision to buy a four-hundred-passenger transport had been made in his own way.

Inasmuch as the 747 has been blamed for much of Pan Am's subsequent financial troubles, a look at its development history is illuminating. First, like virtually every new transport, it kept gaining size and weight as it moved from preliminary design through blueprint, mockup, and then actual production. Pan American, naturally, wasn't the only carrier Boeing involved on the exciting jumbo-jet concept. But Pan Am, as the first airline to commit itself to buying it, carried more weight than the others in determining its size, specifications, and performance. Both United and American liked the airplane but thought it was too big and heavy for its projected engines and their routes; they wanted a lighter and somewhat smaller 747. It was Trippe who insisted on the maximum design—he wanted the biggest, fastest, highest-flying plane in commercial aviation history, and he wanted Pan Am to be the first to fly it in regular service (by at least twelve months!), as it had been with the Clipper flying boats and the original 707. He got both wishes, but he also bought—at a cost of more than $650 million—an aircraft that literally forced the state of the art. The heavier the airplane, the more stress on the engines—and it was the engines that eventually proved to be the 747's Achilles' heel.

Defenders of both Trippe and the 747 have pointed out that in 1966 very few airline economists could foresee a downturn in traffic growth, so severe as to make the goliath the right plane at the wrong time. They argue that at the time Pan Am bought the 747, traffic volume was expanding at a rate of 15 per cent annually and from 17 per cent to 25 per cent internationally. Almost four years elapsed between the Pan Am 747 order and the first scheduled flight of the giant transport—and a lot can happen during the lead time required to buy and then operate a commercial airliner. What happened, of course, was the 1969–71 Nixon recession, which struck shortly after the 747 went into service, depressing traffic growth almost to the vanishing point. The result was the ugliest word in the airline business—overcapacity—and Pan Am, with twenty-five of the jumbos entering its already huge fleet, was worse off than anyone.

Naturally we needed bank financing to help us buy the most expensive transport in history. Its cost was best underlined by a statement American's C. R. Smith made the day the 747 was dedicated, in 1968, after he had been named Secretary of Commerce.

"Thirty years ago," C.R. noted, "the market value of all the airliners in the United States was on the order of $10 million. Today the market value of this single plane is twice that much!"

But the recession-generated traffic slump wasn't the only reason the 747 failed to live up to expectations. It also encountered technical difficulties that ate into its viability, and these could be laid at least partially right on Juan Terry Trippe's doorstep. He did order a plane that was too big with his own marketing experts kept in the dark, but he was not alone in his hopes that by the time the 747 went into service, traffic would justify his huge investment. The chances are that if he had consulted his subordinates, they might have agreed with his own rosy outlook.

The result of an overweight plane and overstressed engines was a long period of delayed flights, in-flight engine shutdowns at the highest rate in the industry, cancelled trips—and early passenger unhappiness with the safest, most comfortable, and most magnificently built plane, in an overall sense.

Typical was the very inauguration of scheduled 747 service—Pan Am's Flight 2, New York–London. An overheated engine before takeoff, partly due to a tailwind blowing into the exhaust, caused a delay of nearly seven hours. Typical was Western's experience in the hotly contested Los Angeles–Honolulu market; Western, with no wide-bodied jets, pitted its relatively ancient 720Bs against Pan Am's, United's, and Continental's new 747s and managed to hold and even expand a reasonably good share of the traffic. It achieved this simply because the 747s poor reliability record kept many passengers away from the plane during the two years it took Pratt & Whitney to lick the engine problems.

Those problems sabotaged Trippe's plan to put the 747 into

service about a year ahead of everyone else. The initial order should have given Pan Am ten to twelve months' lead time over the rest of the industry, but the power plant bugs resulted in Boeing's turning out 747s with engine deliveries delayed while Pratt & Whitney went through some major modifications. The engineless aircraft accumulated in large numbers outside the Boeing factory, and by the time the difficulties were corrected, TWA and the other carriers were getting their 747s delivered only a few days after Pan Am.

The engine fiasco combined with the traffic decline turned this superb machine into the proverbial white elephant. I am definitely not anti-747. The brilliance of its safety record and passenger praise of its comfort and roominess attest to the soundness of its design. I'm guilty of hindsight, but I think the 747 simply came along too soon; we should have retained the 707s and DC-8s until the early 1970s, handling any expanded traffic with stretched 8s; introduced the smaller jumbos like the DC-10 and L-1011 in the mid-seventies and held back on the 747 until 1980. The 747 is really the ultimate in what might be termed conventional jetliners—but we introduced the ultimate prematurely.

The most dramatic evidence is that Pan Am and TWA, the carriers with the first and most 747s, were nearest to bankruptcy, with TWA selling ten to the Shah of Iran at less than book value for survival cash. (All this trouble dogged the Big Birds before OPEC and their trebled aviation fuel prices overwhelmed these flying gas stations.)

Many of the younger Pan Am executives, going back to Sonny Whitney, had resented Trippe's one-man decisions—the 747 being a prime case in point. We knew that eventually we would have the responsibility of integrating the aircraft into the fleet even though we had been given no decisive voice in its purchase. Some of us felt strongly that Trippe had gone overboard not just in buying the plane but also in the size of the original order—twenty-five with an option for ten more. Gray later threw gas on the burning financial pile by exercising part of that option after he became chief executive: He bought another eight, which gave Pan Am the dubious distinction of managing the world's largest herd of white elephants.

In retrospect, however, I wonder how much of the blame I

should shoulder myself. I felt that I would probably be running Pan Am myself one day. Yet side by side with Trippe and Gray, I sat with the outside Directors at Executive Committee meetings, not once standing up to fight the total overloading of the company. It wasn't just the 747 but other obvious financial overcommitments—such as Gray's purchase of a new $98 million maintenance center at JFK and spending $126 million on the Worldport, Pan Am's plush terminal facilities at Kennedy International—the final cost being $76 million over the original budget allocation. The terminal, as a matter of fact, cost more to build than the fifty-seven-story Pan Am Building in midtown Manhattan.

I should have at least tried to blow an early whistle when Gray indicated he was going to buy an additional eight 747s at a time when I was most aware I was about to succeed him. He asked his brand-new president for his concurrence and I gave it, sitting by silently while Pan Am raised its commitment to more than $1 billion in new aircraft and new terminal facilities, all based on the thinnest kind of market projection—so thin that it left no margin for error.

It wasn't because I was afraid that any opposition might destroy my avowed goal of heading this great airline. It wasn't ambition that blinded me, but rather the brainwashing effect of working for Juan Trippe for nearly four years. In slowly subjecting myself to his dominating pressures, I must have lost perspective. I argued with him vehemently over diversification schemes like New York Airways and taking over Teterboro from the Port Authority, and we had major disagreements about his Washington political tactics. But I guess like so many Pan Am people, I couldn't get myself to challenge this giant of the airline industry head-on regarding the size of the newest Pan Am Clipper or the extent of its corporate debt. Down deep I knew he might be making a lethal gamble, but I couldn't bring myself really to believe what my mind was warning me. And the final factor was my Twilight Zone kind of corporate existence—an heir apparent with little previous experience in the very areas where we were making the biggest mistakes. Ignorance and isolation on one hand, my inexperience on the other—this was my status as I prepared to take over command of a leaking, overloaded ship.

CHAPTER EIGHT

I suppose I could sum up my regime as president and chief executive officer of Pan Am as being the right man at the wrong time—somewhat like the 747 in the world's airline industry.

I was seduced into the job by a very charming founder and godfather; introduced by this benevolent despot into the "family" in an awkward, ungracious way and sidetracked by him from the mainline of airline operations into lobbying as "senior vice president of miscellaneous." I was on my own running three diversified businesses when I should have been in training under a wise and experienced airline administrator.

Trippe, unable to retire until a magic moment of his own choosing, and unwilling to indicate his selection of a successor until the last moment, had set a stage for which the actors were not prepared. After months of near resignation and total frustration while I watched major policy decisions and huge expenditures being made with very little participation by me, suddenly Gray had been selected chief executive officer and I had become president on May 8, 1968.

Whether Trippe chose this moment because he realized the airline had stalled out and was beginning a dive, or because he felt that Gray and Halaby were ready, I'll never know. My paranoia about Trippe, however, makes me suspect that he realized the jig was up in Washington and that he should go out at the peak of Pan Am's earnings, having achieved the glory of making the largest and most advanced procurement in airline history. In any case, my corporate epitaph in Pan Am history will probably read:

"Najeeb E. Halaby, a man who did his best at the worst time."

I might have done much better heading Pan Am at a different time under different circumstances, but assuming full command when I did upon Gray's retirement in 1970, I now see it would have taken a man with much greater airline-operating experience and a successful student of Machiavelli to run a company as big as Pan Am, one so involved with self-satisfaction, prior arrogance toward the public and the government, and one internally full of divided loyalties and prejudices. Most of all, the right man in 1970 had to be coldly ruthless in decisively making drastic changes in the whole company. Certainly that didn't describe me. I am still not sure whether ruthlessness is a weakness or a strength in a corporation, but I didn't have it, and I guess I'm glad.

It was difficult to maintain my confidence in my early months at Pan Am during 1965 because I had come in under such a cloud of uncertainty. Who is this newcomer the papers say is going to take over? What is he going to do among all of our familiar heroes of the past? What does he know about running an airline?

These questions were asked all up and down the line. But even more chilling was the feeling of isolation and sidelining that Trippe, Gray, and the other officers had given me during my first weeks.

One of the most thoughtful and co-operative, however, was the outgoing head of Pan Am's marketing division, Willis Lipscomb, and as he approached retirement, he took me at face value and not as a threat to his own position. He encouraged me to fly the line as a passenger and get a firsthand look at sales and inflight service. He was a fine old southern gentleman, who ran his department like a benign tyrant, centralizing authority over all but the most minor decisions in his own office in New York.

It took only a few trips to realize how highly centralized Pan Am had become in all its departments. There was virtually no authority in the field, and this was official policy—I saw pages of manuals requiring referral to New York of what I would consider unimportant nonpolicy decisions. From time to time I visited stations where no senior officer had ever been before, and I even arranged clandestine meetings with pilots and stewardesses alike, listening to their numerous gripes and noting their various suggestions on how to improve our airline. Throughout all this goodwill activity, however, I had to maintain a very low profile to avoid giving the impression that I was starting to take over long before Trippe got around to making his decision.

My task was to perform my assigned staff duties satisfactorily, but I sneaked rides and access to where the real airline action was. I rode in tourist and economy as well as first class, knowing that how the airline treats the non-VIP passengers is where it cuts the mustard. I poked my nose into baggage handling, reservations, dispatch, and just about every phase of the operation I could without creating resentment or suspicion, and if there wasn't any element of the latter, there certainly was considerable curiosity—particularly among employees who inquired, quite frankly, what I was doing and why. I always tried to explain that I was just interested in how the airline was being run, as a member of the Board and as a member of the Executive Committee. Eventually, of course, the word got back to me that maybe I was taking too much interest— "Don't make like you're taking over," one of the Directors advised me.

There was little doubt in my mind that some of the Directors wanted Trippe out of power, or at least wanted a major reduction of his power. But none of them was prepared to take any initiative. Even as my assigned responsibilities were increasing in scope and demand, so were the constraints under which I was trying to gain airline information and background. With my intrusion obviously resented, I more and more became isolated and frustrated during the early years. Some of my most valuable information came from Lindbergh, whom I saw frequently because he was constantly flying the line and knew more about Pan Am's current operations than either Trippe or Gray. What he reported to Gray and Trippe I'll never know, but he was an extra pair of eyes and ears as well as a very wise observer of Pan Am's development. I've always felt

255

that he was a steady ally of mine, and he never failed to give me intelligence, advice, and support.

Another ally was Pan Am's oldest Director, Mark McKee, who had been on the Board for many years and now was ripening at age 79. He often dropped by my office to encourage me, as did Lindbergh.

By the spring of 1968, I had reached the point of resigning. As had been predicted by so many, it looked as though Trippe would never retire and that all of the external forces were developing adversely against Pan Am. Increasingly I expressed this sense of frustration to Trippe and intimated on several occasions that I was beginning to think of other opportunities. Whenever I did this, he would always throw out some enticing suggestions—such as membership on the Business Council, which he promised to instigate and, to his credit, he recommended me to the chairman of the Board of Chrysler Corporation as a suitable successor on that Board of Directors, which I later joined. He was playing for time and was barely able to keep me from jumping ship, but by then I had already invested more than three years, and my alternatives were neither apparent nor attractive.

One day in May 1968, Trippe called me into his office and gave me some sobering news: Harold Gray had cancer of the lymph glands. I recall the meeting because it was just shortly before Trippe announced his retirement as chairman of the Board and chief executive officer, and it was then that he told me he had decided with the Directors' approval to name Gray his successor in both of these positions, while nominating me to be president. My disappointment at not being selected was softened by sympathy for the seriousness of Gray's illness, which at that moment appeared to be responding to treatment. It was obvious that Trippe had thought Gray's time had come and was afraid his longtime associate might die before his lifelong dream had been realized.

It always has intrigued me that so many of the strongest airline chiefs, those autocratic and totally domineering pioneers who ran one-man carriers, struck out when it came to choosing their successors. It is particularly true of those larger airlines dominated by exceptionally strong men—Trippe at Pan Am, Rickenbacker at Eastern, Smith at American, and Patterson at United. In each

256

case, they chose successors who for one reason or another failed to fill the gunboat shoes they stepped into. There seems to be no common denominator nor causal pattern, but I suspect the "captains" simply neglected really to train a successor and establish a solid line of succession. Or maybe they just hated to face the day when they would have to step down from the throne of power, the left side of the cockpit.

In Trippe's case, his choice of Gray was sentimental rather than objectively wise. Gray was undergoing a series of cobalt treatments, but eventually they failed to arrest what proved to be a terminal disease. Thus it was a sick, slowly dying man to whom Trippe loyally turned over the cockpit of Pan American just as it was heading into its worst storms and navigating for its survival.

Moving up from a seat as a passenger in Juan Trippe's Clipper to Gray's copilot was a revelation, and although my copilotship was short, it was extremely eventful.

The first great event was a raid by a small hotel company called Resorts International from Florida, backed by Charles Bluhdorn, president of Gulf + Western Industries, and indirectly supported by the head of the Trust Department at Chase Manhattan Bank. Bluhdorn approached Gray, indicating that he would like to help improve Pan Am and that he would like a friendly reception to his acquisition of stock. He indicated he had already acquired several hundred thousand Pan Am common shares and was planning to acquire more. Instead of throwing him out of his office, Gray indicated he would give the matter careful thought. He talked first to Juan Trippe, who had retired only a few months before but was occupying my old office in the back benches of Pan Am's Executive Suite. He then talked to me. I was unalterably opposed to the takeover by "that pirate," and I counseled Gray to fight it tooth and nail. Trippe shared this view. However, Gray had a couple of more lunches with Bluhdorn, who expressed a desire to meet with me. I told Gray that I was somewhere between unhappy and unwilling to meet with Bluhdorn and that I thought he ought to make a decision, perhaps in consultation with the Board of Directors, on whether to go ahead appeasing Bluhdorn or opposing him.

Meanwhile, the second event was a strike by Pan Am mechanics, which Gray dealt with in his customary tough manner.

257

The third was Gray's three major financial commitments: the aforementioned purchase of eight more 747s for approximately $210 million, the construction of a new maintenance center for about $100 million, and the construction of a new terminal at Kennedy for about the same amount. It fell to Harold to add $400 million to Juan Trippe's $600 million purchase of the orginal 747s. Gray consulted with me, but he made the decision, and my views—uninformed and inexperienced as they were—did not have a great deal of weight.

For example, I favored using the old Pan Am terminal as the center for mobile lounges carrying passengers out to airliners ramped at some distance from the terminal—in other words, transfer of the Dulles scheme up to JFK. This idea was rejected.

As my first months as second-in-command rushed by, revelation of what lay underneath the Pan Am I had seen as a sideline observer hit me with shocking impact. I knew that Trippe had brought his management team together through fear and secrecy rather than through faith and openness. I had an inkling of how highly centralized management was. I had recognized the external threats from the U. S. Government, and its friendly attitude toward our competitors, plus Washington's determination to put the nonskeds on our backs. Finally, I had some idea how tired and petered-out management was but was quite unaware of how really critical the internal union and personnel problems were becoming.

The biggest problem was how to lead and motivate forty-five thousand people to serve the public better than did the competing airlines. Improved personnel relations and greater productivity were the greatest reforms I had to undertake as Pan Am's new president. I didn't fear unions as Gray seemed to, believing that, in general, responsibly led unions do more good than harm. However, with nine strong unions already deeply and resentfully a part of Pan Am, with headquarters in New York, the union capital of the Americas, and with most of our people located at JFK, the least productive and most corrupt airport in the United States, there was—regardless of one's philosophy—no alternative to living with the unions as effectively as possible.

One of the most serious problems that surfaced in this first phase was the fact that I disagreed with a very close personal friend and confidant of Harold's who was the vice president of industrial relations, Everett Goulard—a bright and aggressive lawyer who had been the great defender of the company against encroaching union power. An intelligent, quick-witted, and strongly conservative man, Goulard was the mail around Harold's fist, and it was Goulard's conviction, shared by a majority of industrial-relations men in the airline industry, that the way to cope with the pilots, mechanics, and stewardesses was "to take a strike issue right down to the wire." They were convinced that local, state, and federal governments were on the side of the unions and that union strike power in an airline was almost lethal, with justice impossible to obtain through mediation or arbitration. They believed the only thing that would hold costs down would be to go right up to or through the early stages of a strike, to exhaust all legal procedures, and then, in a final spasm of fatigue and frustration, to get a settlement. Goulard was not alone; he was just one of the two or three leaders playing a defense-attorney role in a union-ridden industry, as I saw it. When Gray became chairman and chief executive, he naturally kept Goulard reporting to him even though the personnel function was at the very heart of Pan Am's problem. Because of the very close personal relationship between the two, every move I wished to make with regard to staff or management appointments had to be cleared with Goulard, who in turn would get Gray's approval.

Only after Harold began to decline in health was he willing to have Goulard report to me, and soon thereafter I was able to help create a job for Goulard in Washington as the principal officer of a new airline industrial conference group that was designed to seek new ways of collective bargaining between the airlines and the unions. The selection of Goulard's successor was, therefore, of the most critical importance, and I spent much time and effort in finding an "up with people" personnel officer.

Management attitude seemed to me to be of foremost importance. The policy had been to fight the union on every front, every step of the way toward a strike or a grievance procedure. It was "we vs. they," whether the union was the ALPA or the Transport Workers or the Teamsters—the latter being the nation's toughest union, which succeeded the Railway Clerks in controlling our

259

sales, accounting, and clerical personnel. What I was trying to achieve was to convince all employees that we were in this competitive struggle for survival together and that we had to communicate and collaborate. Rather cautiously at first, I set about to lessen at least some of the antimanagement feelings so prevalent among employees. I even went to the extreme of acting as Santa Claus for the youngest Pan Americans at my first employee Christmas party as president in 1968!

My major effort was directed toward those who had the most contact with the public. Emphasis on these key personnel was deliberate: If I could do something to better their job environment, their attitude toward the public might change, for improvement of Pan Am's image among its passengers and shippers was a priority goal. To bring home that message that management was ready to admit past mistakes, I visited every Management Club on the system. My evangelism included the practice of tape-recording informative briefings for employees, a new talk every two weeks, telling them what was going on at the upper levels and available to each employee by dialing a telephone number in his town. We also sent video cassettes to field stations informing them what changes were being made and why—a kind of "how goes it" report to let them know the company wanted confidence and loyalty to be a two-way street. We wanted a sense of participation, and we accompanied these appeals with a program of decentralizing management and delegating authority to a single chief in each of the areas served by Pan Am rather than perpetuating several different Pan Ams in each city the airline served. One of the most popular morale moves we made was to liberalize Pan Am's archaic travel privileges. We gave our own people more liberal annual pass privileges and extended them to employees of other airlines to whom we wanted to show our routes and have them judge and criticize our service.

We even hired an industrial psychologist who conducted in-depth interviews with flight attendants, trying to find out what motivated them to do a better job and where we and management had fallen down. What we found resulted in revised training procedures and some badly needed job-environment improvements. For example, we made drastic changes in crew scheduling and in modernizing crew lounges, two areas in which crew resentment had festered into near mutiny and certainly outright indifference toward the person who counted the most: the passenger.

I sat down with the head of every union representing Pan Am employees, including the Pan Am Master Executive Council of the Pilot's Union and all regional councils. I tried to get across the fact that the company really cared about its employees, that we had serious problems that could be solved only if we pulled together, and that we all had to realize the passenger came first—not ourselves, executives, or employees. The toughest union to deal with was the Teamsters. I never did get to first base with the tough Teamster leaders, but the other unions seemed co-operative and anxious to work with management toward common goals. I like to think that the splendid support that Pan Am employees gave their company during the truly dark days of 1974 sprouted at least to some extent from the seeds of mutual respect sown in my early days as president.

The strongest departments in Pan American were flight operations and legal. The latter figured because Trippe never made a move without consulting the lawyers first. The rest of the airline was suffering from executive malnutrition. Gray's tight-fistedness even with operations and maintenance managers was legendary and the primary cause for the outward mobility of maintenance vice presidents, such as Bossange's going to head maintenance at Braniff, Adams to Continental, and George Warde to American (and later to its presidency). In fact, many of the Pan Am alumni, freed of the stifling environment, had been much more successful after "graduation"—a tribute to their original selection but not to development of management.

Within seventeen months, I had to pump new blood into seventeen out of the top twenty-three executive posts. At times it seemed as though the transfusions were direct from my own veins, promoting a few men but hiring the rest, and inevitably I lost some. I made mistakes in some selections. A number of airline officials said that I brought in too many nonairline people—men as inexperienced in the industry as I was, citing as examples my hiring a personnel man from Western Union and a new financial officer who came over from Federated Department Stores, among others. My reply was that the whole industry as well as Pan Am

261

needed new ideas and new managers. It had a lot of operators but few business administrators.

As soon as I really appreciated the magnitude of our management problems, I knew I badly needed professional help. I recognized that to replace the myth of Trippe with a management such as he and Gray should have developed, I could not do it alone. Certainly there was hardly anyone inside who saw the need for a nearly total revolution in managerial power while reforming the attitude within the company and toward its passengers. In this position of dire need, I turned to Booz, Allen & Hamilton and one of its partners, C. A. "Joe" Kalman, who was a senior partner in the New York office and with whom I had had effective working relationships at Servomechanisms in California and the FAA in Washington.

During the period of our acquaintance Kalman had worked closely with United Air Lines, which is one of the better-managed U.S. carriers, as well as Qantas and other airlines. He had had quite extensive experience at Northeast Airlines, and so unlike most other management consultants, he had some direct, practical, hardheaded experience in the airline industry. With his help—I couldn't really bring him in until Harold Gray had retired, since he considered consultants "parasites"—we concluded that our primary need was for a chief operating officer.

Recognizing that it would take some time and be extremely difficult in Pan Am's present circumstances to recruit a man from another airline, I decided to promote Richard Mitchell, who had worked for me as head of the Aerospace Services Division, to the new position of executive vice president and general manager of the airline. He was given the mandate with Kalman's help to reorganize the company and rebuild the management corps in the engineering, operations, maintenance, accounting, and marketing areas, and to help set the stage for a new president and chief operating officer.

In effect Mitchell's job was to come from Florida to New York, reorganize the company, and work himself out of a job as he and I with Kalman's help recruited a new president. Mitchell was most helpful. He had an orderly mind, was a good administrator, and knew where the great problems of Pan Am lay. Since he had nothing to lose, he was clinical, candid, and fearless in his approach. He was absolutely incorruptible and determined to replace cronyism with competence in the key jobs. For example, he brought in "Mitchell's Mafia" from the Aerospace Services Division—young men who were accustomed to investigating and auditing and they went through a number of the least productive units of the company as the Marine Corps went through Nicaragua. Unfortunately Dick was not in good health, and his wife detested Manhattan and the long hours that he was forced to keep. As a result he was only available to me for a few months and could not finish the job he'd so capably begun, for physical reasons. Worst of all, we were unable to recruit a suitable man to take up where Mitchell had left off upon his early retirement. So temporary relief was not enough; permanent strength was required.

The recruiting and placement team was composed of myself, Dick Mitchell, Joe Kalman, and the substantial worldwide Booz, Allen & Hamilton staff, plus Dr. Robert Snowden, the industrial psychologist we had used at FAA. This made a very good team. Our first steps were to take inventory of the company's managerial manpower to take advantage of insiders, as we had with Mitchell. We did some reshuffling, particularly in the process of decentralizing the management—trying, as I had done in the FAA, to decentralize and strengthen field operations. In the course of this, we used all of the techniques of evaluation and appraisal, and for the first time in the history of the company we set up a management-development program designed to bring along young men who were motivated by upward opportunity, and we began to appraise managers on the criteria set down to measure their performance.

This, however, was a long-term program, and we needed people in key positions immediately. We identified those positions and then canvassed first the airline industry and then industrial management at large. This proselytizing team worked quite well, except that it could not find a president and chief operating officer. Our next most difficult executive search was for a chief financial officer—obviously a key position for a company in as much difficulty as Pan Am. There was no one within the company who had developed sufficiently, and nearly all at the top recognized that we had to go outside. The outstanding young financial officer in the industry was Robert Oppenlander of Delta Air Lines, and after meeting him two or three times in Atlanta and at IATA meetings, I invited him to New York to discuss the position. He said he would be interested in being president of Pan Am or even executive vice president but he would not be interested in the narrower job of vice president of finance and treasurer. It was a disappointing reaction because he would have been ideal for the company. He had a breadth of mind, a professional precision, and a very tight profit-and-loss sense. We next turned to the former chief financial officer of TWA, Robert Kerley, who by now had gone on to more lucrative companies. He was a very powerful and capable man and I very much wanted him to come with us but we could not convince him to make the move. We then sought out the treasurer of American Airlines, Richard Bressler; he gave the job careful consideration, but George Spater would not let him go, immediately promoting him and giving him a raise.

We then looked outside the industry and considered a number of very capable men and finally decided on Richard Knight. He had very fine training in General Electric's accounting department and had moved on to successively more important jobs; at the time we approached him he was vice president of finance for Federated Department Stores in Cleveland, Ohio.

Booz, Allen recommended him very highly, and one of our Directors, General Alfred Gruenther—a fine judge of men—thought well of Knight. After a number of interviews in New York and a trial visit by Mrs. Knight, he looked like our man. He would not voluntarily submit to a Snowden interview and psychological evaluation.

"I have been all through that and I'm too old for it," he told me. I didn't insist and, perhaps, that was a fatal mistake on my part, because it might have disclosed things that made his appointment a mistake—mainly his ambition to become president of Pan Am at the earliest opportunity.

At the time Knight was hired he had a fine record, very strong training, and an excellent reputation among the key bankers and insurance executives who provided us with vital credit. In fact, I consulted with all of them at Chase, Citibank, Metropolitan Life, and Equitable Life—they all were quite strong in supporting him for the job whose importance was very great to them.

One might ask at this point why we relied so heavily on the advice of outside management consultants to fill key posts. Frankly, their use is a crutch that should be indulged in only when one's normal facilities are broken or ailing, and then only temporarily until the body of management has healed. This was only too true of Pan Am's situation at the upper levels. As Dick Mitchell got deeper into the Marketing Department, for example, he found that Harold Gray's personal assistant—whom he had chosen to head sales and services was unable to cope with his wide and demanding responsibilities. Willis Lipscomb, who had somewhat reluctantly agreed on the choice of his successor by Gray, concurred in this appraisal. We also felt that to decentralize our marketing and service efforts we would have to move some of the best men out into the field. At about the same time, largely on the recommendation of Joe Kalman, we had decided to bring in as head of all sales and services a very capable former Pan American marketing man— James Leet, president of Northeast Airlines which was about to be absorbed by Delta Air Lines.

Leet, an Irishman who had made a great record of sales for Pan Am in New York and Dublin, was a very strong physical figure of a man and well regarded by his former colleagues. His return was welcomed by those who had chafed under Harold Gray's cold demeanor and rather indifferent approach to problems of selling tickets. Leet saw a future, perhaps the top job in Pan Am, and he saw no future in Delta after Northeast had been acquired. He accepted the job after we let Normal Blake go, and Leet was quite supportive of the idea of bringing in a third consultant—Henry Golightly—to achieve the kind of marketing reforms that the latter had helped achieve at both American and Continental. I barely knew Golightly, a highly regarded management expert, and had no inkling of the role he was to play in Pan Am's future. Golightly was brought in somewhat against the wishes of Joe Kalman, who thought that Booz, Allen & Hamilton could provide as much marketing and management reorganization as Golightly. I suspected that Kalman might be right, but I agreed to let Mitchell and Leet hire Golightly in the belief that he was about tops in the area of corporate marketing decentralization, as he had demonstrated at two other airlines. I did not want him to compete with Booz, Allen & Hamilton, nor did I want Kalman and him to overlap in any way.

Up until this new wave of consultants, the company had always relied on its inner resources, except in the area of public affairs and government relations. There Trippe had always had complete faith in Sam Pryor, his Yale classmate, and Willis Player, his VP for public affairs. Trippe and Pryor had in the forties and fifties developed the largest network of consultants all over the United States and abroad that any company had ever conceived. When I took over, I asked Player for a list of these consultants, Pryor having retired the year before. To my amazement there were over fifty of them, and the tactic worked out by Pryor and Player was to employ them as political operatives.

A firm close to some particularly influential congressman or senator would be hired. Frequently the firm would be permitted to bill Pan Am enough to pay for tables at political dinners, an indirect form of contribution. I was never able to prove it, but I suspected that some of these consultant billings also were covering cash contributions to key politicians. At any rate, I told Player I would not tolerate these arrangements any longer.

I still remembered those 1947 Senate hearings into the Howard Hughes flying boat, a controversy that the adroit Hughes turned into an attack on the integrity of Maine's Senator Owen Brewster. Hughes was then heading TWA and drew the rather obvious conclusion that Brewster was after that airline, not the flying boat. The senator from Maine was known around Washington as "the senator from Pan Am" and had introduced legislation that would have squeezed TWA out of overseas competition. Brewster himself had instigated the Hughes investigation and by doing so stuck his head into a buzz saw; Hughes demolished him during the hearings, and amid the wreckage of the senator's reputation were some tarnished pieces belonging to Pan Am and Trippe. Brewster wasn't the only lawmaker reportedly in Trippe's hip pocket; a similar charge was made against Senator McCarran of Nevada. I was determined to abolish this kind of backdoor maneuvering.

In any case, the widespread consultant network Pan Am had established had lost most of its effectiveness; its principals had grown old, running out of both energy and influence. To put it bluntly, even if their services had been legal and ethical, they were costing Pan Am a fortune without paying any dividends. I began at once to unhook the network.

Here and there abroad, consultants were acquired because of their political influence with the governments where Pan Am wanted routes and favorable rates set. I neither knew these gentlemen nor knew the disciplines under which they were operating, and we rapidly replaced them with full-time Pan Am employees. In fact, I found upon becoming president of Pan Am that the only consultant Pan Am had who was worth more than he was paid was my favorite airman, Charles Lindbergh, who since the 1930s had been receiving five hundred dollars a month for his services!

Over the years up to 1963 Pan Am had been extraordinarily successful in getting what it wanted out of Washington, primarily out of the State Department, the White House, and the Senate, rather than through the regular procedures of the designated regulatory agencies such as the CAB and the FAA. In fact, having gone around end and over the top to get what he wanted, Trippe had earned the deep-seated enmity of most staffers in all of the agencies with whom the company management had to live on a daily basis. Pan Am's success, its status as No. 1 airline in the world, and its "political arrogance" had made enemies all over Washington.

I was fully aware of the Pan Am phobia and hoped to be able to mitigate it. But the most interesting thing that I discovered was that Pan Am's power in Washington was far less than reputed and its method of dealing with the politicians was far less astute than widely believed. Essentially it was based upon Juan Trippe's own personal charm, his legendary reputation, and his use of financial and political power on a personal basis with Presidents, White House staffers, Cabinet officers, and senators. He did this by hiring friends of the current Administration as consultants to the company or naming them to the Board of Directors. He did it by making personal calls, entertaining, flying them in the Pan Am executive aircraft, a converted WWII bomber, rather than through his own personal contribution of funds to political campaigns. I never recall seeing Juan at a political dinner and, as far as I know, he never made any substantial personal contributions to any candidates or parties on behalf of the company. He let Pryor, Player, and the Washington staff do that, and in the process they created the aforementioned network of individual consultants through whom "they took care of their friends." The fact that this was rather wide practice simply justified it in the eyes of the practitioners. If I've heard Trippe say once, with his eyes wide and innocent, "I don't know what Sam and Willis are doing but I'm sure they wouldn't do anything wrong," I've heard it a dozen times. This business of developing political influence is a self-generating thing, and those who get involved tend to self-justification and easy rationalization.

Very little question had been raised officially about the hiring of consultants to acquire political influence until the spring of 1967, when the Internal Revenue Service brought an investigation to a head in California. It involved a public-relations firm, and an audit of its income tax returns had indicated that it was getting substantially more fees than was normal, with some of it traced to political contributions. In other words, the whistle was being blown on this method.

Another method available to international corporations was "laundering the cash." I recall one of my Pan Am "public affairs" colleagues in the course of the presidential campaign of '68 coming to me with a proposal for doing this via our Inter•Continental Hotels in Europe and Mexico. His proposal went along the following lines:

The Inter•Continental Hotel Frankfurt could convert *deutsche* marks into dollars on the Frankfurt exchange. He would pick up the dollars in Frankfurt and bring them here for direct contributions to the Nixon campaign. Pan American would then reimburse its wholly owned subsidiary, Inter•Continental Hotels, and credit the Frankfurt Hotel or, as he said, we can do the same thing at the hotel in Mexico or even in Colombia.

I said I didn't want any part of the idea. It immediately appeared to me to be not only a violation of the Corrupt Practices Act, with which we had become fairly familiar in the government, but also a scheme that would foul up the normal business relationships between the parent company and subsidiary. Finally, I didn't want any individual in any of our companies responsible for handling tens of thousands of dollars in cash. "Furthermore," I told him, "Paul Sheeline, the president of IHC, would have nothing to do with it!"

"Well, I thought it was a pretty good idea," my colleague said sadly when I turned him down.

In the area of kickbacks to contractors and suppliers during my time at Pan Am, there were rumors of people on the take at JFK. So we reviewed and strengthened the company's rules, which are somewhat tougher than the criminal statutes of the state of New York. Each officer and employee of the company had to pledge that he had not and would not accept anything from an outside source for doing his job in the company.

Pan Am's badly weakened influence in Washington had the unfortunate effect of affecting my own performance in the presidency. For example, one of my greatest mistakes was my failure to get my own appointees to work together in harmony on a consistent and daily basis. Among all the newcomers, some friction and feuding was inevitable and even healthy, if held to reasonable proportions, but my people went too far. I should have followed Trippe's example of blowtorch persistency and if I couldn't get this done with faith and pleading, I should have instilled sheer fear.

The result was that we never really did have a team—with all the selflessness and mutual goals that word *team* implies. We didn't even have unity borne of awe and fear as Trippe had inspired. Part of this was my own fault, but it was a personal weakness directly attributable to the lack of time I had to indulge in administrative affairs. To put it bluntly, I was spending as much time and effort in Washington as in New York, lobbying among our own people and exploring mergers with competitors, as well as managing the airline. To paraphrase National Airlines' old slogan, it was no way to run an airline.

A cruel event that befell Pan American was the Transpacific Case. Trippe, recognizing the impending disaster, had violated his pledge to me that I would not have to do any lobbying for Pan Am after leaving the government. He was in mortal fear of losing the case, a fear that turned out to be only too justified. It caused him to

269

dispatch me week in and week out, month after month, trying to put Pan Am's arguments before influential congressmen and the White House itself.

Admittedly, I could wield a bit more influence and prestige as Pan Am's president, though not as much as its chief executive; there were times when I was asked whether Trippe still was really running Pan Am, and I couldn't honestly answer. At any rate, Lyndon Johnson decided the Transpacific Case just before he left office, and the new Nixon administration, after reviewing LBJ's decision, left Pan Am out in the cold.

The Transpacific Case was the lowest point in the long history of the regulatory process—and also the lowest ethically in terms of American air policy. This was the largest, most complicated case in the history of the Civil Aeronautics Board. All trunk airlines (eleven at the time) plus nonskeds, cargo carriers, and local-service carriers applied for routes in the Pacific, some twenty applicants in all. The record of hearings and briefs comprises more than ten thousand volumes weighing about thirty tons. And when the case finally got before the full CAB, the staff and the individual members had been lobbied to a greater extent than ever, and this was just the semifinal round before the finals at the White House, since international routes were involved. And only a decade later did the massive corporate political gifts surface out of Watergate.

A word about the process. In theory, a career professional civil servant reads and listens judiciously and objectively to the facts and makes his recommendations to the Board, consisting of five political appointees divided three for the majority party in power and two for the minority party, with the chairman having been appointed each year by the President.

Servicing the CAB theoretically as "officers of the court" are the members of the Washington bar specializing in civil-aviation matters, often alumni of the CAB staff itself, and generally men who have decided that the partly political, partly judicial process of the CAB gives them optimum opportunity as practitioners of the law and politics. Some of these men have done a great deal to corrupt the whole procedure, making specious and capricious motions, filing fictional briefs, charging extraordinarily large fees and,

270

in general, contributing to the delinquency of the CAB as a quasi-judicial organization.

Outside of the lawyers are the consultants. For example, Player had hired a man solely to find out what was going on in the minds of the individual members. His techniques and procedures were unknown to me, but his purpose was to listen to gossip, trace pieces of paper through the labyrinth of the CAB, and alert and identify confidential ideas and documents so that Pan Am would have a spy inside as well as lobbyists and lawyers outside.

Another approach was to hire a law firm to lobby congressmen and senators who, in turn, would put pressure on CAB members who may have come from their districts or may have been obligated in getting appointment and/or confirmation. One of the best, a very resourceful firm called Corcoran, Youngman and Rowe—Tommy Corcoran of New Deal days and Jim Rowe, a former administrative assistant to FDR and a member of the Hoover Commission—was very capable in this area, particularly with veteran senators such as Mike Mansfield from Rowe's home state of Montana.

One technique was to get one of the senators to make a call of inquiry—never a formal call demanding something but rather a very pointed inquiry that made clear the direction of their thinking. Naturally a Board member who wanted to continue as chairman or just be reappointed would respond favorably. Senator Magnuson, for example, had his favorite airline, Northwest. At one point he had been general counsel of Northwest Airlines, and its principal service was in the Northwest, which included his home state of Washington.

Senator Monroney and Senator Cannon, who were No. 1 and No. 2, respectively, on the Aviation Subcommittee, were quite partial to TWA, who served their respective states and, as a result, seemed anti-Pan Am, TWA's principal competitor. Pan Am had no such support since its headquarters was in New York, and the Empire State's senators couldn't afford to pick from one of the six airlines with headquarters or large offices there. The same was true of California and Florida, where two other main Pan Am bases are located. The Florida senators were for Eastern and National, California senators tended to be for United and later Continental, whose maintenance base or corporate headquarters were there. Even more so was Minnesota's delegation for Northwest and Missouri's for TWA.

The number of lunches and private telephone calls to CAB members during the Transpacific deliberations was the heaviest in the Board's history. Johnson had put in Under Secretary of Agriculture Charles Murphy, former assistant to Harry Truman, as an interim chairman of the CAB but soon moved him over into the White House as an assistant to make way for John Crooker from Houston, Texas. Crooker's appointment had been strongly supported by Braniff and American—the two "Texas airlines" who were very strong with LBJ. Crooker's appointment was a clear indication that the case was going to be a highly politicized one.

In any case, when the Board slowly and belatedly sent its recommendations to the White House, the rush was on to find out what they contained. Lobbyists for all the carriers descended on White House staffers, and Johnson remarked to a friend that he never felt as much pressure from so many during his tenure in the White House. For example, one summer afternoon in 1968 I emerged from the White House as my old boss and beloved friend, Laurance Rockefeller, entered. He was seeing a staff officer to persuade him to recommend Eastern Air Lines for a route across the southern United States and on to Tahiti and the South Pacific—the same man I had been talking to for an hour, urging that new routes shouldn't be awarded to anyone. New lawyers thought to be in solid with the Johnson administration were hired in droves. Continental, for example, hired Clark Clifford, and the Flying Tiger Line grabbed Mike Feldman, JFK's transportation specialist who had left the White House after LBJ took over.

Whole new offensive airline platoons appeared in the fall of 1968 working every level of power—House of Representatives, Senate, large contributors, etc. Since a presidential election campaign was under way, the contributions streamed in, and the fundraisers for both parties were particularly avid in putting the bite on airlines seeking routes in the Transpacific Case.

Ours was clearly a defensive maneuver; we had the routes that the others wanted, and for the domestic carriers it was a golden opportunity to break out of domestic service into what they thought would be very lucrative international operations.

Even the famous "military/industrial complex" entered the free-for-all. The initial role of the airframe and engine manufacturers was to maximize their sales as each applicant tried to outdo the others in placing paper orders for aircraft so they could prove they would have the capacity to carry the passengers on any routes that might be awarded. Inevitably this had a substantial effect on increasing orders, for the jumbos as well as for the long-range 707s and stretched DC-8s. All the forces of the airline and aerospace lobbies were brought to bear on the White House as soon as the CAB sent over its recommendations.

Johnson's decision, made just before he left office, largely rewarded his friends and punished his enemies, in the timeless manner of the lame-duck politician. American Airlines to Hawaii and the South Pacific. TWA on around the world. Five new carriers to Hawaii, etc.

The Transpacific Case still wasn't finished. Shortly after Richard Nixon became President, he announced he would review Johnson's decision, and ultimately he was to make some changes—taking away Continental's authority to serve the South Pacific, for example, and giving it to American. This was the most unexpected revision, for LBJ's award of the route to Continental instead of American was a surprise—C. R. Smith was Johnson's Secretary of Commerce—and Nixon's taking the route away from Bob Six was equally surprising. It didn't make much difference to Pan Am, however—the floodgates of fresh competition were now wide open.

At first I felt that dealing with the Nixon regime might be a refreshing change from the Johnson days. I knew the new President, not well but sufficiently so that I was hopeful of a fairer shake for Pan Am, or at least a new one. I first met Richard Nixon in the spring of 1946, while he was serving his first term as a young congressman. We happened to be in the Naval Reserve together, and another reservist, a good friend of mine named Philip Watts, introduced us. Nixon liked Phil, who had been one of Admiral Ernest King's aides during the war, and apparently liked me, too. Or maybe he liked those Navy wings I possessed—on a couple of occasions, Nixon hitched rides with me to New England that summer in a "double-breasted" Beechcraft for some relief from Washington's stifling heat. When I was working at the Pentagon on Forrestal's staff, he'd call me from time to time and later, after he became a senator and Phil Watts was executive director of the State Department's policy planning staff, Nixon would invite the two of us to his office, where he'd pick our brains on foreign-policy issues.

When Nixon wanted something—information and/or intelligence—he could be extremely affable and even likable. Phil and I once had a drink with him at his Senate office, joined by Rose Mary Woods, who had been Watts's secretary at the State Department before she went to work for Nixon. My politics, openly on the liberal Democratic side, never seemed to bother Nixon, and there were times when both Phil and myself were rather pleased at his conversion to internationalism and even a touch of liberalism—figuring, of course, that we had something to do with it.

Phil used to have Nixon to dinner at his home, deliberately inviting avowed Nixon haters as fellow guests to show them that the man had a better side. Eventually I began wondering if Nixon truly had a better side—it was during the McCarthy hearings that I felt my greatest contempt for Nixon, feeling that he was supporting this sinister and unscrupulous demagogue and that in some ways he actually was like the Wisconsin senator. By 1954, we had drifted apart, and I didn't see him again until shortly after his first election to the presidency. I had supported Senator Humphrey, and about the time that I became Pan Am's president I made an effort to renew our admittedly thin relationship. It was strictly a gesture in behalf of my airline, which already had suffered enough from the machinations of the Johnson administration and LBJ's Texas political crony, John Crooker. So I called Rose Mary Woods, who not only remembered me but was unusually jovial.

"I'd like to see the President for a few minutes, at his convenience," I said.

She said she'd try to arrange it, and it wasn't long after that that Nixon called me. He apologized for not being able to see me right away but said he'd like me to meet his new Transportation Secretary, John Volpe. This led to my seeing Volpe at the Pierre Hotel in New York, a brief but friendly session that ended in my driving out to LaGuardia Airport with him.

"You must know the President very well," he remarked, "because he told me to see you right away."

At that point I was beginning to dream that Pan Am finally might have some sympathetic ears at the White House; as all political seekers say, we didn't want special treatment, but rather an understanding of problems that were not entirely of our own making. I even got on the White House social list, probably the doing of Rose Mary Woods, and was invited to the Executive Mansion on a couple of occasions. Later in the winter, Phil Watts and I were attending the Alfalfa Club's first dinner during the Nixon administration. Emboldened by a few drinks, we went up to the head table to shake hands with the President and his new Secretary of State, William Rogers, to chat a bit about the good old days. It so happened on the same occasion that I was sitting at a table close to H. R. Haldeman, whose family I had known in Los Angeles, and I took advantage of this proximity to make a pitch for Pan Am.

"We need a lot of help from the White House," I told Haldeman, "and I'd like the opportunity to talk to you about it."

He looked at me coldly from under his crewcut.

"Well, switch over to our side and we may be able to help you."

I laughed—it was an unbelieving laugh—and didn't get so much as a smile in return. That remark from Haldeman was a shadow of things to come as the new Administration settled into power, putting Nixon's own stamp on those mediocrities who became the heads of the various agencies and departments. It became only too clear that this would be one of the most partisan regimes in history. Those who had contributed heavily to the campaign, those who had demonstrated the greatest loyalty toward Richard Nixon, were the men running things. And thanks to Trippe's strange insistence on becoming a political eunuch, Pan Am people had contributed nothing so far as I knew. True, the airline's Board of Directors had a heavy Republican tinge, but most of these members were content to use their Brownie points not for Pan Am but for their own more important interests.

275

As I observed earlier, our first crisis under Nixon's administration arose when Harold Gray was advised that Resorts International was going to raid Pan Am via stock acquisition. I heard about it almost too late; Trippe, who had supposedly retired, was aware of the scheme but didn't bother to let either Gray or me know what was happening. This plan was hatched, according to the information we finally received, when Charles Bluhdorn discussed possible acquisition of the airline with a vice president of Chase Manhattan Bank and none other than Charles "Bebe" Rebozo, Nixon's buddy, at a secret meeting in the Bahamas with the head of Resorts International.

It wasn't a complete surprise to Gray, who already had had some discussions with Bluhdorn concerning Pan Am's financial difficulties. Gray actually was not averse to further exploratory talks, but he didn't know that Trippe was not only violently opposed but also scared—to such a degree that he personally went to the White House and told presidential aides, including Robert Ellsworth, that Bluhdorn and his colleagues were trying to take over Pan Am. Without letting us know, Trippe was sounding alarms all over Washington, and Gray finally heard the bells. He decided that I should go to Washington for a counterattack.

I spent several hours with Bob Ellsworth, a former congressman, who unlike some of the men around Nixon seemed to have a heart as well as a brain, and convinced him that with all Pan Am's troubles, a takeover by outside, nonairline interests was the last thing we needed. With Ellsworth's blessings, I also talked to Senators Warren Magnuson and Norris Cotton, the senior members of the Commerce Committee, and we put together a bill that would require public disclosure by anyone acquiring more than 5 per cent of a civil air carrier's stock. The bill had the President's support and eventually was passed and signed into law. It effectively blocked Bluhdorn and his friends—they needed secrecy in order to pick up the stock while it was declining, knowing that if the planned Gulf + Western/Resorts International raid became public, the stock would climb out of the bargain category.

But in a sense our victory was a defeat. I think the President felt he had done Pan Am not only a big favor but also a rather undeserved favor, considering the airline's failure to contribute anything to his campaign. Certainly it was the last thing the Nixon administration did to help Pan Am. When it came time for Nixon to review the horrendous Transpacific decision, he left all the anti-Pan Am provisions virtually untouched. Almost every carrier involved in that most tortuous of all route cases got at least part of what it wanted, with three exceptions: Pan Am, United, and Eastern. Not one of this trio could muster sufficient pressure or influence to pry major revisions out of the White House. For Pan Am, more than for either Eastern or United, it was a crippling blow.

We at Pan Am cheered when Crooker left the CAB, but Nixon's choice of successor was Secor Brown, a transportation scholar from Cambridge who had once done consultant work for Boeing and Pan Am. This previous experience was raised at his confirmation hearing and did Pan Am no good whatsoever, for the disclosure seemed to make Brown lean over backward to avoid any impression that he might be giving Pan Am a break. And Brown, in my opinion, turned out to be surprisingly inept as chairman.

He was extremely pliant in face of the political pressures from the supplemental carriers and, conversely, rock-hard when faced with the arguments advanced by Pan Am and TWA primarily, who kept warning that the nonscheduled airlines were skimming the cream off our most lucrative international routes. It is my belief that Brown, who had served briefly under his fellow Bostonian, Governor John Volpe, as Assistant Secretary of Transportation, was heavily under the influence of people like Bob Haldeman, John Ehrlichman, Peter Flanigan, and Charles Colson—a quartet of solid anti-Pan Am voices. (I always suspected that Brown's goal was to be Secretary of Transportation with Vice President Volpe in 1973.)

My own influence at the White House dwindled to the size of a thimble. Occasionally I was invited there for the swearing-in of a friend or when there was some aviation-award function, such as the Harmon or Collier trophies, and it seemed suitable to extend me an invitation either as a senior Pan Am officer or as an ex-FAA administrator. The closest I got to the President occurred after I had served on a special committee established to mobilize

277

support for Nixon's "New Economic Policy," which I had no reason to oppose. Late in 1971, not long before Nixon took off on his historic trip to Red China and the Soviet Union, he gave a reception for the committee, thus affording me a chance for a quick conversation more or less in private.

We talked briefly about the forthcoming trip to China (I had urged normalization with the PRC since early 1971), and I suggested that he might take along one of our new 747s as the press corps' charter aircraft. He liked the idea and said he would discuss it with his aides. He was in such a good mood that I figured it was an opportune moment in which to strike a blow for Pan Am.

"I realize how busy you've been, Mr. President," I ventured, "so I haven't bothered you previously. I would appreciate a chance to talk to you alone for a few minutes one of these days."

"Call Rose Mary and she'll arrange it," he said promptly.

I did, but nothing immediate came of it.

When I finally was armed with almost complete authority as Gray's successor, I was determined to do something about Pan Am's losing Washington team. I went to Bryce Harlow, an old friend from my Pentagon days who was now Nixon's chief legislative strategist and a crafty, competent man with excellent Capitol Hill connections. Press reports indicated he was ending his temporary stint in the White House, so I offered him the job of Pan Am's Washington representative with the status of a senior vice president. Harlow, I think, was tempted, and I know he considered it carefully. But his decision was negative.

"When I leave the White House, Jeeb," he told me regretfully, "I'm going back to my old company, Procter & Gamble."

"You're probably being wise," I sighed, "but as the price for that refusal would you nominate someone else?"

He promised to find a good man for the Pan Am lobbying job and a few days later came up with the name of a Marine Corps brigadier general, Donald Hittle, who was about to leave his post as Assistant Secretary of the Navy for Manpower. I didn't know Hittle but I checked him out with a number of people whose judgment I trusted—his own deputy, Bob Willy, who had been my chief personnel officer at the FAA; Secretary of Defense Melvin Laird;

278

then Congressman Gerald Ford and several senators who knew him well and praised his performance as a lobbyist for the Marines.

Hittle himself was eager to take the Pan Am post. Coincidentally, he had married an attractive Pan Am stewardess and had a natural affinity for her airline. So I hired him shortly after he resigned from the Navy Department—an action that immediately downgraded the top Washington staff members. Most of them, realizing they weren't getting anywhere with the Nixon administration, resigned gracefully. The one major exception to acceptance of my housecleaning was the retired Director, Sam Pryor. Ironically, Pryor was quite popular socially and had made many friends in the nation's capital, yet his personal and social popularity had never stemmed the anti-Pan Am tide on the White House and legislative fronts (during the early 1960s), where influence really counted.

Pryor was bitter at my decisions to scrub our Washington stables, to clean out a barnful of public-relations consultants he had raised, and to reduce an empire of 125 PR people costing Pan Am over $3 million a year. Pryor warned me that eliminating them would hurt us with Nixon, but I felt that it really would have no effect one way or the other, and as for Pryor himself, I considered him obsolete on the Washington scene. It was only natural that he became extremely embittered toward me—not to mention how he felt when he saw his fifty thousand shares of Pan Am stock decline sharply in value. He had retired in 1965, but even in 1970 he had not given up some of the fringe benefits he had been enjoying, such as a Pan Am telephone extension in his Greenwich, Connecticut, home and the privilege of handing out favors to his friends. Later Pryor was to get his revenge: When I began running into my own troubles and my leadership was not only questioned but also challenged, I found that Pryor was one of the Old Guard who sought to undermine me with certain Directors and Pan Am supporters in the New York community.

Quite early in the game I became aware that the Directors weren't being of much help and that we needed new blood on the Board, with a more balanced representation. My first success came when I persuaded Cyrus Vance to join the Board, and he was a strong addition, indeed. Although a Democrat, he was highly respected by people like Mel Laird, Bill Rogers, Henry Kissinger, and by Nixon himself. The President several times had asked Vance to accept various major government posts but was turned down. To balance out Democrat Vance, I picked former Governor William Scranton of Pennsylvania, a far more liberal Republican than Nixon, and Robert O. Anderson, Chairman, Atlantic Richfield Company.

When Nixon named Arthur K. Watson as ambassador to France, and he resigned from our Board, we invited his brother, Thomas, to become a Director. Again seeking balance, I talked William T. Coleman, a prominent and public-spirited Philadelphia attorney, into accepting a directorship—thus making him the first black in history to join an airline board. Incidentally, we beat American Airlines to Coleman by just two days; Coleman's ability and reputation were to be recognized later when President Ford named him Secretary of Transportation in 1975.

The final addition to the Board was by way of a deliberate effort to get a truly hard-hat Nixon Republican as a member. After seeking advice from Bryce Harlow, Peter Flanigan, and other White House staffers, I was impressed with the credentials of Donald M. Kendall, Board chairman of Pepsico and a longtime friend of Nixon as well as a major GOP contributor. I had met Kendall before but didn't know him very well, and I asked him to lunch one day. He was flattered at the directorship offer and also pleased—he had recently married a Viennese lady who loved to travel, and he had a number of children for whom pass privileges would be welcomed. He told me that his first wife had been the daughter of a Navy admiral who had once served on the Pan Am Board.

I didn't really dig deeply into what kind of person Kendall was. I certainly didn't require any personal oath of loyalty to me or to Pan Am; I selected him solely because of his friendship and influence with Richard Nixon, John Mitchell, Maurice Stans, and Peter Flanigan—all of which happened to be the wrong reasons. He was taken on the Board without my knowing anything about his attitude, his philosophy, and particularly his objectivity with regard to both me and the company.

It was a fatal mistake in two ways. First, we might as well have picked the curator of the Smithsonian as a Director, for all the good Kendall did Pan Am at the White House. He was not only close to Nixon but Flanigan as well, yet there was no record or results of his ever having intervened either with the President or Flanigan on Pan Am's behalf. He made a major effort toward getting his directorship approved by the Civil Aeronautics Board, over the objections of CAB staff members who thought a conflict of interests was involved; Kendall's company, Pepsico, owned a trucking company. His energy in overcoming this obstacle was admirable and promising, but I wished some of it could have been directed toward helping our airline.

My second mistake in choosing Kendall was that I had unwittingly invited an enemy into my camp. Without my realizing it until it was too late, Kendall apparently felt that a principal task as a new Director was to get rid of Halaby—in favor of a man with a more profitable experience as an airline administrator, preferably a Republican. This was his right, of course, but I never dreamed that I had admitted a figurative Trojan horse committed to the early selection of my successor.

Naïve concerning Kendall's intentions and unaware that both Peter Flanigan and Secor Brown were getting set against me, I did my damndest to get our message to the top. There was one bright ray of hope when Rose Mary Woods finally called me to advise that the President would see me—the day before Thanksgiving, in 1971. I was vastly encouraged by the simple fact that he was willing to listen; I was sure that once presented with the cold facts, he had the good sense and judgment to agree that our airline had been the victim of regulatory wrongs, and that he would be willing to correct them. Carefully prepared and coached, I laid out the proposals to save Pan Am. And when I emerged from the Oval Office, I was even more convinced we had won a major battle. The President was not only sympathetic but also promised to do everything possible to help Pan Am. (Someday I want to hear the White House tape recording of that meeting in the Oval Office.)

Flanigan, who had been present, said little during the course of my talk with Nixon but had plenty to say to me privately after it was over. He thought it was dirty pool for me to have gotten into the Oval Office without going through him. He also expressed irritation over the difficult issues I had raised and the fact that the

President had indicated his desire to solve them against Flanigan's wishes to keep them submerged or diffused. At that point I didn't give a damn how Flanigan felt; I thought I had the President of the United States on Pan Am's side. I was wrong.

Nixon had told Flanigan to review Pan Am's case, which I had presented in a handsome blue-leather binder, and, more importantly, "to do what we can now and report back to me the reasons we can't do the rest." I never heard another word out of the White House. In fact, that was my last invitation and my last visit to 1600 Pennsylvania Avenue. According to some very reliable information I received later, Flanigan apparently put the word out that I was to see only him in the future and not to be allowed to see the President again. I also learned later that Flanigan during all this time had been discussing my increasingly shaky status at Pan Am with both Secor Brown of the CAB and Kendall. Flanigan was furious at me for my aggressiveness with the President, and Brown was even more angry when he heard that I bluntly told Nixon that many of Pan Am's troubles could be traced directly to CAB indifference, lethargy, and bias against the airline.

The eventual result was another nail in my corporate coffin. Flanigan and Kendall concluded, I surmised, that so long as I was head of Pan Am, it would get no favors out of Washington—justified or not. Certainly that was the opinion given me by Kendall. Later I found out that my name had been added to John Dean's list of Nixon enemies—quite literally a list of individuals singled out for pressure from the White House gang. I now regard it as not a complete coincidence that for the first time in my life, I had my income tax return audited at this time, and this was repeated for the next two years. My crime in Dean's eyes—the reason for my being on the White House "enemies list"—had been my personal contribution of five hundred dollars and open support of Edmund Muskie for the Democratic presidential nomination, whom I vastly preferred over George McGovern. Now, years later, I wonder if I could have saved Pan Am by abjectly yielding to Haldeman's cynical advice at the Gridiron Club dinner: *"Well, switch over to our side and we may be able to help you."*

At that time it wouldn't have been hard to do, assuming considerable rationalization, conscience-wrestling, and giving Pan Am's welfare higher priority than my own principles. All this was before Watergate, and I guess until that scandal broke, I always felt there was hope for Richard Nixon; that he somehow would rise above his intense ambition and avarice, his distrust of so-called eastern intellectualism, and become a true leader. At first it seemed to me that he was the victim of those around him, largely because he invariably attracted reactionary, ruthless, and cynical people.

I always was impressed by Nixon's internationalism, his grasp and knowledge of world political and military problems. I had no trouble in voting for Hubert Humphrey over Nixon in the 1968 election; Humphrey was my friend and, more important, I considered him a seasoned, honest, and decent human being. But when it was Nixon vs. McGovern, I was badly torn. I frequently debated with friends whether Nixon was better than the men around him. I argued that after he was re-elected, he would rid himself of the Haldemans, Ehrlichmans, and Colsons and become his own man during his last four years in office. It was Burke Marshall, an old friend and former fellow New Frontiersman under Bob Kennedy, who put my thinking straight one night after I had espoused my "Nixon's better than the guys around him" theory.

"You're wrong, Jeeb," Burke told me soberly. "Nixon's really chief of that White House Mafia. The people around him are better than he is but they've been corrupted and misled—and one of these days you're going to find that out."

I did—when the Watergate mess broke just before the Nixon-McGovern mismatch. At that point the President wasn't supposed to have been involved, but I never could swallow that claim. Despite all my reservations about McGovern's ability to lead this country, I voted for him on the simple basis of integrity in government.

And from the purely provincial standpoint of an airman, I'm glad I did. Disregarding all his other shabby deeds, Nixon's record in behalf of civil aviation was as disastrous as Lyndon Johnson's. Both allowed establishment of policies that led to excessive proliferation of routes and competition, susceptibility to political influence, inconsistency, and inferior appointments. Nixon's appointment of Brown to head the CAB, for example, was almost as bad as LBJ's choosing Crooker. Brown's fault was not political cronyism but vainglorious ambition and a yearning to hold onto his job at all costs—which inevitably caused him to be all things to all men. From both Crooker and Brown, civil aviation got the worst of both worlds, overregulation and overcompetition, to such an extent that at this writing, I have serious doubts as to the future of the U.S. international air transportation system and whether it can survive the mistakes made in the 1964–74 decade.

Many of those mistakes were made in the White House itself; the absolute authority given to the President in determining the final outcome of international air-route cases degrades and politicizes the civil-aviation regulatory system. Such cases are primarily a matter of economic regulatory consideration. Yet when they move into the White House, they become less a judicial and more a partisan political matter, a question of who contributes most to the party rather than the public's needs and welfare.

The life-or-death presidential power has been challenged, but without success. No less than the U. S. Supreme Court has ruled that the President's decision in an international route case under the present Federal Aviation Act is absolutely final and not subject to court review. Thus there have been times when months of hearings before the CAB, thousands of words of testimony, and weeks of discussion and debate among CAB members and staff experts all have been tossed aside in favor of a presidential verdict based on political factors and even personal pique.

Admittedly the CAB findings themselves may not always be fair or wise, and it can be argued that the President's power to overrule assures full consideration of our foreign policy and is a safeguard against poor CAB decisions. That has been true in rare cases, but the White House role as a safeguard is more theoretical than actual. It also could be pointed out that statistically Presidents have upheld CAB decisions far more often than they have been overturned. Yet this is a weak defense of the system when one realizes how many times excellent, carefully considered decisions on the part of the Board have been scrapped for political purposes or shaped by the CAB chairman to suit the desires of the White House staff that makes the final recommendation.

In light of past sad experiences dating back almost forty years, it seems to me that White House authority over international air routes should be eliminated. The regulatory authority should have the final say, provided that other departments such as State, Treasury, Defense, and Transportation be allowed to intervene—making sure that the Board is aware of all diplomatic and military interests that may be involved. The final review would be in the federal courts, with a last resort to the U. S. Supreme Court. I am convinced this would remove politics to a considerable extent.

Obviously, any route case—domestic or international—is the target of pressure and influence. I know of one airline president who used to be a CAB chairman himself—Don Nyrop of Northwest. He is a man of integrity, but his old CAB experiences and connections have given him quite an advantage over competitors—as Northwest's lucrative route system would attest. Of course he is also tight-fisted and has had Senators Magnuson, Jackson, Humphrey, and Mondale in his corner but his contacts include many public servants whom he brought into the CAB—fine, able, and honest men who exercised their responsibilities with great care. But they quite naturally listened to a man with Nyrop's experience and reputation. They didn't violate any rules, but they were operating in a gray ethical area, discussing route cases with a man in whom they reposed respect and even affection.

One of the other ways in which White House political activities affect the airlines is with respect to legislation. This, of course, is important in relation to bills either initiated by the Executive Branch or those initiated in Congress or elsewhere on which the President must take a position. More often than not, such a position is derived by interdepartmental consensus. Sometimes the Office of Management and Budget acts as the consensus-maker after obtaining comments on legislation from all interested departments. Sometimes a White House special assistant takes the lead role, and sometimes a Secretary of Transportation does so. And there always are the pressure groups such as the Air Transport Association; the National Air Carrier Association, which represents the supplementals; the Air Line Pilots Association, and other unions getting their licks in through their favorite connections within the various departments and agencies.

Perhaps the basic issue that any airline chief executive faces lies in the Federal Aviation Act itself. When Congress passed the Act and amended it from time to time, it made a compromise between promotion of civil aviation and regulation under its federally subsidized growth and its federal control.

Actually the law says that the Civil Aeronautics Board will be guided by both promotional policies and regulatory policies. Five good men or bad, faced with the unresolved dilemma inherent in the law, have for nearly forty years tried without much success to regulate while promoting the airlines of the United States.

In the beginning the Mail Subsidy Act was the promotional device, and all kinds of routes were subsidized by extraordinary mail payments on an annual basis. Pan Am, for example, thrived on these subsidies for its first thirty-five years, and only in the more recent years did it operate without federal subsidies. Even then the airline was not charged full cost of airport facilities because the federal government, through its Federal Aid to Airports legislation, heavily subsidized local and state airport development. Then, too, absolutely essential air-traffic control is a very substantial federal subsidy, partly on the grounds that it is also used for military operations. Excise taxes and sometimes user charges are attempts to recover some of these costs of these federal subsidies, but they fail by several hundred million dollars to recoup the total cost; the airlines, of course, immediately pass those taxes on to the passenger and the shipper rather than absorbing them themselves. The ultimate beneficiary is still the passenger, who is given the protection and convenience of airports and air-traffic control, while the general taxpayer is paying for the federal subsidy.

The obvious solution is to cut down on these federal expenditures to an efficient yet lean program, and to tax the beneficiaries—the airlines, their passengers, and shippers—so as to recover all of the costs that cannot be justified for national security or for public safety. This debate goes on each year in the Congress and is generally resolved by continuing the federal subsidy. Also buried in the federal budget is a great deal of money for research and development of airplanes and engines by the military and by the National Aeronautics and Space Administration. This, in turn, is made available to the aerospace manufacturers and comes back to the taxpayer in the form of exports of aeronautical products and in the competitive edge provided to American operators of the equipment. I think my main concern is that the public be informed of these "hidden subsidies," see that they are reduced to the minimum, and then accept them on a candidly understood and fully disclosed basis.

There is certainly no longer any reason that 215 million Americans should subsidize the 60 million Americans who regularly use federally subsidized airports. We should keep working toward the beneficiaries paying the full federal cost of aviation services.

A far worse problem has emerged over the past decade as a result of the CAB staff and some of its members proliferating competition while simultaneously regulating fares and conditions of commerce. The Board long ago departed from the original legislative intent—that in return for being granted a monopoly franchise to carry passengers and freight, an airline would have its rates, routes, and rights regulated by a public authority in the public interest. If there were free and open competition, there would be little need for regulation; the regulator would be the marketplace, and five CAB members would not substitute their judgments for those of the buyers and sellers of air services.

In sum, we now have the worst of excessive regulation and the worst of excessive competition.

Current debate over "deregulation" of the airlines is a healthy one, and there is a very good argument to be made that deregulation would result in some momentary chaos, but in the long run would eliminate the weakest carriers and permit the strongest to survive. My view is that we want to get less and less economic regulation and more and more judicial review and control into the process. In other words, I don't think the CAB is either capable or wise at setting airline fares. This should be determined in the marketplace by freely competing carriers. At the same time, I do not believe deregulation should be allowed to create conspiracies or combinations in restraint of trade, thus bringing higher fares. What is needed is a new legislative framework in which basic antitrust principles are applied by a special quasijudicial administrative court. In other words, I would like to see the judicial process supplant the regulatory process, and the test would be that there be no artificial restraints on airline trade and there should be no criminal or malicious activities in the marketplace.

We could gradually cut the federal subsidies for airports within the national system and transfer some of those responsibilities to the states and municipal governments, which, after all, gain the greatest economic benefits from the airports. Through federal taxation, all of the costs of the airways and air-traffic control except the 25 per cent required by the military and other governmental agencies for national security and public safety would be recovered through the FAA-administered "Airways/Airports" Trust Fund.

If such amendments to the Federal Aviation Act were ever introduced, the aviation lobbies would be out in force. I once incurred the wrath of both the airlines and the small-plane operators when we proposed that a substantially increased amount of the costs of air-traffic control should be borne by them in the form of user charges. Through stalwart friends such as Senator Mike Monroney and Congressman John Bell Williams, they prevented the Administration bill from even getting a full hearing. In other words, those airmen who are swashbuckling free enterprisers don't want to lose any of the hidden subsidies, like the oil companies, maritime shipping companies, and the railroads. They want to keep doing their business as usual at the federal trough.

Certainly, the present aviation regulatory system makes the CAB pitiably vulnerable to political pressure from all sides. And for intervention based solely on politics, the place for the action is the White House. This extends not just to international route cases but also to any merger proposal that involves international routes. The Federal Aviation Act literally invites mergers because it permits the CAB to exempt airlines from the antitrust provisions of the Sherman and Clayton acts. And because it also gives the President the right to approve or disapprove mergers between carriers with international routes, such airlines must consider not merely the CAB's attitude but also that of the President.

When Charles Tillinghast and I began discussing a possible TWA-Pan Am merger in the summer of 1971, for example, one of the first calls we made was to Peter Flanigan, sounding him out on what the President's reaction might be if the CAB gave the "marriage" its blessing. This kind of advance reconnaissance is just the first step that must be taken in what I call "mergyrations"—a mobile pinwheel of tentative inquiries and outright lobbying among

288

the various agencies and departments. I hated this aspect of my job during the Nixon days; out of all these activities I can remember only one that gave me a pleasant and productive contact with the White House in the early seventies.

It stemmed from that Juan Trippe tradition of having First Ladies christen the first Clipper of a new Pan Am aircraft series. After much negotiation, we finally persuaded Mrs. Nixon to christen Pan Am's first Boeing 747, *Clipper Young Independence*—apparently the powers-that-be decided that a 747 wasn't as politically partisan as the Democrat who was heading the airline.

The ceremony was held at Dulles on what also happened to be the late Martin Luther King's birthday. I had asked my daughter Alexa, then fifteen, to be on hand, an invitation that produced mixed reaction on her part; she was quite upset to have been taken away from collecting signatures on a petition to make King's birthday a national holiday in honor of the fallen civil rights leader, but she also couldn't resist a teen-ager's delight at being involved in something exciting.

Alexa's job was to hand Pat Nixon an armful of roses after I spoke a few introductory words appropriate to the occasion. Alexa was a perfect little lady as she presented the flowers and curtsied, with a broad smile. As we left the platform and walked toward the airplane, I mentioned to Mrs. Nixon that Alexa wanted to talk to her—knowing this would give my daughter an opening. Alexa had greatly admired Dr. King, was crushed at his murder, and felt it was high time to observe something other than Emancipation Day to honor 11 per cent of our population. The First Lady, in a schoolmarmish tone, said, "Alexa, where do you go to school?"

"Brearley School in New York."

"You have a holiday today?"

Alexa said it was sort of a holiday, that she had taken the day off for the christening but was anxious to get back to New York "to collect signatures."

"Signatures for what?" Mrs. Nixon inquired politely.

"To make today a national holiday in honor of Martin Luther King," my daughter informed her with a touch of belligerent pride.

"Oh that's just a way of taking another day off from school, isn't it?" the former schoolteacher responded.

289

I could see as well as sense Alexa's angry reaction. She didn't reply and I tried to smooth over the incident, although it was obvious my daughter's day had been ruined. She never said another word to the First Lady who, I'm sure, never realized how much the unthinking remark had hurt her. I was somewhat relieved when we reached the christening platform where a band was playing and flags were flying in the wind.

Pan Am's station manager, Frank Stoppa, had concocted a unique substitute for the traditional champagne. Mrs. Nixon was to push a handle that activated three sprays directed at the nose of the 747—one red, one white, and one blue. Frank had his fingers crossed; there hadn't been time to test the device. He finally gave me the signal, I gently nudged Mrs. Nixon's elbow, and she yanked the handle.

Nothing happened; it was stuck in the detent. I reached over and pushed it out of the detent position. She gave another yank and the spraying started—but not in the planned order. First just white, then blue, and finally a stream of red. Only for a second or two did the three sprays come out simultaneously, like a fluid flag.

I asked Mrs. Nixon if she'd like to go aboard and inspect the gigantic aircraft. She got a quick glance at the size of the cabin and nodded when I asked her if she would like to see the cockpit. Followed by four Secret Servicemen, we climbed up the spiral staircase to the first-class upper lounge and went onto the flight deck. A Pan Am veteran captain, Doug Moody, sat in the left seat, Mrs. Nixon occupying the copilot's seat while I parked where the flight engineer is normally stationed. The captain explained some of the primary instruments and controls, and her eyes began to sparkle. Suddenly she turned toward me.

"I have a confession to make. This is the first time I've been in the cockpit of an airplane since my boyfriend was teaching me to fly—it was in 1933, I think."

She was a middle-aged woman who by some magic had become a girl again. She told me about that young man, with whom she had been very much in love before she met a struggling young lawyer named Richard Nixon in Whittier, California. She said she really had loved flying, and this visit to the 747 cockpit had brought back not only that thrill but also the sweet memories of that youthful romance with a pilot. It was the first time I had ever seen her drop that wooden, emotionless First Lady mask and become really human and warm. It was as if entering that cockpit had stripped thirty or forty years from the pressures of being Nixon's wife.

As we gave the mammoth cabin a more thorough inspection, she had to be enjoying herself hugely for she stayed more than thirty minutes over the time allotted to the inspection tour. On the two or three occasions when I subsequently saw her—before I became *persona non grata* at the White House—she always reminded me how much she had enjoyed those two hours at Dulles and the cockpit/cabin visit. We sent her a beautiful photographic album as a souvenir of the christening, and she replied with a most gracious thank-you note. In retrospect, her letter was about the only tangible reward Pan Am got out of the White House during my entire regime.

For it was in this pre-Watergate atmosphere of Administration arrogance that Pan Am, fighting for its very survival, steered toward the merger with its chief U.S. competitor—Trans World Airlines.

CHAPTER NINE

I only wished I could have convinced Mrs. Nixon's husband that the great Clipper she was christening was so overloaded with burdens and disadvantages that Pan Am might never climb above the clouds to cruising altitude again.

The 747, to Pan Am in 1970, was an engineering miracle and an economic monstrosity, but we could have lived with this ahead-of-its-time airplane if it had not been for the intolerably excessive competition piled upon Pan Am by the CAB and the White House.

From the early days of the CAB's regulatory authority, the Board believed that the only way to assure the proper extent of international competition was to certificate, at least in certain markets, two U.S.-flag carriers, mainly because the competition offered by the foreign-flag carriers was weak and inadequate. But by 1960 it became clear that the competence and strength of those foreign carriers was growing tremendously; most of them soon became the equal of U.S. airlines in technical skill, equipment, and service—a few even better. Their success temporarily caused the CAB to slow down certification of U.S. carriers in the international market, and for a time the Board believed that Pan Am should retain its status as the nation's leading international carrier.

During this period, in the early sixties, Pan Am was pitted against other U.S. airlines only in specified areas—TWA in Europe, the Near East, and South Asia; Eastern and Delta in the Caribbean; Braniff in Latin America; and Northwest in the Pacific.

Pan Am could have lived with this kind of competition—a pattern that was confirmed by President Kennedy in his 1963 policy statement. It could not cope with what began to happen under LBJ by the mid-1960s, when the CAB and White House, in rapid succession, released the Flying Tiger cargo line to serve many points in the Pacific; extended Seaboard World Airlines to new points in Europe; put American into the South Pacific to Australia and New Zealand; allowed up to six supplemental airlines to compete in some of our prime markets unfettered by the rules of carriage Pan Am had to observe; added five new carriers to the mainland–Hawaii market; and granted a fistful of new-route certifications in the Caribbean—to Jamaica, the Bahamas, Bermuda, Haiti, San Juan, and a few other points.

For Pan Am it was near disaster. Previously profitable routes turned into ribbons of red ink. U.S. facilities and personnel were wastefully duplicated. Attempts to increase efficiency collided with what might be called government-promoted competitive waste— more aircraft, more airlines flying fewer people for more fuel and higher fares. And all this coincided with foreign carriers steadily improving their competitive positions because they did not have to split their resources and energies. They were able to restrict access to their markets by U.S. international carriers—a process that diffused and divided the latter, while simultaneously protecting their own single national-flag carriers and enhancing their ability to conquer more of the market. For Pan Am it added up to an unhappy but inescapable result: We could no longer afford to carry the flag to a number of important but uneconomic foreign points—and, apparently, the U. S. Government didn't care whether this withdrawal of the American flag was or was not in the national interest.

For example, in the U.S.-New Zealand/Australia market, there was competition among Qantas, BOAC, Air New Zealand, and Pan Am before the CAB decided to let American join the scrap. All that happened was that the Australian Government simply slapped a lid on the number of weekly flights that could be operated there, forcing Pan Am to turn over to American some of the flights they otherwise would have operated. I concede that American is a superb airline, but I doubt seriously whether the public was better off for allowing it into that South Pacific market—one tailored, incidentally, for an aircraft like the 747. A few of the big Boeings should have made money serving Australia and New Zealand. Instead, Pan Am's costs per operation soared—a perfect example of what I mean by government-promoted competitive waste.

It is true that the industry's temperatures rise or fall in direct correlation to the state of the national and international economies. But Pan Am's troubles in recent years have not been cyclical but virtually permanent; its difficulties are based on unique factors that cannot be eliminated by upturns in the economy. In 1974, for example, Pan Am was the only U.S. trunk carrier that lost money. Like all airlines, it had to battle mushrooming fuel costs, general inflation, and the constant demands of labor. But unlike the other carriers, it had other problems inherent in its route structure that no improved economic climate could cure. Pan Am lost $26 million in 1969 and another $48 million in 1970—two years in which the domestic airlines were solidly in the black thanks to overall traffic growth and higher seat traffic. Pan Am had both the latter advantages too, but still fell back in the profit parade due to wasteful overcompetition.

It wasn't that we didn't try to save ourselves. Knowing that our in-flight reputation was almost an industry joke, I hired Dick Ensign away from Western—a relatively small trunk carrier with a reputation for fine service that bore Ensign's trademark. Dick could almost be called a service scientist; at Western he even observed the serving of drinks and meals with a stopwatch in his hand, searching for ways to speed up the operation without sacrificing a gracious atmosphere.

I made Pan Am leaner and hungrier, although not to the extent I desired. In the fourth quarter of 1970, when it became only too clear we were going to finish the year with a huge deficit, we cut eighteen hundred persons from the payroll. We reduced a number of our operations. We applied for permission to suspend all service to Hilo, Hawaii, because excessive competition combined with fares that were below operating costs made it impossible to continue flying there. We cut out six other service points. We deferred delivery of 747s scheduled for the first half of 1971, delaying some of them until late 1971 and the remainder into 1972. The Boeings and supporting facilities, incidentally, were being financed or leased at fixed charges totalling $10 million a month.

But in a sense I was trying to bail out a sinking ocean liner with a sandpail. We could do little about a route structure that involved a high percentage of low-frequency operations. (A typical airline regards five flights a day at a given station as low-density traffic. Only a small proportion of Pan Am's stations have as many as two round-trip flights daily. One third handled only one flight a day or less.)

Landing fees in the United States are bargains compared to the astronomical charges at most foreign airports—and Pan Am is a 100 per cent international carrier, of course. In 1972 it cost $240 to land a 747 at Los Angeles International; $1,814 to land the same plane at London, and $3,483 at Sydney, Australia. Landing fees went up more than $15 million for Pan Am in just the 1970–71 period. Other countries see our huge flying cows coming into their pastures and each one of them reaches up and squeezes a little more cream out of the cow. Their own nationalized carriers often are nothing but flying flagpoles, incapable of viable operations without government support that frequently is nothing but a nationalistic ego trip.

In markets where the CAB controlled the fare structure, we often took a bath. Our average yield in the New York–Puerto Rico market was less than $.04 a mile, compared to Chicago–Los Angeles, where the yield ranged from $.053 in thrift class to nearly $.08 in first class. During the twelve months ending June 30, 1970, Pan Am had an operating loss of $8.7 million in the Hawaii market, which was not surprising in view of an average yield of less than $.035 per passenger mile—40 per cent under the average domestic yield. This is what happens when fares are instituted at ridiculously low rates. And such fares result from the irresponsible promises made by airlines when they seek competitive route authority. Pan Am was not opposed to lower fares—not in my regime

—when such fares could still return a profit. We tried, for example, to introduce a $99 standby youth fare in the Atlantic market.

And Pan Am's position in the area of fares is hampered by the many advantages foreign carriers enjoy. They have lower costs in many major categories, particularly labor. They receive considerable financial support from their respective governments. And when they buy U.S. aircraft, they can borrow from the Export-Import Bank at interest rates far below what a U.S. carrier would have to pay; it was only 6 per cent in 1970, compared to the over 11 per cent that Pan Am and TWA were shelling out on 747 loans. In 1970 our interest payments alone totalled $58 million.

I've heard other airlines argue that Pan Am's poor service is the prime reason it has not been able to withstand fresh competition from other U.S. airlines. Bunk. Even when we improved service, we still were at a tremendous disadvantage. In the series of decisions that permitted domestic carriers to invade our routes, they were almost always in a superior competitive position because their domestic operations fed into their international operations.

The seven U.S. scheduled airlines serving Hawaii have the support of their vast domestic route systems; Pan Am has no domestic route. Three airlines were authorized to fly nonstop between New York and Hawaii; Pan Am was denied this right repeatedly, although it pioneered Hawaii service in 1936. After pioneering service to Puerto Rico, it wound up with American and Eastern also flying to Puerto Rico—two airlines, again, with a huge domestic route backup. TWA was allowed to join Pan Am in providing round-the-world service, but TWA had thirty-nine cities supporting this operation, while Pan Am had only eleven points of departure overseas.

The moral seems to be that the pioneer gets the shaft. As soon as Pan Am pioneered, developed, marketed, and produced a route worthy of penetration, as many as five other carriers were allowed into the act. In all other areas of business—particularly regulated businesses, franchises, patents, defense, NASA contracts, and the like—the company that has done the research, the development, and all the hard work is given a period of time in which to service the market it has developed and to build up reserves for taking on new developmental routes. Not Pan Am.

Pan Am, naturally, fought all this intrusion, and when defeated, it logically sought access to the one major competitive edge the invading carriers enjoyed: domestic routes to feed into its international operations. Every such attempt was rejected. No nonstop service from the East Coast to Hawaii. Negative on New York–Miami rights. We couldn't even get a hearing on an application to provide transcontinental service. And never underestimate the value of a domestic backup—two thirds of all travelers across the Atlantic are American citizens.

All in all, Pan Am faced no fewer than eighty-nine competitors. There were and still are twenty scheduled airlines authorized to fly the Atlantic, and a dozen more countries have bilateral rights to start such service whenever they are able. An additional twelve foreign charter airlines served the Atlantic market along with six U.S. supplementals. In the Orient, Pan Am competed against nine other scheduled airlines, including three U.S. carriers. Six scheduled competitors have been operating to the South Pacific, and it will be seven now that Continental has been granted the access to Japan from Micronesia.

The once-weak foreign airlines are now efficient, well-financed operations blessed with a few advantages peculiar to their flag-carrier status. Many of them don't really have to make money—they were established to "show the flag" and are more institutions of pride than of profit. They command great ethnic loyalty not only by their own citizens but also by foreign nationals now living in the United States. They use passport and currency controls that favor use of their carriers by foreign nationals. They frequently indulge in various back-scratching and under-the-table deals usually frowned on in the United States—including illegal fare-cutting that in 1972 cost TWA and Pan Am some $75 million. To circumvent IATA tariff regulations and protect themselves against homemade competition, airlines like Lufthansa, Air France, Sabena, and KLM have operated separate charter airlines. Many of the foreign-flag carriers also enter into airline pools and relationships to reduce costs and strengthen their operations—such as the British Commonwealth pool, which is so tight in the South Pacific-U.S. market that Air New Zealand, British Airways, Qantas, and related carriers use a single, combined timetable.

It may be a surprise to the reader to learn that by 1968 from the West Coast to Europe, the supplemental airlines were carrying two out of every three passengers. Yet in contrast to the huge responsibilities of the scheduled airlines, they had no public obligation to perform any service at all, anytime, anywhere. What they do is move in and out of markets, skimming the cream in the heavy tourist markets during peak seasons.

After I became head of Pan Am, I took a close look at data for the year 1969 on supplemental airline operations over the Atlantic. They operated 80 per cent of their charters between just two U.S. gateways—California and New York—and five gateways in Europe, all of which were receiving regularly scheduled U.S. service. More than 75 per cent of their transatlantic operations were conducted between June and September—and during those three months they carried more passengers than Pan Am carried on its scheduled service on all its transatlantic routes combined. Those peak summer months provide the only profitable period for Pan Am's Atlantic operations—as ordained by CAB and White House decisions. We needed those profits to cover our losses in maintaining the service for the remainder of the year. It was our only shot at a net profit, and we failed to make it in 1969, 1970, and 1971—the thirty months I served as chief executive officer. The encroachment by the supplementals was not the only factor, but it was a major one. They diverted tens of millions of dollars in revenue.

As I write this, the supplementals are still pushing for expanded authority. If it is granted, the increased unrestrained charter services may drive out scheduled service, and charter costs will go up—for the supplementals are truly parasitic, living off the promotion, the investments in technology, and the fees the scheduled airlines pay day in and day out to support the airport and airways system.

The ability of foreign carriers to "pool"—with the blessings of their governments—is another competitive hurdle for Pan Am. The classic example is the rich London–Paris market, roughly comparable to New York–Washington in terms of traffic generated. British Airways and Air France carry all London–Paris passengers by agreement of the British and French governments. The two airlines split expenses and revenues right down the middle. Contrast this tidy but high-priced arrangement with the chaotic Hawaii situation—eight carriers in a market that could at most support four, maintaining eight sales offices, eight airport stations, eight advertising and public-relations staffs, eight frequencies, and eight different sales campaigns. Each, I submit, is a wasteful, destructive way to regulate an industry whose profit-vs.-loss scales are so delicately balanced that even the altitude at which a captain decides to cruise can mean the difference between a money-losing flight and a profitable one, and to this mess we must add the inroads made by the supplemental carriers.

The only good reasons for an international airline to consider a merger are to reduce duplication and operating costs, thereby holding fares down and maintaining profits while at the same time combining to get a greater share of the world market for the U.S. carriers. Merging to become big is not a good reason, because as many mergers have shown, bigness leads to inefficiencies rather than to higher productivity. Often, due to labor union requirements, one must do less work with the same number of people in the early stages. Certainly the marriage of the managers is a psychologically difficult and sometimes impossible task. The delays involved in getting approval of a merger are enormously wasteful. Often the benefits are not achieved or are at least outweighed by the detriments. So one doesn't entertain the idea of merger lightly.

Airline mergers usually reflect the failure of the regulatory process. Unfortunately, the history of the CAB is one of certification, not decertification. The Board never admits a mistake, nor seriously contemplates a possibility of excessive competition. Its record indicates it is concerned only with giving franchises rather than taking them back in the public interest. Thus, as it did during the Johnson-Crooker and Nixon-Brown regimes, the CAB too often goes on a certification binge. You cannot look to any President or any CAB chairman to correct these excesses, and the only way left for carriers like Pan Am and TWA to save what the government laid waste is merger or route-swapping.

The most ferocious fighter against bigness and less competition, of course, is the Antitrust Division of the Department of Justice. I know that well, since I worked there briefly one summer for Thurmond Arnold, one of the greatest trust-busters of all, while I was one of his law students at Yale. It is the religion of the Antitrust Division to go after bigness and attack any restraints on wide-open, free competition. It doesn't make any difference to them whether the industry is regulated or not or how deeply and broadly it is regulated. Yes, they know that the Federal Aviation Act gives the CAB the power to approve of a merger, a route swap, or a coordination of schedules over their objections. They fought that provision in the statute, and they would like to get it appealed. They don't really believe that the CAB regulators regulate the competition and so, in their fiery zeal, they automatically oppose any efforts to reduce duplication if it results in less competition or a very large company.

They tend to downgrade any foreign competitor and all but ignore the fact of today's aviation life—that a Swiss Air or a Lufthansa or a British Airways is in many respects more capable of competing with Pan Am or TWA than each is with the other. These young lawyers in the Antitrust Division, right out of law school, highly theoretical, zealous to win cases and to go on to politics or partnerships in law firms, have bright analyses and good reasons for all of their activities. They also are the biggest leakers to Congress in any administration and they have their own classmates and contemporaries in the staffs of antitrust leaders on Capitol Hill who immediately take merger proposals into the pits of Congress and the media.

Finally, for every proponent of a merger there are at least ten opponents—mainly those who would claim the route themselves. They oppose the merger or swap and then say that if it is approved, they will apply to take the place of the carrier merged on the route. So anyone who wants to run this gantlet of opposition must have very strong justification; it is no wonder that many mergers are posed but very few achieved.

The first step is to recognize the need and gather up the energy and courage to examine the political and psychological aspects of a merger—in other words, develop the will to put it through. The second is to conduct an analysis of both the costs and the benefits, the risks and the rewards. This has now taken on a very sophisticated, computerized technique, and a number of firms specialize in merger analysis. The third step is to approach the management of the company with which you seek to merge and see if there is interest and agreement in principle. There are several questions demanding immediate answers in the early stages. Who will be chief executive? What would be the exchange of common stock and refinancing plan? How would the managements mix and mesh? How would the labor unions resolve the representational and seniority problems? What will be the economic effect—such as the short-term loss due to confusion and uncertainty while it is in the regulatory phase, and then what are the long-term benefits to be gained? If it is approved and recommended to the President by the CAB and he okays it, what will be the consequences in terms of certification of new competition on the route—in other words, what is the ultimate expected cost?

The only three substantial airline mergers in post-World War II history have been those in which a healthy carrier acquired a sick carrier and there were already two or more carriers on the routes. United Air Lines purchased a failing Capitol Airlines; Delta Air Lines took over a faltering Northeast Airlines; and Allegheny acquired both Mohawk and Lake Central, each a sick company.

All this made me ask why, in the view of all of these obvious obstacles, any sane chief executive of Pan Am would consider in the summer of 1971 a merger with its principal competitor, TWA. Furthermore, having been administrator of the FAA, I was fully familiar with the agony of Alan Boyd's and Mike Feldman's coping with Trippe's and Tillinghast's proposal of merger just eight years before. I had carefully studied Boyd's and Feldman's conclusion that the merged carrier would be too big, would reduce competition too much, and would make the United States Government almost wholly dependent on a single chosen carrier for the Atlantic, Europe, and Middle East routes.

In spite of my previous doubts, I developed all of the data, and they showed that by eliminating duplicate stations, aircraft, facilities, and personnel we could save a minimum of $125 million and a maximum of $200 million a year in operating costs. Moreover, we saw that to compete with forty-nine other carriers on our joint routes, thirty-four of them foreign, we needed to combine to fight

301

them. In other words, merge to compete with the foreign airlines and, thereby, as the principal American carrier, get most of the American patronage for our own. The consequence of this would be a substantial amount of earnings for the U.S. economy in balance of payments at a time when it was going into a foreign-exchange deficit. We, of course, could effectively argue that this was a way to keep a huge fleet of 747s in operation should they be needed for the civil reserve air fleet. We could also go to the government and say that by combining our relative strengths, we could correct the tragic wrongs of CAB action over the previous eight years, and we could save them from another Penn Central or Lockheed situation where the government would either have to pay subsidies or guarantee the credit of each of us. This all added up to what I called the "faltering companies doctrine"—where two companies, as a result of federal misregulation, were approaching bankruptcy. This would justify the CAB's granting an exemption from antitrust laws and policy. About all Tillinghast and I agreed on was that in principle it would make sense and it was worth a thorough exploration in Washington.

We did not agree in advance who would be chief executive officer and how we would rank the top officers. We did not agree upon the stock-exchange ratio; this was going to be the item of greatest interest to the shareholders.

We knew there would be a union problem. Their ALPA chapter representing pilots and stewardesses would fight our ALPA chapter for seniority positions, and it would take months if not years to get agreement on the relative value, rights, and privileges. They had the International Association of Machinists bargaining for their mechanics, and we had the Transport Workers Union for ours and our stewardesses. They had no clerical union and we had the dreaded Teamsters, with their hands on the throats and paychecks of our reservations, sales, accounting, and clerical people, which was anathema to TWA. Nevertheless, we did both think it was worth a full exploration in Washington. Frankly, we were both deeply concerned about survival and saw no satisfactory solution coming from any government initiative.

We discussed the matter first on the golf course up at an IATA meeting in Banff, Alberta, Canada, and then later back in New

York. We took it up with our respective Boards of Directors, and they encouraged us. Juan Trippe, in particular, was ecstatic with the thought that I was going to rejuvenate his longtime effort to "acquire" TWA.

And so, knowing all the risks and hurdles, Tillinghast and I went down to see Peter Flanigan, who by then was the White House staff officer in charge of transportation and regulatory matters.

Flanigan, for the first time, was quite hospitable, which in my suspicious way I attributed to the fact that he had been TWA's investment banker at Dillon, Read before coming into Washington with the victorious Nixonites. He listened to our presentation of the law, the very favorable economics, the improvement in the U.S. balance-of-payments and national-security position, the avoidance of another Penn Central situation, etc.

He set out a procedure for us to follow. He wanted us to go and explore the issue with the chairman of the Council of Economic Advisers, the Attorney General, the Secretary of Transportation, the Secretary of State, the Secretary of Defense—but not the chairman of the CAB. We made it repetitively clear that we were not seeking a direction from the White House to the CAB to favor the merger. We were not seeking any pressure on the members of the CAB. Rather, we wanted an advisory opinion that the White House could always reverse—namely, that if we got a favorable vote on the merits in the CAB, the President would approve their recommendation and would stand firm against the inevitable opposition of other airlines and the pressures that certainly would come from congressmen and union leaders, etc. He said he fully understood this and stated flatly, "We will give you an answer within sixty days."

We went away from that meeting quite encouraged to know that we could get an answer, that it would come promptly, and that the disruptive uncertainty would be short. We began making rounds of the designated officials. The most encouraging meeting was with the new Secretary of the Treasury, John Connally, whom by chance I had previously approached when he was a private citizen with regard to his being a director of Pan American World Airways, prior to his appointment as Secretary of the Treasury.

303

Flanigan arranged for the President to appoint a special committee to deal with international airline policy. On that committee were the Secretaries of State, Treasury, and Transportation, and the Attorney General, with Flanigan an unofficial executive secretary. They selected Charles Baker, Assistant Secretary of Transportation, as the principal staff officer to evaluate the data submitted by Pan Am and TWA, and they required that each of us submit very elaborate statistical data and economic and political estimates of the merger's impact in all areas. It was to this group that Dick Knight submitted the catastrophic deficit projection that Pan Am could suffer in the succeeding eighteen months if there were no merger—a forecast that was exaggerated but conceivable.

Each of these submissions required co-ordination. We set up a merger task force within Pan Am, and Tillinghast did likewise within TWA, each group going into the major issues involved. The two key men turned out to be Ed Smart, senior vice president of TWA for planning and diversified activities (and later TWA chairman), and Dick Knight was my own agent. Since they both had the problem of planning for the survival of each of the carriers, they had plenty of incentive to put together a deal, and they went about it with gusto. I think they privately had agreed that Knight would be chief financial officer of the whole merged company and Smart would be in charge of all of the planning and diversified activities.

One of the most attractive features of a Pan Am-TWA merger was a sleeper—namely, the combination of the Hilton International Hotel chain, owned by TWA, and Pan Am's Inter·Continental Hotel chain—which would have given the U.S. a superb worldwide hotel conglomerate earning the best foreign exchange possible.

Knight and Smart reported back to me and Tillinghast almost daily. They made rapid progress on some issues, and in particular they began to narrow the exchange of stock ratio to realistic proportions, although they never agreed on a final figure.

The summer wore on, and the sixty days we had set as a target passed around July 1. By coincidence, Charles Tillinghast was the guest of one of his Directors, a fellow member of mine at the annual Bohemian Grove outing in California. A further coincidence was that Peter Flanigan was the guest of his brother, who is a member of my camp, Mandalay, at the Bohemian Grove. The result was that there were several opportunities for us to talk to Flanigan and for the three of us to have a brief conversation. Later Tillinghast and I had a long talk on the grass under the Grove's tall redwood trees, and we concluded that it was still a good idea but that the Nixon administration had already passed the promised deadline and it was growing more difficult to hold our troops, competing as they were most of the day, to serious consideration of a merger during the night. Another element was quite worrisome: Our respective Directors were beginning to throw stones at each other. Their Directors were impatient to get the merger on or off and were using some of our statistics to needle the TWA management. Some of our own Directors, Kendall in particular, were using TWA, and especially what they regarded as the superior performance of the TWA president, "Bud" Wiser, to stick the needle in me.

Another problem—one that often occurs in industrial mergers— was that TWA's stock began to go up and Pan Am's stock to go down. Because the recession of 1969–71 was beginning to phase out, TWA's thirty-nine domestic cities were beginning to produce a healthy cyclical increase in revenue and bottom-line result, whereas we had no domestic lift for the Pan Am stock.

We agreed at the Bohemian Grove that we would continue exploration, but not beyond September 13, approximately a month later. So we set a deadline and we advised Flanigan that we had to have an answer by that time. He promised that we would have an answer by August 15.

Throughout the period, Herb Brownell, President Eisenhower's Attorney General and now my special merger counsel, had been submitting memoranda and making visits to the White House and to John Mitchell, while Tillinghast and I had been talking to a number of officials plus congressmen and senators.

I had urged Kendall to make a major effort to help us get a green light from the White House, and I went out to visit him in his baronial office in White Plains after one of my trips to Washington, begging him to throw his "great influence with the President" into the balance. But about all he would do was to make a call to John Mitchell, seeking his reaction to the presentation Tillinghast and I

305

had made. Mitchell told him it was a good job, but as far as I know, that was the only yardage our star draft pick was to make in the Pan Am-TWA game.

On September 13 Tillinghast called Flanigan and then phoned me with the news that Flanigan couldn't give us an answer. I was furious and put in a call to Flanigan myself.

"Jeeb, I'm sorry but we just can't give you an answer," he said.

"You promised us one and you can at least say 'yes,' 'no,' or 'maybe, if,' " I retorted.

"No, it's not possible to give you that."

"Well," I snapped, "I don't understand it or even believe it, but thank you for your efforts."

That ended the conversation. Tillinghast and I went back to our respective companies, announcing to our Boards and employees alike that merger exploration had been discontinued. We knew that without some kind of assurance of probable approval from the White House, we were dead.

In retrospect, I think there were two major points of significance. First, we conducted all these "mergyrations" in the open. At the very beginning, we announced that we were having discussions that might lead to a merger and were exploring the necessary avenues of approval. This was an important step because we let our people in on it right from the start. Naturally, they reacted in individual ways, as they always do; some began figuring out how much power they'd get when functions were combined, while others became fearful of being subordinated to some expert or specialist from the other carrier. Some relaxed a bit, with a kind of feeling that "we're going to get married, so why compete so fiercely?" Still others, seeing no gain for themselves in a merger, began to urge their colleagues and unions to fight the merger.

The other significant aspect was that we also conducted our discussions in Washington in the open. There was never any attempt to hold clandestine meetings, or to deny that we were in Washington for the purpose of exploring presidential approval. To fortify this, we never went near the CAB, and if there were any discussions with the CAB chairman, they would have been by Flanigan or by Charles Baker, not by us. I feel that it was an effort well justified, and I believe Tillinghast did too.

Soon thereafter, Floyd Hall of Eastern approached me again with regard to a merger more or less along the lines, "Well, Jeeb, now that you've failed with the massive merger, as I predicted you would, let's resume discussions of a less massive one."

I told him I was very grateful for his continued interest and that we ought to keep the matter on the back burner but not pursue it aggressively. By then I had more serious internal problems to cope with and more or less closed the mergyration front for an indefinite period.

I am convinced that the best solution to Pan Am's problems, assuming it will never be granted a domestic-route structure, is a merger with an airline that has such routes. The obvious marriage partner is one of the big three: United, the nation's largest domestic airline; TWA, which serves 39 U.S. and 27 foreign cities; or American, which serves 42 U.S. destinations. I believed this when I headed Pan Am and still believe that merger is the logical, fair, and lasting solution. Certainly Trippe thought so, as his 1963 attempt at marriage with Tillinghast demonstrated, and Trippe might even now agree with me in regretting my personal time wasted. In fact, one of the reasons I failed to perform better operationally was the amount of time I spent to consummate a merger when a straight statement of national policy could have spared us that crucial energy.

During my very first week in the chief executive officer's chair, I called American's C. R. Smith and told him frankly that I was "shopping" for a merger partner and wondered whether he thought it was timely for serious discussion with George Spater, then president of American. I invited Spater to meet me at Herb Brownell's apartment in New York. Brownell was a senior partner in the legal firm of Lord, Day and Lord. I liked Herb and respected his integrity and ability. I knew the Justice Department's Antitrust Division would be our biggest obstacle outside of the CAB itself, a view that Brownell—a former Attorney General himself—thoroughly shared. So did Spater; our merger talks continued over several sessions in which we determined that we both would like to do it (I told him in view of his seniority, I would accept him as chief executive officer and serve as chief operating officer), but also agreeing that getting CAB and White House concurrence would be precarious. He too didn't think we could get it passed by the government, and two of the four members of his Management Committee who were opposed to marrying the Pan Am management. Also, American, at that time, unknown to me was having its own troubles, including indictment of a key officer for taking kickbacks, conflict among members of the Committee, and the ever-present influence of Smith.

Harding Lawrence of Braniff wooed me from Manhattan penthouses to Mediterranean villas, but his idea of a merger was for Braniff to absorb Pan Am—a case of the minnow swallowing the whale. (Ironically, both Spater and Lawrence were later charged with making illegal contributions of airline funds to Nixon's re-election campaign.) Eastern also continued to be very interested as my old boss, Laurance Rockefeller, firmly reminded me on social occasions. With Floyd Hall's co-operation, we conducted an elaborate study of what an Eastern-Pan Am marriage would entail, and I concluded it would be worth pursuing if nothing could be worked out with the other members of the Big Four—TWA, American, and United.

I did talk to United, at meetings arranged by General Al Gruenther of our Board, who was close to UAL's top management, but we had to agree that the CAB was most unlikely to approve a merger between the nation's biggest domestic airline and its largest international carrier.

Brief discussions were held with Delta, but here the stumbling block was Delta's traditional nonunion policy. So when we kicked merger around with Delta's management, it was apparent that they wanted no part of Pan Am's heavily unionized personnel, the powerful Teamsters in particular.

My own preference was TWA or American. Interestingly enough, Willis Player urged talks with Continental—he was close to Bob Six and sincerely admired this fiery, explosive pioneer. I couldn't see how Pan Am ever could accommodate Six's domineering personality and besides, at the time, we were bitterly resisting Continental's attempts to move into the Pacific. Also, Pan Am's disease was too massive for this cure.

I sought a merger with a strong domestic carrier because I felt it would cure Pan Am's three major problems, each unsolvable without merger: lack of domestic routes, the burden of excessive competition, and our need for seasoned, stable management, which Pan Am hadn't had for a decade. I think that events that transpired after I left Pan Am proved the wisdom of the "join 'em if you can't lick 'em" course I tried so hard to follow. Both Pan Am and TWA, the latter to a lesser but still major degree, flew into financial storms. In Pan Am's case, it was partly due to managerial mistakes—including my own—but also because of factors beyond management control. War, revolution, hijacking, devaluation, inflation, and the energy crisis all found the two biggest U.S. international carriers even more vulnerable than their domestic compatriots. The combined Pan Am-TWA 1974 fuel bill, for example, went up $400 million over 1973. I have watched Pan Am carefully since I was forced out of office: I had to admit that William Seawell—with Wiser, whom he brought over from TWA as president—has tried just as hard as I to save the airline, and that both Pan Am and TWA management have done everything within ordinary corporate power to keep these two great carriers strong and viable.

What were the alternatives to merger?

We could keep federal hands off both airlines and let their seventy-five thousand employees and two hundred thousand stockholders crash.

We could subsidize them for an indefinite period while groping for an international air policy.

We could nationalize them.

We could dismember Pan Am and distribute the remains among other airlines, thus further disintegrating this nation's portion of the world air transportation system.

Or we could force the companies' Directors and officials, together with their long-term creditors (insurance companies and bondholders) and their short-term creditors (banks) to come up with a reorganization and refinancing program short of bankruptcy, while Pan Am and TWA combine into one healthy, strong competitor.

I proposed this in an Op Ed-page article written for the New York *Times* that was published October 11, 1974, after I had left the airline. To quote its concluding paragraphs:

"I believe the last option should be exercised urgently. To this end, Congress should consider adopting legislation that would authorize, through June 30, 1976, an international air transportation commission composed of the Secretaries of State, Treasury, Defense, Transportation, and all Civil Aeronautics Board members.

"Congress should appropriate, and this temporary body should be authorized to grant, necessary operating subsidies to Pan Am—this was done from 1927 to 1954—and TWA for up to six months. The sum should not exceed $30 million. This should be done provided that the subsidies are to be paid back out of future profits over a long period and that the carriers' creditors defer interest and rent under a combined refinancing plan.

"Further, the commission could commit the government to guarantee long-term indebtedness on realistically favorable terms, giving the merged company time to work its way back to financial health.

"The commission would be authorized in this one case to approve, subject to presidential veto, a merger on such terms and conditions as would assure a balanced, integrated, dynamically competitive United States international air transportation system.

"I anticipate certain arguments against this proposal. First: 'Uncle Sam should not come to the rescue of private corporations in a free-enterprise system. It's not fair to the taxpayers.'

"Reply: Neither Pan Am nor TWA are truly private-enterprise companies. Where they fly, how much they charge, and whom they must compete against are decisions made largely by the United States and foreign governments. And many of these decisions have been, at least with the benefit of hindsight, horrendous. We are not just trying to rescue Pan Am; we are also seeking to correct major regulatory mistakes and to preserve the United States position in overseas aviation.

"With the United States balance-of-payments deficit mounting daily, we must strengthen our exporters of air services who can together earn more than $500 million a year in foreign exchange. Pan Am and TWA are semipublic corporations and, in fact, national assets belonging to all Americans, not just their shareowners.

"A second argument: 'Combining failing companies will produce a massive failure, not success.' Reply: TWA, with a strong, sound structure of routes—it serves thirty-nine United States cities —and seasoned management can ultimately break even and, joined with Pan American, is potentially profitable. More than $100 million could be saved by eliminating duplicated annual costs and by rationalizing the airlines' large jet fleets and marketing organizations.

"More important, the merger would not be more complicated than today's operations of both carriers. In fact, elimination of the competitive jockeying would simplify much decisionmaking, improve schedules, hold down fares, and could result in the world's best airline."

After the article appeared, Tillinghast sent me a nice letter complimenting me for what I had espoused, and so did a couple of Pan Am Directors. (I didn't hear anything from Pan Am's management, however.) I only cite that article to the *Times*, out of chronological context, to demonstrate my conviction, both past and present, that Pan Am must go the merger route to survive.

And in fighting for merger while I was the airline's chief executive officer, I unwittingly sowed the "dragon's teeth" that would lead to my own demise.

CHAPTER TEN

My heavy involvement with merger possibilities made it only too
apparent that as Pan Am's "captain" I needed a good executive
officer to help me run the ship—in other words, a president to
guide day-by-day operations so I could concentrate on long-range
problems, mergyrations, and policies, not to mention the "on-the-
job" training I was undergoing myself.

As I have indicated, my search for a new president started almost as soon as I became Board chairman in 1970. The trouble
was that our mounting losses made Pan Am a poor attraction for
executive talent; the general feeling seemed to be, "Why go with a
loser?"

I would have preferred to have promoted a president from
within Pan Am, in particular from the quartet of new group vice
presidents I had brought in. I've already recounted our hiring of
Jim Leet to head marketing and Dick Knight to take over finance.
I also enlisted Frank Doyle, formerly chief of personnel and public
relations at Western Union, as vice president of personnel and administration, replacing Goulard. I weaned Frank Davis away from
Kaiser Engineers International to become vice president of operations, engineering, and maintenance.

Dick Mitchell was an obvious choice as a "presidential trainee," so to speak; he had done a fantastic job of running Pan Am's Aerospace Division, but his health continued to decline, and he couldn't stay around long enough to lift some of the heaviest burdens from my shoulders.

Leet was another excellent possibility, having been president of a trunk carrier, but he never seemed ambitious enough to reach out for Pan Am's presidency. He preferred to play it cool, stick to his own area of responsibility, and never fully commit himself one way or the other.

I've already mentioned my failure to get my own appointees to work together as a team. Nowhere was this more apparent than with the four group vice presidents, who just didn't get along. So, unable to draw from within Pan Am's own ranks for the presidency, we went outside—combing the entire airline industry.

An early choice was Sam Higginbottom, later president of Eastern, whom I wooed with such intensity that I wound up offering him more money than I was making. He was interested but his family wanted no part of the New York rat race, preferring to stay in Florida, where Sam was working as a top EAL operations man. He also had his craw full of Eastern's earlier stormy management feuds and the airline's long history of Rickenbacker domination. Floyd Hall had done a Pan Am in reverse—he had hired so many good men to repair the Rickenbacker damage that they were fighting among themselves, and Hall had to fire some of them.

"I've lived through that massacre at Eastern," Sam told me, "and I don't want to go through anything like that again. Second, I'm not sure whether you're running Pan Am or whether Trippe still is. Hell, I don't want to walk into another Rickenbacker situation."

Later I heard Higginbottom also wasn't sure if I was capable of delegating full operating authority to him, and I regret that I didn't give him sufficient assurance on that point. At any rate I wasted six months courting Sam, and despite his subsequent termination as Hall's No. 2 man, I still think he would have been good for Pan Am.

There didn't seem to be enough hours in each day to accomplish what I wanted accomplished. I was getting involved in virtually every phase of Pan Am's sprawling, intricate operations. I had

313

given major priority to improving the airline's service reputation, trying to create an image of a fresh new management that had the public's interest at heart. This job alone could have occupied me twelve hours a day. Most airline presidents have to keep themselves immune from direct contact with passengers or they'd never get anything else done; C. E. Woolman of Delta was one of the few air-carrier bosses I ever knew who refused to have an unlisted phone. I was another.

I let myself be used on frequent occasions. I often flew in the coach section of our planes, observing our service there and talking to passengers about Pan Am. When on a flight that was delayed, I sometimes took on the chore of explaining the whys and wherefores to some of the customers. And invariably when I flew Pan Am planes, flight crews would volunteer lengthy lectures on what was wrong with our airline and how it could and should be improved. Some of these sessions were helpful but they also could be painful, particularly when I was trying to relax.

I learned quickly, and had the lesson repeated on numerous occasions, that no head of an airline ever gets a chance really to relax, not when he commits himself totally to his responsibilities. Even when I was away from my office, I never stopped thinking about Pan Am, its problems, and my own responsibilities for trying to solve those problems. The 747 was always in my mind, not only from an economic standpoint but also in the knowledge of what would happen if one went down. I knew it was the safest and strongest transport plane ever built, yet its very size provided the constant nightmare of what a fatal crash would entail in terms of the number of lives lost.

I dreaded the news of an accident, any accident, when I headed the FAA, and at Pan Am the apprehension was even worse; the feeling of personal loss, of soul-searching, of anger that someone or something could have caused a tragedy that didn't have to happen—this is what an airline executive inherits after a crash, along with the very human tendency to start rationalizing, alibiing, or buck-passing. We did suffer three accidents while I was at Pan Am's helm, all of them involving 707s—one a freighter and the others on passenger flights. My fears about the 747, however,

314

proved unwarranted; and my intensive concern and care was re-warded. When it came to safety, the giant Boeings were absolutely superb. Financially ailing though we were, we did not stint one nickel in our 747 crew-training program. That we could introduce and then operate this incredibly complex piece of flying equipment with a perfect safety record—inaugurating 33 planes in half as many months—was an achievement of which I am extremely proud.

We did lose one, but not in a crash. I'll never forget the day it happened. We had rented a house on Fisher's Island off New London, Connecticut, for the Labor Day weekend in 1970. I had been playing golf and had just returned to our little cottage when a state trooper, who happened to have the cottage next door, rushed over.

"Is your name Halaby?" he asked.

"Yes."

"The Halaby of Pan American?"

"That's me," I replied. My heart started to pound. There was something in his demeanor that hinted at bad news. I figured one of our birds must have gone down.

"Your office at JFK has been trying to reach you," the trooper told me. "They finally got to our headquarters and I was told to contact you. Some kind of an emergency—a hijacking, they said."

I raced to JFK in a small plane and was briefed immediately on what had happened. The hijacked plane was a 747, Flight 93, Brussels to New York, with a single stop at Amsterdam—the first jumbo jet, incidentally, to suffer a hijacking. The culprits were two men from the so-called Popular Front for the Liberation of Palestine (PFLP). Each was armed with a revolver and a hand grenade. The first word of their crime came in a teletyped message from Pan Am operations in London to our flight-control center located in a hangar at JFK:

AFTER DEPARTURE AMSTERDAM FLIGHT 93/06 SEP SUFFERED 9052 REPEAT 9052 AND PROCEEDING MIDEAST STOP FINAL DESTINATION NOT KNOWN BUT LAST WORD REPORT CAPTAIN FILED FLIGHT PLAN FOR BEIRUT STOP WILL KEEP YOU AD-VISED STOP

9052 was our code for hijacking. Will Gerkin, a Schedule-Control man who received the message, decided to notify me, and by the time I reached the airport, Flight 93 definitely was heading for Beirut, where the 747 had to circle for two hours; the Lebanese Government didn't want it to land there. The hijackers were insistent—it developed later that they wanted to pick up a demolitions expert waiting for them at Beirut Airport. And Captain John Priddy, in command of Flight 93, wasn't averse to landing at Beirut, either; he felt that once on the ground, the hijackers would at least release the passenger hostages.

At first, airport officials tried to divert the plane to Damascus, informing both Priddy and the hijackers that the main runway at Beirut was closed and that the other runway wouldn't support the weight of a 747. Priddy, however, knew that while the main runway *had* been shortened because of construction work at one end, it still was long enough for Flight 93, and he finally got permission to land. The hijackers at this point had decided to refuel and take off again for Cairo after their demolitions colleague had been taken aboard. From a distance of five thousand miles away I thought we could stop them at Beirut, if we stood firm as we had done in El Paso nine years before.

We had established radio contact with the Beirut tower, where Hal Williams—our manager in Beirut—had been surrounded by a kind of "negotiating committee" consisting of himself, Pan Am's security chief in Beirut, a member of the Palestinian Liberation Organization (PLO) who was acting as a go-between with the hijackers aboard the plane, an official from the U. S. Embassy, the airport manager, and the Lebanese civil-aviation deputy administrator. When Williams advised me that the hijackers wanted Flight 93 refueled for a flight to Cairo, and the demolitions expert permitted to board, I flatly refused.

"I want a Pan Am truck parked in front of that plane," I told Williams. "Don't let it take off."

To make sure Williams and the others in that tower understood how strongly I felt, I sent a confirming cable repeating my instructions to drive a truck in front of the 747 so it could not leave for Cairo. I sent a personal plea to the Arabs in the tower and on the plane. But Williams, under severe pressure from the rest of the "committee," informed me that everyone in the tower—including by then the deputy chief of the U. S. Mission—considered my course of action too risky.

Refueling was completed in forty-five minutes, the "committee" permitted the demolitionist to board, and the aircraft proceeded to Cairo—where, two minutes after landing, it was hastily evacuated and then blown up. Seven passengers were injured in the evacuation but they, along with the others, were lucky. The young demolitionist had started igniting the ten-minute fuses to numerous bundles of dynamite throughout the cabin just eight minutes before Flight 93 landed in Cairo.

It was ironical: the loss of the first jumbo in flames set by the craziest of the homeless, frustrated Palestinians, who missed their assigned Israeli target and hit an airline headed by an Arab-American aviator who had labored long to help get recognition of the rights of the Palestinian people—and in my father's homeland, too!

The two young Arab skyjackers—who had very good manners, according to the stewardesses—had been sent by PFLP to capture and destroy an El Al flight bound from Amsterdam to JFK; the Israeli security and Dutch police had balked them but then failed to notify Pan Am of their suspicions until after the hijackers had boarded the wrong flight.

It was a sad day for commercial aviation but, it seems to me, one with some beneficial results. Worldwide antihijacking measures were stiffened, particularly those involving U.S. and Arab aircraft. (The Israelis had already applied maximum security on El Al.) Hijacking rises and falls throughout the world and could be virtually eradicated if all other governments instituted the tough security precautions existing within the United States. Industry/FAA/airport co-operation in the United States shows what can be done to solve a major aviation problem with a concerted, united effort in which the FAA—with vigorous initiative and support from the airlines—showed the way.

We managed to recover the hull insurance we had on our destroyed 747, *Clipper Fortune,* but only after some protracted and unpleasant negotiations with Lloyds of London. I had always considered Lloyds to be more of an institution than just an insurer—

quick judgment and quick pay—but they degraded their reputation in this case. They all but admitted liability, but they delayed payment so long that I finally had to fly to London with my very able insurance broker, Al Tahmoush, and assault Lloyds in their fortress—to no avail. It took four years to collect.

But dealing with, or trying to deal with, a crisis like the fate of Clipper Flight 93 was at least the kind of straightforward and tangible issue with which I had previously coped. But Pan Am's mounting financial worries, debts, and corporate politics were something else. Always I felt I had the formidable figure of Juan Trippe looking over my shoulder. I had asked Trippe to move off the main-headquarters floor and to drop off the Executive Committee, but I had not asked him to leave the Pan Am Building and to retire from the Board itself. It is now clear that I should have made these conditions for my taking the job as chief executive. There was no way that a man who had founded and lived with the airline for all those years could detach himself completely, especially one as mercurial and manipulative as Juan Trippe. But more important, I did not replace his cronies on the Board at the earliest opportunity—in particular at the 1971 Annual Meeting, when I missed a crucial chance to eliminate several old-timers who were intensely loyal to Trippe.

I acquiesced to their staying on the Board, and they turned out to be the group on which Trippe relied for his bloc of votes against me in what would be a final showdown. If I had replaced them with more helpful, effective, and loyal Directors, as I should have, it might have been a different story.

Within management, an early ally who turned into an enemy was Willis Player, Pan Am's vice president for public relations. It was disappointing that what started out as friendly collaboration changed to animosity, for Pan Am sorely needed a modern communications man. Pan Am had hired Player away from American, and previous to that he had been with the Air Transport Association. He knew Pan Am and he knew the airline business and at first I relied heavily on his advice and counsel. But now that it had become painfully clear that Pan Am's public and political relations were crashing around us, he was committing me to far too many speeches and public appearances, almost as if he, too, were trying to replace the image that had made the names Trippe and Pan Am synonymous. Even more serious to our relationship was my conclusion that his empire of 125 employees and dozens of consultants was uncontrolled and not producing results, and finally my growing belief that he was spending too much time on non-Pan Am activities. Eventually I removed Player from his command, made him a staff assistant and encouraged him to seek his future elsewhere.

And now here I was, having started the revolution—the reforming of attitude toward service, the reduction in force working toward higher productivity, a whole new (if quarrelsome) management team, decentralization, and delegation of authority. All of the steps were under way, but what about outside? We were now deeply into the morass of Vietnam, and the mud of the rice paddies splashed against us because as the principal carrier from the United States to Vietnam, Pan Am was not only there in full force, perhaps the largest private American activity in the country, but also we were carrying equipment in and warmakers in and out. There developed across the country an anti-Pan Am offshoot of the anti-Vietnam movement, with picketing at some of our principal offices.

The flood of transpacific competition was now in full tide and bursting upon us.

Just as we acquired thousands of new 747 seats, the 1969–71 economic recession depressed traffic growth to 1.5 per cent per year, at the moment Trippe and Gray had been counting on it to continue rising at 17 per cent per year.

Furthermore, the supplementals were beginning to get rich enough to buy additional equipment surplus to their Vietnam needs, and throw that at us from the West Coast to Europe and from the East Coast to Europe.

Then the 747, supposed to be a dream machine with all the decades of experience of Boeing behind it and millions of hours on Pratt & Whitney engines, developed very costly power-plant bugs that deterred passengers, interrupted trips, canceled flights, and added $2.5 million a month in additional operating costs. Finally, hanging over us was $1 billion worth of debt and huge interest and rental charges.

The storms were thickening, and as the gallant Clipper plowed ahead, the news media began to focus attention on its struggle for survival. As they poked and probed, so did the fright of the Directors increase. They saw their prestige and even their personal fortunes possibly at stake in what began to look like another Penn Central. Every week another revelation about that railroad's Board or management appeared, and stockholder suits against officers and Directors of the railroad commenced.

I had been under press pressure before but in private life it takes on a different aspect. It is extremely hard to call a news conference to answer an insinuation; it is very difficult to get the attention of one periodical to answer an article in another periodical. Then an element new to me appeared: disloyalty from within, leaks appearing in obviously inspired articles. One series of articles is worthy of special note because it clearly came from within the Pan Am PR staff. There began to appear in *Business Week,* under the by-line of Brent Welling, a very devastating series on Pan Am in which nearly all of its problems were attributed to my shortcomings. *Business Week* created enough of a stir for *Time* and *Fortune* to pick up the pursuit, and *Fortune* assigned two of their toughest editors to do stories on Pan Am's troubles.

By then, Frank Doyle had taken over PR, and he got off on the worst possible foot by restricting the *Fortune* writers' access to me and to others, and by advising me to tape any interview I might have with them. They talked to Player and people who had been let go by Doyle in a bloodbath that reduced the PR staff from 125 to about 40, and the annual budget from about $3.5 million to about $1.5 million—all at my direction but with his implementation.

TWA was having its troubles, too, and it was in that spring of 1971, perhaps out of my own sense of searching for a miraculous solution, perhaps out of a feeling that two faltering companies could get approval for a merger, that I plunged into the previously recounted effort with Charles Tillinghast to convince the Nixon administration it should not only permit but also promote the merger. By September our hopes for this solution had been dashed, and we went into the winter of 1971–72 under pressure from the rear, the right flank, the left flank, and head on—I had ignored a cardinal lesson of my FAA experience: Concentrate on one front at a time.

One of our most ominous obstacles ahead was a bankers' deadline for refinancing the credit arrangement we had arranged two years earlier. In the years since Trippe had committed Pan Am to the 747 fleet, followed by Gray's additional 747 order and the terminal and maintenance base projects, our investment bankers, Lehman Brothers had been very aggressively selling very high-priced bonds and convertible debentures, resulting in a high and barely tolerable debt-equity ratio.

So, money, that fuel of every corporation, was running low and there was no money for all the other long-range schemes I had dreamed about—for example, going into the small-airport hotel business in a big way; buying land around rapidly developing airports and developing it for a gain; further expanding our technical-assistance program for developing country airlines, which had been neglected but quite profitable and quite prestigious around the world; and setting up trading companies in the Soviet Union and the People's Republic of China. All of these were on my Pan Am 1980 blueprint but now had to be shelved. Only hotel expansion could be pursued, fortunately into my favorite region, the Middle East.

It was clear to all friends of Pan Am that the number one priority and most pressing problem was to recruit a president and chief operating officer. I simply could not carry the multi-headed, monstrous role that had been thrust upon me—keeping the Directors and shareholders happy, holding the bankers at bay, negotiating a merger with Tillinghast, lobbying in Washington and running the day-to-day operation of an international airline, not to mention being a husband and a father.

Some thought that I desired to retain power and had been delaying the recruiting of a president. Far from it; I simply had been unable to attract a suitable, qualified person, even with the help of Booz, Allen & Hamilton and various Directors who were sympathetic and helpful. It was clear that the Directors were getting impatient, and at a Board meeting in September of 1971 I was given an ultimatum to bring in a new president regardless of conditions and price or else the Board was going to take the problem into its own hands. In the course of a long and sympathetic talk

321

with Governor Scranton, I recognized the challenge and the threat—and the necessity for immediate action. I must admit I was getting desperate on a number of counts, and perhaps in my desperation I moved too fast.

In any case, I consulted again with Joe Kalman of Booz, Allen & Hamilton, who had been working on the problem for over a year and had been unable—except in the case of Higginbottom—to come up with a suitable and available candidate.

Henry Golightly, our marketing consultant, who knew the cast of characters in the airline industry as much as anyone, went over with me the list that we had been considering, and we decided that it was probably worth an effort to explore William Seawell's candidacy in depth.

Seawell's track record was good. He was a former Air Force general, and at the time I approached him about the Pan Am presidency, he was president of the North American subsidiary of the British Rolls-Royce Aircraft Engine Company. Prior to that he had been a senior vice president of American Airlines.

Before inviting him to have lunch, I talked about him to several trusted friends and advisers who had known him at American Airlines—in particular C. R. Smith, George Spater, and James H. Douglas, a longtime American Director and outside counsel. They all gave Seawell very good marks, especially Douglas, who had Seawell as his executive officer when he was Deputy Secretary of Defense. He was very high on him and thought he would fit in quite well.

Spater was complimentary, but later told me that he thought I was considering Seawell for *executive* vice president. C. R. Smith, who had originally hired Seawell out of Douglas's office in the Pentagon, was quite strong in his support of Bill, and this was encouraging.

Golightly made some inquiries on his own and reported back that he thought that Seawell would fit into the picture very well. At my request, Golightly wrote me a letter to that effect, and that same letter later was useful in convincing the Executive Committee and the Board of Directors that the man I had selected was fully qualified. At the same time, Seawell and Golightly became inevitable allies, since Golightly had helped Seawell get the job, and Seawell could help Golightly keep his job as a consultant. Interestingly enough, Seawell and Player had become well acquainted while they were both at the Air Transport Association and American. I've no doubt that this made the triumvirate of Golightly, Player, and Seawell a natural one and contributed later to Seawell's demand that Player be retained despite my having given him his walking papers and his keeping Golightly as a consultant after I had concluded his work had been done.

One must remember that while all these developments were occurring, Pan American World Airways was hemorrhaging from operating deficits. Traffic was off in 1970 and 1971, while expenses were up due to inflationary wage settlements forced upon us and the unexpectedly high cost of operating thirty-three Boeing 747s. We were eating away at the stockholders' equity and we also were eating away at the foundations of Pan Am's financial structure.

A word at this point about the financial foundation of an airline may be relevant. Airlines are notoriously weakly financed, with a thin equity capital and very high debt. A man like Richard Knight shuddered on recognizing that the ratio of debt to equity when he took charge of the Pan Am balance sheet was about 70 per cent debt to 30 per cent equity. The debt ratio kept climbing, affecting all the credit agreements with the banks and insurance companies. There was a covenant that management would not let the net worth go below a certain absolute amount and that the debt-to-equity ratio would be held to a fixed formula limit. The structure of Pan Am's debt and obligations was roughly as follows. There were three groups of creditors: Holders of long-term notes largely in the hands of insurance companies all over the country. One issue of debt had over thirty-five insurance companies involved, and if we had to amend any portion of that credit agreement, we had to obtain the unanimous consent of all of them. The second was a midterm debt, five to ten years in duration, with a nationwide consortium of banks. A third type of creditor was the owner and lessor of aircraft and facilities; many of the airplanes that Pan Am operated were leased from various aircraft leasing institutions such as Citibank and other financial companies. The same was true of the new terminal and the maintenance base.

323

Adding up the obligations of the company in terms of long-term debt, short-term debt, and leases of aircraft and facilities, the total amount exceeded a billion dollars. There were many landlords, lessors, bank creditors, and insurance-company creditors demanding their annual interest. These fixed charges, of course, came out of operating revenue and were a very heavy burden indeed to bear and to contemplate in the future. So the next financing move was a very important and urgent one, and we spent many days getting the insurance companies and the banks lined up to continue financing Pan Am under these very difficult conditions. Our negotiations with our lead bank, which I had selected in the summer of 1971—Citibank—were proceeding satisfactorily, although I felt sure that Walter Wriston, their chairman, was uneasy. His president, Bill Spencer, was quite friendly and co-operative but the No. 3 man, Ed Palmer, was the most demanding and difficult. I think it is fair to say that the Directors stood in greater awe and fear of the bankers than they did of the regulators in Washington.

It didn't make things any easier for the very same bankers to be testifying en bloc before Congress supporting the emergency credit legislation for nearly bankrupt Lockheed and government subsidies for the successor to the bankrupt Penn Central. They were all in the same transportation divisions of their banks and were the leading experts in aerospace, airline, and other transportation financing. It was natural for them as well as their Directors and mine to have a deepening concern for the effects of government action or inaction on two other transport-oriented giants who were ailing or failing.

The lack of an experienced, resourceful chief financial officer was almost as serious in these stormy conditions as a lack of a president. And one was not at hand.

Juan Trippe's son, Charles Trippe, had been the apple of his father's eye. A fellow Yale alumnus, as well as a Harvard MBA, young Trippe came into the company and worked under various bosses until he was named an assistant to John Gates in Inter·Continental Hotels. That's when I first met him, finding him a very bright, quick-witted young man, as intense as his father but without the latter's mesmeric charm. He was totally dedicated to Pan Am and I'm sure could dream of becoming the second Trippe to head the company. Surely his mother and father, who were indeed very proud of him, must have harbored such a dream.

I liked Charlie very much. Gray had great respect for his mental ability—though with concern about his immaturity in dealing with his colleagues—along with Gray's natural sense of obligation to a proud father who wanted his son to do well. So Gray, in concert with his chief financial officer and closest friend in the company, Robert Ferguson, made Charles Trippe treasurer of Pan Am with a view to his succeeding Ferguson, who was at retirement age after long and faithful service to the company. Unhappily, however, shortly before his retirement Ferguson told Dick Mitchell and me that he did not really think Charles Trippe was qualified to be chief financial officer. He joined us in conducting a search outside the company, which finally wound up with the selection of Knight.

Because I felt that Charlie was one of the most imaginative officers in the company and because of a desire to get away from the fix-to-fix, seat-of-the-pants financial navigation of the past, I mobilized from within Pan Am a new planning organization for him to head, and in the course of his work there he came up with the first five-year plan that Pan Am had ever had. It was carefully researched, concurred in by all, and presented to me in the form of a handsome brochure. It projected for the years 1969–74 net profits of over $200 million, and to my eternal regret I accepted the plan and published it as the best available estimate—adding, however, that it would be used for "planning purposes but not for expenditure purposes." This was a qualified acceptance of an elaborate piece of work. Even this didn't fully satisfy Charlie, although he understood my reasons for caution. (Losses for this period exceeded his estimate of profit!)

As part of the planning function, we gave him a very substantial control over scheduling of the airline, and the small staff of two principals, who had previously reported to Gray, now reported to him. At about this time an outstanding expert in scheduling and financial planning became available. His name was William Crilly, and he had previously been one of the top officers of Eastern Air Lines; according to Floyd Hall, he had done an outstanding job, particularly in the planning and scheduling area. He was also very highly regarded in the financial community as a man of his word and a man of wide experience in the airline industry. He had lived through some of the internal travails of Eastern and was, therefore, a seasoned officer. So I brought him in, put him over Trippe in charge of all planning and scheduling, and, in particular, assigned him the task of restructuring the route system in the light of our financial problems. I told him to take an X ray and a scalpel and do the first major surgery on the airline in its forty years of life. He had just about completed this monumental task when Knight departed Pan Am and I had no alternative but to press Crilly into service as the chief financial officer as well as his other duties. Meanwhile Charlie Trippe was working for him on planning and special assignments.

So through a rather tortuous and painful route, we were entering the worst part of the storm with a new copilot and a new financial engineer. One of the most ironic things about Knight's departure involved the discussions in Washington over the feasibility of a Pan Am-TWA merger. Pan Am had been requested to forecast its cash flow and deficit so the analysts in the CAB and the Department of Transportation could determine whether or not it was a "failing company" within the meaning of the antitrust exemption that would permit a failing company to merge with another company, as had been the case in Capitol's absorption by United. Knight, an artist with arithmetic, had prepared, just a few months after Charlie Trippe's optimistic five-year plan, an entirely different forecast showing that in the single year 1972, under certain fairly miserable assumptions, Pan Am would lose $150 million—quite a contrast of conclusions out of the same computer and financial staff! In any case, neither of them was right, but unfortunately Knight was much closer to right than Trippe. I refused to send Knight's estimate to the government because I felt it was based upon unrealistic assumptions and, moreover, if it leaked out, it would destroy both our credibility and creditworthiness. Nevertheless, Knight having received an official request for the figures, they were given in confidence to an Assistant Secretary of Transportation, who fortunately kept them confidential—and, I guess, found them quite incredible.

The circumstances of Bill Seawell's selection and placement as the fourth President of Pan Am are remarkable in several respects.

They contrast sharply with my own recruitment and introduction, in his requirements for a contract and, finally, in the response of the Pan Am Directors.

I discussed his selection with the Executive Committee in advance of the November 1971 Board meeting, and although they knew little more about him than I told them, they were satisfied to concur in my selection, although they were concerned about the rapidity with which he could take on the very difficult operating task. I then discussed the matter with the five key people reporting to me. At least four out of the five had strong yearnings to be president themselves, but I think they realized they had not yet demonstrated to me and the Board the requisite achievements. They accepted my choice, albeit reluctantly. I then presented his name and credentials to the Board of Directors, who had been urging the appointment of a new president. There was, to my surprise, quite a bit of critical questioning, and I later discovered it was largely because of Kendall's desire to select my successor himself. Nonetheless, in a fairly long and somewhat tense Board meeting, Seawell was approved and his hiring announced.

Immediately thereafter we sat down to negotiate the employment contract that he had requested and that I had promised as a condition of his coming into such a risky situation. To my amazement, he brought with him his brother-in-law, a lawyer from Little Rock, Arkansas, and they had some very specific demands not only for the terms of employment but also regarding the assignment of functions to Seawell. I think this reflected his own concern about his role in the company and advice he had been given that I might be reluctant to delegate full authority to him. So in what must be a unique document in airline history, he not only got a contract guaranteeing him salary, options, retirement benefits, etc., but also specifying the functions he would perform and those that I would retain among my prerogatives.

This irritated me somewhat, but I assumed it would make Seawell secure and satisfied; I had great faith in him, his self-discipline, and his obligation to duty, which had been tested in the Armed Services. His distinguished background—graduate of the Harvard Law School, commandant of the Air Force Academy, senior officer of American and ATA, and head of the Rolls-Royce

327

subsidiary in the United States—gave me confidence that he had been tested.

The most serious problem and the one that disturbed the Directors and the press a great deal was the fact that the new management team I had chosen was not working together effectively, and so I told Seawell that this was the area in which we should make our first decisive moves. He decided that he would widen Henry Golightly's consulting responsibility and diminish the use of Booz, Allen & Hamilton. I told him I felt that we'd had enough outside consultants in our hair and that we should get rid of all of them at the earliest practicable moment. He said that he would try but that he very much needed Golightly.

There followed several weeks, from approximately November 16 to the end of the year, during which time he was getting familiar with the company and the officers involved. As far as I know, Jim Leet, Frank Davis, and Frank Doyle all were fully co-operative and their working relationships were satisfactory. Having been hired by me, they still gave me their primary loyalty, but I'm convinced they were quite obedient to Seawell. He soon reached the conclusion that he wanted Willis Player to remain with the company, and to this I was strongly opposed. After we talked it out, I understood very clearly that he had accepted my termination of Player and the arrangement that I had made to give him time to find another job, but making it appear publicly that he had worked his way out of a job at Pan Am into new opportunities.

The second major personnel argument that divided us was over Frank Doyle. Doyle was a rather progressive, experimentive manager who was willing to try new things and new situations. He had been particularly adroit in selecting a vice president of industrial relations and in obtaining co-operation and even concessions from the pilots and Teamster-affiliated employees. I was very pleased with the work he had done even though his manner of slashing the PR staff had caused me great difficulties with the press. When Seawell indicated he would probably like to replace Doyle with his own man, I demurred.

"Get to know him a little better, Bill," I urged, "and give this further consideration before you make up your mind."

Seawell said he would and shortly thereafter told me he

had had a long talk with Doyle and had decided to keep him. I relaxed because I felt Doyle was not only good for Pan Am but also would be helpful to Seawell. But apparently Golightly and Player were opposed to Doyle's retention because a few days later Bill came back and said he had changed his mind: Doyle had to go. "I lack confidence in him," he explained.

"You're free to have your own man in charge of personnel," I replied. "This function is too important to be manned by anyone in whom you lack confidence. I'll tell you what I'd like to do, though: I'll take Doyle on my own staff temporarily while he looks for another job. I talked him into coming to Pan Am and I think I should grant him the courtesy of a graceful exit."

Seawell agreed to this and I thought the matter had been settled. As it turned out, it was far from settled.

I planned right from the start to lean heavily on Seawell. His appointment as president seemed to be what I needed. He had the airline operation experience I so sorely lacked and I had planned a change of command under which he would take over the day-to-day operations of Pan Am while I concentrated on long-range policy and other phases of the company's interest. I had emphasized publicly when he was named president that he would report directly to me as the chief executive officer and would be given full authority to act for the company. I hoped we could form a team capable of pulling our great airline out of its tailspin, recognizing that there might be inevitable conflicts and clashes but believing that our leadership in tandem would work. Bob Six had done it successfully at Continental, when Harding Lawrence ran the airline while Six devoted most of his time to policymaking, long-range planning, and politics.

As far as I knew, the only serious differences that Seawell and I had in our early days were with regard to Player and Doyle. I realized that he had a very difficult role to perform, gaining the confidence of a somewhat doubtful Board; working with me, who had been both president and chairman for twenty-two months; and working with a new team that was still unsettled itself.

This might have been a good time for me to take thirty days off "inspecting the airline" and let Seawell get fully involved without having me coaching and questioning him. That might have been a smart thing to do, but with all fronts open and under pressure, it didn't seem too smart at that moment. Seawell proceeded in his own way to organize and manage the airline, and I did not attempt to second-guess him. I occasionally would sit in on staff meetings and would request progress reports from him.

Bill didn't know at this stage how close he had come to not getting the Pan Am job. Back in October 1971, the Board of Directors had appointed a Special Committee to examine the organizational and leadership problems about which the press had spoken and about which various members of management had complained to various Directors. This committee was composed of Donald M. Kendall, Frank Stanton, and Thomas J. Watson, Jr.

I learned much later that the committee assumed the role of recruiting a new president and with the help of headhunters like Golightly and McKinsey sought F. C. "Bud" Wiser from our main rival, TWA. This recruitment went as far as making Wiser an offer, unknown to the full Board of Pan Am and kept completely secret from me. Wiser informed Tillinghast who, in turn, recommended to the TWA Board that Wiser's contract be sweetened. Wiser came back to the committee and declined the offer. I didn't learn this for several months, but it occurred at just about the time I was placing Seawell in the presidency; it may account for some of Kendall's initial opposition to Seawell's nomination.

My good friend Bill Scranton, who had by now had to resign from the Board because he had been appointed a member of President Nixon's Wage-Price Commission, and Cyrus Vance both advised me to make a maximum effort toward the most unified and harmonious leadership and to convince the Board of Directors that this was the case. So in my own way I had gone to great pains to assure very good communication between Seawell and me. I generally dropped by his apartment at Seventy-ninth Street and Lexington Avenue each morning and we drove to work comparing notes on the previous day and the day ahead. It was obviously a very tough job for him, nor was it easy for me to get completely out of the daily operational area, but I tried very hard. One of the things Seawell and I did was agree to swap schedules for sixty days ahead, but before I picked him up one morning in March of 1972, he advised me that he was going on an inspection tour that very day. I wrote him a note expressing my surprise at his being away for two weeks and I'd hoped he'd reconsider and shorten his trip if at all possible.

"The downward communications between us are a little better than the upward communications," I commented as a concluding observation to the handwritten note. I left the note with Ivan Dezelic, the efficient and discreet chauffeur for Pan Am chief executives who would be driving Seawell to the airport after he dropped me off.

Seawell flew first to London, then on to Frankfurt and Rome. He told me later that he received a phone call in Rome, requesting him to return at once for consultation with the members of Pan Am's Special Committee. He did not tell me what I subsequently learned—that the call was initiated by Henry Golightly, who apparently had taken it upon himself to see Kendall and report to him that I was interfering with Seawell's operation of the company. Whether he talked to either Seawell, Player, or both before taking this action, I don't know.

What seems to have stirred up Golightly was my firing of Player and my "rehiring" of Doyle. Golightly evidently considered that the Player and Doyle matters constituted a major breaking point between Seawell and myself. I considered them normal differences that had been resolved between us.

Seawell rushed back to New York—without my knowledge, incidentally—and immediately met with Kendall, Tom Watson, and Frank Stanton, the members of the Special Committee. Stanton and Watson believed that the session was at Seawell's request, but Seawell informed me it was held at Kendall's. After the meeting, Bill came to my office and told me he had been questioned sharply by all three Directors and that he had given them all the facts about our differences over Player and Doyle.

"Did you discuss any other differences?" I asked.

"No, I did not."

"Well, did you characterize these differences as ones we had solved or not?"

331

"I said they were simply a poor omen for the future," Seawell replied.

I was mad. "You hadn't told me that, Bill. I thought we had amicably settled these matters."

"All I said was that they were a poor omen for the future," he repeated. (I recently learned that he had actually threatened to resign, thereby putting the members under terrible pressure.)

I questioned him again as to whether they had insisted on his returning early, and he said flatly that they had.

A few days later, I received a report that the three-man committee had taken Seawell's remarks most seriously, concluding that they must recommend my resignation to the full Board. One of them, I was told, observed that I had been "very unperceptive in permitting any kind of disagreement to exist with Seawell." Another told a friend of mine that the Player/Doyle incidents proved beyond any doubt that "Halaby could not give up power." The third member was Kendall, who from all available evidence had decided six months before that I must go; the Player/Doyle business had given him the opportunity. But at this moment I still refused to believe that Seawell was behind this backstaging; he seemed so sincere and straightforward in his approach to me, I could not conceive of his either conspiring against me or being the willing victim of a conspiracy.

After the shock I received from the reports concerning Seawell's meeting with the Special Committee, I got another jolt: The Committee requested me to call a special meeting of the Board on March 22, 1972, prior to the regular Annual Meeting, so the Directors could hear the Committee's report. My immediate response was to request a hearing before Kendall, Stanton, and Watson before they made their recommendations final. Kendall refused to attend. My second act was aimed at enlisting Seawell's support at what decidedly would be a showdown between the factions on the Board: Trippe and the Old Guard; Kendall; those loyal to me; and Stanton, Watson, and the rest of the Directors who were concerned to do what was right for the shareholders.

So I invited Seawell for a long lunch at the River Club. I wanted both of us to sit down away from the office for several hours and thrash out hitherto undisclosed differences or misunderstandings. He agreed to talk things over with me, and I started out with a recap of the whole picture as I saw it, and then asked him to fill in his side of it and see if we could get things settled. Far from complaining about how our relationship had developed, Bill expressed surprise at the great to-do being made over some relatively minor differences. More significantly, he agreed with me that we definitely had to go into that special Board meeting unified, lest those who wished to do so would divide us, to the embarrassment of both.

We talked for about three hours amid what seemed to be a very friendly, harmonious atmosphere. One decision we reached was to have breakfast together the morning of March 22, to make certain of a unified presentation. I came home from my meeting with Seawell reassured, but when I recounted the story to Doris—as I did each evening—she reiterated her deep concern over Seawell's ambitions.

Her own doubts bothered me to the extent of discussing the situation with two Directors who were special friends of mine. It was their firm advice to come into the special Board meeting with an absolute show of unity between Seawell and myself. I assured them I was planning to do just that and told them I was meeting Bill at breakfast prior to the Board session.

He didn't meet me.

And thus began my last day at Pan Am.

CHAPTER ELEVEN

I'll never forget that morning of March 22, 1972, nor what was to follow.

There was an ominous air of urgency about the meeting, called for 1:00 P.M. that day against the gloomy backdrop of Pan Am's worsening financial posture. Over the previous three years, the airline had lost $120.3 million—about half of which occurred during my chairmanship. In January and February of 1972, Pan Am had operated at a deficit of $23.7 million—a loss so huge that not even the heaviest summer traffic could stem the red-ink torrent.

A renewal of our loan agreement was crucial. I was confident we could get one. In fact, we already had negotiated with the banks an extension plan that would have meant Pan Am's paying a higher than prime interest rate and also would have instigated a series of additional economy moves, including an effort to sell our passenger terminal at JFK Airport. Neither Pan Am nor the lending institutions had ratified this new arrangement, but I was sure it would be approved.

Apparently some Directors with their eyes on Lockheed and Penn Central lacked my confidence, and with the March 31 bankers' deadline looming ahead like a violent storm front, the

March 22 meeting had boiled down to the question of my own immediate survival.

On that very day I got fresh indications that Bill Seawell wanted to avoid standing with me in the crossfire of the Board room and to keep his personal options completely open. The night before the special Board meeting, I had dropped off at his apartment a copy of a statement I intended to read to the Directors, outlining what I thought was necessary to save Pan Am and expressing Seawell's complete concurrence. It was this statement that we had agreed to discuss at breakfast the following morning. At 7:15 A.M., while I was shaving, he phoned to say he was sorry but that he couldn't have breakfast with me.

"This is a very, very important breakfast, Bill," I said, "and I think we should go ahead with it."

"I simply don't want to discuss the matter," Seawell said bluntly.

"Well, do you agree with the statement?"

"I don't want to say I agree with it or disagree with it. I just don't want to discuss it."

Silence followed for a few seconds; then in the background I heard his wife say, "Just tell him you can't possibly have breakfast with him." And Seawell concluded our futile conversation. "I simply cannot have breakfast with you, Jeeb," he said with cold firmness, "and there's no place you can reach me between now and the meeting. I won't be in the office or near a telephone." Then he hung up.

I stood there, lather still on my chin. I finished shaving in a fog and told Doris what had happened. She is a lady, but her verbal reaction would have fried asbestos. Instead of going out, I had breakfast with her and we talked about what was likely to happen. We both were in a kind of "cheer up—things will get worse before they get better" mood. I noticed she had prepared a somewhat more sumptuous breakfast than usual, and while I refrained from mentioning it to her, that old chestnut about condemned men eating hearty meals kept invading my thoughts.

One of my best friends on the Board, Tom Watson, called just before I left for the office saying he wanted to drop in for a few moments before the meeting. I told him that would be fine—he was always welcome. Then I called another Director who had given me much support, Cyrus Vance, and told him what had happened with Seawell. Vance and Watson had been the two Directors who so strongly advised me to come into the meeting with solid evidence that Seawell and I were unified. Now, of course, my perception of unity had been shattered. Vance was amazed at Seawell's refusal to discuss the statement I had prepared, and he was most concerned—but he warned there was little he could do about it. After I had made him and his firm our outside counsel, he had to respond objectively to the Board and not personally to me.

I had asked Kendall, Stanton, and Watson to meet with me one hour before the Board session; as members of the Special Committee they had yet to hear my side of the supposed differences between Seawell and me. I got in early—about ten minutes before eight—and Watson arrived at eight-thirty. We talked about what had happened since the Special Committee was formed, and I told him about my phone conversation with Seawell earlier that morning. He was astounded that Bill had hung up on me and concluded there was no possibility of our working together harmoniously and effectively in the future. But he added he was terribly disappointed that I hadn't been more careful to avoid disagreements with Seawell.

"I don't see how any chief executive can yield at every point of disagreement with his chief operating officer," I argued.

Watson nodded. "I suppose that's true," he said.

While waiting for Stanton and Kendall to arrive, I read him the statement I planned to present to the Board. He listened carefully and called it "about as good a summing-up as I can imagine."

Stanton arrived and after an awkward wait for Kendall, who never showed up, the two of them listened to me sympathetically and without comment. My intuition told me Kendall wouldn't come. Ever since we had flown back together from a meeting of the Advisory Council on Japan-United States Economic Relations, which I chaired in San Francisco, I had known he was a determined foe.

We were in the Pepsico Falcon flying across the country. At the Council meeting, he had done a lot of table-pounding (at which he is an internationally acknowledged expert!), and as chairman I had to quiet him down and soothe our friends, the top Japanese business leaders, by reassuring them that even though he was a Nixon intimate his threats were not U. S. Government policy. After a Pepsico vodka on the rocks, we started talking about Pan Am, of which he now had been a Director several months.

He indicated that ever since he had met with the TWA Directors concerning a Pan Am-TWA merger and listened to them state that Wiser, president of TWA, wanted to be chief executive of Pan Am and would not willingly work for me, as he had for Tillinghast at TWA, Kendall's doubts about my leadership had grown. Knight, he said, also had expressed dissatisfaction with my management and, apparently, I had done nothing to drive him into line.

"If you can't get all these new guys to work together as a team, you can't be the captain," Kendall added bluntly.

The second count of his indictment was that I couldn't get anything done in Washington. He intimated that he had talks with his pal Flanigan as well as other unnamed members of the Nixon administration, and he had concluded that so long as I was heading Pan Am, the airline would get nothing from Washington. From a Nixon confidant this was a lethal chop.

His third criticism was that morale in Pan Am was very bad. He had recently been on a flight in which the crew filled his ears with complaints about cutbacks, economies, and failure to get any relief from Washington.

After another vodka, I tried to give him my defenses to these complaints, but his icy eyes told me he had already made his judgment.

After the perfunctory "hearing" by two thirds of the Special Committee, my fate was decided a few hours later in the properly appointed Board room on the forty-sixth floor of the Pan Am Building. There were twenty-one men in that room, including myself and Seawell. Fifteen were the "outside" Directors—those who served the airline solely as Board members and not as representatives of management. Crilly, Davis, Doyle, and Leet were the other insiders.

As chairman, I opened the meeting by suggesting that we dispose of the least controversial items on the agenda first and get to the main business at hand: the question of the company's leadership. There was rather perfunctory discussion and action on those routine matters, followed by an uneasy, tense silence, which I broke by asking the Pan Am executives present to leave while I read my prepared statement—the same one I had left with Seawell the night before.

"Except for Bill Seawell," I added. "I'd like him to stay and hear this."

The tension in the room tightened as I read. I remember that Seawell sat at my left and tough old Juan Trippe on my right, both expectantly silent while I talked.

To repeat what was in that lengthy statement would merely repeat what I already have written herein as to what was wrong with Pan Am and what was necessary to save it. The most important item to the Directors, of course, was *who* would save it. What I did was hand them three courses of direction:

1. Give me their confidence another two years to let me run Pan Am and complete the turnaround I sincerely believed we had started in motion.

2. If they lacked such confidence, I would be willing to stay on until a new chief executive officer was named.

3. I would resign forthwith.

When I finished, I glanced at the sober, even grim faces of this jury of my peers.

One Director, Alfred Gruenther—once Dwight Eisenhower's chief aide in the European Theater during World War II—broke in.

"Before you leave," he said, "I want to ask you gentlemen [meaning Seawell and myself] whether there are any disagreements or serious differences between you. Bill, do you have any disagreements with Jeeb?"

Seawell hesitated, but only for a second.

"No," he replied, "I don't think there's anything I should discuss about that, General. I'd rather not comment in any way."

"Well, how about you?" Gruenther asked me.

"Well, General, there have been reports of differences between the chief operating officer and me, but he has registered no complaints, and I am aware of only two serious differences of views that we have had, and both of them have been resolved. One was his desire to keep Willis Player and to assume control of all public relations, as opposed to my desire to terminate his services. This matter had been resolved by a letter from me to Player advising him of a rather liberal termination arrangement in which Seawell concurred.

"The second and more important difference, General Gruenther, was the matter of Senior Vice President Frank Doyle, whom Seawell at first confirmed in office and later advised that he did not have sufficient confidence in him to keep him as chief of personnel and industrial relations. Since this function had been assigned to Seawell, it was clear that he should be free to have a man in the job of his own choosing. On the other hand, since Doyle's performance had been superior and our labor relations had improved more than at any other time in the history of the company, I knew of no reason why he should be dismissed forthwith and, in fact, desired him to stay. Nevertheless, once Seawell had decided he could not use him in his professional field, I stated I would take Doyle on my own staff temporarily to give him time to turn around and get another job. The matter had been resolved by a letter from me to Doyle indicating the terms of his termination—leaving Seawell free to select a man of his own choice.

"I repeat: The only differences that I knew were those two, and I thought that they had been resolved between us."

Another Director, Stillman Rockefeller, asked Seawell to cite any differences with me other than the two personnel conflicts I had detailed. Again, Seawell declined to comment.

There were no further questions or comments; a rather embarrassed silence permeated the Board room. I suddenly had a distinct aversion to leaving that room—as if I were giving up without a fight. I told the Directors I'd rather stay before them.

"Put all the questions and comments and criticisms right on the table," I said. "Have it settled once and for all, because I don't think the Board should adjourn without establishing a clear-cut leadership."

Some discussion followed that plea, but it was apparent that

339

most of the members wanted an executive session without Seawell and Halaby. Bill and I both left, reluctantly on my part. I went to my office and Seawell to his.

I don't know how long I must have sat there, thinking of the unhappy recent past, the threatening present, and the uncertain future. I felt like a prisoner locked in a cell of self-recrimination and anger, waiting for a jury to decide. Of the fifteen men deliberating, one face stood out above all others—that of a Director who also was a friend, a trusted adviser, and a legend in his own right. We had not always agreed, but we respected each other's views. I couldn't resist glancing at him as I left the room. What was written on that strong, still handsome face? Sadness? Sympathy? Unspoken support? Loyalty to Trippe? I couldn't tell. It was a mask dropped in front of a man's inner emotions. But then, not many people could tell at times what Charles A. Lindbergh was thinking.

(Anne Lindbergh later told me that he was a strong ally!)

An hour passed. Two hours and a half. I sat there musing why I hadn't sought out Directors more loyal to me, Directors more interested in the business and less interested in the business of prestige and politics; why I hadn't insisted on dropping all those "over seventy-two" Directors, who were cronies of Trippe's, at the previous Annual Meeting; and why I hadn't made sure Trippe himself went off the Board when he organized the Old Guard cabal the previous year. I had, indeed, sown the seeds of my own defeat.

And defeat it was. My door opened and Cyrus Vance walked in, a look of sympathy on his face—so pronounced that I knew he really didn't have to say a word. He sat down in a chair facing my desk.

"Jeeb, it breaks my heart to report this, but the Board has decided it would like to accept your resignation."

All I did was nod.

"There was considerable debate and all aspects were considered," Vance continued. "They also asked me to ask you to remain on the Board and to stand for re-election with the slate that will be presented with the proxy statement. So I'd like to go back to the Board room, where they're all waiting, and give them your decision."

I tried my damndest to retain my composure, choosing my

words carefully. "Well, Cy, I guess this is a disappointment but not a total surprise. At this point, there's no use in going into all the details of the debate and so on. Do you really want me to stay on the Board? Because my impulse is to get off the Board and tell them to go to hell."

"Yes, I think they do want you to stay. I think they feel you could contribute, and it certainly would look better for you and for the company if you stayed on."

"Did the Kendall-Stanton-Watson committee make their report?" I asked.

"They did. They recommended that your resignation be accepted."

"Cy, let me think about it for a few minutes."

"Okay, I'll leave you alone. I'll be in the little Board room next door."

As soon as he left, I called Doris and told her the news.

"Why, those bastards!" she snapped.

"Do you think I should stay on the Board or not, Doris? I guess it would be better for the family if I did, and perhaps it would be better for Pan Am people to feel there's an orderly transition."

"Who's going to be elected chief executive?" she wanted to know.

"I don't know yet."

"How about your benefits?"

"I don't know about the benefits yet. What concerns me more is the possible loss of those stock options I've earned for the past six years."

"Well," Doris said with wifely firmness, "they just have to absolutely assure you that you won't lose any of your benefits."

There was a rather tense, uncomfortable silence for a few seconds before Doris gave me her own verdict. "If they do," she said, "I guess it probably would be better if you stayed on."

I sighed. "I'll see you tonight."

It was late in the afternoon by then, and I knew Vance was waiting patiently if uneasily for my decision. But I took the time to jot down some notes on what I wanted to say when I went back into the big Board room. I decided that the most important thing was to pin the Directors down on the preservation of those vital

341

benefits before formally submitting the resignation I had offered and they had accepted.

"Cy, I guess I see no alternative under the circumstances to offering my resignation formally. I'll agree to remain on the Board and to stand for re-election." Vance looked relieved. "But I took a quick look at my employment contract and I want to eliminate any doubt that during the period between now and December 1, 1973, I do retain and maintain to the fullest extent all of my benefits, which I have earned under that contract. So would you please make sure the Board has agreed to my retaining all my benefits?"

"I think that's fair," Vance assured me, "and I'll go in and make sure."

With his usual very quick, sure manner, he went back to the Board room, told them what I wanted and needed, and came back to my office in a few minutes.

"That is agreeable to the Board," he smiled.

So I walked into the Board room with as much dignity as I could command.

It was very still in the large, paneled room with the unusually long table. I glanced about and sensed immediately that everyone's eyes were on me to see how I would take the blow. I could see great sympathy and support in the eyes of Al Gruenther, Slim Lindbergh, Cy Vance, Tom Watson, Stillman Rockefeller, and Bill Coleman.

I called the meeting to order. "I have been informed by Mr. Vance that among the three alternatives I had offered, the Board has selected immediate resignation, and I accept their decision. As a matter of fact, my resignation had been submitted, undated, the day I was first elected chief executive. Although I have not been given reasons for the decision, I see no point in debating it at this point, since you have been in session for nearly three hours and I presume all sides of the matter have been carefully discussed. I'm sorry not to have had a hearing before the Special Committee studying the matter and I have a number of other regrets, but the facts of life are before us. It is my understanding that all my present benefits will be continued through the term of my employment including the exercise of stock options."

As I mentioned stock options, I noticed that Stanton looked

slightly surprised and turned to Vance and asked him a question I didn't catch. (Stanton later explained to me that he had simply said to Vance, "I didn't know he could exercise options after resigning as chief executive.")

I looked around the Board and there were no objections. In fact, most of the Directors nodded that my statement was correct. I then said that I presumed the next order of business was the election of a new chief executive. Trippe promptly nominated William T. Seawell as chairman and chief executive. There was some brief discussion about whether he was to continue as president as well or whether he should be president and chief executive and leave the chairmanship open. It was finally decided that the motion was intended to make him president, chairman, and chief executive. There was no dissent; I abstained from voting. Seawell was invited in and—looking a bit flustered—took charge of the meeting, sitting on my left with Trippe continuing to sit on my right. About this point, Stanton said, "We'd better get somebody drafting a press release." I said I would be glad to do a first draft.

Seawell seemed briefly to choke up with emotion as he thanked the Directors for electing him as the fourth chief executive of Pan Am and then gained control of himself and the situation. Meanwhile, I wrote out the following press release:

> The Board of Directors of Pan American World Airways, Inc., accepted effective today the resignation of Najeeb E. Halaby as chairman and chief executive officer.
>
> William T. Seawell was elected to succeed him and will serve as chairman, president, and chief executive officer.
>
> Mr. Halaby has accepted the invitation of the Board to continue as a Director and to stand for re-election at the Annual Meeting. He plans to enter the field of international trade and venture capital and will shortly announce the creation of a new activity in this area.

This was handed to Stanton, Vance, Seawell, and others and, with a few minor changes, approved in the spirit of putting the resignation in the best possible light. The whole idea was to make it appear an orderly transition and not an abrupt or disruptive action.

In particular, the Directors had decided to make it as easy as possible for me—apparently out of their concern for my future and, perhaps, a sense of guilt for having made me the scapegoat of a situation that had obviously gotten beyond their control or mine.

After the press release was cleared by the Directors, Seawell beckoned to Jim Leet and said, "Get that to Will Player as soon as possible and tell him to process it." This came as a huge surprise to me. Since I had written the letter to Player some three weeks before in effect terminating his employment, Player had been away most of the time—I had heard job-hunting. By a strange coincidence he returned on this particular day. Seawell, obviously, knew that he had returned and had asked him to handle the press release.

Seawell completed the relatively routine work on the preparation for the Annual Meeting of Shareholders and adjourned the meeting. I turned to him and rather weakly wished him the best of luck. Several other Directors, of course, congratulated him on his election. Then, most of them—notably excluding Trippe, Kendall, and Anderson—came by to express their sympathy and gratitude to me.

My very loyal colleagues, Davis and Doyle, came to express warm and friendly feelings, and Jim Leet called on the phone to say how much he regretted the events of the day. Many others did likewise. Tom Watson and Stillman Rockefeller came by on their way out and, in effect, said, "It will pass, and if there is any way we can help you get started again, let us know."

I was concerned with what Player would do with the release. Since I had already promised Robert Bedingfield of the New York *Times* and Stewart Pinkerton of the *Wall Street Journal* that I would let them know if there were ever any major development of this nature, I decided that I had best call each of them. Pinkerton was in Canada and Bedingfield was away, and no one knew who would cover this story.

I had a long and, for her, somewhat tearful discussion with my secretary, Joan Nixon, and I advised Miss Martha Sullivan, my first secretary at Pan Am, what had transpired. I also tried to reach Lisa, Alexa, and Christian so my children would hear the story first from me. None of them were available, but I finally reached my mother and she, who had had faith in the Board of Directors until the very end, was stunned. Her only question was, "Did Lindbergh support you, son?"

I had to tell her I didn't know, but I hoped so. Her response was, "Well, he's the only one that really counts in that crowd."

I drove home, and on the way I told my good friend Ivan, the Yugoslav driver, about how American corporations worked. He knew that I was having troubles but it was beyond his belief that such a thing could happen to any big shot anywhere, and he simply could not believe that he would soon have another boss to drive around. He was genuinely shaken, I suppose because of his friendship for me as well as his natural concern over his own future.

When I got home, I finally was able to reach my son, Chris.

"Are you really out of that rat race, Dad?" he asked.

"Yes."

"Well," he said with open relief and enthusiasm, "welcome back to civilization!"

By now I had poured myself a rather large Bourbon on the rocks and was feeling somewhat less pain. Doris was fending off incessant calls from the news media—I didn't want to talk to the press at that point—but one call was from Robert Lindsey of the New York *Times,* and he was insistent on talking to me. I decided he might be the best source of finding out whether Player had released the official announcement prepared at the Board meeting, or had been peddling his own line.

"Bob, what have you got?"

"I have a story that you were dismissed by the Board of Directors."

"Dismissed?"

"Yes. That you were forced to resign."

"Who the hell did you talk to in the company?"

First he said he couldn't tell me but a few minutes later admitted it was Player.

"Did you talk to any of the Directors who were present? Or to Seawell?"

345

"No, sir, I didn't."

"Well, did you read the release?"

"Yes, I did. Player just elaborated on it."

I was furious. It wasn't that Player had lied—to all intents and purposes, I *had* been asked to resign. But the official announcement was deliberately worded to avoid giving any impression of bitter feuding and instead to present a picture of unity and orderly transition of power. Player, I felt, had no right to go beyond the carefully prepared press release.

"I'll have to give you the facts, Bob," I said without bothering to hide my anger. "I was there and this is what happened. I opened the meeting by offering the Directors three alternatives. One, if they would give me their confidence and two years in which to complete the turnaround of Pan Am, I would remain as chief executive. If they could not, I would be glad to remain as chairman and presiding officer until a new chief executive was appointed and put into place. Third, I would resign forthwith if I did not have both the necessary time and necessary confidence. After a 2½-hour debate within the Board, they decided to pursue alternative three. I took the initiative in putting all this to the Board, and you should let your readers judge whether I was dismissed or forced to resign, or whether I resigned. Those are the facts."

"Did this have anything to do with the pending negotiations with the banks?" Lindsey inquired.

"Nothing. And I might add that to my knowledge there was no pressure from the bankers for my resignation. I think you should carefully verify anything Player tells you."

But the damage had been done. The headline in the *Times* the next day read:

PAN AMERICAN REMOVES HALABY FROM TOP POST, NAMES SEAWELL

And the first two paragraphs might as well have been dictated by Player.

Najeeb E. Halaby resigned as chairman and chief executive officer of Pan American World Airways yesterday after

the airline's board of directors gave him an ultimatum to quit
or be dismissed.

Mr. Halaby was blamed by the directors for the airline's
deepening financial crisis. The company has lost more than
$120 million since he took over as president in May
1968. . . .

I didn't blame Lindsey. Player's version made more interesting
reading. And Lindsey at least had the decency to quote some further remarks I had made during our telephone interview. I had
told him I was "relieved to be freed from the strains on myself and
my family of the day-to-day problems of running the airline and
taking care of thirty-six thousand people"—the last a reference to
Pan Am employees. He further quoted me:

A chief executive likes to leave a company better than when
he found it and I believe I have. The accomplishments have
been the quality and the efficiency of the airline, such as improved productivity.

The *Wall Street Journal,* to whom I also had talked the previous
night, treated me a bit more fairly, and the story this newspaper
ran I considered relatively objective, under the circumstances. It
started off:

After months of rumors and rumblings about his future with
financially troubled Pan American World Airways, Najeeb E.
Halaby, one of the most colorful and controversial of modern
airline chief executives, resigned as chairman of the big carrier. It was clear the move came under pressure. . . .

The *Journal* article went on to say that I had refused directly to
answer a question as to whether my resignation was tendered
under pressure. They did quote my admittedly guarded answer:

"I was brought in as the architect of change and the manager
of transition from the Pan Am of the past to the Pan Am of
the future. . . . That transition is far enough along so that I

347

feel free to pursue other interests. I think I have gone as far as I could with Pan Am, and there are other things I want to do." Asked whether he felt he had been a victim of the changes he had wrought, he replied: "I didn't say that. That's your judgment."

I could find no fault with the way the *Journal* phrased the events leading to my resignation:

> Despite strong support from certain members of the Pan Am Board, Mr. Halaby's position was said to be in jeopardy even prior to the Board's election of Mr. Seawell to the presidency, replacing Mr. Halaby in that post, last November 16. Almost immediately, some close observers of the company questioned how long the dual arrangement could last. . . .
>
> Sources close to Pan Am said they understood Mr. Halaby's resignation was prompted by one or more recent conflicts which had arisen from the dual-management arrangement involving Mr. Seawell, who has been directing sweeping organizational changes and recently ordered the elimination of over five hundred additional management and management-related positions in the airline. However, a Pan Am spokesman said he didn't believe such reports were accurate. . . .

Reading my "obituary" notices didn't afford nearly as much pleasure as the flood of telegrams, telephone calls, and letters that began coming in. The gist of them was that I had an impossible job, I had done the best I could, and I was lucky to be out of it. I had to agree, for there followed a feeling of tremendous relief. I hadn't realized how much I had made Pan Am the center of my life. How totally responsible I felt for Pan Am. How much I felt the risk and the danger of every flight, such as the loss of a fully loaded 747. How much I felt responsible for each and every one of the employees. How the Washington politics of Pan Am had gripped me. How the governmental attitudes were no longer looked at as objective facts but as almost personal neglect. How I was absorbing all setbacks with a sort of "What else can go wrong? Who else can attack Pan Am?" reaction. All of this I had taken as personal blows, and when I was relieved of command, it just fell away. Later, of course, the regrets began to rise, but the initial feeling was one almost of euphoria, the exhilaration of being freed of a heavy burden.

And then I began to worry about what would happen to all the people whom I had brought in and who might be regarded as "Halaby people" and, therefore, fair game for dismissal—Joan Nixon, Frank Davis, Frank Doyle, Dick Ensign, Lee Amaya, all of the seventeen officers I had brought in to replace retirees, Trippe contemporaries and cronies, and deadbeats. And then, what about the ones I had plucked out of their secure positions in the company to take unusual jobs—like my black friend Earl Estwick, and like the design co-ordinator and the consumer-action office? What could I do to help them? How could I protect them without hurting them?

At first, my family took it much harder than I did—that is, my wife and mother took it harder. The kids seemed genuinely pleased that I was no longer "a big-business tycoon." Whether that meant they wanted to see more of me or that they were embarrassed by trying to explain away Pan Am to their friends, I do not know. But for Mother it was a terrible blow, although she had long felt that Trippe was never going to let go and would continue to pull the strings wherever he could. She felt it was terrible treatment of her beloved only son.

My wife, on the other hand, was besieged by questions and comments and was under constant pressure of her back ailment. She was absolutely outraged at what she regarded as a plot to take over. Then, to my surprise, everyone became very concerned that they would lose their travel privileges.

Without mentioning it, they were doubtless also concerned about the reduction in pay. They were relieved to know that Pan Am had committed to pay me at the rate of $127,500 a year until December 1, 1973.

About this stage, I began to reflect and recall deeply the previous year and even beyond. As lawyers are wont to do, I went back from effect to cause. More and more it had become clear that the cause of Pan Am's leadership problem was in the failure of Juan

349

Trippe to perceive the needs of his fellow human beings, in his insensitivity to the feelings and incentives of his colleagues in the company. He simply spent all his time on the power and the politics, the route structure and the public relations—and unsuccessfully since 1962—and he spent almost no time in planning and developing the careers of his management people. Thus it became a club rather than a company; members instead of managers. And, of course, he dominated it without any shadow of doubt or sharing of power. Trippe was one of America's great transport pioneers, a fabulous promoter but a miserable manager and predecessor!

He did, back in 1961, reach out and select Roger Lewis as a potential leader, but through a combination of frustration and what seemed to Lewis to be a superior offer to head up General Dynamics, Lewis left in 1964. Trippe had to reach out and get General Kuter, but Kuter, having had a successful career in the Air Force, was not in the mood to make a fight for leadership in Pan Am. Thus he was left with his trusted lieutenant, Harold Gray, and he made him president in 1965 mainly because Gray was able and entirely reliable, but partly because he had no alternative.

I suppose if I had any idea how bereft of management depth and strength the company was, I would not have considered Trippe's insistent offers in mid 1965—but on the other side, the job of rebuilding had to be a unique challenge.

I have already recounted spending my first four years with Pan Am entirely outside the operation of the airline. Never in corporate history had a man come in to be head of a huge company with less business experience, not to mention less experience within the company he was chosen to lead, than I.

But now the ordeal was over. My last official act at Pan Am was to transcribe a final message to employees on the Pan Am "line"—one of the management-employee communication innovations I had instituted. I have a copy of it in front of me as I write—and on the top, scribbled in longhand, is a note to Bill Seawell: "Bill: If you have no objection to this, I will tape it later today. If you have any problems with it, let me know. Jeeb." He raised no objections. And this was my farewell to the thirty-six thousand loyal men and women of a great air carrier:

Fellow Pan Americans, this is Jeeb Halaby on the Pan Am line, March 24, 1972.

Last Wednesday I offered my resignation as chairman and chief executive to the Pan Am Board of Directors and, after some discussion, they accepted it and elected Bill Seawell as my successor. He is now not only president but also chairman and chief executive, and I wish him all possible good fortune as he lifts up all of the burdens of leading the company.

I feel I owe you, with whom I have served so actively for the past twenty-seven months as your boss, a statement as I say farewell. It has been an exciting, challenging, and in many respects proud period for me. You and I well know the number of challenges and problems that have been accumulating for Pan Am. You also know that someone had to be the architect of change from the old order in this company to the new. As the manager of that transition I felt—first, we had to change some basic attitudes toward each other and our customers and, I believe, much progress has been made in improving employee relations and customer relations. Next, it seemed to me that our productivity had to be increased. And I am very pleased to say that in these two years we are producing substantially more revenue-ton miles with five thousand fewer people than before. That we are selling and treating our customers better is testified by our rising traffic, which is now showing healthy increases month by month. That we have preserved our balance sheet and credit is testified by the willingness of our banks to continue adequate loans available during the coming year. That we have introduced the great 747 fleet without a fatality and brought into being the most modern maintenance and passenger facilities of any airline in the world is a source of pride as well. So, in my judgment, despite all our dollar deficits, I leave you fundamentally a better company than I found and despite all the serious and difficult challenges ahead, I think Pan Am is better prepared to meet them. My greatest regret is that although I believe we have established a better recognition, understanding, and sympathy of our problems in Washington, our regulators have not corrected the errors of the past and are not moving rapidly and

351

vigorously enough to restore **Pan Am's** proper opportunity to compete. Much, much remains to be done, but I believe the new team that I have brought in is more capable of doing these things than any we have had before.

The Board asked me to remain as a Director and I am doing so because I want to do everything possible to help this team succeed. Therefore, I am not giving up the struggle for Pan Am's recovery; I am simply waging it from a new position.

Then I said that in view of the newspaper reports, I thought I owed them a word about the manner of resignation, and I summarized the Board-meeting drama. I concluded:

And so it is good-bye—not farewell—for I will continue to be thinking, working and praying for the great idea that is Pan Am and for those who make it so—all of my fellow Pan Americans.

Thank you very much.

POST SCRIPT

I left Pan Am feeling that I had suffered a defeat and a disappointment but not a failure.

Now, more than five years later, I have pulled out of that Pan Am dive, restored control of my ship and re-trimmed for cruising to new destinations. A marvelous period of personal rediscovery and self-renewal—despite a painful but amicable divorce last year—has occurred.

With that public career in Pan Am behind me, I'm happier and more private and carefree than I have been for years. As an international lawyer and head of a foreign venture-capital firm, I'm leading a private life completely on my own, making a much more comfortable living than anyone could at Pan Am.

Oddly enough, I have been doing just what I said in that hastily drafted announcement of my resignation from Pan Am. We formed an international venture-capital group with participation by some old friends and fellow Pan Am Directors and my old boss, Laurance Rockefeller. Halaby International is concentrating in the Middle East and Southeast Asia, using American technical assistance and technology and all the things we've learned about helping others to help ourselves.

With the moral support of Herb Brownell and Cy Vance, I got

admitted to the New York bar in 1973, and I have put out my shingle and hold myself out as an international negotiator and problem solver, and have a string of legal associates throughout the Arab states, Iran, and Southeast Asia.

As *pro bono publico,* I'm supporting the best American institution in the Middle East, American University, Beirut, as a trustee and as founder and chairman of its developmental company, providing health and agricultural advice and assistance to the Arab states. And I enjoyed a great experience with a group at the Brookings Institution in preparing a report, "Toward Peace in the Middle East," which has been a foundation of the Carter-Vance policies in the Arab-Israeli conflict.

It's been a joy to serve as trustee of such great centers of thought as my old alma mater, Stanford; the Aspen Institute; and the Asia Society; and of the International Executive Service Corps (the "Paunch Corps"); as well as serving corporations such as Bank-America, Chrysler, Uniroyal, and Whirlpool as a Director.

The airman in us has come full cycle. The lift of wings has resumed, and I'm in the air again. Incidentally, at this writing my son, Chris, has been soaring in a sailplane and after graduation from Stanford last year he's swinging with a guitar as a progressive jazz musician. Our daughter Alexa is trying for her private pilot's license from the FAA. Our first-born, Lisa, has been serving as design adviser to the chairman of the Royal Jordanian Airline.

And the story of her job may be worth telling as this memoir closes. It tends beautifully to reveal life's marvelous cycle constantly regenerating.

It all began in the aftermath of my leaving Pan Am when Ali Ghandour, the very imaginative and courageous chief executive of ALIA, suggested to His Majesty King Hussein that he should invite Mrs. Halaby and me to Jordan for a refreshing visit and to offer me the role of chairman of an International Advisory Board for the national airline. We were delighted guests, particularly after an inspiring audience with the King in the spring of 1973 during which he decorated me with the Jordanian Medal of Independence and Doris with a ruby and diamond brooch by Schlumberger. The King let me have his Falcon jet and we toured Jordan in style— the seaside resort of Aqaba, the fabled red caves of Petra, the

354

graceful Roman ruins of Jerash and Philadelphia. Naturally, I agreed to act as one of Jordan's civil aviation advisers and it has been great fun because the King and Ghandour, with unusual vision and audacity for such an austere, troubled country, embarked on a course of rapid expansion of Jordanian civil aviation. They were starting an air cargo carrier; building hotels in Amman and Aqaba; and developing an executive jet service called Arab Wings which was not unlike the Falcon Jet Service that I had helped start at Pan Am. The King encouraged and backed Ghandour in the growth of civil aviation and they developed, with occasional help from me, what we called the "ArabAir America" concept for service between Arabia and America. And in 1976 President Ford authorized non-stop service by ALIA and SyrianAir between Amman, Damascus, and New York. Of course, they would fly my favorite "oversized" 747s twice weekly between our two homelands, America and Arabia. We soon formed a new aviation technical company called ArabAir Services Corporation Ltd. owned by ALIA and Halaby International. We conceived an ArabAir Academy to train pilots, mechanics, controllers, and other civil airmen for all of the Arab world.

To help in this work, we hired a lithe, blond, Princeton planner/architect, Lisa Halaby, to help design the first Arab University of the Air. And then, as she progressed, Chairman Ghandour lured her away from ArabAir and gave her a lofty title and put her to work on developing a Dulles-like Amman Intercontinental Airport and other facilities for ALIA. The day Boeing delivered the first 747 to Amman, Lisa and I came out to watch Ali Ghandour and his powerful airman patron, King Hussein, receiving the beautiful new giant. The King waved hello to me and Ali graciously introduced Lisa. True to "romance in aviation," an airport acquaintance grew over several months of working, water skiing, motorcycling, dining, and caring. One day, a few weeks ago, His Majesty called me and in a most engaging, old-fashioned way said, "Sir, I wish to ask you for the hand of your daughter in marriage." She had already intimated her love to me and after the three of us talked it over and they consulted with her mother, it was announced by the King to a surprised and pleased world. A New

York *Daily News* editorial proclaimed, "Something pleasant out of the Middle East at last."

And so life cycles around again. The Phoenician spirit of her forefathers, the Western liberal arts cum technical education, the aviation fever, and then back to where we all began.

As I write these final words, it is now 1978, more than a dozen years after I started this memoir of an airman; more than thirty since I shared the sweet victory of World War II; more than twenty since my successful tour of duty in international security affairs; some seventeen years after John F. Kennedy appointed me to the FAA; and a half-dozen summers since my last stand in the Pan Am Board room.

Each chapter of a career has an ending and a beginning, and the present one does too. Life—and the struggle of the individual with the institution—goes on and on. The divine inner core thrusts upward again and one's awareness of his all-but-infinite capacity lifts him onward.

INDEX

H. stands for Najeeb E. Halaby.

357

358

361

362

218–19, 321, 345, 349;
finances (income), 18, 53,
59, 85–86, 173, 174, 212, 213,
349; friends, 21, 31, 38, 43,
64, 82, 96, 149, 151, 154, 179,
185, 191, 201, 203, 215, 272,
273, 283, 322, 330, 340, 345,
349; goals, 252; hobbies, 5, 11,
137, 165, 315; homes, 66, 86,
96, 218–19; honors, 53, 65,
179; ideals, 37; lawyer, 18–20,
69, 85, 122, 123, 211, 353 ff.;
marriage, 36–37, 38–39, 86,
333, 335, 340; nickname, 10;
philosophy, 19, 356; pilot,
21–22, 91–93, 130–31,
169–70, 186; politics, 62–65,
161–63, 278, 282–83, 285;
presidential adviser (*see*
under Kennedy, J. F.); religion, 9–10, 16; "security risk,"
51 ff.; self-analysis, 66, 110,
211, 252, 349–50; travels,
51 ff., 160, 163, 164 ff., 173.
See also under names of Presidents *and under* CAB, FAA,
Pan Am, *and* Public service
Halaby, Najeeb Elias (father),
2–4, 5–7, 12; death, 9–10
Halaby, Rose (aunt), 3
Halaby, Salim (grandfather), 3
Halaby, Salim (uncle), 3
Halaby Galleries, 5, 6, 10
Halaby International, 353, 355
Haldeman, H. R., 275, 277, 282
Hall, Floyd, 58, 202, 308, 313
Hambleton, John, 223, 225, 226
Hanes, John W., 64, 65
Hannah, Dr. John, 150–51
Hannifin, Jerry, 179
Harding, Charles B., 58
Harding, William B., 58, 59, 62,
65, 76, 186; Commission, 59,
60–62, 68
Harlow, Bryce, 278, 280

Harlow, Jean, 12
Harriman, Averell, 49, 53, 159,
193
Harris, Oren, 82, 208
Hartke, Vance, 92–93
Hartranft, J. B., Jr., 107–8
Harvard University, 223, 324;
Business School, 60; Law
School, 327
Havana, 225 ff. *See* Cuba
Hawaii, 247, 295, 296, 299
Hawkins, Willis, 187
H-bomb, 48, 76
Helicopters, 58, 248
Heller, Walter, 188
Hepburn, Katharine, 11
Hereil, Georges, 191
Heroes, 3, 17
Higginbottom, Sam, 313
Hijackings, 152–55, 309, 315 ff.;
H., 154 ff.
Hitler, Adolf, 19, 47
Hittle, Donald, 278–79
Hodges, Luther, 158, 188
Hoffman, David, 211
Hong Kong, 234, 238
Hoover, J. Edgar, 45, 48, 51, 53,
153
Hoover Commission, 271
Hough, Richard, 119
Howard, Daggett "Bud," 95, 97,
122
Hoyt, Dick, 226
Hughes, Howard, 11, 214, 266
Humphrey, Hubert, 274, 283,
285
Hussein, King, 354–55

IATA tariff regulations, 297
Ibn Saud, King, 39–41
ICAO (International Civil Avia-
tion Organization), 39, 167,
170
ICC, 162
Imperial Air Lines, 128, 131, 134

Nyrop, Donald, 87–88, 285

O'Donnell, Kenneth, 69, 158
Ohly, John H. (Jack), 43–44, 45, 49, 50, 213
O'Neill, Ralph, 230–31
One World concept, 19
OPEC, 251
Oppenlander, Robert, 264
Orenge, George, 165
Orient, 297
Osborne, Stanley, 201
OSS (Office of Strategic Services), 38

Panagra, 230, 231
Panama Canal, 231, 241
Pan American, 102, 157–58, 164, 172, 180 ff., 214 ff., 225 ff., 236, 241 ff., 252, 319; characteristics, 214 ff., 217, 248, 252, 254; "Clippers," 235–36 (see First Lady); competition, 215, 230 ff., 241, 244–45, 273, 292 ff., 298, 319; Concorde, 197–200; consultants, 266 ff., 271, 277, 323, 328; directors, 2, 3, 220 ff., 240, 251–52, 255 ff., 279–81, 303 ff., 318, 330 ff., fear, 320, 324, 328, "outside," 337; finances, 251, 258 ff., 264–65, 294, 298, 309, 319 ff., 334; founder (founding), 157, 226 ff., 240; -government, 235, 238, 258, 267, 269–70, 277 ff., 280–81; H., x–xi, 2, 57, 118, 202 ff., 219, 243, 255–56, 279, 281, accomplishments, 315, blueprint, 321, 329, Chief Executive, 312 ff., 336, enemies, 318, 336–37, farewell, 350–52, goals, 260, 307, leadership, 349 ff., mistakes, 264, 269, 280, 307, 313 ff., 340, ouster,

309, 311, 318, 332 ff., 340 ff., President, 252–55, 278 ff., 300 ff., strategy, 269, 274, 279–93, successor, 321 ff., 326, 343 (see Seawell), team, 328, 337; hotels, 172, 217, 220, 248, 268–69, 321; image, 260, 314, 319; management, 258 ff., 265, 312 ff., 318, 325, crisis, 337 ff.; morale, 337; Old Guard, 279, 340; pilots, 236–37, 290, 316; problems, 242 ff., 257 ff., 293, 307–9, 320 ff.; profit, 243; reputation, 235, 238, 240, 243–44, 267, 292; 747s, 248 ff., 258, 278, 289 ff., 314, 319, 321; -TWA merger, 288, 291, 301 ff., 309, 320, 326, 337; unions, 257 ff., 302, 308; Vietnam, 319. See also FAA; Lindbergh and Trippe
Pastore, Senator, 73–74, 82, 83
PATCO (Professional Air Traffic Controllers Organization), 106, 118
Patterson, Romney, 165, 166, 246, 256
Pearl Harbor, 20, 241
Pearson, Drew, 46–47
Pell, Claiborne, 82, 83
Penn Central, 302, 303, 320, 324, 334
Pentagon, 43 ff., 50, 76, 274; H., 53, 62, 69
Pilots, 13 ff., 16–17, 57, 68, 101–2, 108, 120, 126–27, 171–72, 215–16, 223, 225, 230, 236–37; authority, 136–37; FAA, 108 ff., 165; ferry, 20; "greatest," 30; H., 108, 110 ff., 120, 179, 182, 194 ff., 211, 215; jets, 101; regulation, 101, 162; retirement,

367

371